BLACK MONDAY
and the
FUTURE OF FINANCIAL
MARKETS

BLACK MONDAY
and the
FUTURE OF FINANCIAL MARKETS

ROBERT J. BARRO
EUGENE F. FAMA
DANIEL R. FISCHEL
ALLAN H. MELTZER
RICHARD ROLL
LESTER G. TELSER

Edited by:
Robert W. Kamphuis, Jr., Roger C. Kormendi, and
J. W. Henry Watson

Dow Jones-Irwin, Inc.
Homewood, Illinois

Mid America Institute
for Public Policy Research, Inc.
Chicago, Illinois

Jacket designer: Michael Finkelman
Printer: R. R. Donnelly & Sons Company

Library of Congress Cataloging-in-Publication Data

Black Monday and the future of financial markets.

Includes index.
1. Stock Market Crash, 1987. 2. Stocks—Prices.
I. Barro, Robert J. II. Kamphuis, Robert W.
III. Komendi, Roger C. IV. Watson, J. W. Henry.
HG4551.B465 1989 332.64′2 88–25749
ISBN 1–55623–138-5

Printed in the United States of America

2 3 4 5 6 7 8 9 0 DO 5 4 3 2 1 0 9 8

PREFACE

Mid America Institute for Public Policy Research (MAI) has been lending support to academic research that generates new ideas and new findings of fact in the financial services area since 1985. In mid-1987, for example, MAI published *Financial Innovations and Market Volatility,* by University of Chicago finance professor Merton H. Miller. Though completed before October events in the stock market, the insights in this paper provide a broad framework for thinking about the perceived increase in market volatility associated with the explosive growth in new and innovative financial products.

When this issue, and the differences and interaction between the stock and futures/options markets, became a major policy focus of most of the reports being prepared on the October 19 stock market crash, we established the MAI Task Force on Black Monday and the Future of Financial Markets to bring fresh thinking and perspective to the debate. To this end we invited six outstanding research scholars–all leading university-based experts in one or more of the relevant areas (finance, macroeconomics, market structure, and regulation)–to analyze the events surrounding the mid-October crash and present their findings. Funding for their work was provided entirely by the Lynde and Harry Bradley Foundation.

The MAI task force was formed in December of 1987. The members met and were in contact through April of 1988 to discuss and interact on their individual research efforts. By design no attempt was made to forge a single consensus document; some common themes and interrelationships among the papers are drawn out by Allan Meltzer in the first paper. When it became apparent—not only to us, but to the few highly knowledgeable individuals who viewed the early drafts—that the major findings of the MAI task force members would bring an entirely new dimension to thinking about the crash, we approached Dow Jones-Irwin. This volume is the result.

Black Monday is divided into two parts. Part I contains the MAI task force papers, which are not available elsewhere. The paper by Richard Roll provides a good example of the innovative research of the task force. He shows that the market crash was global in nature, that it probably did not originate in the United States, that the U.S. market suffered the fifth smallest decline of 23 major markets, that the typical sensitivity of a country's market to changes in global market conditions (that is, its "beta") was by far the most statistically significant explanatory variable in its decline, and that given the beta, the institutional structure of a country's market bore no relation to the size of its decline.

All the papers note that while the current debate in the United States seems to accept without question that existing rules and institutional form were somehow related to the crash, there is little theory and virtually no evidence to support such a view. Likewise, the papers find virtually no evidence that the existence or absence of forward trading, stock index futures and options, portfolio insurance and index arbitrage carried out through program trading, margin requirements, and the like, were related to the crash. Also, they find virtually no evidence that a given country's interest rates, the size of its fiscal or trade deficit or surplus, or other macroeconomic factors had much of anything to do with the extent of market decline.

As background to the MAI task force papers, and so that this volume serves as a single-source reference, Part II contains excerpts from six other reports on the crash. These excerpts provide a basic account of what happened and contain the various policy responses now being debated. Of special interest is "Miller," the findings of the Committee of Inquiry convened by the Chicago Mercantile Exchange. Other than the MAI task force papers, this is the only report to provide an academic analysis of the crash. These researchers were given complete independence by the Chicago Mercantile Exchange and were provided open access to trading data. The report contains cogent discussions of margins and program trading, as well as extensive intermarket analysis.

Also of special interest in Part II is the information on the British experience (excerpted from *The Quality of Markets Report*, Winter

1987/88). This is instructive because while the British market declined as steeply and as fast as the U.S. market, the policy implications drawn differ so markedly from some reports on the U.S. market.

The conventional wisdom about the mid-October crash, which has barely changed from what it was right after the crash, is perhaps best expressed in a major piece that appeared in *The New York Times* on October 26. That story cited the market for stock index futures and options as a major factor in the crash. It said that this market has "been interacting with the stock market *explosively* for three years—but never so much as on Monday" and that "the plunge could not have grown to its awful dimensions" without "...an *efficiency* enhanced by computers that accelerate the process of digesting information and executing decisions" (emphasis added).

We believe that a careful reading of the papers in this volume renders the conventional wisdom, and the policy recommendations based on it, highly suspect. In particular, the charge that *efficiency* ran amuck in mid-October, wrecking havoc everywhere, is not supported by any evidence that the MAI task force members were able to discover.

The MAI task force papers suggest a number of possible reasons for the sharp decline in mid-October that stand in sharp contrast to the conventional wisdom. The papers do not, however, pinpoint one specific cause of the crash of '87, which is hardly surprising. After more than a half century we still do not know what caused the crash of '29. This is significant, in light of the current pressure to identify the "villains" of the crash of '87 and "do something" about them. The crash of '29 led to the imposition of an extensive regulatory framework that did little to reassure individuals (as Telser notes, trading volume did not regain pre-crash levels until the '60s). Moreover, that structure today seems to hamper the ability of U. S. financial institutions to meet consumer demands and compete internationally.

Black Monday raises a number of critical issues that have received a wide variety of responses, but there is still a clear and pressing need to examine capital markets from a perspective broader than that of a single day or week. A broader perspective would include research on (1) market performance, aimed at identifying impediments and restrictions that inhibit efficient functioning, and (2) market mechanisms that can, over the longer run, better accommodate the trading needs of the public, both individual institutional investors. This is an important focus of MAI's ongoing research program.

MAI is indebted to many individuals and organizations for their valuable contributions to this volume. Above all we would like thank the MAI task force members, all of whom produced truly outstanding papers in record time, the Lynde and Harry Bradley Foundation for quickly and generously responding to our request for funding of this effort (especially Michael Joyce), and Dow Jones-Irwin (especially Ralph Rieves) for their initial and continuing enthusiasm.

We would like also to thank especially MAI board members Gary Ginter of Chicago Research and Trading Group, Ltd., Richard Rosett of Washington University, and Ann Wood Farmer for their support of our efforts to bring independent, top-quality academic analysis to bear on these issues.

We also wish to acknowledge with deep appreciation three individuals whose generous support of the MAI vision at crucial times has made it possible for MAI's initiatives to go forward: Gaylord Donnelley, M.A. Self, and Richard Stephenson. For his initial encouragement and support of MAI involvement in financial services issues, we are heavily indebted and very grateful to Philip M. Knox, Jr., recently retired general counsel of Sears, Roebuck & Co.

For their attention to the work of the MAI task force as it progressed, we thank Michael Darby, Robert Davis, Edward Fleishman, George Gould, Wendy Gramm, Alan Greenspan, Joseph Grundfest and Manuel Johnson.

We acknowledge with gratitude the permission to reprint parts of their reports granted by the International Stock Exchange of London and the CME Committee of Inquiry.

We also wish to thank Ida Walters for her time and valuable insights, and especially for preparing the highlights of the task force reports.

Bernadine Gibson and Beverly Taylor of MAI labored long and under trying circumstances to put the full manuscript into its present form. Others who helped significantly were Carol Lobbes, Roderick Smith, Gregory Simoncini, James Schroeder, Beatrice Vander Vlies Kamphuis, and Betsy Jansen Kamphuis.

Robert W. Kamphuis, Jr., Mid America Institute

Roger C. Kormendi, The University of Michigan School of Business Administration and Mid America Institute

J.W. Henry Watson, The University of Chicago School of Public Policy and Mid America Institute

June 1988

The Mid America Institute is a relatively new (1984) non-profit 501(c)(3) organization created to generate and disseminate original academic research on economics-related policy issues. Current priorities include four major areas: (1) the financial system, (2) fiscal policy and economic growth, (3) manufacturing, and (4) human capital. MAI's offices are at the Columbia Building, Suite 107, 5220 South Harper Street, Chicago, IL 60615.

CONTENTS

PART ONE

BLACK MONDAY AND THE FUTURE OF FINANCIAL MARKETS

*The Mid America Institute
Task Force*

Robert J. Barro

Eugene F. Fama

Daniel R. Fischel

Allan H. Meltzer

Richard W. Roll

Lester G. Telser

Highlights

Overview
by Allan H. Meltzer

This opening paper (1) critiques seven major reports (CBOT, GAO, Miller, CFTC, NYSE, SEC, and Brady) that examine aspects of the October events in the U.S., particularly their recommendations regarding changes in market regulations, new regulations, and new arrangements for coordination, (2) examines the three key aspects of the October crash—the size and cause of the decline, the speed of the decline, and the performance of the markets during and after the decline, (3) discusses two reports that examine the London market during the October crash, and (4) makes recommendations. Some of the discussion draws from findings in the other task force papers and from analysis and recommendations in the institutional reports.

1. Seven reports on the U.S. market. A striking and generally disregarded feature of the recommendations offered in these reports is that, often, no claim is made and no evidence is offered that the events of October would have been different if the recommended changes had been in effect. Indeed, in some reports, there is little relation between the problems described and some of the solutions proposed.

2. The three separate aspects of the October crash.

• **The Size and Cause of the Decline.** All relevant explanations can be grouped under three headings: reductions in anticipated future earnings, rising interest rates, and increased uncertainty, particularly the effect on volatility and uncertainty of computerized trading and index arbitrage. A fourth explanation, attributing the decline entirely to chance, has two problems: the decline was universal and prices did not recover to anywhere near their pre-crash levels in the following five months. The international nature of the decline also makes it hard to attribute it to internal exchange processes such as computer directed trading, the use of index futures or derivative securities, and the like that have received most of the attention, as these differ greatly across countries. As to interest rates

1

(on long term bonds), these were much more highly correlated to stock prices than usual in the days prior to October 19, but this explanation is partial and incomplete. The decline did not have a single cause, but was influenced partly by the rise in interest rates, partly by uncertainty, and partly by changed beliefs about anticipated future earnings.

• **Speed of the Decline.** The entire decline in the U.S. was compressed into four trading days with most of the adjustment on a single day, Monday, October 19. Negotiated commissions, block trading, and the development of futures markets in which claims to entire portfolios can be purchased and sold have markedly lowered transaction costs. This and improved information technology allow markets to respond much more quickly than in the past. Was the response excessive? There is slight evidence of overreaction. Transactors appear to have valued securities in the days, weeks, and months after the crash about the same as they did on October 19.

• **Market Performance.** On October 19 and 20, the value of trading was far in excess of any previous experience, and the exchanges have received favorable comments on the quality of their performance under the circumstances. There were problems, however. Some people were unable to reach their brokers. Specialists were unable to set prices for some securities for relatively long periods during the trading day. Some market makers are reported to have withdrawn from trading in the OTC and other markets. Reporting of transactions prices and transactions to buyers and sellers was delayed for long periods. Spread between spot and futures market prices widened during the decline. Particular attention has been directed (in several of the reports) to the relatively large difference between the market price of S&P 500 futures and the spot price of the securities in the S&P 500 index, which persisted from October 19 to 23. This suggests that arbitrage between the S&P 500 futures traded on the CME and the spot securities traded on the NYSE was insufficient to keep the spread between the two markets within the usual (one percent) trading range. One explanation attributes the spread to the non-availability of the NYSE's Designated Order Turnaround (DOT) system. Another (the Brady Report) attributes some of the differences to concerns about the solvency of clearing market firms and customers. Also, some part of the discrepancy may have resulted from the "up tick" rule and the slow and uncertain execution of orders on the NYSE. No full explanation of the persistent discount is likely to be found. However, CME settlements are due the morning following execution, whereas the NYSE settles after five days. No later than October 21 it was apparent that all CME settlements for the days of the crash had been made, but there was no way to be certain that there would be full settlement of all NYSE transactions. There is another risk difference between the CME and NYSE. Every loss on the CME is balanced by a gain. On the NYSE, transactors as a group experienced large losses in market value.

3. The London Market. During the decline in London most securities traded continuously, quotations moved in step with actual transactions. There are significant differences in the relative size of futures markets in the U.S. and the U.K., as well as major differences in operating rules, so comparisons cannot be precise. Nevertheless, comparison of the two countries helps to isolate some of the reasons for the relatively poor performance in the U.S. market. First, since the liberalization of trading known as "Big Bang," in October 1986, the London market has competitive market makers who are required to make two way price quotations available on all computer screens, with stiff penalties for suspending trading. Second, there is no "up tick" rule for short sales in London. Third, the increased capital following Big Bang enabled market makers to take sizable positions.

4. Recommendations. There should not be a rush to judgment. Development of the S&P 500 contract and other futures contracts permit portfolio adjustments to be made by selling a basket of securities. These and other changes have pushed transactions costs down to a fraction of what they were 15 to 20 years ago, and trading volume is considerably higher. Restrictions on futures trading, proposals for higher margin requirements, and limits or bans on portfolio insurance, for example, reverse the direction of change by raising transactions costs or limiting opportunities for portfolio adjustment. Proposals for limits on daily price changes change the risks faced by transactors. Dynamic hedging strategies and other recently developed portfolio management techniques permit transactors to manage risk more efficiently.

• Exchanges should be encouraged to make, as they appear to be doing, the required investments in sufficient back-up computing power to handle a multiple of the average daily transaction volumes on each market, to process an extraordinary surge in trading volume.

• Changes should be adopted to permit portfolios to be traded, on or off the NYSE floor. Capital requirements of specialists, block traders, and market makers should not be set at an arbitrary level. Perhaps an alternative to the specialist system, more along the lines of the London system, with competitive market makers and severe penalties for withdrawing, would be more efficient.

• To increase confidence, recommendations made to develop a more unified clearing system to reduce risk by consolidating information on net positions, and to clarify the responsibility of parent firms for the liabilities of clearing subsidiaries or affiliates, and where useful, increase capital, are worth considering.

• Margin requirements should be left to exchanges to set. So-called "circuit breakers" to slow the rate of price change should not be adopted.

• The GAO recommendation to develop intermarket contingency plans involving public regulators and self-regulators appears more useful than the Brady Report "single public regulator" recommendation.

The International Crash of October 1987
by Richard Roll

All major world markets declined in October 1987. There was wide disparity in stock market performance across 23 major countries during calendar year 1987; such disparity is typical. There have been few, if any, months over the past 20 years when every major market in the world moved in the same direction, but in October 1987 market movements across major countries were all negative.

Of the 23 major markets, the U.S. had the fifth smallest decline, that is, the fifth best performance. Markets in 19 of the 23 countries fell 20 percent or more. In local currency units, the minimum decline was 11.4 percent (Austria), the maximum was 45.8 percent (Hong

Kong). Restated in a common currency, the U.S. was eleventh because the dollar declined against most major currencies in October 1987.

The U.S. market was not the first to decline sharply. Non-Japanese Asian markets began a severe decline on October 19, their time, and this decline was echoed first on a number of European markets, then in North America, and finally in Japan. This provides evidence against the widely-expressed view that the U.S. market pulled down all the others on October 19. However, because the U.S. experienced one of the largest declines in the previous week, there remains the possibility that other market crashes, though generally occurring before the major U.S. crash, were in fact precipitated by the relatively modest U.S. decline from October 14 through 16.

No link between computer directed trading and market decline found. In local currency units, the average decline of five countries in which computer directed trading is prevalent (Canada, France, Japan, the U.K. and the U.S.) was 6.6 percentage points less than the average decline of the 15 countries where it is not prevalent. Taken in isolation, computer directed trading such as portfolio insurance and index arbitrage, if they had any impact at all, actually helped mitigate the market decline.

Various institutional characteristics across markets were empirically examined with respect to the extent of the price decline. In a multivariate comparison, the presence of a specialist and computer directed trading were associated with *less* severe October declines. Continuous as opposed to single auctions were marginally associated with a larger October decline. Automated quotations, forward trading, options and futures trading, transactions taxes, limits on price moves, and margin requirements all had no perceptible influence on the extent of the crash. The response coefficient, or "beta," which measures the relative magnitude of the response of a given country's market to changes in a world market index, was *by far* the most statistically significant explanatory variable in the October crash. It swamped the influences of all institutional market characteristics.

Thus, no evidence was found to support the view that arrangements in place during October in the U.S. were related

to the crash. The current debate in the U.S. is mainly over the rules needed to prevent another crash. The debaters seem to have accepted without question that existing rules and institutional form were somehow related to the crash, though there is virtually no evidence to support such a view.

The global nature of the October crash debunks the notion that some basic institutional defect in the U.S. was the cause, and it also seems inconsistent with a U.S.-specific macroeconomic event.

Perspectives on October 1987, or What Did We Learn from the Crash?
by Eugene F. Fama

Rational Prices

Interpreted from a rational pricing perspective, the October price shock has the look of a permanent adjustment in response to changes in fundamental values.

Evidence from the S&P 500 dividend/price ratio. At the end of September 1987, the dividend/price ratio for the S&P 500 was 2.7 percent, compared to its average value for the 1957-86 period of about 3.8 percent, suggesting that prices at that time were forecasting extended good times. At the end of December 1987, the ratio was 3.71 percent, below but close to its 30-year mean, suggesting that the crash was a shift from prices that were forecasting extended good times to prices that are forecasting that future times will be about average.

Other evidence is found in the default spread. At the end of September 1987, the default spread (measured as the spread of A-Baa yield over Aaa yields) was 27 basis points, about half its mean value of 55 basis points for the 1957-86 period. At the end of December 1987, the default spread was 50 basis points, below but close to its 30-year mean. Like the dividend yield, this suggests that the October shock reflects a shift in expected returns from low levels prior to the crash, reflecting low risk, to higher expected returns, reflecting risk assessments closer to the historical mean.

Irrational Prices

One cannot say for sure that price behavior around October was rational because there is no scientific way to show that security prices are rational or irrational. One can say:

• A large irrational component might be suspected if the October 19 price drop was later substantially reversed, but it was not. Moreover, the drop resulted in dividend/price ratios close to but still below historical averages, making it difficult to argue that the drop was an over-reaction.

• If the five-year, orderly increase in market prices is taken to be largely irrational, then most analyses of the period around October 19 are misdirected and most proposed "reforms" are irrelevant. There is no evidence or convincing argument that the preceding rise was due to program trading, index arbitrage, portfolio insurance, different margin requirements on futures than on the underlying stocks, or any of the other purported villains of the crash. Nor is there evidence that these created unusual volatility ("noise") that was unrelated to variations in fundamental values.

Taking the rational view, the market moved with breath-taking quickness to its new equilibrium, and its performance during this period of hyperactive trading is to be applauded. Taking the view that the October price swing was irrational, then it is the preceding upside swing that is questionable, not the crash itself. Thus, even in this view, changes in market structures and rules motivated by the crash are largely irrelevant.

The Stock Market and the Macroeconomy:
Implications of the October 1987 Crash
by Robert J. Barro

• **Given the relatively weak stock return in 1987** (total return of 2.8 percent, as compared to an average of 11 percent since 1926), the market forecasted growth rate for real GNP of 1.4 percent in 1988 suggests a mild recession. Whether the stock market's forecast for 1988 falls into the category of successfully predicted recessions or into the category of called recessions that never appeared is as yet unknown.

There are two, not necessarily mutually exclusive, theories of the interplay between the stock market and the macroeconomy.

The first theory begins with the idea that real factors (possibly unobservable to researchers) lead to variations in the prospective real rate of return on capital. These changes cause responses, in the same direction, of real stock prices and of business's desired quantities of capital goods. The shift in desired capital leads to a change in business investment. Moreover, since investment depends on the gap between desired and actual capital stocks, the proportionate movement of investment is much greater than that of desired capital. This theory is consistent with the finding that stock returns lead aggregate economic activity. Moreover, the association should be stronger for the part of GNP that goes to business investment than to the part for household investment or consumption.

The second theory begins with the idea that the initial change in stock prices reflects a movement in discount rates, possibly resulting from a shift in the perceived riskiness of the return on capital or in individual's willingness to absorb risk. Other things being equal, an increase in real stock prices creates an excess of the market's valuation of existing business capital over the cost of that capital, and thereby motivates firms to expand investment. As with (1) above, this approach predicts a positive correlation between stock returns and subsequent economic activity, especially business investment.

- **The important finding is the similarity of the conclusions for these two approaches.** (1) Stock returns are positively correlated with subsequent changes in real economic activity; hence, stock returns can forecast the economy's overall performance, and (2) stock returns would exhibit an especially strong association with the subsequent growth of business investment.

- **To what extent can poor market performance be explained by bad news about the macroeconomy?** Given the relation of stock returns to subsequent economic growth rates—especially of real business investment—it is possible (with hindsight) to "explain" a good deal of the historical movements in stock returns as a "response" to changed expectations about future economic activity. Whether this relationship holds up for late 1987 depends on the economy's behavior in 1988. The shortcoming is that it does not distinguish the stock market's position as a signal of altered expectations from the market's possible role as a causal element in the macroeconomy.

If one restricts attention to contemporaneous and lagged variables, then it is harder to explain stock returns. However, much of the explanatory power comes from the contemporaneous association which could not be used to forecast the stock market.

Some of the usually cited determinants of stock prices (from a statistical analysis of long term interest rates, net exports, federal budget surpluses, and the like) can account for unusually low stock returns in late 1987, but not for returns that are nearly as low as those that occurred.

October 1987 and the Structure of Financial Markets: An Exorcism of Demons
by Lester G. Telser

The unprecedented events of the crash of 87 have inspired a plethora of searches for causes, and a tendency to seek scapegoats who can be blamed and therefore punished. It will better serve the general interest, however, to examine with as much objectivity as we can muster the most probable causes of the Crash, eschew a search for scapegoats and on this basis consider the remedies, if any, that are most likely to be helpful.

In October 1929, a close runner-up to October 1987, there was no program trading, no futures index contracts, no portfolio insurance and no stock options, to name only a few of the culprits mentioned as responsible for the 87 Crash. Any theory of the 87 Crash that relies on these special factors must explain the 29 Crash. In addition, any explanation of the 87 Crash in U.S. markets that focuses on the nature of U.S. trading practices must explain why prices fell in all worldwide markets with their different trading rules.

The most plausible of theory of the Crash asserts that a speculative bubble, expanding on all world markets, burst in October 1987. No economic theory can reveal the correct price, but only whether the rules of the market help or hinder the forces converging on that market that determine the price. Accepting the hypothesis that a bubble burst in October 1987 does not preclude a belief that other difficulties were present as well. The volume of trading was huge and swamped market makers, brokers, floor traders and specialists. One must recognize, however, that the cost of handling such rare events may exceed the benefits.

Differences in institutional form and rules between options/futures and stock exchanges, which were a major concern of the investigations into the October crash, can and should be exorcised. While formal rules regarding trading practices *are* quite different, in reality trading practices on an exchange or individual security market (such as the S&P 500 index or Exxon) are more dependent on volume than on rules. For example, as volume has risen on the NYSE, the trading techniques for the higher volume stocks more closely resemble those that have proven successful in the Chicago exchanges.

The Specialist System vs. Open Outcry. A NYSE specialist is supposed to maintain "orderly" markets in their stocks, whereas in OTC and futures markets, no one bears this responsibility. In practice, the difference among these markets is less than the difference their rules would suggest. A crowd of NYSE floor traders surrounds the specialists of an actively traded stock and bidding is spirited, with the practical result that the mode of trading is like in a pit of a Chicago exchange. Trading in the 200 most heavily traded stocks tends to resemble the Chicago pit, with the specialist effectively serving as an auctioneer who keeps track of trades.

Limit Price Move Rule. This futures market rule can be regarded as the alternative to the NYSE specialist. The rule does not change the ultimate price, which is still driven by market forces, but it slows the process. Without the rule it would be more costly for nonmembers to trade futures and so would mean less trade.

Block Trading. These have risen to 50 percent of total volume and occur off the floor of the NYSE among agents of principals who bargain among themselves, much like the bilateral auction in the pit of a futures market. But in a futures pit, the bargaining is visible, whereas at the NYSE block trading is not visible to the public or even to the members on the floor. Block trading was developed in response to the needs of traders and survives in the face of competing alternatives.

Hedging and Program Trading. The NYSE is to the Chicago exchanges as a spot market is to a futures market. When a hedger opens a cash position, he simultaneously opens a short position in futures, thereby foregoing a profit or loss from a change in the price level, but exposing himself to the risk of changes in the relation between the spot and the futures price, known as the basis. Program trading arbitrages between the cash and futures markets, resulting in the prices of both moving more closely together. By virtue of their greater ability to handle large volume, the Chicago exchanges had more continuous trading, alleviating the congestion problems on the NYSE. In fact, in the absence of reliable price quotations from the NYSE, program trading could not do its job and the basis between the spot and futures price widened to unprecedented levels.

Margins. The forces of competition and brokers' own self-interest impel brokers to set appropriate margins, which they did long before any federal controls. The Federal Reserve Board began regulating stock margins in 1934 because of the belief that the 1929 crash resulted from inadequate margins. The evidence shows that margins were not the culprit in 1929, nor were they in 1987.

Trading volumes did not regain levels existing before the 1929 crash until the late 1960s. This may happen again, but like then, new regulations are unlikely to reassure potential investors.

Should One Agency Regulate Financial Markets?
by Daniel R. Fischel

The Brady Report proposes one-agency (Fed) regulation of all financial markets, seemingly based on the following rationale: markets for stocks, stock index futures and stock options are one market; Black Monday can be traced to failure to recognize links among these markets; one agency is necessary to reduce "market breaks" and deal effectively with them; and a one-market concept points to one-agency regulation.

The logical premise of a one-agency proposal is that regulatory failure produced or exacerbated Black Monday. However, there is not one shred of evidence in the entire Brady Report that suggests that this premise is accurate. Roll convincingly demonstrates that the crash was international in nature, much of it preceding events in the U.S. market. Fama makes the point that if prices fell on new information, then it is not clear there was a failure of any kind, regulatory or otherwise, and no problem to address. The relative stability of prices since suggests that the crash was a response to information. Uncertainty over exactly why prices fell is not surprising; there is still argument over what caused prices to fall in 1929.

Difficulty in executing transactions, a problem that did occur due to unprecedented volume, is something best dealt with by exchanges. There is no direct connection evident between this problem and the one-agency proposal. It is unlikely that regulators could have predicted volumes and associated transaction execution problems any better than exchanges themselves. To the extent that mechanisms for executing transactions were inadequate, exchanges will modify them accordingly. Exchanges, not regulators, have the expertise and incentive to operate exchanges in ways that are in the best interests of investors.

The one-agency proposal implies that competition among regulators is harmful, but there is no evidence of this. Regulators, like exchanges, compete to supply rules and regulations that facilitate providing transactions services. The SEC, for example, has consistently opposed "futures" products that developed under the CFTC. Also, there is no consensus that different rules and organizational structures (margin requirements, trading halts and price limits, for example) among different exchanges have caused harm. Regulatory cooperation, when desirable, can occur without a single agency.

The economic theory of regulation raises questions as to what is motivating the one-agency proposal, given the proposal's lack of rationale. The NYSE, which has opposed new products and growth of other exchanges, has advocated a bigger role for itself and more regulation for competitors since the October crash. The SEC, which wants more control over substitute products, is taking the same position. A notable exception is Fed chairman Alan Greenspan, who has shown little interest in either the one-agency proposal or in the Fed being that agency.

Legislation in response to the October crash that is enacted in this climate is unlikely to resolve the problems connected with the October crash and thus is likely to impose undesirable social costs.

Overview

Allan H. Meltzer[*]

From the opening on October 14, 1987 through the market close on October 19, major indexes of market valuation in the United States declined by 30 percent or more. On October 20, the major indexes recovered part of their loss. For the next four months, these indexes remained within a narrow range, though they were often subject to relatively large daily changes.

Seven groups—the Chicago Board of Trade (CBOT), the Chicago Mercantile Exchange (Miller), the Commodity Futures Trading Commission (CFTC), the General Accounting Office (GAO), the New York Stock Exchange (NYSE), the Presidential Task Force on Market Mechanisms (Brady), and the Securities and Exchange Commission (SEC)—have reported on aspects of the October events in the United States and, in some cases, recommended courses of action including changes in market regulations, new regulations and new arrangements for coordination. The seven reports differ in quality, in depth of analysis as well as in their recommendations. In part, these differences reflect the different missions undertaken. The diversity of the reports and the differences in recommendations suggest that an independent review of the reports and their recommendations may be useful.

In addition to these reports about the performance of the United States markets, the International Stock Exchange (London) and the Bank of England (Bank) report on the performance of securities markets in London. Differences in performance and in organization, under broadly similar circumstances, permit helpful comparisons to be made, so these reports are discussed also.

---

[*] I have benefited from discussions with Franklin Edwards.

This volume is the result of an effort to review the analysis of the October events and the responses to them. Of particular interest is the relation between the reports on United States markets and the recommendations. A striking but generally disregarded feature of the recommendations made is that, often, no claim is made and no evidence is offered that the events of October would have been different if the recommended changes had been in effect. Indeed, in some reports, there is little relation between the problems described and some of the solutions proposed.

There are three separate aspects of what is called the October "crash." First is the size of the market decline. What can be said about the cause or causes of the decline? Second is the speed of decline. Third is the performance of the markets for shares and derivative products during and after the decline or crash.

CAUSES OF THE DECLINE

Although there are a large number of competing explanations of the size of the market decline, all relevant explanations can be grouped under three headings—reductions in anticipated future earnings, rising interest rates and increased uncertainty. Of particular interest, in view of the attention it has received, is the effect on volatility and uncertainty of such market arrangements as computerized trading and index arbitrage. A fourth explanation, attributing the decline entirely to chance, is difficult to reconcile with two different observations—the universal decline in share prices and the fact that three to five months after the decline, stock price indexes in all countries remained below their previous peak. This pattern of change in all markets suggests that some systematic change, or changes, occurred to lower share prices in all markets.

The international nature of the decline also helps to dispose of some principal explanations of the decline that attribute the decline to uncertainty arising from the stock market's internal processes—mainly computer trading in the United States—or to the development of new trading techniques—particularly the use of index futures or derivative securities. The problem with these explanations is that neither the use of the computer in executing trades nor the development of futures markets and derivative securities is universal, whereas the market decline is.

Richard Roll's paper, later in this volume, compares the decline in 23 stock markets around the world. He finds that trading procedures, trading rules and market organizations differ along several dimensions. Some countries have developed futures and forward markets. Some have continuous auctions, margins or computerized trading. Others do not. Roll finds very little relation between these organizational factors and trading arrangements and the size of the decline when he allows for the interaction of the many differences in market arrangements.

One possible reason for this weak association is that the decline may have started in the United States. On this commonly advanced explanation, computerized trading or futures market initiated a sharp decline in the United States that spread to other countries. Roll's data permit us to reject this explanation for the major decline on October 19. On Monday, October 19, markets in some countries declined before the United States market opened. The countries include Belgium, France, Germany, Hong Kong, Malaysia, Singapore, but there are others as well.

Further, if computer trading procedures or the use of derivative securities in the United States had been responsible for the decline by increasing variability, risk and uncertainty, there is no reason for markets in other countries to decline and certainly no reason why some markets would decline relatively more than the United States markets. Increased risk in United States markets should cause a decline in the United States market relative to foreign markets; securities used in program trading or traded in the futures market should decline relative to other securities in United States markets. This is not what occurred. Roll reports that the October decline in the United States S&P 500 index is near the mid-point for the 23 countries in dollar value and is one of the smallest when declines are measured in each country's currency. The October decline in the S&P 500 index was about the same as the decline in the American Stock Exchange index but smaller than the decline in the more actively traded over-the-counter market (NASDAQ) or in the over-the-counter market as a whole (SEC, p. xi). Since these smaller markets have different risk characteristics than the New York Stock Exchange, it seems unlikely that the relative decline in United States markets can be explained satisfactorily by differences in market risk arising from computer directed trading, or derivative securities.

Any surprise, or shock or macroeconomic change affecting the United States would also affect markets in the rest of the world. For example, a recession concentrated in the United States would lower world demand and, therefore, affect markets around the world. The largest effects should be felt in countries most dependent on exports to the United States. There is some evidence of a strong response in countries like Hong Kong, Singapore and Mexico with relatively large exports to the United States, but the explanation fails for Japan, where the decline is relatively small, and does not explain the sizeable decline in Germany or France, countries that depend relatively little on trade with the United States. There is a relatively high degree of correlation between stock prices in major countries—the United States, the United Kingdom, Germany and Japan. Pairwise correlations of daily prices on these markets for the period September 15 through November 15 are typically 0.9 or above.[1] Earlier periods surrounding major changes in dollar exchange rates, July 1 to August 30, 1979 and February 15 to March 30, 1973, show either weak positive or negative correlations.[2] These latter patterns are the patterns expected at the time of a major change affecting principally the United States. Roll finds that, even when measured in a common currency, monthly changes in stock prices typically are not highly correlated. In contrast, stock price indexes fell in all countries in October 1987, as would be expected from a common shock.

No complete explanation of the shock affecting world markets is likely to be found. However, we know that interest rates on long-term bonds and stock prices in the United States are closely correlated (-0.95) for the October trading days prior to the October 19th decline. The correlation is much higher than usually found between these variables. Whatever caused the rise in rates produced similar increases in all major markets at the time.

The rise in interest rates became a source of contention between countries, particularly between Germany and the United States, since the rise in rates abroad necessitated an increase in the United States. The reason is that, under the so-called Louvre agreement, major countries had

---

[1] An exception is the correlation between the Dow Jones Industrial and the Nikkei index, 0.81. Prices are measured in local currency.

[2] Japan and the U.S. are an exception in 1979.

agreed in January to maintain a band on exchange rates. To maintain the band, in the face of rising interest rates abroad, the United States was expected to increase rates further. United States long-term rates on Treasury bonds reached a peak of 10.5 percent on the morning of Monday, October 19, then declined.[3]

This explanation is incomplete. Interest rates and stock prices have a low, positive correlation from October 19 to the end of the month. In this period, the movement of stock prices in the United States may have been influenced more by uncertainty or anticipated income than by interest rates.[4]

In sum, the decline was international in scope. Stock prices fluctuated around the new lower level until, months later, evidence of lower interest rates, stronger growth and reduced uncertainty contributed to a new moderate rise in some countries.[5] The movement in stock prices in October is suggestive of a change in valuation, not a random movement or a response solely to market arrangements such as the existence of markets for futures or derivative securities.

Fama's and Telser's papers, below, consider the possibility that the decline on October 19 was a bubble, or purely random movement

---

[3] The SEC report reaches a similar conclusion about the effect of interest rates, but their discussion refers to short-term rates. See SEC, p. 3-9 and 3-10. The Governor of the Bank of England lists the possible collapse of the dollar and rising interest rates as the immediate cause of the decline in stock prices. See R. Leigh-Pemberton, "Addressing the Stock Market Crash," February 11, 1988, p. 2. The Federal Reserve Bank of New York reports: "As interest rates moved higher abroad, market participants took the view that, given the commitment to exchange rate stability, interest rates in the United States must move up at least as much to maintain sufficient interest rate differentials. In this context, the announcement on October 14 of another large U.S. trade deficit for August at first had a much more pronounced impact on securities and equities markets than on the exchange markets." ("Treasury and Federal Reserve Foreign Exchange Operations," *Quarterly Review,* Federal Reserve Bank of New York, Winter 1987-88, p. 50.) The article continues with discussion of concerns about possible breakdown of the Louvre accord and the decline in the dollar during the week ending October 17.

[4] If one interprets short-term movements of the gold price as reflecting uncertainty, the correlation between gold and stock prices should be negative. From October 19 to the end of the month, there is a negative correlation of -0.66. From October 1 to 16, the correlation is +0.01.

[5] At the October 26 close, the Dow Jones Industrials were only 55 points above the level reached at the October 19 close and 842 points below the October 1 close.

unrelated to any news, information or event. Telser cites the size of the decline, and the asymmetry between the speed of decline and the rate of rise as a possible support for the bubble hypothesis. Both Fama and Telser note, however, that economic theory does not predict the precise price at which markets clear, so it is difficult to reject, directly, arguments about bubbles or purely speculative changes. On the other hand, it is difficult to explain why such changes would occur on the same day in all markets and, having occurred, would persist for weeks or months.

THE SPEED OF DECLINE

A notable feature of the October decline in the United States is the concentration of the price change within a very short period. Even if we date the beginning of the decline as October 14, the entire decline in the United States (but not in all countries) was compressed into four trading days with most of the adjustment on a single day, Monday, October 19. In some other countries, limits on price movements distributed the decline over several days. In some, costs of transacting are higher than in the U.S., so adjustment to "news" may be slower. The similar size of the October decline in several of these countries suggests that the main effect of price limits on price movements is to spread the movement over several days. Once again, this is consistent with a persistent price correction, not a transitory or purely random change.

Costs of buying and selling securities in the United States have declined markedly since the early 1970s. Some of the reasons for the reduction include the introduction of negotiated commissions, block trading, and the development of futures markets in which claims to entire portfolios can be purchased and sold. As a result of these changes, transactions volume has increased to many times the levels achieved a decade or even a few years ago.

One effect of lower transactions costs and improved information technology is to concentrate the response to new information within a smaller time frame. It should not be surprising, therefore, that when new information implies lower (or higher) prices, U.S. markets respond more quickly than in the past.

Fama's paper argues that it is socially desirable for markets to respond more quickly. The reason is that more rapid adjustment allows new information, "news," to affect prices promptly. There is less chance that people will buy or sell at prices that do not fully reflect events that have occurred or are anticipated to occur in the future. Higher volatility is a possible offset to the gain from lower transactions costs. As Fama notes, lower transactions costs may increase volatility.

There is no way to establish beyond doubt either that share prices did not fully reflect "news" or that prices responded excessively to new information.   To test either conclusion formally, we would have to be precise about the particular news that drove the markets. Several pieces of new information arrived during the period immediately preceding the market decline that could substantially change securities prices in major markets. Rising interest rates were mentioned earlier. Monthly trade figures for the United States, announced on October 14, showed a record trade deficit thereby raising concern about a further decline in the dollar or a rise in U.S. interest rates. There were rumors and fears of increased involvement by the United States in the conflict in the Persian Gulf. A conflict in the gulf that disrupted oil supply or that juxtaposed the United States and the U.S.S.R. would have potentially large effects. During the days preceding the market decline on October 19th, open disagreements about interest rate and exchange rate policies between United States and West German officials became known. Doubts arose, therefore, about the direction of monetary policy in major countries and about the future of the so-called Louvre agreement on bands for exchange rates. In addition, news affecting individual countries occurs with high frequency. An example was concern in the London market about the large sale of BP shares by the government in October.

Even if the markets' responses were entirely a response to news, it is not an easy task to link specific responses to specific events. As the Barro and Fama papers note, research has produced better evidence of effects of the stock market on the economy than the reverse. Further, the evaluation of "news" changes. What at first appears important, or unimportant, is often perceived differently at a later time. Questionnaires that ask people, after the event, to cite events important at the time must face this and other problems.

Despite these well-known problems of explaining market movements, we can reach some judgment about the degree to which markets overreacted to news on October 19 and 20. An excessive response would be followed by a reversal; market prices would rise. Those who had sold near the bottom of the decline would, in retrospect, find that they had been too hasty.

Market prices in the United States show only slight evidence of overreaction for the next three months. The intraday low point for the Dow Jones Industrial average during the decline is 1708.70 on October 20 (SEC, p. 2-1). The industrial average ended the week at 1794, only 55 points higher than the close on "Black Monday," October 19. During the next three months, the industrial average remained between 1800 and 2000 with rare exceptions, so the intraday low point is less than 100 points (5.5 percent) below the bottom of the range within which the market fluctuated, and the close on October 19 (1738.74) is less than 3.5 percent below that range. These data suggest that transactors, with hindsight, appear to have valued securities in the days and weeks after the crash not very differently from valuations that prevailed on October 19 and 20. By the end of March 1988, none of the market averages had reached its previous peak. Although the Nikkei average for Japan was within two percent of its peak, most averages remained between 20 percent and 40 percent below their previous peak. Indeed, some continued to fall through late March (see Figure Roll-10). The speed of the market's decline does not appear to have been a cause of substantial overshooting of the major indexes.[6]

MARKET PERFORMANCE

On October 19 and 20, the value of trading was far in excess of any previous experiences. Several of the reports comment favorably on the quality of performance under the circumstances prevailing at the time. Quality of performance was marred, however, by problems on which several of the official reports comment. Some people who would have liked to trade on October 19 and 20 were unable to reach their brokers.

---

[6] Individual stock prices would provide additional information on the presence or absence of overshooting.

Specialists were unable to establish prices for some securities for relatively long periods during the trading day. Some market makers are reported to have withdrawn from trading in the over-the-counter and other markets on these days, thereby reducing the public's opportunities to transact (Brady, pp. VI, 49-50).

Volume of trading became so heavy that reporting of transactions prices and transactions to buyers and sellers was delayed for long periods, in some cases for days. Some reports note that the absence of information on transactions and prices may have inhibited trading. This could occur if potential buyers did not know what they had purchased or sold, the prices to which securities had fallen or the prices at which purchases could be made.

Much attention has been focused on market organization and trading procedures as causes or contributors to problems that transactors experienced during the market decline. Computerized trading, portfolio insurance and index arbitrage have been singled out for attention.

A problem with discussions of this kind is that markets all over the world declined. Only a few countries have computerized trading, index arbitrage, and portfolio insurance. Further, as Telser notes in his paper, none of these techniques or procedures were present in previous large sudden market declines—1914, 1929, 1962 and other periods.

The spread between spot and futures market prices widened during the market decline. Several reports including Brady, the CFTC, Miller, and SEC comment on or direct attention to the relatively large difference between the market price of S&P 500 futures and the spot price of the securities in the S&P 500 index. Several of the reports note that part of the difference can be explained by delays in information about spot prices, particularly the price of securities in which trading had stopped.[7] A considerable difference in the spread remains from October 19 to October 23 even after adjustments are made to allow for securities that did not trade.

---

[7] GAO (p. 55) reports that there were 195 trading delays and halts on October 19 and 280 delays and halts on October 20. For stocks in the S&P 500, the average halts were 51 and 78 minutes.

The data suggest that arbitrage between the futures, traded on the Chicago Mercantile Exchange (CME), and the spot securities traded on the New York Stock Exchange (NYSE) was insufficient to keep the spread between the two markets within the usual (one percent) trading range.[8] During most of the week of October 19 to 23, the CME index was below the NYSE index much of the time. The discrepancy between the two market prices increased uncertainty about prices. Transactors could not know whether the discrepancy was likely to be removed by a further, at times relatively large, decline in spot prices or a rise in futures prices.

Two main explanations of the unusual discrepancy have been offered. One attributes the spread to the non-availability of the NYSE's Designated Order Turnaround (DOT) system. The other, suggested by the Brady report, attributes some of the differences to concerns about the solvency of clearing market firms and their customers. In addition, some part of the discrepancy may have resulted from the "up tick" rule requiring short sellers on the NYSE to sell at a price higher than the previous transaction, and part may have resulted from slow and uncertain execution of orders on the NYSE (Miller, pp. 26-7).

Again, no full explanation of the persistent discount is likely to be found. The fact that the discount on the futures market persisted through Friday, October 23 suggests that it cannot be explained fully by temporary closing of trading in components of the index or by the up tick rule. The latter may have been a hindrance to short sales on October 19 or early on October 20, but it cannot explain why relatively large discounts persisted when the market averages rose on October 20 and later in the week.

Concerns about settlement and the viability of the clearinghouses, or clearing firms, would raise the risk for transactors. The risk is not the same for CME and NYSE transactions. Every loss on the CME is balanced by a gain. On the NYSE transactors as a group experienced large losses. If the losses had any effect, they should have caused the NYSE to sell at a discount.

---

[8] The spread depends on the dividend rate on the spot shares, the short-term interest rate and transaction costs.

The persistence of the discount on the CME is a problem. No later than October 21, it should have been apparent that CME settlements for the days of the crash had been made. Since these settlements are due on the morning following execution, and the clearing corporation cannot by charter extend credit to a clearing firm, it should have been apparent that defaults were limited. (In fact, there were none.) Perhaps some residual uncertainty remained about whether banks would continue to lend (on collateral). NYSE transactions settled after five days, so many of the Monday and Tuesday transactions on the NYSE remained to be settled. There may have been questions and rumors about the prospects for these settlements. If so, the NYSE should sell at a discount to the CME index. Generally, the NYSE sold at a premium in the October 19 week.

Many transactors trade in New York, Chicago and elsewhere. Clearing is not centralized. The same person may have net credit or debit balances in more than one market. Concern that transactors would be forced to liquidate futures positions to satisfy clearing balances in New York could explain a discount of the futures index. I know of no evidence that these concerns arose or, if they arose, that they were sufficiently important to explain the discount.

The closing of the DOT system to arbitrage transactions—restrictions on so called computerized trading—raised the cost of arbitrage transactions and reduced the volume of such transactions. Since futures prices were below equivalent spot prices, arbitragers would have purchased futures and sold on the spot market to reduce the discount. In the absence of "computer trading," arbitragers had to sell each of the 500 stocks separately. Further, trading interruptions and inability to get current spot price information limited arbitrage and other trading on October 19 and 20, but, as previously noted, this explanation is not relevant for the discount that remained later in the week.

In summary, there is clear evidence in the Brady, CFTC, Miller, and SEC reports of problems in the execution of transactions and the dissemination of information about prices and market transactions. Recommendations for changes in market operations and regulations should attempt to find solutions to these problems.

THE LONDON MARKET

The International Stock Exchange (London) and the Bank of England studied the performance of the London markets during the market decline.[9] Although there are significant differences in the relative size of futures markets in the United States and the United Kingdom, and differences in operating rules, comparison of the two countries' markets helps to isolate some of the reasons for performance problems in the United States.

Futures markets in the United Kingdom are small whether judged relative to the size of the London market or relative to the United States futures market. Futures option trading on market indexes is currently about 20 percent of the volume of trading in the London equity markets. For the United States, the ratio of trading in the S&P 500 futures to trading in the NYSE has been about two to one (London, p. 36). Nevertheless London futures markets were active during the crash, and trading was at record volume. As in the United States, futures prices traded at a discount to the spot market much of the time, but the difference between cash and futures prices ranged from 60 to -350 points, the latter a very short-lived event lasting three to four minutes (London, p. 41).[10] For the week as a whole, the discount was in the neighborhood of five percent.

London, unlike New York and Chicago, has very little portfolio insurance in force. Index arbitrage occurs, but it is limited, in part by differences in tax treatment (London, p. 43, Bank, p. 9). These features, often blamed for the discount in the United States, were small or absent in London. Hence, they cannot explain the discount in the United States.

The International Stock Exchange report suggests that the principal reasons for the discount include two factors that were a feature of the United States markets also (Ibid). First is the rate of price decline. This reduced the

---

[9] The report of the International Stock Exchange can be found in *Quality of Markets Quarterly* Winter 1987/88, pp. 1-83. The Bank of England study is from Bank of England *Quarterly Bulletin*, February 1988, pp. 2-9.

[10] The London market was closed on Friday because of a hurricane. Holders short put options and futures apparently dumped their positions at the opening.

opportunity to sell in the cash market at or near (last) quoted prices. Some transactors turned to the futures market. Second, there was uncertainty about the possibility of executing in the cash market. "[T]he experience of those trading simultaneously in both the cash and futures markets suggests that, because of access difficulties in the cash market, some investors may have chosen to deal in a discounted market because it was more accessible and so provided certainty of execution" (London, p.43).

These attempts at explanation are partial. They do not explain why the discount persisted on average, in London and New York, after October 20. And, they do not explain why more transactors did not attempt to profit from the discount by selling in the cash market and buying futures. The comparison does point out, however, that computerized trading and portfolio insurance are not sufficient to explain the discount between the two markets.

The International Stock Exchange dismisses clearing difficulties as a possible explanation of the discount. As noted, the futures markets are relatively small, so the risk of large exposures in both cash and futures markets is limited (London, p. 36).

An important difference between the United Kingdom and the United States is that most securities traded continuously in London. Spreads between bid and ask prices widened, and quotation sizes fell. However, "market makers' quotations provided a fair representation of the market" (London, p. 37).[11] For shares regarded as highest quality, bid-ask spreads rose as high as 3.4 percent, from an average of 1.2 percent prior to October 19. Average quote size declined to one-half of normal size. For other shares, spreads are typically higher at 2.5 percent to three percent. These spreads doubled to five percent and six percent; average quote size declined to 12,000 shares from 50,000 before October 19 on medium quality shares and from 7,000 to 2,500 shares on lower quality shares (London, p. 17).[12]

---

[11] Under the prevailing uncertainty, the quality of quotations was underestimated, as noted previously.

[12] Average volume per quotation declined by half to 145,000 by October 21 (Bank, p. 8).

Quotations moved in step with actual transactions. In the London market, "fast markets" are periods in which transactions volume is so heavy that market makers cannot keep quotations up to date. During these periods, price quotations on computer screens are indicative only and must be confirmed prior to transacting. Only two "fast markets" were declared on October 19, for 13 minutes and one hour, and on October 20, for approximately 120 and 90 minutes. Even during these periods, there is no evidence of excess divergence between quotations and transactions prices (London, pp. 13 and 19). A general conclusion of the studies of the London market is that the volatility of the Dow Jones index for the United States "was higher during the crash than that of either the FTSE (London Financial Times index) or the [Tokyo] Nikkei Dow. This contrasts with the third quarter data which show little difference in the price volatility in each market" (Bank, p. 4).

Several major differences between the rules of United Kingdom and United States markets may have contributed to the more orderly decline in London. First, since the liberalization of trading known as "Big Bang" in October 1986, the London market has competitive market makers who are required to make two way price quotations. Quotations are available on all computer screens. Second, the penalty for suspending trading is a three month suspension of the right to trade.[13] Although spreads widened and quotation size declined, as noted, the reported changes do not suggest that market markers circumvented the rules by making extreme bids and offers—in effect, closing their market while observing the rules. Third, there is no "up tick" rule for short sales in London. Fourth, increased capital following Big Bang enabled market makers to take sizable positions. On October 19, market markers' net long positions increased by about £250 million.

EFFECTS ON THE ECONOMY

Robert Barro's paper, later in the volume, investigates the effects of the stock market decline on the economy. He finds that the decline in October 1987 lowered the rate of return on stocks from above average to

---

[13] In January 1988, NASDAQ adopted a rule calling for twenty day suspension for failure to maintain markets.

below the average rate of return for the years 1927 to 1987. He finds, consistent with earlier work, that changes in the expected rate of return are a useful predictor of changes in real GNP in the following year. These predictions are far from exact, but they appear to be as reliable as other commonly used methods of forecasting.

Barro estimates that the October decline lowered the forecast growth rate of 1988 GNP to 1.4 percent. This suggests that any recession caused by the market decline will be mild. He warns, however, that forecasts of GNP from past stock market returns, like other forecasts, are subject to relatively large errors.

RECOMMENDATIONS

The most important recommendation of this report is that there should not be a rush to judgment. The October experience focuses attention on the markets and provides an opportunity to make changes that lower risk and increase welfare. Some changes may reduce the risk of repeating the October experience. Other proposed changes, though widely publicized, and advocated in some reports, have limited merit or may be counterproductive.

In the past few years, securities markets have developed a limited capacity to permit portfolio adjustment to be made at relatively low cost. The development of the S&P 500 contract and other futures contracts permit portfolio adjustments to be made by selling a basket of securities at transaction costs that are a small fraction of the costs paid 15 or 20 years ago. By encouraging the use of negotiated commissions on the NYSE, and other exchanges, and by permitting trading in options and futures, the exchanges and the regulators have contributed to these improvements in markets. Costs of transacting are now substantially lower, and trading volume considerably higher, as a result of these, and other, changes in regulations and procedures.

Some proposals for change reverse the direction of change by raising costs of transacting or by limiting opportunities for portfolio adjustment. Restriction on futures trading, proposals for higher margin requirements, and limits or bans on portfolio insurance are examples. Proposals for limits on daily price changes change the risks faced by transactors.

Dynamic hedging strategies and other recently developed portfolio management techniques permit transactors to manage risk more efficiently.[14] Few who argue for controls or bans on these techniques argue that markets would function more efficiently if portfolio managers returned to stop-loss orders and other techniques that the new methods have supplanted or shifted arbitrage and hedging operations to foreign markets.

There is little doubt that markets did not function effectively on October 19 and 20. In part, the problem arose following the breakdown of the computerized order system called DOT. To reduce the risk of future breakdown and to process an extraordinary surge in trading volume, the exchange should be encouraged to acquire sufficient back-up computing power to handle a multiple of the average daily transaction volumes on each market and to avoid a breakdown. The exchanges appear to be making the required investments.

The rules of the NYSE do not permit that market to service the demand for portfolio trading in a fully efficient manner. The DOT system is a compromise that permits buy or sell orders for each of the stocks in a basket, such as the S&P 500, to be placed at one time, but each separate order must be routed to a specialist in the particular stock. The SEC report suggests that consideration be given to the creation of posts at which specialists would trade entire portfolios. Presumably, posts would be established for each of several portfolios such as the S&P 100, S&P 500 and other actively traded portfolios off the floor of the exchange. Changes to permit portfolios to be traded, on or off the NYSE floor, should be adopted.

Several reports discuss the capital requirements of specialists, block traders and market markers. Capital requirements should not be set at an arbitrary level. Consideration should be given to the development of risk related capital requirements for market makers.

---

[14] To the extent that the insurers underestimated the cost of the insurance prior to the crash, the role of insurance and dynamic hedging will decline. It is not clear why regulation would be needed.

The SEC and the Brady reports provide details on the performance of exchange specialists and other market makers.[15] Neither report suggests an alternative to the present system, although both reports criticize the performance of some specialists on October 19 and 20. The larger issue is whether the specialist system should be replaced, in part or whole, on the NYSE. The volume of trading and size of turnover in large capitalization stocks has increased to levels at which an alternative method of trading may now be more efficient for many securities. The performance of the London market system, discussed earlier, suggested that the London system, with competitive market makers and severe penalties for withdrawing from the market, functioned continuously, albeit with increased spreads between bid and ask prices. A study, including outside experts as part of the study group, should be undertaken of alternatives to the current, specialist system for large capitalization stocks and possibly for others as well.

Two recommendations have been made to increase confidence in the financial position of market makers, market participants and clearing firms. One calls for development of a more unified clearing system. A more unified clearing system would reduce risk by consolidating information on net positions. The scope of present day trading limits the possibility of complete coverage of international markets with different closing times, but information can be increased. A related recommendation would strengthen the financial position of clearing firms by clarifying the responsibility of parent firms for the liabilities of clearing subsidiaries or affiliates and, where useful, by increasing capital.

Higher margin requirements raise the cost of transactions. Proposals to equalize margins in financial futures with stock exchange margin requirements treat the two margin requirements as equivalent. They are not. Margin requirements on stocks are a down payment, paid by a purchaser of shares who borrows the balance of the purchase price. Futures margin is a performance bond, paid by both the buyer and the seller, to assure that the transactor can cover any losses resulting from price changes. Settlement is made at least daily, and intraday margin calls are made in periods of substantial price change. The use of stock margin

---

[15] Brady, pp. 49-50 has a succinct summary.

typically indicates a leveraged position, while much of the trading in futures markets, particularly arbitrage transactions, does not involve leverage. Further, the effect of margin requirements is uncertain. A study of stock market requirements by the staff of the Federal Reserve, several years ago, did not develop a rationale for margin requirements.

The setting of margin requirements should be left to the exchanges. The system worked satisfactorily during the October break. Margin requirements on futures were adjusted, flexibly, in relation to volatility and risk. As Telser notes, margin requirements originated as a solution adopted by borrowers and lenders. Markets have increased the use of intraday margin calls and, in the futures market, margin requirements have been raised.

The Brady report recommends "circuit breakers" to slow the rate of price change. Telser argues that daily limits on price changes in futures markets reduce the cost to a non-member of trading in futures. The broker or dealer has time to contact the non-member when there are large price changes and to get new instructions or additional margin. Fama argues that trading halts can increase volatility by inducing trading in anticipation of a trading halt. The Governor of the Bank of England argues that closing one market may shift pressure to other markets. He concludes:

> I have yet to be persuaded of the need to introduce artificial breaks in the markets. I can see that they might impose a semblance of orderliness, but this would have to be at the expense of...liquidity.[16]

It seems clear that, despite the appeal of the name "circuit breaker," there is considerable difference of opinion about their effect. The evidence in Roll's study shows no significant effect of price limits. Indeed, once allowance is made for differences in volatility, price limits on cash markets have no effect at all.

---

[16] Speech given by the Rt. Hon. Leigh-Pemberton, Governor of the Bank of England at the City University, February 11, 1988, p. 7.

The Brady report recommends a single public regulator to coordinate intermarket issues. The report presents no evidence that regulatory failures played a part in the October decline. Self-regulation receives little criticism and much praise in several reports. However, rumors of a possible SEC decision to recommend a closing of the stock exchanges contributed to the uncertainty experienced in mid-October.

GAO recommends the development of intermarket contingency plans involving public regulators and self-regulators. This recommendation seems a more useful way of dealing with intermarket and international coordination. Public regulators would coordinate their own activities and monitor the markets.

The International Crash
of October 1987

Richard Roll[*]

INTRODUCTION

The sharp drop in the U.S. stock prices around October 19, 1987 gave birth to at least one industry: the production of explanations for the crash. Among the most popular explanations are those related to the U.S. market's institutional structure and practices; e.g., computer-assisted trading, portfolio "insurance," the organized exchange specialists, concurrent trading in stock index futures, margin rules, and the absence of "circuit breakers" such as trading suspensions and limitations of price movements. These institutional arrangements are the central focus of several commission reports about the crash.

Regulatory agencies and potential regulatees have been debating the most appropriate rules for preventing another crash. A striking feature of the debate is its almost complete focus on institutional form. The debaters seem to have accepted without question that the arrangements in place during October actually were somehow related to the event.

Yet there is virtually no evidence to support such a view. The institutional structure of the U.S. market cannot have been the sole culprit, or else the market would have crashed even earlier. There must have been an underlying "trigger." Some have pointed to the U.S. trade deficit, to anticipation about the 1988 elections, to fears of a recession. But no one

---

[*] Many thanks to Jim Brandon for assistance and advice beyond both compensation and the call of duty. The comments and suggestions of Robert Barro, Michael Brennan, Eugene Fama, Robert Kamphuis, Roger Kormendi, Allan Meltzer, and Maggie Queen are gratefully appreciated.

has been able to substantiate convincingly the true underlying cause of the October market decline.

The likely impact of both market structure and macroeconomic conditions can perhaps be deduced by comparing circumstances in the United States with circumstances prevailing in other markets around the world. Indeed, we are blessed with a natural laboratory experiment, for conditions varied widely across countries. To the extent that institutions and economics influence the stock market, we should be able to detect those influences by comparing behaviors in various markets during October 1987. This paper presents a first look at this international evidence.

THE COMPARATIVE PERFORMANCE OF MAJOR STOCK MARKETS IN 1987

During the entire calendar year 1987, there was a wide disparity in stock market performance across major countries. Table Roll-1 gives the total percentage change in the major stock price index for each of 23 countries, both in local currencies and converted into U.S. dollars.[1] The number one dollar performer in 1987 was Japan, (+41.4 percent), while the worst performer was New Zealand, (-23.8 percent). The calendar year results expressed in local currency units are quite different than the dollar-denominated results. For an extreme example, Mexico had a 5.5 percent dollar-denominated return in 1987, but when expressed in pesos, Mexico was up 158.9 percent!

The wide disparity in 1987 calendar year returns is typical. Table Roll-2 shows the simple correlation coefficients of monthly percentage changes in the (local currency) indexes over the most recent period just prior to the crash when simultaneous data were available for all countries. The intercountry correlations are mostly positive, but moderate in size. Correlations above .5 are relatively rare and there are only two above .7 in

---

[1] The data source was Goldman Sachs & Co., "FT-Actuaries World Indices," various monthly editions. The indices are the most widely followed in each country. For instance, the U.S. index is the S&P 500, (consisting of the 500 largest companies), and the British index is the Financial Times-Actuaries All Shares Index. A complete list for each country is contained in Goldman, Sachs & Co., "Anatomy of the World's Equity Markets."

the entire table.[2]   These modest correlations are in marked contrast to the usual correlation found between any two well-diversified portfolios within the same country.   Randomly selected portfolios of U.S. stocks for example, generally have correlations above .9 when there are 50 or more individual issues included in each portfolio.

TABLE ROLL-1
Stock Price Index Percentage Changes in Major Markets
Calendar Year 1987 and October 1987

	Local Currency Units		U. S. Dollars	
	1987	October	1987	October
Australia	-3.6	-41.8	4.70	-44.9
Austria	-17.6	-11.4	0.70	-5.8
Belgium	-15.5	-23.2	3.1	-18.9
Canada	4.0	-22.5	10.4	-22.9
Denmark	-4.5	-12.5	15.5	-7.3
France	-27.8	-22.9	-13.9	-19.5
Germany	-36.8	-22.3	-22.7	-17.1
Hong Kong	-11.3	-45.8	-11.0	-45.8
Ireland	-12.3	-29.1	4.7	-25.4
Italy	-32.4	-16.3	-22.3	-12.9
Japan	8.5	-12.8	41.4	-7.7
Malaysia	6.9	-39.8	11.7	-39.3
Mexico	158.9	-35.0	5.5	-37.6
Netherlands	-18.9	-23.3	0.3	-18.1
New Zealand	-38.7	-29.3	-23.8	-36.0
Norway	-14.0	-30.5	1.7	-28.8
Singapore	-10.6	-42.2	-2.7	-41.6
South Africa	-8.8	-23.9	33.5	-29.0
Spain	8.2	-27.7	32.6	-23.1
Sweden	-15.1	-21.8	-0.9	-18.6
Switzerland	-34.0	-26.1	-16.5	-20.8
United Kingdom	4.6	-26.4	32.5	-22.1
United States	0.5	-21.6	0.5	-21.6

Mexico is the only country whose currency did not appreciate against the dollar during 1987. The currencies of countries indicated in bold face (Australia, Canada, Mexico, New Zealand, and South Africa) depreciated against the dollar during October 1987.

NOTE: Annual average dividend yields are generally in the two to five percent range except for Japan and Mexico, which have average dividend yields less than one percent.

---

[2] Between Canada and the U.S. and between Malaysia and Singapore.

TABLE ROLL-2
Correlation Coefficients of Monthly Percentage Changes in Major Stock Market Indexes
Local Currencies, June, 1981 - September, 1987

	Australia	Austria	Belgium	Canada	Denmark	France	Germany	Hong Kong	Ireland	Italy	Japan	Malaysia	Mexico	Netherlands	New Zealand	Norway	Singapore	South Africa	Spain	Sweden	Switzerland	UK
Austria	0.219																					
Belgium	0.190	0.222																				
Canada	0.568	0.250	0.215																			
Denmark	0.217	-0.062	0.219	0.301																		
France	0.180	0.263	0.355	0.351	0.241																	
Germany	0.145	0.406	0.315	0.194	0.215	0.327																
Hong Kong	0.321	0.174	0.129	0.236	0.120	0.201	0.304															
Ireland	0.349	0.202	0.361	0.490	0.387	0.374	0.067	0.320														
Italy	0.209	0.224	0.307	0.321	0.150	0.459	0.257	0.216	0.275													
Japan	0.182	-0.025	0.223	0.294	0.186	0.361	0.147	0.137	0.183	0.241												
Malaysia	0.329	-0.013	0.096	0.274	0.151	-0.134	-0.020	0.159	0.137	0.082	0.109											
Mexico	0.220	0.018	0.104	0.114	-0.174	-0.009	0.002	0.149	0.159	-0.020	-0.021	0.231										
Netherlands	0.294	0.290	0.344	0.545	0.341	0.511	0.318	0.395	0.352	0.114	0.333	0.151	0.038									
New Zealand	0.389	0.275	0.230	0.247	0.148	0.318	0.263	0.373	0.314	-0.111	0.136	0.231	0.058	0.239								
Norway	0.355	0.009	0.233	0.381	0.324	0.231	0.173	0.356	0.306	0.042	0.156	0.262	0.050	0.239	0.405							
Singapore	0.374	0.030	0.133	0.320	-0.085	0.133	0.037	0.219	0.102	-0.038	0.066	0.891	-0.013	0.196	0.212	0.201						
South Africa	0.279	0.159	0.143	0.385	-0.113	0.267	0.007	-0.095	0.024	0.093	0.225	-0.013	0.260	0.058	0.196	0.038	-0.056					
Spain	0.147	0.018	0.050	0.190	0.019	0.255	0.147	0.193	0.175	0.290	0.248	-0.071	0.059	0.170	0.095	0.075	0.056	-0.088				
Sweden	0.327	0.018	0.158	0.376	0.131	0.159	0.227	0.196	0.122	0.330	0.115	0.103	0.000	0.324	0.136	0.095	0.180	0.157	0.181			
Switzerland	0.334	0.161	0.276	0.551	0.283	0.307	0.675	0.379	0.290	0.287	0.130	0.099	0.026	0.570	0.397	0.136	0.237	0.331	0.192	0.334		
United Kingdom	0.377	0.073	0.381	0.590	0.218	0.332	0.263	0.431	0.467	0.328	0.354	0.193	0.068	0.534	0.313	0.250	0.168	0.112	0.168	0.339	0.435	
United States	0.328	0.138	0.250	0.720	0.351	0.390	0.209	0.114	0.380	0.224	0.326	0.347	0.063	0.473	0.083	0.377	0.218	0.070	0.218	0.356	0.500	0.513

Table Roll-1 also reports total percentage market movements for each country during the month of October 1987. They are all negative! This alone is a cause of wonder. During the period of data availability (calendar years 1981-1987 inclusive), the *only* month when all markets moved in the same direction was October 1987; but in that month, every stock market fell, and most fell by more than twenty percent. When just the last three months of 1987 are added to data from the previous 76 months used in Table Roll-2,[3] the average correlation coefficient increases from .222 to .415.

Austria, the world's best performing country in October, experienced an 11.4 percent local currency decline and Japan's decline was 12.8 percent, but the currencies of both countries appreciated significantly against the dollar. The worst performer was Hong Kong which had the same result in local currency and in U.S. dollars, -45.8 percent. The rank of the U.S. improves considerably (from eleventh to fifth), when the results are expressed in local currency, because the dollar depreciated against most countries during October.

Given the generally low intercorrelations among countries, the uniformity during October 1987, even in local currency units, is all the more striking. There seems to have been a truly international trigger that swamped the usual influences of country specific events.

During the month of October, the declines experienced in all markets were concentrated in the second half of the month. Figures Roll-1 to 6 present the day-to-day *closing* index numbers for each market over the entire month of October, restated to 1.0 currency units on October 1. Figure Roll-7 plots equal-weighted regional indexes over a shorter period around the crash, beginning on October 14 and ending on October 26. Figure Roll-8 gives a similar portrayal of the six largest individual markets.

---

[3] June 1981 through September 1987, inclusive.

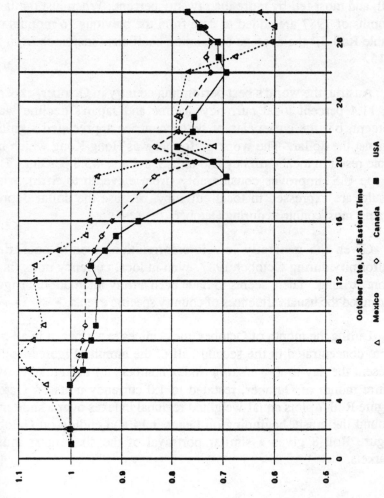

FIGURE ROLL-1
Stock Prices, October 1987
North American Markets

△ Mexico   ◇ Canada   ■ USA

October Date, U.S. Eastern Time

Value of One Currency Unit Invested on October 1

FIGURE ROLL-2
Stock Prices, October 1987
Ireland, South Africa, United Kingdom

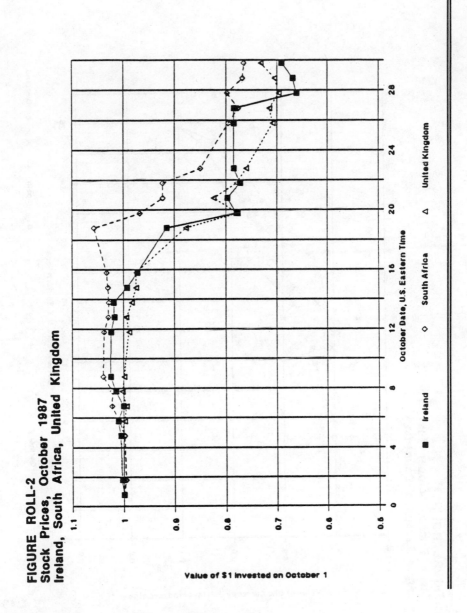

FIGURE ROLL-3
Stock Prices, October 1987
Larger European Countries

Value of One Currency Unit Invested on October 1

October Date, U. S. Eastern Time

■ France   + Germany   ◇ Italy   △ Spain   × Switzerland

FIGURE ROLL-4
Stock Prices, October 1987
Smaller European Countries

Value of One Currency Unit Invested on October 1

October Date, U. S. Eastern Time

■ Austria　+ Belgium　◇ Denmark　△ Netherlands　× Norway　▽ Sweden

FIGURE ROLL-5
Stock Prices, October 1987
Asian Markets

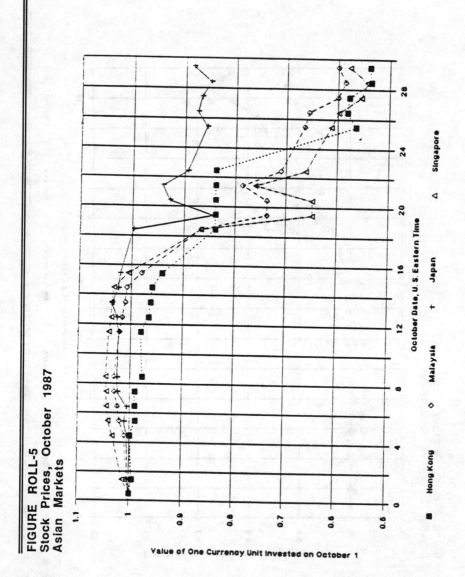

Value of One Currency Unit Invested on October 1

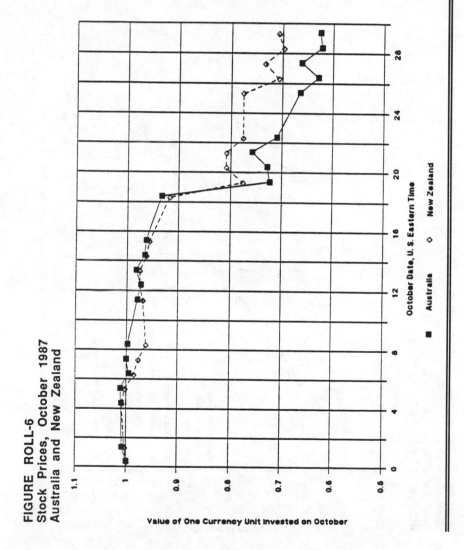

FIGURE ROLL-6
Stock Prices, October 1987
Australia and New Zealand

FIGURE ROLL-7
Regional Indexes Around the Crash
October 14-October 26, 1987

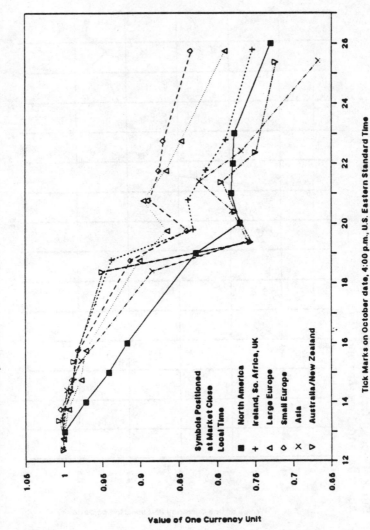

FIGURE   ROLL-8
The Six Largest Markets Around the Crash
October 14-October 26, 1987

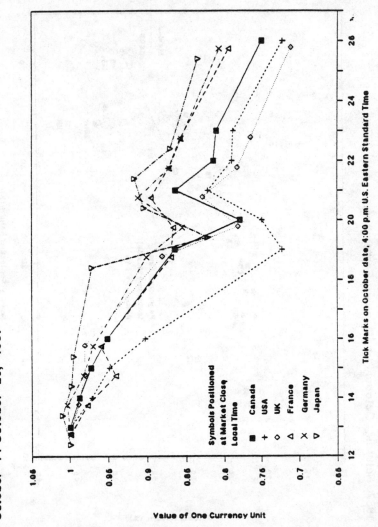

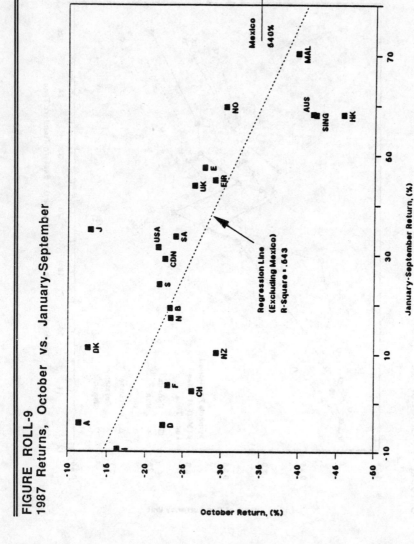

FIGURE ROLL-9
1987 Returns, October vs. January-September

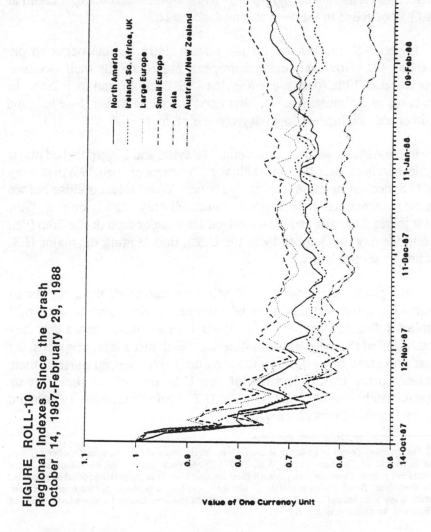

FIGURE ROLL-10
Regional Indexes Since the Crash
October 14, 1987-February 29, 1988

North America
Ireland, So. Africa, UK
Large Europe
Small Europe
Asia
Australia/New Zealand

Value of One Currency Unit

All eight graphs are plotted in actual world time;[4] the tick marks are located on the indicated October date at the New York market closing, 4:00 p.m. U.S. Eastern Standard Time. Since each graph is on the same vertical scale and plotted for the same world time, they can easily be compared.

The earliest significant decline in any market occurred on October 14, (in the North American markets, and early in the morning U.S. time in France, the Netherlands, and Spain). Most world markets experienced at least some decline in the week ending October 16.

In the U.S. market, by far the largest daily decline occurred on October 19. However, many European markets split their declines between *their* 19th, (thus *preceding* the U.S. decline), and their 20th. In the cases of Belgium, France, Germany, the Netherlands, Sweden, and Switzerland, the biggest down day was their 19th.

In the Asian markets, Hong Kong, Malaysia, and Singapore had major declines on *both* their 19th and 20th; the movement on their 19th *preceding* the U.S. decline by more than twelve hours. These markets close before the North American markets open. Japan fell only slightly on their 19th, but it joined Australia and New Zealand for a major drop on the 20th (i.e., late in the day on October 19 in the U.S.), thus lagging the major U.S. decline by several hours.

On a given calendar day, the North American markets are the last to trade. Thus, the fact that most of the other markets around the world displayed dramatic declines on October 19, their time, means that they foreshadowed the crash in North America. With just a few exceptions, the most important being Japan, other countries experienced most of their declines prior to the opening of the U.S. market on the 19th or approximately equally straddling the U.S. market's October 19 session, i.e., on October 19 and 20, local time.

---

[4] For instance, Tokyo is 14 hours ahead of New York, so its observation for October 1 Tokyo time is plotted as October .41666, (i.e., 10/24), New York time. The non-Japanese Asian markets are plotted Japanese time, though they are one hour later. Similarly, Mexico is plotted New York time. South Africa is plotted British time, and New Zealand is plotted Australian time. Mexico is one hour behind New York while South Africa and New Zealand are two hours ahead of Britian and Australia, respectively.

This seems to be some evidence against the widely-expressed view that the U.S. market pulled down all the others on October 19. However, it *is* true that the U.S. experienced one of the largest declines in the previous week; cf. Figure Roll-8. So there remains the possibility that other market crashes on their 19th, though generally occurring before the major U.S. crash, were in fact precipitated by the relatively modest U.S. decline from October 14 through 16.[5]

There was a one-day advance in most markets on their 21st, (including the U.S.), and Figure Roll-7 shows that this advance began first in the Asian and Pacific markets, then spread to Europe, and finally to North America.

Many markets resumed a substantial decline after October 21. From the 22nd through the end of October, every market except the U.S. fell and every decline except that of Canada was substantial (in local currency units).[6] Some of these cases were at least partial holdovers from market closures on the 19th (e.g., Hong Kong), or drawn out by the successive encounters of exchange price limits. In Europe and Asia, however, the weekend from the 23rd to the 25th was just as bad, and in a few cases worse, than the great crash weekend of October 16 to 19. See Figures Roll-3, 4, and 5 or 7.

The overall pattern of intertemporal price movements in the various markets suggests the presence of some underlying fundamental factor, but it debunks the notion that an institutional defect in the U.S. market is the cause, and it also seems inconsistent with a U.S.-specific macroeconomic event. If anything, the U.S. market lagged the initial price movements that began in earnest on October 14 and it also did not participate in further declines that occurréd during the last weekend in October. This would not be the observed empirical pattern if, for instance, portfolio insurance and

---

[5] Looking closely at Figures Roll-7 and 8, most other markets did decline even earlier than the U.S. on each day from the 14th through the 16th. The U.S. decline was only slightly more pronounced.

[6] Canada's decline from October 22 through October 30 was only 1.62 percent. Thirteen countries had at least ten percent declines during this same period.

program trading in New York and Chicago were the basic triggers of the world-wide crash.

OCTOBER 1987, BEFORE AND AFTER

October vs. January-September 1987

The strong market decline during October 1987 followed what for many countries had been an unprecedented market increase during the first nine months of the year. In the U.S. market, for instance, stock prices advanced 31.4 percent over those nine months. Some commentators have suggested that the real cause of October's decline was over-inflated prices generated in a speculative bubble during the earlier period. Of the 23 countries in our sample, 20 experienced stock price increases over the January-September period. There was, however, wide disparity in the extent of the advance.

One symptom of a speculative bubble might be an inverse relation between the price increase and the subsequent extent of the crash. A cross-country comparison of the January-September 1987 return versus the October decline is shown in Figure Roll-9.[7] There is in fact a significant negative cross-country relation. The regression lines shown on the figure indicate a statistically significant association with an R^2 of .543.

However, there is a conceptual difficulty in ascribing these results to the existence of a speculative bubble: the same pattern would arise if there were underlying *common* factors driving stock price changes in all countries. Suppose, for instance, that there is a fundamental macroeconomic factor related to world industrial activity, that it influences the market in every country, but that each country's amplitude of response is different. If that factor happened to be relatively stable, we would have observed price advances in most countries, but of widely varying amounts. If the same factor happened to decline dramatically in October, those countries with the greatest amplitude of reaction would display the largest

---

[7] Mexico was excluded from the figure and the regression line shown on the figure because its return during January-September 1987, was 540 percent in local currency units, (though only 271 percent in dollars); it seems to be an outlier. The arrow pointing to its position off the graph is located vertically at its October return, -35 percent.

stock price declines. The overall result would be a cross-country negative relation such as that indicated in Figure Roll-9. In other words, high "beta" countries do better in worldwide bull markets and worse in bear markets, thus inducing a cross-country negative relation when a bull market period is compared cross-sectionally to a bear market period.

To ascertain whether 1987 was really a speculative bubble followed by a crash, as opposed to a simple manifestation of the unusual world market behavior, one would be obliged to identify and estimate a factor model over an entirely different period and use the *pre-fitted* response coefficients with fundamental macroeconomic factors measured during 1987.

Since the Crash

In the aftermath, some have alleged that the crash was actually an overreaction and that it will soon be reversed; i.e., that it represented just the opposite of a corrected speculative bubble (but was still irrational). If this be true, strong and sharp price increases should occur sometime. However, as shown in Figure Roll-10, there is no evidence of such a rebound during the successive four calendar months. Certain regions have performed better than others. Asia, North America and the smaller European countries have experienced moderate price increases, particularly after the first of December 1987. Conversely, other regions have performed rather poorly, (Australia/New Zealand), or have shown little movement in either direction from the level established at the end of October. The interocular test in Figure Roll-10 reveals an ordinary pattern, one that could be expected over just about any four-month interval; some differences across markets, but certainly no dramatic and worldwide reversal anywhere close to the size of October's decline.

A world index constructed by equally-weighting the local currency indexes and normalized to 100 on September 30, 1987, fell to 73.6 by October 30. By February 29, 1988 the index stood at 72.7. Thus, the price level established in the October crash seems to have been a virtually unbiased estimate of the average price level over the subsequent four months. If a sizeable correction is going to occur, it is apparently going to take quite a while.

TABLE ROLL-3
Institutional Arrangements in World Markets

Country	Auction	Official Specialists	Forward Trading on Exchange	Automated Quotations	Computer Directed Trading	Options/ Futures Trading	Price Limits	Transaction Tax (Round Trip)	Margin Requirements	Trading Off Exchange
Australia	Continuous	No	No	*Yes	No	Yes	None	.6%	None	Infrequent
Austria	Single	Yes	No	No	No	No	5 %	.3%	100%	Frequent
Belgium	Mixed	No	Yes	No	No	No (1)	10%/None (2)	.375%/.195%	100%/25% (2)	Occasional
Canada	Continuous	No	No	Yes	Yes	Yes	None (3)	0	50% (4)	Prohibited
Denmark	Mixed	No	No	No	No	No	None	1%	None	Frequent
France	Mixed	Yes	Yes	No	Yes	Yes	4%/7% (5)	.3%	100%/20% (6)	Prohibited
Germany	Continuous	Yes	No	No	No	Options	None	.5%	None	Frequent
Hong Kong	Continuous	No	No	No	No	Futures	None (7)	.6% +	None	Infrequent
Ireland	Continuous	No	No	Yes	No	No	None	1%	100%	Infrequent
Italy	Mixed	No	Yes	No	No	No	10-20% (8)	.3%	100%	Frequent
Japan	Continuous	Yes	No	Yes	Yes	No (9)	-10%	.55%	70% (10)	Prohibited
Malaysia	Continuous	No	No	No	No	No	None	.03%	None	Occasional
Mexico	Continuous	No	No	No	No	No	10% (11)	0	None	Occasional
Netherlands	Continuous	Yes	No	No	No	Options	Variable (12)	2.4% (13)	None	Prohibited
New Zealand	Continuous	No	No	No	.10	Futures	None	0	None	Occasional
Norway	Single	No	No	No	No	No	None	1%	100%	Frequent
Singapore	Continuous	No	No	Yes	No	No (14)	None	.5%	71%	Occasional
South Africa	Continuous	No	No	No	No	Options	None	1.5%	100%	Prohibited
Spain	Mixed (15)	No	No	No	No	No	10% (16)	.11%	50% (16)	Frequent
Sweden	Mixed	No	No	Yes	No	Yes	None	2%	40%	Frequent
Switzerland	Mixed	No	Yes	Yes	No	Yes	5% (17)	.9%	None	Infrequent
United Kingdom	Continuous	No	No	Yes	Yes	Yes	None	.5%	None	Occasional
United States	Continuous	Yes	No	Yes	Yes	Yes	None	0	Yes	Occasional

Footnotes

(1) Calls only on just five stocks.
(2) Cash/forward.
(3) None on Stocks. 3-5% on Index Futures.
(4) 10% (5%) for uncovered (covered) futures.
(5) Cash/Forward, but not always enforced.
(6) Cash/Forward. 40% if forward collateral is stock rather than cash.
(7) "Four spread rule:" Offers not permitted more than four ticks from current bids and asks.
(8) Hitting limit suspends auction; Auction then tried a second time at end of day.
(9) Futures on the Nikkei Index are traded in Singapore.
(10) Decreased to 50% on October 21, 1987 "to encourage buyers."
(11) Trading suspended for successive periods, 15 and then 30 minutes; effective limit: 30-40%.
(12) Authorities have discretion. In October, 2% limits every 15 minutes used frequently.
(13) For non-dealer transactions only.
(14) Only for Nikkei Index, (Japan).
(15) Groups of stocks are traded continuously for ten minutes each.
(16) Limits raised to 20% and Margin to 50% on October 27.
(17) Hitting limit causes 15-minute trading suspension. Limits raised to 10-15% in October.

INSTITUTIONAL ARRANGEMENTS
AND MARKET BEHAVIOR

Our world laboratory experiment provides suggestive insights into the possible influence of each major element of the market's institutional structure. The stock markets around the world are amazingly diverse in their organization; Table Roll-3 provides a list of some of the particular features in place during October 1987.[8]

Among the features that have figured prominently in post-crash discussions are the extent of computerized trading, the auction system itself, the presence or absence of limits on price movements, regulated margin requirements, and off-market or off-hours trading. Additional features that could be of significance include the presence or absence of floor brokers who conduct trades but are *not* permitted to invest on their own account, the extent of trading in the cash market versus the forward market, the identity of traders (i.e., institutions such as banks or specialized trading firms), and the significance of transaction taxes.

Some markets have trading for both immediate and forward settlement. When forward settlement exists, the forward contracts often have a greater volume of trading than cash contracts. For instance, on the Paris *Bourse*, there is a once-a-day auction in the cash market conducted by designated brokerage houses, but there is continuous forward trading in the larger stocks from 9:30 to 11:00 a.m. and repeated call auctions thereafter in forward contracts for all stocks. The limit moves are different too; they are seven percent in the forward market and four percent in the cash market.[9]

---

[8]The data presented in Table Roll-3 are not easily available. Jim Brandon telephoned every country on the list and interviewed a person knowledgeable about each market. For giving generously of their time, the author thanks Neville Thomas and Michael Crowley, Australia; Robert Schwind, Australia; Mme. Moeremhout, Belgium; Jim Darcel, Canada; Jorgen Brisson, Denmark; M. Duzy, France; Michael Hanke, Germany; Patrick Leong, Hong Kong; Tom Healy, Ireland; Alessandro Wagner, Italy; Moriyuki Iwanaga, Japan; Mr. Izlen, Malaysia; Armando Denegas, Mexico; Paul Koster, the Netherlands; Cathy Cruschow, New Zealand; Melvin Tagen, Norway; Gillian Tam, Singapore; Brigette Borsch, Switzerland; and Matthew Hall, United Kingdom.

[9] The French market exhibits a unique concept of price limits. They are not enforced if the entire market seems to be moving in the same direction. According to our informant, enforcement applies only when an individual stock "appears to be manipulated."

TABLE ROLL-4
Local Currency Returns in October 1987 and Market Characteristics

Characteristic:	Auction	Official Specialists	Forward Trading on Exchange	Automated Quotations	Computer Directed Trading	Options/ Futures Trading	Price Limits	Transaction Tax	Margin Requirements	Trading Off Exchange
Variable Value	Continuous=1 Otherwise=0	Yes=1 Otherwise=0	Yes=1 Otherwise=0	Yes=1 Otherwise=0	Yes=1 Otherwise=0	Yes=1 Otherwise=0	None=0 Otherwise=1	Non-Zero=1 Otherwise=0	None=0 Otherwise=1	Prohibited & Infrequent=0 Otherwise=1
Group				_Average October Local Currency Return for Countries in Zero/One Variable Group, (%)_						
1	-29.69	-19.53	-24.70	-28.99	-21.25	-27.31	-22.08	-26.31	-23.54	-25.94
0	-21.39	-29.47	-26.93	-23.14	-27.89	-25.50	-29.25	-27.08	-30.22	-27.38
Difference	-8.31	9.94	2.23	-5.85	6.63	-1.80	7.17	0.78	6.68	1.44
T-Value	-2.66	3.53	0.51	-2.05	2.31	-0.57	2.25	0.22	2.20	0.41
				Multiple Regression of October Local Currency Return on Zero/One Variables						
Coefficient	-7.324	6.528	-2.867	-6.065	7.518	1.194	1.638	1.845	2.111	1.452
T-Value	-1.304	1.068	-0.417	-0.954	1.110	0.222	0.232	0.298	0.449	0.258
TS T-Value	-1.762	1.628	-0.592	-1.287	1.631	0.267	0.335	0.343	0.594	0.406

Intercept = -26.5, Adjusted R-Square = 0.254.

However, there are *no* limits on the price movements of foreign securities. All trading is done by registered stock brokers, a requirement of French law. Block trading is conducted between the previous day's high and low prices and there is heavy block volume, constituting about one-half of all equity trading.

To judge the importance of any particular institutional characteristic, one could compare the market behavior in Table Roll-1 or in Figures Roll-1 to 6 with the presence or absence of the characteristic, as given in Table Roll-3. For example, computer directed trading is prevalent in Canada, France, Japan, the United Kingdom, and the United States. In local currency terms, these five countries experienced an average decline of 21.25 percent during October; the 18 countries without widespread computer directed trading experienced an average decline of 27.89 percent. Thus, taken as a characteristic in isolation, computer directed trading such as portfolio insurance and index arbitrage, if it had any impact at all, actually helped mitigate the market decline.

The Quantitative Impact of Market Arrangements on the Extent of the Crash

To obtain a quantitative estimate of the impact of each qualitative institutional characteristic, the entries in Table Roll-3 were converted into zero/one values and then both univariate and multivariate results were computed based on the converted numbers. Table Roll-4 defines the zero/one variables and presents the basic results.

The top panel of the table shows simple cross-country means for the countries in each univariate zero/one category. For example, if the auction in a particular country is conducted on a continuous basis, that country is assigned to group one, while if there is a single daily auction or a mixed auction, the country is in group zero. Table Roll-4 shows that continuous auction countries had October declines of -29.69 percent on average while the non-continuous auction countries had October declines that averaged -21.39 percent.

The "T-Value" of the difference provides a statistical measure of significance. If the T-Value is above 1.65 (in absolute value), the odds are roughly ten to one that the variable is significant, when judged on a univariate basis, i.e., in isolation.[10]   Thus, six of the ten variables were related to the magnitude of the crash. Continuous auctions and automated quotation systems were associated with large declines while the presence of an official specialist, computer directed trading, price limits, and margin requirements were associated with smaller declines. Forward trading, options and futures, transaction taxes, and trading off the exchanges were not associated significantly with the size of the crash.

Any univariate test may lead to an inappropriate conclusion because the characteristic in question may be proxying for some other characteristic which is the actual cause of the observed difference. This is certainly possible here, not only because the different institutional characteristics are correlated across countries, but also because other relevant influences may have been omitted.

The first problem is addressed in the bottom panel of Table Roll-4, which presents a multivariate comparison in the form of a cross-country regression of October returns (in local currency units) on all of the zero/one variables. The explained variance, (adjusted $R^{2)}$), was 25.4 percent but none of the ordinary T-Values from the cross-sectional regression indicate statistical reliability. This reveals the presence of multicollinearity in the explanatory variables, which makes it difficult to assess the relative importance of each one.

Moreover, there is a potential problem in this cross-sectional regression in that the observations may not be cross-sectionally independent. This will bias the ordinary T-Values though the direction of bias is impossible to determine without knowledge of the covariance structure of the residuals. In an attempt to repair both multicollinearity and cross-sectional dependence, another T-value was constructed by using the time series of cross-sectional returns for the period prior to October. The method is explained in the statistical appendix.

---

[10] An explanation of the statistical methods used to obtain the T-Value is contained in the statistical appendix.

Using the Times Series derived "TS T-Values," several characteristics have at least marginal statistical reliability: the presence of an official monopolistic specialist, and computer directed trading were associated with *less* severe market declines in October. Continuous auctions were marginally significant and associated with greater market declines. Note that these three variables have coefficients with roughly the same magnitude in both the univariate and the multivariate computations while variables such as price limits and margin requirements have much larger coefficients in the univariate calculations.[11]

Although the regression in Table Roll-4 indicates some statistically significant associations between certain market characteristics and the October decline, one should hesitate to conclude that even a strongly associated variable actually *contributed* to the decline. Markets differ in their amplitudes of response to the same underlying trigger and certain institutional features may have been adopted *because* of a high amplitude. As an example, it is conceivable, though perhaps improbable, that price limits are abandoned in markets with great volatility. This could have given rise to an association between the absence of price limits and the severity of price decline in October 1987, without there actually having been a mitigating influence of limits.

The Typical Market Response to World Movements and the Crash

In addition to institutional arrangements, another potential explanation for the variety of declines in different markets is that an underlying fundamental worldwide triggering variable caused the crash and that the relative movement of each market was simply the usual relation between that particular market and the underlying factor. In order to assess this possibility, data for February 1981 through September 1987 were used to construct a world market index[12] equal-weighted across countries using

---

[11] The univariate difference in means across zero/one groups is identical to the slope coefficient in a cross-sectional regression of the October return on a *single* zero/one variable; (for a proof, see the statistical appendix). Thus, the effect of multicollinearity can be directly gauged by comparing the slope coefficient in the second panel of Table Roll-4 with the corresponding group mean differences in the first panel.

[12] Goldman, Sachs & Co. provided monthly market index levels beginning in January, 1981. However, their data base does not include Mexico until May, 1981. The first month is lost by

local currency denominated returns.[13]   Then a simple "market model" was fit to the available time series of monthly returns for each country,

$$R_{j,t} = a_j + b_j R_{M,t} + e_{j,t},$$

where $R_{j,t}$ is the monthly percentage change in the index of country j for month t, $R_{M,t}$ is the world market index percentage change, $e_{j,t}$ is an unexplained residual, and a_j and b_j are fitted coefficients. The slope coefficient b_j is the so-called "beta" which measures the relative magnitude of response of a given country to changes in the world market index. The statistical appendix gives details of these regressions for each country. Every country exhibits a statistically significant relation with the world market index, and the average R-Square is 0.243.

The market model fitted for each country up through September 1987 was used to predict the country's return in October 1987, conditional on the world market index movement in October. The prediction errors (or out-of-sample residuals) were then cross-sectionally related to market characteristics, i.e., to the zero/one variables used previously. The results are given in the top panel of Table Roll-5.

No coefficient is statistically different from zero. Thus, *none* of the institutional market characteristics was associated with an unusually large or small October return after the worldwide market movement was taken into account. In other words, the magnitude of each market's decline was explained by that market's ordinary relation with world market events.

---

calculating the monthly percentage change in the index. Thus, the index includes 22 countries from February 1981 and 23 countries from June 1981. Dividend yields are available for the latter part of the data period, but dividends have little variability and were thus omitted from the calculations without harm. Due to this omission, the index percentage change for a given month differs slightly from the monthly total return.

[13] Indexes were actually constructed both on a common currency basis and a local currency basis and both equal-weighted and value-weighted (by the dollar value of total country capitalization). Time series regressions between individual country returns and the various indexes yielded surprisingly similar slope coefficients, ("betas"). There were differences in R-Squares, of course, because the exchange rate adjustment essentially adds a noisy but relatively uncorrelated random variable to the local currency return. The intercepts also differed, by roughly the difference in mean returns in local currency and in dollars.

Nothing was left to be explained by the particular institutional arrangements in place.[14]

The second panel of Table Roll-5 gives some additional evidence about the overwhelming influence of the world market "factor." In the cross-sectional regression reported there, the October index return (not the residual) was related to the institutional zero/one characteristics *plus* the market model slope coefficient (or "beta") from the time series regression for each country calculated up through September. This panel differs from the cross-sectional multiple regression in Table Roll-4 only by the inclusion of the "beta." Comparing the two regressions, we observe that *none* of the market characteristics remains even marginally significant. In contrast, the "beta" is highly significant and its coefficient (-16.6 percent) is a large fraction of the average world market portfolio return [15] and it is more than three times the magnitude of any other estimated coefficient in the regression.

Because this regression uses total percentage change during October, it may be subject to cross-sectional dependence; thus, a time series T-Value was also computed using the methods described in the statistical appendix. The results are qualitatively the same: only the market model "beta" is a statistically significant variable in explaining October 1987 returns.

There is, however, one remaining problem: it seems at least conceivable that the typical magnitude of response of a given country to a world market movement is itself a function of the institutional arrangements in that country's stock market. For example, perhaps margin requirements or limits on price movements reduce the "beta" in the market model from the level it would otherwise achieve in their absence. If this be true, the dominance of the "beta" in the October return cross sectional regression in Table Roll-5 and the absence of a statistically significant market characteristic in the cross-sectional regression for market

---

[14]Notice that cross-sectional dependence is probably not material in this regression, simply because the principal source of that dependence, general worldwide market movements, has already been removed.

[15] Even this coefficient is probably understated in absolute magnitude because the beta is only an estimated coefficient and is thus an error-contaminated regressor.

residuals during October may still not entirely remove the suspicion that some of the institutional arrangements had an influence on the crash. Instead of showing up directly, their influence could have been exerted by reducing or increasing the estimated magnitude of response.

To check out this possibility, another cross-sectional regression was computed, but this time the dependent variable was the estimated "beta" itself while the explanatory variables were the zero/one market characteristics. See the bottom panel of Table Roll-5 for the results.

There are two marginally significant characteristics: continuous auctions and forward trading. Forward trading, however, did not show up as an influence on either the total returns in October nor on the October market model residuals. Thus, though it may be an influence on the typical response of a market to world movements, it seems to have not played a role in the crash. There is greater suspicion that continuous trading was a culprit. Countries whose stock markets conduct continuous auctions did worse during the crash. They are also associated with larger "betas" and thus tend to swing more widely in response to worldwide market influences.

If we were willing to accept this result as evidence of causation, we might go on to speculate on why continuous auctions might be prone to larger price swings. A continuous auction conducts trading throughout the day, as orders are received, while a non-continuous auction collects orders over a 24-hour interval and clears all of them at a given time. The continuous auction is more dynamic and it certainly offers a larger inducement for a trader to act quickly. Quick decisions are less important in a non-continuous regime because others may reach similar conclusions before the appointed time for the auction. Acting quickly could lead more often to error and even to panic in attempting to beat others to the next trade. Perhaps haste made waste in October 1987.

TABLE ROLL-5
Local Currency Market Model and Market Characteristics

Characteristic	Auction	Official Specialists	Forward Trading on Exchange	Automated Quotations	Computer Directed Trading	Options/ Futures Trading	Price Limits	Transaction Tax	Margin Requirements	Trading Off Exchange	Beta
Variable Value	Continuous=1 Otherwise=0	Yes=1 Otherwise=0	Yes=1 Otherwise=0	Yes=1 Otherwise=0	Yes=1 Otherwise=0	Yes=1 Otherwise=0	None=0 Otherwise=1	Non-Zero=1 Otherwise=0	None=0 Otherwise=1	Prohibited & Infrequent=0 Otherwise=1	

Market Model Prediction Errors in October, 1987 vs. Market Characteristics

	Auction	Official Specialists	Forward Trading on Exchange	Automated Quotations	Computer Directed Trading	Options/ Futures Trading	Price Limits	Transaction Tax	Margin Requirements	Trading Off Exchange
Coefficient	1.688	3.540	8.529	-4.381	1.670	-3.614	-2.201	-5.669	0.551	-0.951
T-Value	0.361	0.697	1.491	-0.828	0.297	-0.809	-0.376	-1.103	0.141	-0.203

Intercept = 5.89, Adjusted R-Square = 0.088.

Multiple Regression of October Local Currency Return on Zero/One Variables and on Typical Response

	Auction	Official Specialists	Forward Trading on Exchange	Automated Quotations	Computer Directed Trading	Options/ Futures Trading	Price Limits	Transaction Tax	Margin Requirements	Trading Off Exchange	Beta
Coefficient	-1.443	4.010	4.080	-5.460	4.218	-1.476	0.020	-3.088	1.338	0.179	-16.642
T-Value	-0.281	0.786	0.654	-1.046	0.741	-0.326	0.003	-0.571	0.346	0.039	-2.615
TS T-Value	-0.351	1.046	0.779	-1.169	0.945	-0.339	0.004	-0.638	0.387	0.049	-2.251

Intercept = -6.42, Adjusted R-Square = 0.498.

Market Model Betas, January, 1981 - September, 1987 vs. Market Characteristics

	Auction	Official Specialists	Forward Trading on Exchange	Automated Quotations	Computer Directed Trading	Options/ Futures Trading	Price Limits	Transaction Tax	Margin Requirements	Trading Off Exchange
Coefficient	0.353	-0.151	0.417	0.036	-0.198	-0.160	-0.097	-0.296.	-0.046	-0.077
T-Value	1.691	-0.665	1.631	0.154	-0.787	-0.803	-0.371	-1.288	-0.266	-0.366

Intercept = 1.21, Adjusted R-Square = 0.255.

Market Liquidity

"Liquidity" is another possible influence on inter-country differences during the crash. Liquidity is an ill-defined term, but most market observers seem to regard smaller markets as less liquid and thus potentially more prone to price volatility, subject to greater psychological influences, and probably less "efficient." To examine this idea, the aggregate dollar value of stocks traded on each stock exchange, and appearing in the index, was used as a proxy for liquidity.

On September 30, 1987, the 23 national markets in our database differed widely in aggregate capitalization. The smallest was Norway, $2.65 billion, and the largest was Japan, $2.03 trillion. The United States market capitalization was $1.85 trillion.

Since market capitalization differs across countries by almost a factor of 100, its logarithm was used in the statistical estimation. Log(Market Cap) was introduced as an additional regressor in the cross-sectional model reported in Table Roll-5, panel 2; i.e., it was used along with the zero/one institutional characteristics variables and the estimated market model "beta" to explain the cross-sectional differences in return during October 1987. It was completely insignificant, having a T-Value of only .348, and leaving all the other coefficients virtually unchanged.[16]

Given the previous information about returns around the crash, the lack of a liquidity effect is probably not all that surprising. Some of the smallest markets performed relatively well in October (e.g., Austria and Denmark), while others did badly (Malaysia and Mexico). Similarly, some larger countries had small declines, (Japan), and others were more severely affected (the UK). Overall, the relative extent of the October crash was related to characteristics other than sheer size.

---

[16] In particular, the coefficient of "beta" was about the same (-15.6) and still highly significant (T-Value = -2.16). Cross-sectionally, the "beta" estimated from February 1981 through September 1987 is moderately correlated with the Log of market capitalization at the end of September 1987. A cross-sectional regression of beta on log size gives a slope coefficient of -.147 with a T-Value of 1.68. But when *both* variables compete in a cross-sectional regression predicting the October decline, the "beta" wins in the sense of being uniquely significant.

Conclusions

Differences across countries in stock market behavior constitute a natural laboratory experiment to assess causes of the stock market crash in October 1987. All major world markets declined substantially in that month, which is itself an exceptional fact that contrasts with the usual modest correlations of returns across countries. In local currency units, the minimum decline was in Austria (-11.4 percent) and the maximum was in Hong Kong (-45.8 percent). Out of 23 countries, 19 had declines greater than 20 percent. The United States had the fifth *smallest* decline, i.e., the fifth best performance, in local currency units. However, because the dollar declined against most currencies, the U.S. performance restated in a common currency was only 11th out of 23.

The United States market was not the first to decline sharply. Non-Japanese Asian markets began a severe decline on October 19, their time, and this decline was echoed first on a number of European markets, then in North America, and finally in Japan. However, most of the same markets had experienced significant but less severe declines in the latter part of the previous week. With the exceptions of the U.S. and Canada, other markets continued downward through the end of October, and some of these declines were as large as the great crash on October 19.

Various institutional market characteristics were empirically associated with the extent of the price decline. Each of ten characteristics was examined one by one. The presence of an official specialist, computer directed trading, price limits and margin requirements were associated with less severe stock market declines in October 1987. The presence of a continuous auction and automated quotations were associated with larger declines. Forward trading on the exchange, options and futures trading, transaction taxes, and trading off the exchange were unrelated to the extent of the crash. These are all univariate results that omit the interactions among the variables and ignore their dependence on other factors.

In multiple regressions, several of the variables that had significant univariate associations with the crash were discovered not to matter, their univariate importance apparently deriving spuriously from their correlation with other variables. Two important examples are limits on price moves and margin requirements. Their statistical influence is entirely eliminated when other market characteristics are taken into account.

Finally, an attempt was made to ascertain how much of October's crash could be ascribed to the normal response of each country's stock market to a worldwide market movement. A world market index was constructed and found to be statistically related to monthly returns in every country during the period from the beginning of 1981 up until the month before the crash. The magnitude of market response differs materially across countries. The response coefficient, or "beta" was *by far* the most statistically significant explanatory variable in the October crash. It swamped the influences of the institutional market characteristics.

Only one institutional variable, continuous auctions, had even a marginally significant influence on the estimated "beta."

STATISTICAL APPENDIX

T-Values for the Univariate Differences in Group Means

The first panel in Table Roll-4 presents a T-Value for the differences in the mean returns of countries in homogeneous institutional groups during October 1987. This T-Value was computed as follows:

1. For *each* institutional characteristic, two portfolios were formed corresponding to whether the group variable was zero or one. As an example, when the institutional characteristic was computer directed trading, the first portfolio consisted of an equal-weighted combination of the countries with computer directed trading (Canada, France, Japan, the United Kingdom, and the United States; see Table Roll-3), and the second portfolio consisted of an equal-weighted combination of the other countries (the 18 without computer directed trading). There is a total of twenty such portfolios, two for each of ten institutional characteristics.

2. The return was calculated for each of the twenty portfolios for all available data periods before October 1987. Except for Mexico, this was February 1981 through September 1987. For Mexico, it was June 1981 through September 1987. Thus, during the first four of 80 months, Mexico was missing from the ten portfolios to which it later belonged.

3. For each month and institutional characteristic, a return *difference* was formed by subtracting the portfolio return for group 0 from the portfolio return for group 1. This is tantamount to buying long those countries with a "1" and shorting those countries with a "0" *for a particular characteristic*. There were thus ten time series of return differences, one for each institutional characteristic.

4. The standard deviation of the return difference was calculated from the ten time series.

5. The T-Value was calculated as the return difference in October 1987 divided by the calculated time series standard deviation.

Univariate Regression on Zero/One Regressor

The slope coefficient from the regression of y on a zero/one variable x is simply the difference in group means of y.

Proof:

Define,

N = Total sample size

n = Number of observations with x=1.

$p = n/N$.

Y, Y_1, Y_0 = respectively, the sample mean of y, y with x=1,

and y with x=0.

Then,

it is straightforward to show that the ordinary least squares bivariate regression slope coefficient of y on x is

$$b = \{p(Y_1 - Y)/[p(1-p)]\}$$

$$= \{Y_1 - [pY_1 + (1-p)Y_0]\}/(1-p)$$

$$= Y_1 - Y_0.$$

Time Series T-Values, Multiple Regressions

The second panels of Tables Roll-4 and 5 present T-Values obtained from a time series not including the cross-section month (October 1987). The method was as follows:

1. For every month when all countries had available data, June 1981 through September 1987, a cross-sectional multiple regression was calculated between the actual monthly index percentage changes and the explanatory variables, the zero/one variables (corresponding to Table Roll-4) and the zero/one variables *plus* the country's market model beta (corresponding to Table Roll-5). The vector of 10 (11) cross-sectional coefficients corresponding to panel 2 of Table Roll-4 (Table Roll-5) for month t, formed a single time series observation.

2. The standard deviation of each element in the vector of coefficients was computed across all time series observations.

3. The "TS T-Value" was the estimated cross-sectional coefficient in October 1987 divided by its corresponding standard deviation as computed in steps 1 and 2.

Market Model Results For Local Currency Returns

Table Roll-1A gives means, standard deviations, and market model regression results for local currency returns using an equal-weighted local currency world market index.

TABLE ROLL-1A
Local Currency Index Percentage Changes
and Equal-Weighted World Portfolio
February, 1981-September, 1987

Country	Sample Size (Months)	Average % Change (per Month)	Standard Deviation (%/Month)	Market Model Regression Slope (T-Values)	Intercept	Adjusted R-Square
Australia	80	1.634	5.896	1.218 (7.208)	-0.563 (-0.938)	0.3921
Austria	80	0.985	5.128	0.563 (3.152)	-0.031 (-0.048)	0.1016
Belgium	80	1.899	5.191	0.808 (4.785)	0.442 (0.736)	0.2170
Canada	80	0.855	4.931	1.116 (8.492)	-1.159 (-2.481)	0.4738
Denmark	80	1.463	5.306	0.579 (3.127)	0.419 (0.637)	0.1000
France	80	1.748	5.602	0.901 (4.995)	0.123 (0.191)	0.2326
Germany	80	1.503	4.923	0.739 (4.567)	0.171 (0.297)	0.2009
Hong Kong	80	1.439	9.248	1.533 (5.201)	-1.326 (-1.266)	0.2480
Ireland	80	1.926	6.445	1.193 (6.074)	-0.226 (-0.324)	0.3124
Italy	80	1.911	7.783	1.192 (4.688)	-0.240 (-0.266)	0.2098
Japan	80	1.989	4.651	0.557 (3.483)	0.983 (1.729)	0.1235
Malaysia	80	0.433	8.108	1.137 (4.197)	-1.618 (-1.681)	0.1738
Mexico	76	6.555	16.110	2.135 (3.914)	2.655 (1.345)	0.1603
Netherlands	80	1.529	4.988	1.050 (7.440)	-0.365 (-0.728)	0.4076
New Zealand	80	2.190	6.609	1.019 (4.726)	0.352 (0.460)	0.2127
Norway	80	1.656	6.381	1.110 (5.553)	-0.346 (-0.487)	0.2742
Singapore	80	0.874	7.858	1.251 (4.930)	-1.383 (-1.534)	0.2278
South Africa	80	2.181	7.247	0.713 (2.790)	0.895 (0.985)	0.0791
Spain	80	2.352	6.443	0.716 (3.196)	1.060 (1.331)	0.1045
Sweden	80	2.513	6.109	0.872 (4.290)	0.940 (1.302)	0.1805
Switzerland	80	1.010	3.876	0.795 (7.117)	-0.424 (-1.068)	0.3860
United Kingdom	80	1.888	4.567	0.950 (7.288)	0.176 (0.379)	0.3975
United States	80	1.221	4.243	0.856 (6.933)	-0.324 (-0.738)	0.3734

Perspectives on October 1987

or
What Did We Learn
From the Crash?

Eugene F. Fama[*]

INTRODUCTION

There has been a rash of work on the decline in stock prices in October 1987. Much of it is concerned with how market structures should be changed to improve the performance of the market during its hyperactive periods, or to dampen future price shocks. Common questions include: (a) Should margins like those required in stock transactions be imposed on derivative securities like stock options and index futures? (b) Should the derivative securities be banned? (c) Should steps be taken to discourage portfolio insurance, or index arbitrage, or program trading?

In the discussions of these issues, a central point is overlooked. The appropriate view of market performance in October depends on whether the price decline was irrational or whether it was a rational adjustment to a new equilibrium, that is, to rational perceptions of changes in fundamental values. If the price decline was irrational, it is interesting to ask whether changes in market structures can make pricing more rational during similar future episodes. But if the price shock was a rational response to changes in fundamental values, the appropriate response to the October performance of the market is applause.

[*] The comments of Robert Barro, Bradford Cornell, Kenneth French, Roger Kormendi, Allan Meltzer, and Richard Roll are gratefully acknowledged.

THE ISSUE: RATIONAL OR IRRATIONAL PRICES

In a market economy, prices are signals for resource allocation. Rational prices, prices that are unbiased estimates of fundamental values, contribute to economic efficiency by directing resources toward their highest-value uses.

This signalling role of prices has an unavoidable implication. If the driving forces in the economy (for example, prospects for capital investment, or for tax changes) produce large shocks to fundamental values, then economic efficiency is served by the immediate adjustment of prices to the new fundamental values. Slow price adjustment benefits some investors, but the winners are offset by the losers. More important, slow adjustment of prices to a new equilibrium is socially inefficient: unreliable signals from prices imply less efficient allocation of the economy's real resources.

In short, rational prices are not necessarily less volatile prices, and less volatile prices are not necessarily better than more volatile prices. The appropriate view of the October price shock depends critically on whether it was a rational response to changes in fundamental values.

RATIONAL PRICE MOVEMENTS AND NEWS

In many analyses of the period, whether by academics, the media, or the expert panels set up to study market performance, there is a presumption that the October price shock has a large irrational component. The reason is that there was no news immediately preceding October 19 that would seem to imply a decline of more than 20 percent in fundamental values.

In the common valuation models, changes in rational prices have two sources: (a) changes in expected earnings, and (b) changes in the anticipated or expected returns investors require to get them to hold securities (more precisely, changes in the discount rates used to price expected earnings). It would seem that if the October price shock was rational, it should be traceable to news about the earnings prospects of stocks and/or to news about expected returns. The task, however, has problems that are due in large part to our lack of knowledge about how markets absorb information about business conditions.

Stock Returns and Forecasts of Real Activity

Among my academic colleagues, much of the frustration from the October drop relates to strong empirical evidence that, historically, stock returns are good predictors of real activity. For example, depending on the time period examined, this year's stock return explains 50 percent to 70 percent of the variance of next year's growth of real GNP. (See Fama 1981, Kaul 1987, and Robert Barro's paper in this volume.) From this evidence, it is natural to presume that a price drop like October's is a forecast that real activity (and corporate profits) will not be as strong as previously anticipated. The frustration comes from not being able to identify the news that gave rise to the forecast.

The frustration, however, is not special to the October experience. Financial economists are skilled at measuring the response of security prices to firm-specific information, like earnings announcements, changes in dividends, and takeover announcements. In contrast, although there is evidence that stock returns and other financial market prices forecast real activity, existing research is silent on how the forecast power comes about, that is, how the market puts together different bits and pieces of information to forecast general business conditions. Our inability to identify the precise causes of the October price drop can be viewed as part of a generally poor record in identifying the causes of market-wide price changes on an on-line basis, even though it is clear from the historical record that stock returns forecast real activity and corporate profits.

It would seem nevertheless that, if rational, a price change as large as October's must be associated with big news. There are, however, scenarios in which this is not the case. My favorite is given by Benoit Mandelbrot (1966). His paper is one of the first formal statements of how rational security prices react to news. He gives a simple example in which rational forecasts of economic conditions depend on past conditions. Specifically, the longer a period of good (or bad) times has run, the longer it is rational to forecast that it will continue. In a long period of continuing good times, security prices will be high relative to observed earnings or dividends because prices rationally forecast extended good times. In this situation, information that times have simply changed from good to average produces a large price decline because prices must be purged of previous (rational) forecasts of extended good times.

Mandelbrot presents his model as an example of how prices are linked to rational forecasts of economic driving variables. The specific scenario for how rational forecasts of economic conditions depend on recent past conditions may or may not be realistic. But the example suffices to make the point that large adjustments in rational prices do not necessarily require striking pieces of news.

Mandelbrot's model does, however, capture the broad outlines of the recent market scenario. The crash was preceded by a long period of sustained growth. Prior to the crash, ratios of earnings or dividends to stock prices were low relative to historical values, suggesting that prices were forecasting extended good times. For example, at the end of September 1987, the dividend/price ratio for the S&P 500 was 2.78 percent, compared to its average value for the 1957-86 period of about 3.8 percent.

The loss of wealth in October was traumatic. But now that the dust has settled and the wounds have been bandaged, one can argue that, as in the Mandelbrot story, the shock was just a shift from prices that were forecasting extended good times to prices that are forecasting that future times will be about average. A suggestive piece of evidence is that at the end of December, the dividend/price ratio for the S&P 500 was 3.71 percent, still below but not far from its mean, 3.8 percent, for the last 30 years.

Changes in Expected Returns

Changes in the anticipated or expected returns investors require to hold stocks can also produce large price changes. For example, if expected future earnings remain the same, a permanent change from ten percent to 12.5 percent in the level of expected returns (interpreted as discount rates for future earnings) causes a 20 percent drop in prices.

There is much evidence that the level of expected stock returns changes through time. (See, for example, Fama and French 1987a, b.) Dividend yields on diversified portfolios, like the S&P 500, work well in tracking this variation in expected returns. When the dividend yield is high, future returns are on average high. When the dividend yield is low future returns are on average low (which does not mean negative). The fact that dividend yields (or any other variable known in advance) forecast returns is evidence that expected returns vary through time.

Again, in large part due to the October price shock, the dividend yield on the S&P 500 rose from 2.78 percent at the end of September to 3.71 percent at the end of December, which is close to its average (about 3.8 percent) for the 1957-86 period. The evidence that the dividend yield tracks variation in expected returns then suggests that the October shock reflects a shift in expected returns from low levels prior to the crash to values closer to historical averages.[1]

There is other evidence for this view. Another variable that tracks variation in expected stock and (bond) returns is the default spread, that is, the spread of yields in lower-grade bonds over yields on high-grade bonds. At the end of September 1987, the default spread (measured as the spread of A-Baa yields over Aaa yields) was .27 percent (27 basis points), about half its mean value (.55 percent) for the 1957-86 period. The default spread rose sharply around October 19th, and at the end of 1987, the spread, at .50 percent, was still below but close to its 1957-86 mean. Thus, like the dividend yield, the behavior of the default spread suggests that the October shock reflects a shift in expected returns from low levels prior to the crash to values closer to historical means.

What caused the shift in the level of expected returns investors require to hold stocks? The question is interesting and relevant, but the current state of the evidence on such issues allows only a vague answer. In particular, there is evidence that expected stock returns vary with business conditions. Expected returns (and dividend yields and default spreads) are

---

[1] NYSE data for the 1927-86 period, provided by the Center for Research in Security prices, do not suggest that low dividend yields, like that observed at the end of September 1987, are typically followed by strong negative returns. When the end-of-quarter dividend yields on the value-weighted portfolio of NYSE stocks are ranked by size, the average of the smallest ten percent of the yields (the smallest 24 in the sample of 240) is 2.84 percent, close to the value observed in September 1987. The average return for the 24 quarters following these low yields is -1.8 percent.

higher when business conditions are weak and lower when business is strong. In this light, the change in dividend yields and default spreads around the October price drop suggests that expected returns increased because of market assessments that business conditions were moving from good to average.

What caused this shift in expectations? I do not know. But I am not alone in my ignorance, and it is not special to the October experience. While there is evidence that expected returns are related to business conditions, the evidence is silent on how the relation comes about, that is, the details of how the market processes information about business conditions. Our inability to identify the causes of the October price drop is again part of a generally poor record on this score, even though, from the historical record, it is clear that prices forecast business conditions, and that the pricing process produces a relation between the evolution of expected returns and business conditions.

Summary of the Rational Pricing View

In short, interpreted from a rational pricing perspective, the October shock has two complementary explanations, both driven by a change in expectations about conditions. (1) An extended period of economic growth produced expectations of continued growth in earnings and thus high stock prices. For reasons we do not understand, expectations about growth changed, and stock prices fell. (2) The fall was reinforced by a discount rate effect.   The deterioration of expectations about business conditions meant that the expected returns investors require to hold stocks rose from low levels, typical when times are good, to higher levels. The rise in expected returns (the discount rates for earnings) produced a drop in prices.

AN IRRATIONAL PRICE MOVE?

Financial economists live with an unpleasant fact. There is no scientific way to show that security prices are rational (or irrational). (See, for example, Fama 1970.) The problem is simple. To show that the market sets prices equal to fundamental values, one must know the fundamental values or the "true" model that generates fundamental values. There is, unfortunately, no way to know whether a particular model is the true model. In short, we cannot say for sure that price behavior around October was rational. It is well, then, to also examine the period from the perspective that at least some of the price behavior was irrational.

If the price drop on October 19th was then quickly reversed, one might suspect that it had a large irrational component. There was a rebound on October 20th, but thereafter the market flirted several times with the close on October 19th. Prices were quite volatile after the 19th, but this can be attributed to uncertainty about new fundamental values when there is consensus that they have changed. Moreover, the fact that the price drop resulted in dividend/price ratios close to but still below historical averages makes it difficult to argue that the drop was an over-reaction.

Perhaps, then, it was the preceding increase in prices that was in large part irrational. (This seems to be the view of many market observers, including Chairman Greenspan of the Federal Reserve Board.) If this is the case, most analyses of the period around October 19th are misdirected and most proposed "reforms" are irrelevant. The rise in prices preceding October 19th took place over a long (five-year) period. It was orderly and world-wide. I am not aware of claims that much, if any, of the rise was due to the purported American villains of the crash—program trading, index arbitrage, portfolio insurance, different margin requirements on futures than on the underlying stocks, etc.

Changes in market structure suggested in response to the crash, like trading halts during volatile periods, were irrelevant during the price rise. Moreover, if the upside of the alleged bubble could not be avoided, changes in market structures that (for the sake of argument) might slow the decline in prices to rational levels are ill-advised. If there are bubbles, economic efficiency is served by letting them burst rather than leak.

"NOISE"

Much of the recent discussion of the October period is concerned with reducing "noise", that is, price volatility unrelated to variation in fundamental values. Noise is socially wasteful. It obscures the information in prices about resource allocation. It can increase the expected returns investors require to hold stock, which means higher costs-of-capital for firms and less capital investment.

There is some amount of noise in the variation of stock prices. Unfortunately, there is no convincing evidence on how much. The October period emphasizes the point. In spite of many detailed (and often fascinating) reports, prepared by the best business and academic minds, there is no clear evidence about how much of the volatility of the period is noise. It is nevertheless fun to join in the discussion of market structures that might reduce noise. The cast of popular villains to be scrutinized includes program trading, index arbitrage, and portfolio insurance.

The Villains

Index Arbitrage and Program Trading. Stock index futures have many benefits in improving risk-sharing among market participants. For example, index futures allow investors, especially large institutional investors, to hedge the risks of their stock portfolios at lower trading costs than similar transactions in the underlying stocks. The futures market accomplishes its tasks most efficiently when the futures price is linked closely to the value of the underlying index. The link is largely assured by index arbitrage.

This is the classic process whereby arbitragers buy stocks and sell futures when stock prices produce an index value that is low relative to the futures price, and conversely.

Index arbitrage is in turn facilitated by program trading, which allows investors to simultaneously issue orders for bundles of stocks through a computer. Program trading is in general an efficient mechanism for order transmission. It seems certain to become more important, and it is safe to predict that markets will compete to find ways to improve its performance.

Index arbitrage is a consensus villain in current discussions of market "reforms." But convincing evidence, or even arguments, that index arbitrage creates noise in prices are lacking. It should have the opposite effect. By linking stock and futures prices, index arbitrage should reduce the noise in the combined signals from the two markets. (Grossman and Miller 1987 give an excellent discussion of this point.) Conversely, changes in market mechanisms that reduce the efficiency of index arbitrage destroy some of the economic value of the futures market by increasing the variance of discrepancies between stock and futures prices.

Current proposals to restrict index arbitrage during periods of high volatility (by restricting arbitrageur access to the program-trading system) seem especially misguided. Breaking the links between stock and futures prices can only add to the informational chaos of high volatility periods—a fact that was obvious on October 19th and 20th. A better approach would be to improve the efficiency of program trading in handling the large trading volumes typical of volatile periods, that is, to strengthen rather than weaken the link between stock and futures prices during these periods.

Portfolio Insurance. Another popular villain of the October period is portfolio insurance. In simple terms, this is a strategy of selling stocks (or futures) when prices decline in order to "insure" that the value of a portfolio does not go below some "floor" level, and buying stocks or futures when prices rise and push the portfolio safely above its floor. Since the strategy is not based on analysis of fundamentals, and since it generates trading that reinforces price movements, it has the potential to extend price movements, both on the upside and on the downside.

Price pressure created by portfolio insurers is offset, in whole or in part, by other traders who understand the motives of the insurers and take opposite positions. The important point, however, is that even if some price pressure remains, it is a cost of portfolio insurance. When prices fall, the extension of the fall due to the trading of portfolio insurance means that other traders get to buy from insurers at prices that are lower than otherwise, and conversely when prices rise. Thus any price pressure created by portfolio insurance is more a marketing problem for insurance vendors than a market problem. Aware of the problems, portfolio insurers seek mechanisms (like sunshine trading) that allow them to advertise their trading plans, so other traders can reduce the resulting price pressure by preparing to take the opposite side. (A good discussion of this point is in Grossman 1987.)

The "Reforms"

"**Circuit Breakers.**" One of the changes in market rules commonly proposed to reduce noise or unnecessary volatility in prices is the mandatory suspension of trading during periods of high volatility, so-called circuit breakers. This amounts to reducing the supply of a commodity, liquidity, when demand for the commodity is strong. Moreover, one can argue that mandatory trading halts increase rather than reduce volatility by inciting trading in anticipation of halts. My guess is that trading halts simply delay the adjustment of prices to changes in fundamental values. Richard Roll's paper in this volume is consistent with this view. He finds that the October crash was as strong in markets that imposed trading halts on or around the 19th as in those that did not.

The success of a market is largely determined by the mechanisms it offers to lower trading costs and improve trading efficiency. Markets compete with one another by providing different menus of trading mechanisms. This is not an area where prescience of government regulatory authorities should be assumed. If trading halts (or computer trading, or other market structures) on balance improve market efficiency, markets that provide them will have a competitive edge over those that do not. If trading halts are inefficient, markets that do not have them, in the U.S. or elsewhere, will gain over those that do. Moreover, it is well to point out that personal trading halts are available to any investor who wants time to analyze market events.

Uniform Margin Requirements. Another of the changes in market rules touted as a way to reduce volatility is uniform margin requirements for stocks, index futures, and stock options. Regulated margins on stocks were instituted in the 1930's because of a belief that trading stocks on margin increases volatility. The current argument is that unregulated (lower) margin requirements on futures and options creates volatility that spills into the stock market. Instituting required (higher) margins on options and futures will thus reduce volatility. Unfortunately, although required margins on stocks have existed for more than 50 years, the argument that they reduce volatility is at best a belief. There is no convincing evidence.

On the other hand, the October period was a dramatic experiment in the performance of markets in volatile periods. The crash had the tools to expose any problems in the rather flexible way margins are set in futures and options markets. The futures and options exchanges rightly emphasize, however, that there were no defaults on trades. In light of this, perhaps it is indeed time to re-examine margin requirements. But rather than extending required margins to futures and options, perhaps settling collateral in all stock transactions should be left as a contractual matter between borrowers and lenders, as it is in most other borrowing-lending arrangements.

WHAT DID WE LEARN FROM THE CRASH?

I argue that the October price drop has the look of an adjustment to a change in fundamental values. In this view, the market moved with breathtaking quickness to its new equilibrium, and its performance during this period of hyperactive trading is to be applauded.

Even if one takes the opposite view that the price swing around October was in large part irrational, it is the long, orderly upside of the swing preceding October 19th that is questionable, not the crash itself. Thus, even in this view, changes in market structures and rules motivated by the crash are largely irrelevant.

The loss of stock market wealth in October was traumatic. We should, however, avoid trauma-induced judgments about the performance of markets during the period. We should especially avoid trauma-induced prescriptions about how market mechanisms and rules should be changed.

REFERENCES

Barro, Robert J., "The Stock Market and the Macroeconomy," this volume.

Fama, Eugene F., 1970, "Efficient Capital Markets: A Review of Theory and Empirical Work," *Journal of Finance* 25 (May): 383-417.

Fama, Eugene F., 1981, "Stock Returns, Real Activity, Inflation, and Money," *American Economic Review* 71 (September): 545-65.

Fama, Eugene F., and Kenneth R. French, 1987a, "Dividend Yields and Expected Stock Returns," Unpublished manuscript, (University of Chicago, Chicago IL), November. Forthcoming in the *Journal of Financial Economics*.

Fama, Eugene F., and Kenneth R. French, 1987b, "Forecasting Returns on Corporate Bonds and Common Stock," Unpublished manuscript, (University of Chicago, Chicago IL), December.

Grossman, Sanford, 1987, "An Analysis of the Implications for Stock and Futures Price Volatility of Program Trading and Dynamic Hedging Strategies," *Journal of Business*, forthcoming.

Grossman, Sanford, and Miller, Merton H., 1987, "Liquidity and Market Structure," Unpublished manuscript, (University of Chicago, Chicago IL), December. Forthcoming in the *Journal of Finance* .

Kaul, Gautam, 1987, "Stock Returns and Inflation: The Role of the Monetary Sector," *Journal of Financial Economics,* 18 (June): 253-76.

Mandelbrot, Benoit, 1966, "Forecast of Future Prices, Unbiased Markets, and 'Martingale' Models." *Journal of Business* 39 (January): 242-55.

Roll, Richard, "The International Crash of October 1987," this volume.

The Stock Market and the
Macroeconomy:
Implications of the October 1987 Crash

Robert J. Barro*

The forecasting ability of the stock market often suffers from a bad press. For example, a popular joke is that the market has predicted nine out of the last five recessions (or similar numbers). In fact, considering how difficult it is to make accurate macroeconomic forecasts, the explanatory power of the stock market is outstanding. Over the period from 1927 to 1987 (excluding the war-dominated years from 1941 to 1946), the previous year's rate of return on stocks can account for 62 percent of annual variations in the growth rate of real gross national product (GNP).[1]

Forecasting 62 percent on average of the variation in annual real GNP growth means that much of business fluctuations remain unpredicted. Two types of errors arise; sometimes the stock market misses forecasting actual recessions (or booms), and sometimes the market predicts downturns (or upturns) that fail to materialize. Table Barro-1 summarizes the performance with respect to actual and predicted recessions since 1927. Of the nine periods that are generally designated as recessions (say by the National Bureau of Economic Research), the stock market successfully predicts eight. The notable error is for 1980-82, where the forecasted

---

* I am grateful for research assistance from Xavier Sala-i-Martin.

[1] The 62 percent figure applies when last year's value of real GNP growth is also considered. However, most of the explanatory power comes from the stock return—this variable alone accounts for 55 percent of variations in annual growth rates of real GNP. The findings are similar if the nominal returns are adjusted for inflation to calculate real returns. See the Appendix for the details of these and other results.

average growth rate for real GNP of 3.2 percent per year is well above the actual of -0.3 percent.[2]

TABLE BARRO-1
The Stock Market as a Predictor of Recessions

I.   Actual Recessions (as labeled by the National Bureau
     of Economic Research)

Period	Average Annual Growth Rate of Real GNP (%) (mean, 1926-87 = 2.9%)	Forecast of Growth Rate (%)	Annual Stock Return (%), lagged one year (mean, 1926-87 = 11.0%)
1930-33	-8.8	-4.6	-20.6
1938	-4.5	-4.8	-39.6
1949	0.0	1.9	3.9
1954	-1.3	1.4	0.7
1957-58	0.0	0.6	-0.7
1960-61	2.4	2.4	7.2
1970	-0.3	-0.6	-9.4
1974-75	-0.9	-2.8	-22.7
1980-82*	-0.3	3.2	15.9
1988?	--	1.4	2.8

II. Forecasted Non-Recessions

Period	Average Annual Growth	Forecast	Stock Return
1963	4.0	0.2	-8.5
1967	2.8	0.3	-8.6
1978	5.2	0.7	-4.5
1988?	--	1.4	2.8

*For 1980-81, the average growth rate is 0.9% with a forecast of 4.7%
and a lagged stock return of 25.6%. For 1982, the growth rate is
-2.6% with a forecast of 0.2% and a prior stock return of -3.4%.

NOTE: See Appendix Table A-1 for more details on these results.

The second section of Table Barro-1 shows that the stock market also erred in predicting three recessions that did not occur—for 1963, 1967, and 1978. Given the relatively weak stock return in 1987 (total return of

---

[2] The discussion treats 1980-82 as a single recession. Alternatively, if one follows the National Bureau's classification and separates the experience into two recessions, the market misses the downturn of 1980-81 (actual average growth rate of 0.9 percent, forecast of 4.7 percent) but successfully calls a recession for 1982 (actual growth of -2.6 percent, forecast of 0.2 percent).

2.8 percent, as compared to an average of 11.0 percent since 1926), the market (as of the end of December 1987) predicted a slowdown of economic growth for 1988. However, the forecasted growth rate for real GNP of 1.4 percent suggests a recession that is milder than all previous ones shown in Table Barro-1, except for 1960-61 (which Richard Nixon nevertheless thought was sufficient to cost him the Presidential election). Whether the stock market's forecast for 1988 falls into the category of successfully predicted recessions or into that of called recessions that never appeared is as yet unknown.

THE STOCK MARKET AND THE MACROECONOMY— THEORETICAL ASPECTS

There are two, not necessarily mutually exclusive, views of the interplay between the stock market and the macroeconomy. One model, consistent with the research of Fama (1981), begins with the idea that some real factors (typically unobservable to researchers) lead to variations in the prospective real rate of return on capital. Given the discount rates for owners of capital, an increase in prospective returns raises real stock prices. Therefore, the market valuation of capital exceeds its replacement cost, which causes an increase in business's desired quantities of capital goods.[3] The shift in desired capital leads to a change in business investment—moreover, since investment depends on the gap between desired and actual capital stocks, the proportionate movement of investment is much greater than that of desired capital. (As an example of this "accelerator" effect, suppose that investment is normally ten percent of the capital stock. Then a decision to raise the capital stock by an additional five percent over one year means that investment would be 50 percent above normal for the year.) In practice, because of the costs of making rapid adjustments to capital stocks, the effects on investment tend to be spread out over time. Therefore, movements in real stock prices tend to lead the changes in business's real investment spending.

Good news about the returns to capital amounts to an increase in wealth (as reflected in the higher real value of stock holdings). This higher wealth motivates households to raise their consumption. However, the

---

[3] This effect is stressed in "q-theories" of the investment process.

proportionate effect on consumption tends to be small because the increase in this single component of wealth has a relatively minor effect on the long-run full income of households, which is the principal determinant of consumption. Moreover, a higher rate of return on capital tends to raise real returns on all financial assets, which motivates households to save more; that is, to postpone consumption. Overall, this reasoning leads to an ambiguous contemporaneous relation between stock returns and consumption, but to a positive association between stock returns and the subsequent growth rate of consumption. Empirically, this effect turns out to be weak, at least if consumption is measured by households' expenditures on non-durables and services.

Much of an economy's investment represents purchases of durable goods by households, rather than "businesses." The national accounts classify residential construction as a part of total investment, but treat purchases of other consumer durables as a component of personal consumption expenditures. In fact, these durables—which include automobiles and appliances—are like the producers' equipment portion of business capital. Together with housing, these capital goods enable households to produce a flow of consumer services over many years. (The only difference from businesses is that these home-generated consumer services are typically not sold on markets.) It follows from an economic standpoint that it is best to think of purchases of consumer durables as a part of total gross investment.[4]

The previous discussion suggested a strong interplay among the prospective return on business capital, stock returns, and subsequent business investment. If the prospective return on household capital were closely (and positively) correlated with that on business capital, then the analysis would predict a positive relation between stock returns and subsequent household investment (on residential construction and other durables). To the extent that the returns on business and household capital are independent (or even negatively correlated), the analysis predicts a weaker (and conceivably inverse) relation between stock returns and household investment.

---

[4] Investments in human capital, such as education and training, could also be included. But serious measurement problems arise here.

Putting the results together, the theory is consistent with the finding that stock returns lead aggregate economic activity, as the results in Table Barro-1 indicated. However, the suggestion is that the association will be stronger for the part of GNP that goes to business investment than to the part for household investment (residential construction and purchases of consumer durables) or consumption (say purchases of consumer non-durables and services).

Another approach to the interplay between the stock market and the macroeconomy begins with a shift in the discount rates for owners of business capital. (The change could reflect a shift in the perceived riskiness of the returns on capital or in individuals' willingness to absorb risk.) A fall in discount rates implies an increase in real stock prices, which creates an excess of the market's valuation of existing business capital over the cost of that capital, and thereby motivates firms to expand investment. Hence, as with the first line of theory, this approach predicts a positive correlation between stock returns and subsequent business investment. Carrying through the rest of the analysis leads also to similar results about household wealth, consumption, household investment, and overall economic activity.

The important finding is the similarity of the conclusions for the two approaches,[5] namely:

1) Stock returns are positively correlated with subsequent changes in real economic activity; hence, stock returns can forecast the economy's overall performance, and

2) Stock returns would exhibit an especially strong association with the subsequent growth of business investment.

---

[5] Another approach treats the changes in stock prices as bubbles unrelated to fundamentals; that is, to shifts in prospective returns on capital or in discount rates. Economic theorists can rule out bubbles in some circumstances, but not in others. It is unclear that a bubble in stock prices would lead to changes in business investment or in other components of real economic activity. Therefore, the finding that stock prices are strongly correlated with subsequent economic growth may be evidence against the importance of bubbles.

It is also worth noting that, in either approach, the positive relation between stock returns and business investment does not depend on the extent to which business uses new stock issues to finance investment. In the first approach, a shift in the prospective rate of return on capital has positive effects on current stock prices and subsequent business investment. In the second approach, businesses adjust investment to the gap between the market's valuation of capital (real stock prices) and the cost of creating new capital. In either approach the results follow if stock prices bear a positive relation to prospective net cash flows, and if business investment decisions are guided by the desire to maximize shareholders' wealth (or, at least, if businesses attach some positive weight to this objective). The method of finance for investment is then irrelevant for the results.

THE STOCK MARKET AND THE MACROECONOMY—SOME EVIDENCE

Table Barro-2 shows how stock returns relate to forecasts of real GNP and some of its major components. The results are based on statistical relationships estimated from quarterly U.S. data from 1950 to 1987. (The national-accounts numbers are the standard, seasonally-adjusted values.) The table reports how the forecast of next year's growth rate of real GNP and its components would change if this year's stock returns were higher (uniformly through the year) by ten percentage points.[6] Note that the GNP growth rate rises by 1/2 percentage points, but the growth rates of the investment components rise by much more. In particular, the growth rate of real business investment increases by 2.9 percentage points, while that for real consumer expenditure on non-durables and services rises by only 0.1 point. In terms of levels, the shift in business investment accounts for 68 percent of the movement in GNP, whereas the change in consumer non-durables and services accounts for only 12 percent. These results follow from the much greater sensitivity of real business investment even though this category represents only 11 percent of real GNP on average from 1950 to 1987, while consumers' real purchases of non-durables and services comprise 54 percent on average.

---

[6] The estimates hold constant the behavior of interest rates, as measured by yields on three-month U.S. Treasury bills. Changes in interest rates have significant explanatory power for growth rates of real GNP and some of its components, especially over the last two decades.

TABLE BARRO-2
Stock Returns and Forecasts of Real Economic Activity

Effect of an increase by 10 pct. points in previous year's stock return on the following:

Component of real GNP	Growth rate (pct.pts. per year)	Level (billions of 1982 dollars starting from 1987 value)
Overall GNP	0.5	26.9
Business Investment*	2.9	18.3
Residential Investment	1.1	3.9
Consumer Durables	0.8	4.7
Consumer Non-Durables and Services	0.1	3.2

* Fixed investment (plant and equipment) plus change in business inventories.

NOTE: Results are based on a statistical relation fit from quarterly observations for 1950 to 1987. The equation uses 8 lagged values of the stock return and four lagged values of the yield on 3-month U.S. Treasury bills. The responses shown in the table assume that interest rates do not change.

NOTE: See Appendix Table A-3 for details of these results.

Table Barro-3 uses the statistical results to forecast real GNP for 1988 and 1989 (based on data available through the end of 1987). As already noted, the stock market crash in the fourth quarter of 1987 leads to the prediction that real GNP will grow relatively slowly in 1988; the projected growth rate for the full year relative to 1987 is 1.4 percent The table shows that the forecasted growth rate for the first quarter of 1988 is 2.1 percent—only slightly below average—and the projected slowdown is concentrated in the second quarter, where the forecast is for essentially zero growth.

While these results may capture the most likely outcome for economic growth, it is worth stressing that these types of forecasts are subject to substantial margins of error. For example, the forecast of annual real GNP growth of 1.4 percent for 1988 has an error range of roughly ±2 percentage points, whereas each of the quarterly growth forecasts shown in the table have a margin of error of about ±3.5 percentage points (at an annual rate).

TABLE BARRO-3
Forecasts of Real GNP for 1988-89

(1)	(2)	(3)	(4)
Date	Growth Forecast (% at annual rate)	Growth Forecast without October crash	Shortfall in billions of 1987 dollars associated with crash
1988-I	2.1	4.5	23.1
1988-II	-0.1	3.7	60.7
1988-III	2.7	3.5	69.8
1988-IV	1.0	2.3	83.4
1989-I	3.5	3.1	79.7
1989-II	3.4	3.0	76.3
1989-III	4.9	3.1	59.6
1989-IV	3.7	3.0	53.2

NOTE: Forecasts assume that interest rates on 3-month U.S. Treasury bill for 1988-89 equal the value for the fourth quarter of 1987 (5.9% per year) and that stock returns for 1988-89 equal the average value of 11.0% per year.

Column 2 of Table Barro-3 shows the forecasts of real GNP growth that would have arisen if the stock return for October 1987 had been average (11.0 percent per year), rather than the actual value associated with the crash (-293 percent per year). The forecasted growth rate for all of 1988 over 1987 would have been 3.5 percent, instead of 1.4 percent (the excess of 3.5 percent over the mean growth rate of 2.9 percent reflects the favorable performance of the stock market earlier in 1987). Column 3 of the table translates the differences in projected growth rates into shortfalls of real GNP (in billions of 1982 dollars and at an annual rate for each quarter). The estimated reduction in real GNP associated with the stock market crash is $59 billion for 1988 and $67 billion for 1989.

Figure Barro-1 shows the results graphically. The solid line uses a proportionate scale to plot the forecasted values of real GNP—actual real GNP through the fourth quarter of 1987, and the projected values

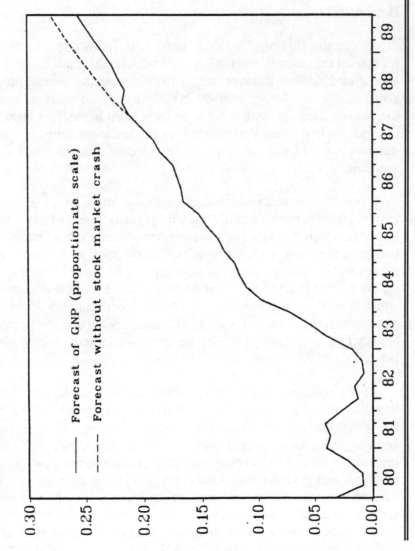

FIGURE BARRO-1
Forecasts of GNP

—— Forecast of GNP (proportionate scale)
---- Forecast without stock market crash

thereafter. The dotted line shows the alternative (counter-factual) projection, which corresponds to the absence of the stock market crash in October 1987.

Given the findings in Table Barro-2, it follows that most of the forecasted reduction in real GNP associated with the crash corresponds to a predicted decline in investment. Considering the overall projected shortfall of real GNP for 1988-89 ($126 billion), the fractions arising in the various components turn out to be 69 percent in business investment, nine percent in residential investment, 14 percent in purchases of consumer durables, and 12 percent in purchases of consumer non-durables and services.[7]

Thus far, the analysis has dealt with the implications of the stock market crash for predictions of economic growth. A related question is the extent to which the poor stock market performance can be explained by bad news about the macroeconomy. Given the relation of stock returns to subsequent economic growth rates—especially of real business investment —it is possible to "explain" a good deal of the historical movements in stock returns as a "response" to changed expectations about future economic activity (as in Fama, 1981, and Appendix Table Barro-A-2). Whether this relationship holds up for late 1987 depends on the economy's behavior in 1988.

If one restricts attention to contemporaneous and lagged variables, then it is much harder to explain stock returns. For example, stock returns are not significantly related to their own lagged values or to contemporaneous or lagged growth rates of real GNP, real business investment, and so on. (These growth rates are also not good predictors of subsequent growth rates.) Other economic "fundamentals" mentioned frequently as determinants of stock prices include corporate profits after taxes, interest rates, the current-account balance, and the federal budget deficit. Stock returns are, in fact, significantly related to some of these variables, especially over the last two decades. I considered the current

---

[7] The fractions need not add to one because two parts of GNP are omitted—government purchases and exports less imports—and because of statistical errors.

four quarterly lagged values of long-term interest rates (measured by the yield on Aaa corporate bonds), the excess of exports over imports (national accounts basis) expressed as a ratio to GNP, and the federal budget surplus (national accounts basis) as a ratio to GNP. (Given these variables, short-term interest rates, and—surprisingly—corporate profits after taxes as a ratio to GNP did not contribute significantly to explaining stock returns.[8]) The three sets of variables included can explain 32 percent of the variation in quarterly stock returns from 1950 to 1987. However, if only lagged values of the explanatory variables are used—that is, if the contemporaneous values for each quarter are eliminated—then the fraction of explained variation drops to 14 percent.[9] Thus, much of the explanatory power comes from the contemporaneous association (which could not be used to forecast the stock market).

For the fourth quarter of 1987, which includes the October crash, the stock return at an annual rate was -103 percent. Using a statistical relation estimated from 1950 through the third quarter of 1987—and including as explanatory variables the current and four lagged values of the long-term interest rate, and the variables for net exports and the federal budget surplus—the fitted value of the stock return for the fourth quarter of 1987 is -14 percent.[10] Recall that the mean stock return is 11 percent—that is, this fitted value is 25 percentage points below the mean. The primary element behind this low estimate for stock returns is the increase in long term interest rates after the first quarter of 1987. The main message is that the usually cited determinants of stock prices can account for unusually low stock returns in late 1987, but not returns that are nearly as low as those that occurred.

---

[8] Monetary growth rates, based on the monetary base or M1, were also not very important in explaining stock returns.

[9] See Appendix Table A-4 for the detailed results. Cutler, Poterba, and Summers (1987, Table 2) report similar findings over various sample periods.

[10] If the contemporaneous values of the explanatory variables are excluded, the fitted value becomes -1 percent.

REFERENCES

Cutler D.M., J.M. Poterba, and L.H. Summers, "What Moves Stock Prices?" presented at the meetings of the American Finance Association, December 1987.

Fama, E.F., "Stock Returns, Real Activity, Inflation, and Money," *American Economic Review*, 71, September 1981, 545-565.

APPENDIX

Notes to Tables:

National accounts variables are the standard figures from the U.S. Department of Commerce, measured in 1982 prices. Quarterly values are seasonally adjusted. The variables are GNP: gross national product, I (Business) gross investment in business plant and equipment plus accumulation of inventories, I (Business, fixed): gross investment in business plan and equipment, I (Resid.): gross private investment in residential structures, C (Dur.): purchases of consumer durables, C (Non-dur., Services): consumer expenditure on non-durables and services, Indust. Prod.: Federal Reserve Board index of industrial production. The growth rates are for the value during the current period relative to that for the prior period (all expressed at annual rates). In Table Barro-A2, DIN is the growth rate of I (Business, fixed), DGNP is the growth rate of GNP, and DIP is the growth rate of industrial production.

NYSE is the total, value-weighted nominal return for the period (at an annual rate) for all New York Stock Exchange issues, as reported by the University of Chicago's Center for Research in Security Prices. Values for 1987 are from D.R.I. and the Standard & Poor's 500 dividend yield. NYSE (real) is NYSE less the CPI inflation rate (January to January). The CPI less shelter is used since 1970. R is the average yield for the period (annual rate) on three-month U.S. Treasury bills, traded on secondary markets. Values before 1931 are for 3-6 month maturity U.S. notes. RB is the average yield on Aaa corporate bonds. EXP is the ratio of the current account surplus to GNP. SUR is the ratio of the federal budget surplus to GNP.

Standard errors of coefficients are in parentheses. σ is the standard error of the regression. DW is the Durbin-Watson Statistic.

TABLE BARRO-1A
Annual Data, National Accounts Variables

Sample	Dep. Var. (Growth Rate)	Const.	Lagged dep. var.	NYSE(-1)	R(-1)	R(-2)	σ̂	R²	DW
1927-40, 1947-87	GNP	.003 (.005)	.249 (.077)	.160 (.020)			.029	.62	1.6
"	GNP	.007 (.005)		.171 (.021)			.032	.55	1.2
"	GNP	.010 (.007)	.273 (.081)	.155 (.021)	-.37 (-.36)		.029	.64	1.6
1931-40, 1947-87	GNP	.006 (.004)	.288 (.063)	.151 (.018)		.19 (.36)	.025	.69	1.6
"	I (Business)	-.083 (-.029)	.147 (.087)	1.006 (.126)			.181	.59	2.2
"	I (Business, fixed)	-.039 (-.012)	.446 (.069)	.504 (.052)			.075	.74	1.5
"	I (Resid.)	-.021 (-.024)	.186 (.076)	.462 (.103)			.148	.37	2.0
"	C (Dur.)	.004 (.012)	.225 (.082)	.296 (.050)			.072	.49	1.9
"	C (Non-dur. Services)	.010 (.003)	.390 (.078)	.067 (.010)			.015	.63	2.0
"	Indust. Prod.	.004 (.010)	-.043 (.091)	.339 (.044)			.063	.55	1.8
1950-87	GNP	.012 (.006)	.234 (.128)	.108 (.022)			.021	.41	1.3
"	GNP	.020 (.005)		.102 (.023)			.022	.36	1.0
"	GNP	.027 (.009)	.269 (.125)	.069 (.022)	-.91 (.26)	.70 (.26)	.018	.59	1.3
"	I (Business)	-.019 (.023)	-.078 (.127)	.500 (.114)			.104	.40	1.6
"	I (Business, fixed)	-.011 (.014)	.335 (.139)	.284 (.062)			.054	.38	1.6
"	I (Resid.)	-.012 (.028)	-.077 (.159)	.347 (.143)			.133	.14	1.6
"	C (Dur.)	.020 (.015)	.017 (.150)	.202 (.067)			.064	.21	1.7
"	C (Non-dur. Services)	.020 (.005)	.239 (.142)	.031 (.010)			.010	.26	1.5
"	Indust. Prod.	.007 (.011)	-.054 (.122)	.250 (.045)			.042	.47	1.5

TABLE BARRO-2A
Annual Data, Stock Returns

Sample	Dep. Var.	Const.	DIN	DIN (+1)	DGNP	DGNP (+1)	DIP	DIP (+1)	∂	R^2	DW
1930-39, 1946-86	NYSE	.086 (.017)	-.58 (.13)	1.32 (.14)					.121	.66	1.8
"	NYSE (real)	.061 (.018)	-.76 (.13)	1.29 (.14)					.126	.64	1.6
"	NYSE	.050 (.025)	-.51 (.16)	.83 (.30)	.00 (.44)	1.65 (.95)			.119	.69	1.8
"	NYSE	.091 (.027)	-.62 (.19)	1.43 (.46)			.00 (.31)	-.17 (.61)	.124	.66	1.8
1950-86	NYSE	.118 (.023)	-1.15 (.29)	1.37 (.29)					.115	.51	1.5
"	NYSE (real)	.073 (.025)	-1.21 (.30)	1.55 (.30)					.121	.52	1.4
"	NYSE	.074 (.039)	-1.07 (.51)	.85 (.47)	.19 (1.22)	1.67 (1.31)			.115	.54	1.5
"	NYSE	.080 (.030)	-.70 (.55)	-.14 (.67)			.00 (.63)	1.73 (.83)	.111	.57	1.5

TABLE BARRO-3A
Quarterly Data, 1950-87, National Accounts Variables

	Contemp. variables		No contemp. variables	
Const.	.22	(.06)	.14	(.07)
RB	-28.8	(6.6)		
RB(-1)	21.7	(10.5)	-14.3	(7.3)
RB(-2)	-6.0	(10.6)	7.2	(11.5)
RB(-3)	19.3	(10.6)	9.8	(11.6)
RB(-4)	-7.7	(7.1)	-2.9	(7.8)
EXP	24.7	(7.7)		
EXP(-1)	-2.9	(10.6)	15.3	(8.4)
EXP(-2)	-34.2	(10.6)	-34.4	(11.6)
EXP(-3)	19.2	(10.5)	24.3	(11.5)
EXP(-4)	-0.6	(7.3)	-2.4	(8.0)
SUR	-4.5	(3.0)		
SUR(-1)	8.2	(4.2)	2.0	(3.3)
SUR(-2)	-7.7	(4.2)	-3.8	(4.6)
SUR(-3)	-4.1	(4.2)	-3.8	(4.6)
SUR(-4)	3.5	(3.1)	4.8	(3.4)
$\hat{\sigma}$	.280		.310	
R^2	.32		.14	
DW	1.9		1.9	

TABLE BARRO-4A
Quarterly Data, 1950-87, Stock Returns

Dep. Var. (growth rate)	Const.	Lagged Dep. Var.	NYSE(-1)	NYSE(-2)	NYSE(-3)	NYSE(-4)	R(-2)	R(-12)	θ	R²	DW
GNP	.031 (.007)	.161 (.079)	.026 (.010)	.036 (.010)	.005 (.011)	.012 (.010)	-.55 (.15)	.30 (.13)	.037	.34	1.9
I (Business)	.032 (.048)	-.082 (.081)	-.040 (.073)	.281 (.074)	.166 (.077)	.029 (.074)	-2.79 (1.03)	1.94 (.96)	.268	.21	1.8
I (Business) fixed	.017 (.018)	.278 (.079)	.009 (.027)	.100 (.027)	.052 (.027)	.022 (.027)	-.94 (.38)	.73 (.35)	.096	.32	2.0
I (Resid.)	-.003 (.033)	.324 (.082)	.228 (.050)	.052 (.053)	-.024 (.051)	-.048 (.049)	-1.57 (.75)	1.53 (.69)	.182	.37	2.0
C (Dur.)	.015 (.029)	-.201 (.084)	.087 (.043)	.127 (.045)	-.002 (.044)	.052 (.044)	-1.35 (.62)	1.54 (.59)	.160	.16	1.9
C (Non-dur., Services)	.038 (.005)	-.011 (.086)	.013 (.006)	.002 (.006)	-.001 (.006)	.009 (.006)	-.27 (.09)	.11 (.08)	.021	.15	1.9
Indust. Prod.	.025 (.014)	.306 (.077)	.058 (.021)	.085 (.021)	.028 (.022)	.010 (.021)	-.95 (.30)	.61 (.28)	.076	.41	1.8

October 1987 and the Structure of Financial Markets:

An Exorcism of Demons

Lester G. Telser

POSSIBLE CAUSES

The Crash of 87 set many records and rudely shocked the public. Few shareholders had ever before experienced so sharp a price decline in so brief a compass of time. These unprecedented events have inspired a plethora of searches for the causes. Some of these studies show a tendency to seek scapegoats who can be blamed and therefore punished. Behind such an approach is the view, simplistic yet formally correct, that some people trading in certain markets who were selling on a large scale caused prices to drop. Had there not been this selling there would not have been the price declines. Or, on a slightly more sophisticated level, those who had some responsibility to buy when the waves of selling engulfed the market, fled their posts and failed to cushion the decline. The more sanguine investigators of the Crash hope that by means of appropriate reforms, new rules and regulations, it will become possible to avoid a future repetition. On one major premise we can all agree. Every market needs rules and none can function without them. A free market is not anarchy. It will better serve the general interest, however, to examine with as much objectivity as we can muster the most probable causes of the Crash, eschew a search for scapegoats and on this basis consider the remedies, if any, that are most likely to be helpful.

Certain facts must be kept in the forefront. First, the October 87 Crash although the record holder so far is not without a close runner-up. There was a Crash in October 1929 when many of the factors blamed for the recent Crash did not exist. In October 1929 there was no program trading, no futures index contracts, no portfolio insurance and no stock options, to name only a few of the culprits mentioned as responsible for the 87 Crash.

Any theory of the 87 Crash that relies on these special factors must explain the 29 Crash.   Second, while prices fell in New York, prices simultaneously fell sharply on markets throughout the world. In these markets there are different rules such as rules on limit price moves. Despite these differences, prices in all of these markets moved down in tandem. Any explanation of the 87 Crash in U.S. markets that focuses on the nature of U.S. trading practices must explain why prices fell in all of the other markets with their different trading rules. Before embracing explanations specific to U.S. trading practices, it would be better to consider theories with a wider range of explanatory power.

A BUBBLE BURST

The most plausible of these theories asserts that a speculative bubble burst in October 1987. This bubble was expanding on all the world markets. Then like many bubbles in the past a selling wave engulfed the markets one after the other and prices collapsed everywhere. Similarly, in October 29 the bubble burst on the New York Stock Exchange. Indeed more recently, we saw a silver bubble bursting in January 1980. To suppose there was a speculative bubble that burst is not without its difficulties. In a stock market in which there are only rational traders reckoning prices on the basis of expected earnings there would be no speculative bubbles. Only those who, perhaps unconsciously, believe in the greater fool theory, would buy at prices they regard as excessive in the expectation they will be able to sell at even higher prices to even greater fools. Eventually, the supply of greater fools dries up and the bubble bursts. A skeptic asks whether economics can say whether a rising price indicates the presence of a bubble. If it could then economists would be the most successful speculators of all. They are not. No economic theory can reveal the correct price. It can say whether the rules of the market help or hinder the forces converging on the market that determine the price. Admitting this more modest role for economics is not to abandon the theory that a speculative bubble burst in October 1929 and again in October 1987.

The most striking fact consistent with the bubble hypothesis is the nature of extreme percentage price changes. According to the economic theory of markets with rational traders there ought to be symmetry so that a large percentage price increase is as likely as a large percentage decrease of the same magnitude. However, the record shows that the biggest percentage downward moves are larger than the biggest percentage upward moves in single trading sessions or even in periods of as long as two weeks. There is asymmetry. Prices do not rise as rapidly as they fall. This supports the hypothesis of a speculative bubble.

Accepting the hypothesis that a bubble burst in October 1987 does not preclude a belief that other difficulties were present as well. The volume of trading was huge. It swamped market makers, brokers, floor traders and specialists. The market machinery was strained because volume was far above the level it was designed to handle even under plausible estimates of the peak load. One must recognize that the cost of handling rare events may exceed the benefits. It would be very costly to have enough capacity available at all times to meet the crush of trading at three times the average level.

THE SPECIALIST SYSTEM

A major concern of the investigations of the Crash is the differences between the futures markets and the stock markets. The New York Stock Exchange and the futures markets have some different rules. In the NYSE there are specialists who are supposed to maintain "orderly" markets in their stocks. They are supposed to buy when the public is a net seller and sell when the public wants on balance to buy. If so, the inventory of stocks that the specialist handles would go up and down inversely to the selling pressure from the public. In return for this duty imposed on the specialist by the NYSE, the NYSE confers a monopoly on the specialist so that there is only one specialist for each stock traded on the NYSE. Only this specialist knows the buy and sell orders at prices away from the current one. That is, only the specialist sees the order book of his stock. In the Over-the-Counter (OTC) market there are no specialists and actively traded stocks have many market makers. In futures markets a member of the exchange can trade any listed contract. Bids and offers occur by open outcry as a bilateral auction. No one bears responsibility to maintain an orderly market in a futures contract or on the OTC market. However, in practice, the difference among these markets is less than their different rules would imply.

The specialist system evolved on the NYSE in response to the needs of the traders. About 2000 stocks are traded on the Exchange and most of the volume is concentrated in about 200 stocks. Trade is thin for the remaining 1800 stocks. To have someone hold an inventory of these less active stocks and use it as a buffer to absorb shocks while keeping prices within a range consistent with the cost of holding the inventory furnishes a solution to a genuine problem. It is also important to point out that a specialist who makes a profit over a time in which his beginning and ending inventory of the stock is the same does stabilize the price of the stock without changing the mean price over that time interval. Moreover, the less he loses, the more he stabilizes the price. Therefore, one can judge how well the specialist succeeds in stabilizing the price by looking at his profit or loss. That specialist who loses the least or profits the most is the one who comes closest to the stated mission of the specialist, to maintain an orderly market in the stock. For the same reason a floor trader in a futures market who makes a profit over an interval such that he begins and ends with the same net position stabilizes the price without affecting the mean price over that interval (Telser, 1959).

LIMIT PRICE MOVE RULE

The limit price move rule in futures markets, that is, the rule that limits the size of the maximum price move in a single trading session, can be regarded as the futures market's alternative to the specialist. By extending a large price move over more than one session and slowing the rate of change per trading session, the futures markets achieve another side of stability. The limit price move rule does not change the ultimate price which is still driven by the market forces; the rule only slows the process. I have argued elsewhere (Telser, 1981) that the main effect of this rule is to reduce the cost to a nonmember of trading in a futures market. Their agents, the exchange members, obtain time to consult their principals, the nonmembers, when there is a large price move, in order to get new instructions or additional margin. Without the limit price move rule it would be more costly for nonmembers to trade in the market.

It is important to note that most spot markets in the U.S. do not have limit price move rules. The spot markets in soybeans, wheat, corn, gold, silver, and Treasury bonds, to name only a few examples which are also actively traded on organized futures markets, have no limit price move rules. This is probably because the participants in these markets are mostly principals trading for themselves. It is not that the spot market by its nature needs no such rule. The usefulness of such a rule depends on who trades in the market. A spot market such as the New York Stock Exchange with many transactions made by agents acting under instructions from principals may find useful such a rule.

BLOCK TRADING

As the volume of trade has grown on the New York Stock Exchange, the role of the specialist has diminished. This is shown by the rising importance of block trades, trades in excess of 10,000 shares. During the past 15 years, block trades have risen to 50 percent of the total volume. Block trades occur "upstairs," off the floor of the NYSE. The block traders bargain among themselves under the instructions from their principals much like the bilateral auction in the pit of a futures market. However, and this is an important point, in contrast to the trading in the futures market, block trading is not visible to the public or even to the members on the floor of the NYSE. Only those directly involved in the bargaining see the bids and offers. After mutually acceptable terms are agreed upon by those involved in a block trade it may be taken down to the floor of the NYSE where it is recorded by the specialist who often has no role in the block transaction.

According to economic theory a block trade is an efficient technique. Those who do not participate directly themselves in the block and use agents to trade on their behalf are not likely to give their agents discretion to trade at whatever block price emerges: instead they would tell their agents what prices would be acceptable and the final block price would not violate these bounds. Thus, the buyer in a block would pay a price not above his maximum acceptable and the seller in a block would get a price not below his minimum acceptable. The active participants in a block trade agree on a single price so that all the sellers in the block trade get the same price per share and all the buyers in the block pay the same price per share. Bargaining and the forces of competition determine the price of the block. For these reasons block trading is efficient. It developed in response to the needs of the traders. It survives in the face of competing alternatives and thereby proves its desirability for some purposes. It can be and is used for the less actively traded stocks. For these, a block trade requires that many small orders would be batched together so that blocks would trade less often and a block transaction would take more time to consummate.

The NYSE imitates the Chicago Exchanges in another important respect. A crowd of floor traders surrounds the specialist of an actively traded stock. Bidding is spirited. The practical result is a mode of trade like that in a pit of a Chicago Exchange.

WHY TRADING PRACTICES DIFFER BETWEEN THE STOCK MARKET AND THE FUTURES MARKET

This analysis shows that the major factor explaining the differences between the trading practices on the New York and the Chicago Exchanges is the volume of trade. This volume is very much larger on the Chicago Exchanges than on the NYSE for even the most actively traded stocks. Even so as volume has risen on the NYSE, changes have occurred such that the trading techniques for the higher volume stocks more closely resemble those proven successful in the Chicago Exchanges.

HEDGING AND PROGRAM TRADING

The NYSE is to the Chicago Exchanges as a spot (or cash) market is to a futures market. Just as there is a spot market in soybeans and a futures market in soybeans so too there is a spot market in stocks and a futures market in stocks. The parallel is nearly perfect when it is recognized that the spot market in soybeans trades particular kinds and grades of actual soybeans while the soybean futures market trades a generic standardized contract in this commodity. A stock index future is a contract in a portfolio of stocks. The NYSE trades shares of individual companies. The price of a share in a company depends on factors specific to the company as well as on general factors that affect all companies. A mutual fund or a pension fund with a portfolio of many stocks exposes itself to the common forces that affect all of the stocks in its portfolio, and the company specific factors tend to cancel each other out. Pursuing this analogy, holders of inventories of actual soybeans can insulate themselves from changes in the price of soybeans by selling soybean futures contracts.

Upward and downward changes in the cash price are closely matched by corresponding movements in the futures price. The closer together the spot and futures price movement, the less vulnerable is the inventory holder of the actual commodity to changes of its price. This is hedging. It enables the inventory holder to specialize in the business he knows best, the merchandizing of the commodity, and to leave to others speculation on the price of the commodity.

Similarly, holders of portfolios of stocks can insulate themselves from changes in the levels of stock prices by taking a short position in stock index futures. Here one must be clear about the nature of hedging. A hedger does not sell futures when he thinks prices are going down and buy when he thinks prices are going up. A hedger does not speculate on the price level. When he opens a cash position in the commodity, he simultaneously opens a short position in futures. He thereby foregoes profit and loss from changes in the price *level*. He does expose himself to the risk of changes in the relation between the spot and the futures price, known as the basis. A hedger incurs a *basis* risk and avoids a *price* risk. The basis risk is smaller, the more parallel are the movements of the spot and the futures prices. Here is where program trading enters the picture.

Program trading looks at the difference between the stock index futures and the index of the spot prices of the stocks. The latter is composed of the prices of these stocks on the NYSE. The former is, say, the S&P 500 futures index traded on the Chicago Mercantile Exchange. The difference between these two indexes equals the (marginal) cost of carrying the portfolio of the 500 actual stocks in the index up to the maturity date of the futures index contract. Changes in these carrying costs cause changes in the basis. For instance, changes in interest rates or expected earnings cause changes in the basis. Program traders look at the differences. They buy or sell the index futures contracts and the market baskets of actual stocks depending on the difference between the spot and the futures price. Sometimes they buy stocks and sometimes they sell stocks. Sometimes they buy the futures index and sometimes they sell the index futures contract. It does not illuminate understanding of how spot and futures markets are linked to blame program trading for price drops or price turbulence. On the contrary, program trading by arbitraging between the cash and the futures markets makes the cash and the futures prices move more closely together. It thereby lowers the risk of hedging. In this way it helps secure the benefits of hedging for those who want it.

It is not hedging when a holder of a portfolio of stocks sells futures while prices are falling. He could have sold the stocks in the spot market. He chose to sell the futures probably because of difficulties in executing trades on the spot markets, the NYSE, the American Stock Exchange, regional exchanges and the OTC market, during the Crash. The Chicago markets by virtue of their greater ability to handle large volume had more continuous trading and thereby alleviated the congestion problems on the NYSE. In the absence of reliable quotations from the NYSE, program trading could not do its job and the basis between the spot and futures prices sometimes widened to unprecedented levels. It was not the presence of program trading but rather its absence that aggravated the situation during the Crash.

Effective program trading uses computers. The public fears computers. Neither computers nor program trading deserve blame for the Crash.

PROFESSIONAL TRADERS

Professional traders are present in all exchanges. Especially in futures markets they are essential for the maintenance of orderly, liquid markets. Professionals constantly watch the bids and offers in order to detect profitable opportunities. These occur when the bids and offers depart from a level the professional regards as normal. He expects prices to fluctuate around some level during a trading session. A professional tries to take advantage of prices he believes are too far from the normal and trades accordingly. If he judges well he closes his position at a price closer to the normal than the one at which he began. To the extent he is successful he makes a profit and by so doing tends to stabilize the price although stability is not his intention. A professional has a very short term horizon. When he sees more offers than bids and prices moving down, he cannot tell whether this signals the beginning of a downward trend or is a temporary aberration. If he buys and it is the former then he will lose. If he buys and it is the latter then he will profit. An experienced professional trader must have the skill to discriminate between these alternatives or he would not have survived in his calling. Not very often does such a trader buy during a falling market or sell during a rising one. They deserve no blame when the public commences sales on a large scale and they step aside in order to see which way the market will go before reaching a new plateau.

MARGINS

Margins are pervasive in futures markets. Everyone with an open position must deposit margin with his broker. Even if the rules of the exchange did not require margin and, indeed, before rules of the exchange required margin, the broker required his customers, long or short, to deposit funds as security against the chance they would renege. It is that most powerful of interests, self-interest, that impels brokers to require margins of their customers. A broker must judge nicely how much margin to ask for. Asking too much will cause a loss of business to competitors. A broker must set the margin neither too low nor too high to survive and prosper. No one has a more powerful incentive to acquire the necessary information for doing so than the broker himself.

Outsiders, no matter how well intentioned, who wish to impose higher margins than would result from competition among the brokers would affect the market differently than they intended. Their action would impose a selective control over credit and thereby reduce trading in the market.

Futures exchanges themselves have developed an elaborate structure on their own based on their long experience going back more than a century. In the course of this accumulation of knowledge about how to run an organized market, the exchanges developed an institution, the clearinghouse. A clearinghouse is equivalent to a bank. It keeps the accounts of its members. A member with a short position in a futures contract incurs a liability to the clearinghouse and one with a long position has an asset from the clearinghouse. Each member of the clearinghouse has a margin account with the clearinghouse. This cash account is marked to the market at the end of each trading session. Those with profits are credited and those with losses debited. Anyone whose cash position falls below a prescribed level is subject to a margin call. He has a limited time to satisfy the call or his position will be liquidated. Losses are not allowed to accumulate. The futures market is a zero-sum game. For every loser there is a winner.

Because open futures commitments are marked to the market daily, so that a trader's cash account is kept current, competitively determined margins depend on the size of an extreme price change that can occur during a small number of trading sessions, often perhaps as few as two sessions. This explains why margins on futures commitments are a small fraction of the value of a contract. The fraction equals the probable size of an extreme price move over a few sessions. In the stock market there are also open positions on margin. To the extent that these positions would be marked to the market on a daily basis so that the practice for stocks would be the same as for futures, left to themselves, the brokers would require margins on stocks equal to the margins on futures. In fact, margins on stock are much higher than on futures. This is because stock margins are regulated by the Federal Reserve Board which began regulation of margins on stocks on October 1, 1934. It is an inheritance of the October 29 Crash and the belief that the cause of that Crash was excessive speculation made possible by stock margins that were too low. Neither evidence nor solid analysis supports that belief. No Federal agency now regulates margins on futures contracts. The Exchanges themselves set minimum margins on these trading instruments. Raising margins on futures by Federal regulation to the same level as is imposed on stocks would be an error. On the contrary, margins on stocks should be relieved of Federal control. The self-interest of brokers constrained by the forces of competition can establish margins at the appropriate level far better than can any Federal regulator.

Because every open position in a futures market must have a security deposit, the margin, and is marked to the market daily, losses cannot accumulate. A futures market is a zero-sum game. There is a winner for every loser. The losses of the losers are transferred to the accounts of the winners. There is no effect on net wealth. In contrast, the stock market is a spot market in which there must be a positive net long position in stocks. This means that a price increase raises the net wealth of shareholders and a decrease lowers it. The same is true for the inventory holders of actual commodities. There is a positive net long position in gold, wheat, copper, soybeans, silver, corn and so on. A rise in the prices of these commodities raises the wealth of those who are holding the inventories. Conversely, a fall in the price lowers the wealth of the inventory holders. Changes in the futures prices of these commodities, however, do not affect the aggregate wealth of those with open positions in futures. It is cold comfort to the losers to be told that the game is zero-sum and that others were the winners. Empirical study of the effects of the October 29 Crash shows that a generation of Americans shunned the stock market. The velocity of trading, that is, the volume relative to the number of outstanding shares, dropped after the 29 Crash and remained low. It did not climb to the pre-Crash level until the late 60s. This will probably happen again. Many who thought that buying stocks was a one way ticket to the Big Rock Candy Mountain now know differently. No new regulations can reassure them. The losses and the suffering they cause are among the costs of a free enterprise system. We must take care that proposed changes do not harm this engine of economic growth and wealth.

REFERENCES

Telser, Lester G. 1959. A theory of speculation relating profitability and stability. *Review of Economics and Statistics*. 41: 295-302.

Telser, Lester G. 1981. Margins and futures contracts. *Journal of Futures Markets*. 2:225-53.

Should One Agency Regulate Financial Markets?

Daniel R. Fischel

Recently the President's Task Force on Market Mechanisms, chaired by Nicholas Brady, issued its findings on the October stock market crash and its proposals for reform. One of the most important aspects of the so-called "Brady Report" is the proposal that one regulatory agency should have jurisdiction over all financial markets. The Brady Report goes on to suggest that the Federal Reserve Board be this agency. This proposal is in marked contrast to the current system where such agencies as the Federal Reserve Board, the Securities and Exchange Commission, and the Commodity Futures Trading Commission all share regulatory authority.

What is the basis for this sweeping proposal? Analysis of the Brady Report reveals that the proposal for one agency is based on a series of interrelated propositions:

1. That, from an economic viewpoint, what have been traditionally viewed as separate markets—the markets for stocks, stock index futures and stock options—are, in fact one market;

2. That the problems of mid-October can be traced in part to the failure to recognize the interrelationships among these different markets;

3. That regulatory changes, derived from the one-market concept, are necessary both to reduce the possibility of destructive "market breaks" and to deal effectively with such episodes should they occur again; and

4. That the primary regulatory change to be derived from the one-market concept is the notion of one regulatory agency.

The Brady Report's proposal for one agency has sparked enormous interest among the different exchanges, the regulatory agencies themselves, and policymakers generally. Because of the interest created by the proposal, Congress is currently investigating the issue.

In light of the importance of the one-agency proposal, it is useful to analyze its logical underpinnings. For the reasons that follow, I am not at all persuaded that the Brady Report's proposal for one agency would be desirable social policy and therefore conclude it should be not implemented.

WAS THE OCTOBER CRASH CAUSED BY REGULATORY FAILURE?

The logical premise of the Brady Report's one-agency proposal is that there was a regulatory failure that produced, or at the very least, greatly exacerbated, the October stock market crash. For if there were not regulatory failure, there would be no basis for proposing a massive regulatory change as a response. Notwithstanding the central nature of the regulatory failure premise, however, there is not a shred of evidence in the entire Brady Report that suggests that this premise is accurate. Does anybody seriously contend that the October crash would not have occurred if the United States had a single regulatory agency as the Brady Report recommends? As Richard Roll's paper in this volume convincingly demonstrates, the crash was international in nature and much of it preceded what happened in the United States. Thus, it is implausible to assume that the regulatory structure in the United States can be blamed for what happened in October.

There is an even more fundamental point. As Eugene Fama's paper in this volume demonstrates, it is not clear that there was a failure of any kind in October, regulatory or otherwise. The key issue is why prices fell. If the reason is that new information became available to market participants (as suggested by the Brady Report itself in its discussion of the effects of the proposed anti-takeover legislation and adverse information concerning the trade deficit), then there is no problem that needs to be addressed. On the contrary, that prices adjusted to new information so quickly is something to be applauded. As several contributors to this volume have noted, the fact that prices have stayed relatively stable since the October crash suggests that the crash was a response to new information.

To be sure, it is frustrating not to be able to identify precisely what this new information was. While frustrating, the uncertainty concerning what exactly caused prices to fall is not surprising. After all, economists and historians are still arguing about what caused the prices to fall in the Great Depression (notwithstanding over 50 years of study devoted to this question).

But, no matter how frustrating, the difficulty of identifying precisely what caused prices to fall provides no justification for a massive regulatory overhaul of American financial markets. To the extent there is uncertainty about what caused the October crash, the more appropriate response is caution. This is particularly true, where, as here, it is not clear that there is any problem that needs to be addressed. Rushing to make wholesale regulatory changes without any understanding of whether any problem exists, whether there is any relationship between the assumed problem and the proposed regulatory changes, and what the consequences of the proposed regulatory changes would be, is rarely a good strategy and this situation presents no exception. Until the Brady Report or anyone else can provide some answers to these unresolved issues, there is no reason to implement the one-agency proposal.

THE PROBLEM OF TRANSACTION EXECUTION

The one problem that did occur in connection with the October crash was that the unprecedented volume made it difficult to execute transactions. Again, however, there is no connection between this problem and the one-agency proposal. There is no reason to believe that regulators would have been better able to predict the difficulties created by unprecedented volume than the exchanges themselves. In fact, there is every reason to believe the opposite because exchanges have a strong incentive to adopt rules and regulations that facilitate the execution of transactions.

Organized exchanges facilitate transactions between buyers and sellers of securities. They do this by providing a centralized location, such as an exchange floor, for trades to take place, or by providing an electronic system to perform the same function. As with all marketplaces, the primary benefit of exchanges is that they save traders the cost of independently searching for someone on the other side of the transaction. A competitive broker or arbitrager in the market demands less of a discount when purchasing a security and charges less of a premium when selling a security if, on average, he does not have to hold it in inventory for very long or incur large search costs to find buyers or sellers. The lower costs are reflected in low bid/ask spreads and high liquidity.

A related benefit is that organized exchanges provide a forum that allows customer orders to be executed with minimum delay. Thus brokers can usually execute a customer's order quickly because the exchange provides swift access to other buyers and sellers. This immediacy is extremely important for purchasers and sellers of securities since prices can move between the time of the order and the time the transaction is consummated. By providing liquidity, exchanges minimize the risk of price fluctuations borne by investors during trading delays.

In addition to providing a centralized location or electronic system to facilitate trades of securities, exchanges provide a set of ancillary services. For example, exchanges police the conduct of member firms to ensure that they are adequately capitalized, do not act fraudulently toward consumers, or otherwise act in ways that harm the reputation of the exchange. Exchanges also may promulgate rules for listed firms governing financial disclosure, annual meetings, or corporate structure.

Exchanges market these transaction and ancillary services by selling access to a trading floor or to an electronic quotation system. The value of access to an exchange is a function of the commission income (and trading profits) that can be earned by members. This income is in turn a function of the ability of the exchange to facilitate trading of securities. The higher the quality of transactional and ancillary services (at a given cost), the more investors will be willing to trade. For this reason, exchanges have strong incentives to provide transactional and ancillary services that are in the best interest of investors.

In this sense, exchanges face the same incentives to provide high-quality products (i. e., transactional services) as any other business. Just as a manufacturer of automobiles has strong incentives to make a product that consumers want in order to maximize its profitability, an exchange has incentives to design transactional and ancillary services that investors prefer. Moreover, the exchange is not in business for one year, but rather for the long term. For these reasons, it has every incentive to set up operations to convince customers (traders) that it will produce high quality transaction services.

In other words, the self-interest of exchanges will induce them to adopt rules that facilitate the execution of transactions in the most efficient manner possible. To the extent that the October crash demonstrated that the then existing mechanisms for executing transactions were inadequate, the exchanges will modify them accordingly. If the exchanges do not satisfy customers that trades can be executed efficiently, their profitability will drop and substitutes will develop. The important point, however, is that the problem of transaction execution is one that should be dealt with in the market place. Exchanges, not regulators, have the expertise and the incentives to design transaction execution mechanisms that meet investors' needs.

COMPETITION AMONG REGULATORY AGENCIES

The implication of the one-agency proposal is that competition among regulatory agencies is harmful. This issue has been studied in a variety of different contexts and the consensus is very much the opposite. The areas of corporate law, banking regulation, and the introduction of new financial products, are all governed by multiple regulatory authorities which in some sense compete with each other. In each of these areas, there have been recurrent proposals to substitute a single regulatory agency for the current system of multiple and competing agencies. None of these proposals have gotten very far and properly so.

The reason why competition among regulatory agencies has proven desirable in a variety of contexts is that it has promoted innovation. For example, the wide array of financial products developed in the 1970's and 1980's may not have existed today if the Securities and Exchange Commission had jurisdiction over all organized exchanges. The SEC has consistently opposed the development of these new products but it has had only limited success because the futures markets are regulated by a differerent agency, the CFTC. Without the CFTC, the new financial products that have developed, and the organized exchanges on which they are traded, would probably exist in other countries as opposed to the United States.

In other words, regulatory bodies, like the organized exchanges they regulate, compete to supply rules and regulations that facilitate the provision of transaction services. To the extent that one regulatory body does a poor job in providing such rules and regulations, investors will shift to other exchanges governed by different and superior rules where substitute financial products are traded. Thus, competition among regulatory agencies creates an incentive to provide rules and regulations that benefit investors and at the same time limits the size of the regulatory tax that any agency can impose.

Critics of regulatory competition assume that there is some externality created by competition among regulatory agencies. The exact nature of this externality, however, is rarely specified. The Brady Report is no exception. This is not to suggest that regulatory bodies, and the exchanges that regulate, all have the same rules and organizational structure. The question, however, is whether the existence of different rules is necessarily harmful. For example, the Brady Report suggests that the different margin requirements on different exchanges that currently exist is socially undesirable. But why? There is no consensus that margin requirements are stabilizing. Indeed, economists have long studied the economic effect of margin requirements and have yet to come up with a coherent rationale why margin requirements should be the subject of regulation (as opposed to private contract), let alone why all margins should be the same.

The same is true for trading halts and price limits. Currently, exchanges maintain considerable discretion in deciding when trading can occur and how much prices can move in a given period. The Brady Report suggests that these types of decisions should be made more uniform under the guise of a single regulatory agency. However, there is again no consensus on what the effects are of trading halts and price limits and no assurance that the proposal for one agency will make things better as opposed to worse. For example, it may be that the threat of a single agency having the power to stop trading in all markets (at least in this country) will create panic, rather than eliminate panic, during periods when prices are changing rapidly. If traders anticipate that all markets may be shut down, they may rush to trade before the time that would be otherwise optimal with the result being greater buy-sell imbalances and sharper price moves. Until there is some basis for believing that the one-agency proposal will not have this effect, it makes no sense to implement the massive regulatory change proposed by the Brady Report.

It should also be emphasized that in situations where regulatory cooperation is desirable, this can occur without there being a single agency. After all, the number of regulatory agencies is small, thereby making it relatively simple for them to reach agreements where appropriate.

THE ONE -AGENCY PROPOSAL AND THE ECONOMIC THEORY OF REGULATION

The absence of any convincing rationale for the one-agency proposal raises questions as to whether something else is motivating the proposal. The economic theory of regulation suggests that there may well be. One possibility is that various entities are attempting to use the October crash to justify anti-competitive proposals that have as their aim not the prevention of future crises, but rather the enactment of proposals to gain an advantage over competitors. For example, it is probably no accident that the New York Stock Exchange, which has long campaigned against the introduction of new financial products and the growth of other exchanges, has advocated a bigger role for itself and more regulation of its competitors in light of the October crash. Similarly, it is probably no accident that the Securities and Exchange Commission, which has also long lobbied for more regulatory authority over substitute products, is taking the same position now but using the crash as a justification. The one notable exception to this inevitable tendency of using fear and uncertainty to justify anti-competitive proposals is the Federal Reserve Board, and particularly Chairman Greenspan. Notwithstanding the Brady Report's suggestion that the Federal Reserve Board assume far greater regulatory authority, Chairman Greenspan has thus far shown no interest. For this he is to be commended. As discussed above, there is simply no connection between what happened in October and the one-agency proposal.

The danger, however, is that in the rush to do "something," interest groups will succeed in getting some legislation enacted. Exactly what this legislation will provide is unclear. But of one thing we can be fairly confident—any legislation enacted in this climate is likely to have no connection to the problems connected with the October crash and will impose social costs in the process.

About the Contributors

Robert J. Barro is Professor of Economics at Harvard University. He was previously on the faculties of The University of Rochester, The University of Chicago, and Brown University. He is a leader in "rational expectations" macroeconomics with expertise on deficits, monetary policy, business cycles, and economic growth. The first edition of his *Macroeconomics* (1984) has been translated into German, Spanish, French, and Japanese. A second edition was published in 1987. Books by Barro to be published in 1989 include *Essays on Macroeconomic Policy* and the edited collection *Modern Business Cycle Theory* .

Barro is also Associate Editor of *The Journal of Monetary Economics* and a Fellow of the Econometric Society and the American Academy of Arts and Sciences. He serves on the Executive Committee of the American Economic Association, the Arbitration Panel of the New York Stock Exchange, and the Advisory Committee for the Hoover Institution.

Eugene F. Fama is Theodore O. Yntema Distinguished Service Professor of Finance at the Graduate School of Business of the University of Chicago. His *Foundations of Finance* (1972) is a standard authority on "efficient markets," especially with respect to portfolio decisions of investors and securities prices. Among his studies to be published in 1988 are "Permanent and Temporary Components of Stock Prices," "Dividend Yields and Expected Stock Returns," and "Business Cycles and the Behavior of Metal Prices" (all with Kenneth R. French).

Fama is the Advisory Editor of *The Journal of Financial Economics* and a Fellow of the Econometric Society. He also serves on the Board of Directors of Dimensional Fund Advisors.

121

Daniel R. Fischel is Director of the Law and Economics Program at the University of Chicago, where he holds a joint appointment as Professor of Law and Business at the Law School and at the Graduate School of Business. He teaches regulation of financial markets and has written studies such as "Regulatory Conflict and Entry Regulation of New Futures Contracts," and "Customer Protection in Futures and Securities Markets." In 1988 Harvard University Press will publish *The Economic Structure of Corporate Law*, written with Frank H. Easterbrook.

Fischel was Law Clerk for Associate Justice Potter Stewart of the United States Supreme Court, 1978-1979, and he is currently also Executive Vice President and Principal of Lexecon, Inc.

Allan H. Meltzer, John M. Olin Professor of Political Economy and Public Policy at Carnegie-Mellon University, has had broad teaching experience. He has been a Visiting Professor at Harvard, University of Chicago, University of Rochester, the Yugoslav Institute for Economic Research, the Austrian Institute for Advanced Study, the Getulio Vargas Foundation in Rio de Janeiro and the City University, London. His reputation in the field of money and capital markets has brought frequent assignments with Congressional committees, as a consultant to the President's Council of Economic Advisers, the U.S. Treasury Department, the Board of Governors of the Federal Reserve System and to foreign governments and central banks. Currently, he is Honorary Adviser to the Institute for Monetary and Economic Studies of the Bank of Japan and a member of the President's Economic Policy Advisory Board.

Meltzer's writings have appeared in numerous journals, including the business press here and abroad. He is the author of more than 150 papers on economic theory and policy and several books, including *Keynes's Monetary Theory: A Different Interpretation* (1988) and *Monetary Economics* (1989, with Karl Brunner). His career includes experience as a self-employed businessman, management adviser, and consultant to banks and financial institutions. He is a director of Cooper Tire and Rubber Company, the Sarah Scaife Foundation and the Commonwealth Foundation. He is currently co-editor of the Carnegie-Rochester Conference Series on Public Policy and an Associate Editor of *The Journal of Monetary Economics*.

Richard Roll holds the Allstate Chair in Finance at the Graduate School of Management, U.C.L.A., and is a principal of Roll and Ross Asset Management Corporation. His recent business experience includes two years, 1985-87, with Goldman, Sachs & Company, where he was the founder and director of the mortgage securities research group. He has also been a consultant for many U.S. corporations and law firms. He has been a board member at Dimensional Fund Advisors and was on the technical advisory board of Wells Fargo Investment Management.

Roll's academic career began with a Ph.D. from the University of Chicago in 1968. He was subsequently on the faculty at Carnegie-Mellon University, The European Institute for Advanced Study in Management in Brussels, and the French Business School, Hautes Etudes Commerciales, near Paris. He came to U.C.L.A. in 1976. Roll has published two books and more than sixty articles in technical journals. He is an associate editor of *The American Economic Review, The Journal of Finance*, and *The Journal of Financial Economics*. He was president of the American Finance Association during 1987.

Lester G. Telser is Professor of Economics at the University of Chicago. He is a leading theorist on the nature of competition and equilibrium in a market economy, and he is an authority on futures markets. In 1986 he served with D. Gale Johnson as coordinator of a major scholarly investigation of the performance and regulation of futures markets. For that project he wrote "Futures and Actual Markets: How they are Related." In 1988 he published *Theories of Competition* (North Holland) and in 1987 *A Theory of Efficient Cooperation and Competition* (Cambridge University Press).

Telser is Associate Editor of *The Review of Economics and Statistics*, and a member of the Editorial Board of *The Journal of Futures Markets*. In addition, he is a Fellow of the Econometric Society and a Fellow of the American Statistical Association.

About the Editors

Robert W. Kamphuis, Jr., is co-founder and executive director of the Mid America Institute for Public Policy Research. In addition to his work on economics-related issues through MAI, Kamphuis is currently preparing a new edition of *Lord George Bentinck: a Political Biography*, by the 19th century British statesman Benjamin Disraeli, the Earl of Beaconsfield.

Roger C. Kormendi is Associate Professor of Economics at the School of Business Administration of the University of Michigan. He is also co-founder and Director of Research for the Mid America Institute. He is co-editor of *Deregulating Financial Services: Public Policy in Flux* (1986, with George G. Kaufman). He is the author of "Earnings Innovations, Earnings Persistence and Stock Returns" (with Robert Lipe) Journal of Business, 1987. His "Fiscal Policy and Private Sector Behavior Revisited" (with Philip Meguire) is forthcoming in *The American Economic Review*, and "Taxation, Aggregate Activity and Economic Growth: Cross-Country Evidence on Some Supply Side Hypotheses" (with Reinhard Koester) in *Economic Inquiry*. Kormendi is a research consultant to the Department of Health and Human Services, and to The Urban Institute. He has served as a consultant to the World Bank.

J. W. Henry Watson is Assistant Professor of Economics and Public Policy in the School of Public Policy at the University of Chicago, where he teaches financial markets, public finance and industrial organization. He is also Associate Director of the Mid America Institute, and a principal of Phoenix Metals Corporation, an innovative powdered metals producer in the Detroit, Michigan area.

PART TWO

Excerpts from
REPORTS ON THE CRASH

Brady
The Presidential Task Force on Market Mechanisms

Miller
The Final and Preliminary Reports
of the CME Committee of Inquiry

Britain
The International Stock Exchange of London

CFTC
The Final Report to the Commodity Futures
Trading Commission

SEC
The Report to the Securities and Exchange Commission

GAO
Preliminary Observations on the Crash
U. S. General Accounting Office

BRADY

Presidential Task Force on Market Mechanisms

Executive Summary

Introduction. From the close of trading Tuesday, October 13, 1987 to the close of trading Monday, October 19, the Dow Jones Industrial Average declined by almost one third, representing a loss in the value of all outstanding United States stocks of approximately $1.0 trillion.

What made this market break extraordinary was the speed with which prices fell, the unprecedented volume of trading and the consequent threat to the financial system.

In response to these events, the President created the Task Force on Market Mechanisms. Its mandate was, in 60 days, to determine what happened and why, and to provide guidance in helping to prevent such a break from happening again.

The Market Break. The precipitous market decline of mid-October was "triggered" by specific events: an unexpectedly high merchandise trade deficit which pushed interest rates to new high levels, and proposed tax legislation which led to the collapse of the stocks of a number of takeover candidates. This initial decline ignited mechanical, price-insensitive selling by a number of institutions employing portfolio insurance strategies and a small number of mutual fund groups reacting to redemptions. The selling by these investors, and the prospect of further selling by them, encouraged a number of aggressive trading-oriented institutions to sell in anticipation of further market declines. These institutions included, in addition to hedge funds, a small number of pension and endowment funds, money management firms and investment banking houses. This selling, in turn, stimulated further reactive selling by portfolio insurers and mutual funds.

Portfolio insurers and other institutions sold in both the stock market and the stock index futures market. Selling pressures in the futures market was transmitted to the stock market by the mechanism of index arbitrage. Throughout the period of the decline, trading volume and price volatility increased dramatically. This trading activity was concentrated in the hands of a surprisingly few institutions. On October 19, sell programs by three portfolio insurers accounted for just under $2 billion in the stock market; in the futures market three portfolio insurers accounted for the equivalent in value of $2.8 billion of stock. Block sales by a few mutual funds accounted for about $900 million of stock sales.

The stock and futures market handled record volume of transactions and had a generally good record of remaining available for trading on October 19 and 20. However, market makers were unable to manage smooth price transitions in the face of overwhelming selling pressure.

Clearing and credit system problems further exacerbated the difficulties of market participants. While no default occurred, the possibility that a clearinghouse or a major investment banking firm might default, or that the banking system would deny required liquidity to the market participants, resulted in certain market makers curtailing their activities and increased investor uncertainty. Timely intervention by the Federal Reserve System provided confidence and liquidity to the markets and financial system.

One Market. Analysis of market behavior during the mid-October break makes clear an important conclusion. From an economic viewpoint, what have been traditionally seen as separate markets—the markets for stocks, stock index futures, and stock options—are in fact one market. Under ordinary circumstances, these marketplaces move sympathetically, linked by financial instruments, trading strategies, market participants and clearing and credit mechanisms.

To a large extent, the problems of mid-October can be traced to the failure of these market segments to act as one. Confronted with the massive selling demands of a limited number of institutions, regulatory and institutional structures designed for separate marketplaces were incapable of effectively responding to "intermarket" pressures. The New York Stock Exchange's automated transaction system, used by index arbitrageurs to link the two marketplaces, ceased to be useful for arbitrage after midday on October 19. The concern that some clearinghouses and major market participants might fail inhibited intermarket activities of other investors. The futures and stock markets became disengaged, both nearly going into freefall.

The ability of the equity market to absorb the huge selling pressure to which it was subjected in mid-October depended on its liquidity. But liquidity sufficient to absorb the limited selling demands of investors became an illusion of liquidity when confronted by massive selling, as everyone showed up on the same side of the market at once. Ironically, it was this illusion of liquidity which led certain similarly motivated investors, such as portfolio insurers, to adopt strategies which call for liquidity far in excess of what the market could supply.

Regulatory Implications. Because stocks, futures and options constitute one market, there must be in place a regulatory structure designed to be consistent with this economic reality. The October market break illustrates that regulatory changes, derived from the one-market concept, are necessary both to reduce the possibility of destructive market breaks and to deal effectively with such episodes should they occur. The guiding objective should be to enhance the integrity and competitiveness of U.S. financial markets.

Analysis of the October market break demonstrates that one agency must have the authority to coordinate a few critical intermarket issues cutting across market segments and affecting the entire financial system; to monitor activities of all market segments; and to mediate concerns across marketplaces. The specific issues which have an impact across marketplaces throughout the financial system include: clearing and credit mechanisms; margin requirements; circuit breaker mechanisms, such as price limits and trading halts; and information systems for monitoring activities across marketplaces.

The single agency required to coordinate cross-marketplace issues must have broad and deep expertise in the interaction of the stock, stock options and stock index futures marketplaces, as well as in all financial markets, domestic and global. It must have broad expertise in the financial system as a whole.

The Task Force compared these requirements with possible alternative regulatory structures, including: existing self-regulatory organizations, such as the exchanges; existing government regulatory agencies, namely the Securities and Exchange Commission and the Commodity Futures Trading Commission; the Department of the Treasury; the Federal Reserve Board; a combination of two or more of these; and a new regulatory body.

Conclusions. Our understanding of these events leads directly to our recommendations. To help prevent a repetition of the events of mid-October and to provide an effective and coordinated response in the face of market disorder, we recommend:

- One agency should coordinate the few, but critical, regulatory issues which have an impact across the related market segments and throughout the financial system.

- Clearing systems should be unified across marketplaces to reduce financial risk.

- Margins should be made consistent across marketplaces to control speculation and financial leverage.

- Circuit breaker mechanisms (such as price limits and coordinated trading halts) should be formulated and implemented to protect the market system.

- Information systems should be established to monitor transactions and conditions in related markets.

The single agency must have expertise in the interaction of markets—not simply experience in regulating distinct market segments. It must have a broad perspective on the financial system as a whole, both domestic and foreign, as well as independence and responsiveness.

The Task Force had neither the time nor the mandate to consider the full range of issues necessary to support a definitive recommendation on the choice of agency to assume the required role. However, the weight of the evidence suggests that the Federal Reserve is well qualified to fill that role.

Other Issues. Certain other issues were discussed by the Task Force without reaching definitive conclusions. The Task Force identified the following issues as warranting review by the appropriate authorities:

- **Short Selling.** There are restrictions on short selling in the stock market, but not in the futures or options markets. Linkages, such as index arbitrage, among these markets may operate to incapacitate the short selling restriction. This issue should be reviewed from an intermarket perspective.

- **Customer vs. Proprietary Trading.** Under certain circumstances, broker-dealers and futures market makers can act as principal for their own account as well as execute customer orders. Potential problems posed by the opportunity to trade in anticipation of customer orders in different marketplaces should also be reviewed from the intermarket perspective.

- **NYSE Specialists.** The adequacy of specialist capital and specialist performance in meeting their responsibility to maintain a fair and orderly market are issues raised by the October market experience.

- **NYSE Order Imbalances.** When there are serious imbalances of orders, consideration should be given to favoring public customers in execution over institutional and other proprietary orders through the DOT system and to making the specialist book public to help attract the other side of the imbalance.

CHAPTER ONE: INTRODUCTION

From the close of trading on Tuesday, October 13, 1987, to the close of trading on October 19, 1987 the Dow Jones Industrial Average fell 769 points or 31 percent (see Figure Brady-1). In those four days of trading, the value of all outstanding U.S. stocks decreased by almost $1.0 trillion. On October 19, 1987, alone, the Dow fell by 508 points or 22.6 percent. Since the early 1920's, only the drop of 12.8 percent in the Dow on October 28, 1929 and the fall of 11.7 percent the following day, which together constituted the Crash of 1929, have approached the October 19 decline in magnitude.

The significance of this decline lies in the role that the stock market plays in a modern industrial economy, both as a harbinger and a facilitator of economic activity. Stock price levels can have an important effect on the confidence and, hence, the behavior of both businesses and households.

FIGURE BRADY-1
Dow Jones Industrial One Minute Chart
October 14, 1987 to October 20, 1987

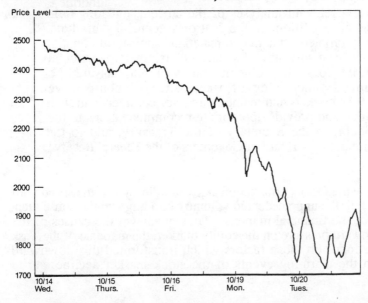

Further, equity markets are a primary means by which businesses and industries raise capital to finance growth and provide jobs. Gross sales of newly issued common stock increased substantially over the course of the 1982 to 1987 bull market, reaching $56.3 billion in 1986 and $27 billion in the first six months of 1987. However, the importance of stock sales is greater than simply the amount of funds raised. New equity capital and public equity markets are essential to financing innovative business ventures which are a primary engine of the nation's economic growth.

Moreover, publicly traded equities are a repository of a significant fraction of U.S. household wealth. Households directly own about 60 percent of all U.S. publicly owned common stock, which was worth approximately $2.25 trillion before the October market decline. Households hold another $210 billion of common stock through mutual funds and $740 billion through pension funds. Thus, in the early fall of 1987, the stock market accounted for approximately $3.2 trillion worth of household wealth.

Equity markets are also inextricably tied to the wider financial system through the structure of banks and other financial institutions. Given the importance of equity markets to the economy and to the public, effectively structured and functioning equity markets are critical.

Consequently, in response to October's extraordinary events, the President created a Task Force on Market Mechanisms, the purpose of which was to:

> ...review relevant analyses of the current and long-term financial condition of the Nation's securities markets; identify problems that may threaten the short-term liquidity or long-term solvency of such markets; analyze potential solutions to such problems that will both assure the continued functioning of free, fair, and competitive securities markets and maintain investor confidence in such markets; and provide appropriate recommendations to the President, to the Secretary of the Treasury, and to the Chairman of the Board of Governors of the Federal Reserve System.

What made the October market break extraordinary was the speed with which prices fell, the unprecedented volume of trading and the consequent dislocations of the financial markets. Thus, whatever the causes of the original downward pressure on the equity market, the mandate of the Task Force was to focus on those factors which transformed this downward pressure into the alarming events of the stock market decline and to recommend measures to ensure, as far as possible, that future market fluctuations are not of the extreme and potentially destructive nature witnessed in October 1987.

Fundamental causes of the recent market decline should not, of course, be ignored. To the extent that existing imbalances in the budget, foreign transactions, savings, corporate asset positions and other fundamental factors are perceived to be problems, they merit attention.

The events of October demonstrated an unusual frailty in the markets. Only three percent of the total shares of publicly traded stock in the U.S. changed hands during this period, but it resulted in the loss in stock value of $1 trillion. That such a relatively small transaction volume can produce such a large loss in value over such a short time span suggests the importance of determining the extent to which market mechanisms themselves were an important factor in the October market break. The work of the Task Force, therefore, focused on the individual marketplaces and the interrelationship of existing market mechanisms, including the instruments traded, the strategies employed and the regulatory structure.

The Task Force's findings and conclusions are based significantly on the primary transaction data and information that we accumulated. Recognizing the importance of determining as much as possible about each transaction, the Task Force spent much of its time gathering and then analyzing transactions on the New York Stock Exchange, Chicago Mercantile Exchange, Chicago Board of Trade, American Stock Exchange and the Chicago Board Options Exchange.

As a vehicle for expanding on, and cross-referencing, this exchange data, the Task Force analyzed information on transactions supplied to the Securities and Exchange Commission and the Commodity Futures Trading Commission. In addition, we received information directly from certain major investment banks and institutional investors.

Finally, the Task Force spoke in person with hundreds of market participants in order to understand better their perspectives on individual transactions and all the events of the October 1987 decline.

CHAPTER TWO: INSTRUMENTS, MARKETS, REGULATION AND TRADING STRATEGIES

This chapter is designed to serve as a brief introductory guide for readers less familiar with the instruments, marketplaces and trading strategies important to understanding the events of mid-October.

Stock, Futures Contracts and Options Contracts.   Shares of stock are claims of ownership in corporations. The price of a stock in effectively operating stock markets depends largely on the current performance and future earnings prospects of a corporation. Futures contracts and options contracts are not corporate ownership claims. They are "derivative" instruments whose value depends primarily on the underlying price of the stock or portfolio of stocks from which they are derived.   The most heavily traded equity-related futures and options contracts are based upon certain standardized portfolios of stock such as the Standard and Poors 500 Stock Index, the Standard and Poors 100 Stock Index and the Major Market Index of 20 stocks.

Exchanges and Market Making. Stocks are traded on the New York Stock Exchange and American Stock Exchange, as well as on several other exchanges throughout the country. Other stocks are traded in the over-the-counter market, a dealer market connected by computer and telephones.

The S&P 500 futures contract is traded on the Chicago Mercantile Exchange, and the MMI futures contract is traded on the Chicago Board of Trade. The preponderance of the daily volume of index futures trading takes place on the CME. Although the value of open interest in the futures contracts is only a small fraction of the value of NYSE stocks, the value of the stocks represented by the volume of futures contracts traded on the CME daily is typically about twice the value of stocks traded on the NYSE daily.

Options contracts on the S&P 100 are traded on the Chicago Board Options Exchange. The Amex trades an option on the MMI. Options whose value is related to individual stocks are also traded on various exchanges.

A specialist system is used by the various stock exchanges for exchange-listed stocks. Under the specialist system, a single dealer is given the right to make the market in a specific stock or option on the exchange. In return, the specialist assumes the responsibility to make an "orderly" market by buying and selling from inventory. In the competitive market maker system, competing dealers set the price of an options or futures contract in an auction process. A competitive market maker system is used by the CBOE for options, and the CME and the CBOT for futures. The OTC also uses a competing dealer system to make markets. A hybrid system employing both specialists and competing market makers is used for options sponsored by the stock exchanges.

Regulation. The stock, futures and options exchanges organize, manage, promote and oversee the individual stock and derivative contract markets. They set and enforce rules regarding trading practices, monitor the financial resources and obligations of participants and supervise the settlement of transactions.

There is a system of federal regulatory oversight which requires or prohibits particular rules and practices, approves rule changes, and audits the exchanges' trading and financial surveillance. The Securities and Exchange Commission has responsibility for stocks and options; the Commodity Futures Trading Commission oversees futures.

Margin. Customers of futures commission merchants and broker-dealers in stock markets must post collateral, called "margin," consisting of cash and securities, against their obligations. These obligations are twofold. First, they are loans from a broker-dealer to purchase stock. Second, they are obligations create by a short sale of stock, the purchase or sale of a futures contract and the sale of an options contract.

The equity balance of a customer's margin account, equal to the difference between the market value of securities and the amount of the loan or other obligation, is calculated each day. The equity value must be greater than the margin requirement; otherwise the broker-dealer may call for more margin or sell the customer's positions.

The Federal Reserve has final authority for setting initial margin requirements for stock and options. The individual commodity exchanges have the authority to set margins in the futures contract traded on their floors.

Clearing. Trades executed on an exchange are guaranteed by a "clearinghouse," whose performance is in turn guaranteed to varying degrees by the clearing members (broker-dealers or futures commission merchants) of that exchange. Most U.S. stock exchanges clear their transactions through a single stock clearinghouse. Similarly, all U.S. options exchanges clear through a single options clearinghouse. In contrast, each of the largest futures exchanges maintains its own clearinghouse.

Trading Strategies. The price of an index futures contract and the price of the stock index portfolio underlying it are directly related. Normally, the price of a futures contract exceeds the price of the underlying portfolio by an amount reflecting the "cost of carry," which relates to the difference between the Treasury bill rate and the dividend yield on the portfolio.

An index arbitrageur attempts to profit when the price difference is abnormal, either by simultaneously buying futures contracts and selling the index portfolio of stocks or by doing the reverse. When the futures price is at a discount, the arbitrageur engages in index substitution by selling an index portfolio of stocks and replacing it with futures contracts. This is typically done by a pension fund which owns an indexed portfolio of stocks. In executing this arbitrage, the institution takes on whatever greater credit risk there is owning the futures contract rather than the stock themselves. When the futures contract is at a premium, the arbitrageur may execute a "synthetic cash" transaction, buying the stock portfolio and selling futures. Typically, a corporation holding short term money market investments would perform this arbitrage to increase its yield.

There are also a number of non-arbitrage trading strategies which involve stock and futures contracts. First, when trading-oriented investors want to trade on the direction of the market as a whole, they often buy or sell index futures because futures transactions can be executed more quickly and cheaply than transactions involving a diversified portfolio of stocks. Lower transaction costs and lower margin requirements make this possible. Second, longer term investors often find it faster and initially cheaper to initiate portfolio position changes through the futures market. Eventually, the futures position is replaced with stocks. Third, block traders, exchange specialists and investment bankers marketing new stock issues can use index futures to hedge their positions.

Other strategies are designed to react mechanically to market movements by selling in a falling market and buying in a rising market. One such strategy, "portfolio insurance," is designed to allow institutional trading to participate in a rising market yet protect their portfolio as the market falls. Using computer-based models derived from stock options analysis, portfolio insurance vendors compute optimal stock-to-cash ratios at various stock market price levels. But rather than buying and selling stocks as the market moves, most portfolio insurers adjust the stock-to-cash ratio by trading index futures. Indeed, several major portfolio insurance vendors have been authorized to trade only futures and have no access to their clients' stock portfolios. Some option hedging strategies employed by options traders use the same method of buying futures as the market rises and selling futures as the markets falls.

Underlying many of these strategies is the ability to use stock index futures to trade the entire "stock market," as if it were a single commodity. Futures contracts make it possible to do this quickly, efficiently and cheaply. However, to the extent they do this, traders and investors treat the stock market as if it were a single commodity rather than a collection of individual stocks.

CHAPTER THREE:
THE BULL MARKET

All major stock markets began an impressive period of growth in 1982. Spurred by the economic turnaround, the growth in corporate earnings, the reduction in inflation and the associated fall in interest rates, the Dow rose from 777 to 1,896 between August 1982 and December 1986 (see Figure Brady-2). Other factors contributing to this dramatic bull market included: continuing deregulation of the financial markets; tax incentives for equity investing; stock retirements arising from mergers, leveraged buyouts and share repurchase programs; and an increasing tendency to include "takeover premiums" in the valuation of a large number of stocks.

Despite the dramatic rise in the market, stock valuation at the end of 1986 was not out of line with levels achieved in past periods. (Figures Brady-3 and 4 show two common stock valuation measures, the price-to-earnings ratio and the ratio of price-to-book value per share, for the stocks in the S&P 400 Index from 1950 to 1987.)

1987. Stock in the U.S. continued to appreciate rapidly during the first eight months of 1987, despite rapidly increasing interest rates (see Figure Brady-5). When the Dow reached its peak of 2,722 in August, stocks were valued at levels which challenged historical precedent and fundamental justification (see Figures Brady-3 to 6). Factors which contributed to this final rise included, in addition to those listed earlier, increased foreign investment in U.S. equities and growing investment in common stock mutual funds.

The rapid rise in the popularity of portfolio insurance strategies also contributed to the market's rise. Pension fund managers adopting these strategies typically increased the fund's risk exposure by investing more heavily in common stock during this rising market. The rationale was that portfolio insurance would cushion the impact of a market break by allowing them to shift quickly out of stocks.

During this period, the OTC market also advanced rapidly, and institutional participation and trading volume rose. The OTC and NYSE increasingly moved in parallel, with relative price levels in one matching those in the other.

FIGURE BRADY-2
U.S. Market - S&P 500 Index
January 1982 to November 1987

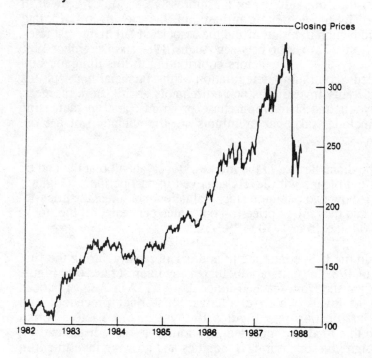

Moreover, volatility in all the U.S. equity markets increased somewhat during this period. However, prior to October, it was not substantially high by historical standards and increases in U.S stock market volatility were comparable to increases in volatility in foreign markets.

International Equity Markets. Foreign stock exchanges enjoyed bull markets similar to the U.S. during this period. As in the U.S. stock valuation in these markets by 1987 began to rise above levels apparently justified by historical precedent or economic factors. In Japan, for example, stocks were selling at a ratio of 70 times earnings in October 1987, more than double the price-to-earnings ratio in the beginning of 1986.

FIGURE BRADY-3
U.S. Market - Price/Earnings Multiple vs Long Term Government Bond Yield
January 1950 to November 1987

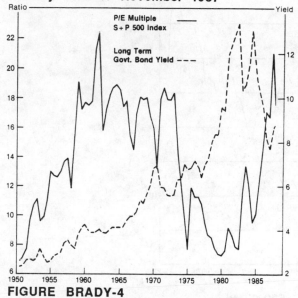

FIGURE BRADY-4
U.S. Market - S&P 400 Price-to-Book Ratio
January 1950 to November 1987

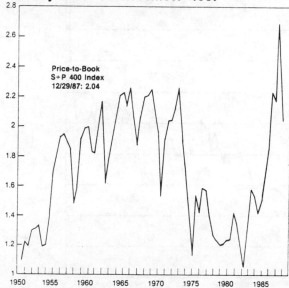

FIGURE BRADY-5
U.S. Market - Price/Earnings Multiple vs Long Term Bond Yield
January 1982 to November 1987

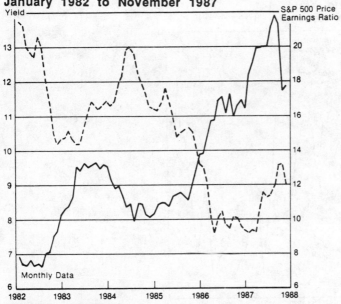

FIGURE BRADY-6
Ratio: Bond Yield/S&P 500 Yield
January 1947 to December 1987

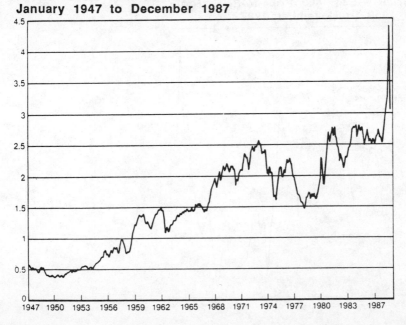

Aided by significantly improved computer and communications technology, cross-border investment increased rapidly during this period. The communications networks of four key data providers alone cover over 100,000 equities, connect over 110 s and include 300,000 terminals in over 100 countries. In the first nine months of 1987 alone, Japanese investment in U.S. equities increased by about $15 billion. As cross-border investment grew, so did U.S. investors' sensitivity to foreign common stock performance. Investors made comparisons of valuations in different countries, often using higher markets. Consequently, a process of ratcheting up among worldwide stock markets began to develop. In the midst of this globalization of equity investment, trading volume on U.S. markets continued to dominate worldwide trading. Trading on U.S. markets tended to lead other markets around the world.

This economic and financial panorama was the backdrop to the October market break in the U.S.

THE OCTOBER MARKET BREAK:
OCTOBER 14 THROUGH OCTOBER 20*

Introduction. On August 25, 1987, the Dow Jones Industrial Average reached a record high close of 2,722. The Dow had risen by more than 40 percent during the year, and expectations were favorable toward stocks for the remainder of 1987. In slightly more than two months those expectations were shattered. The unprecedented five year bull market that had more than tripled stock prices was over, ending in the worst week in history for U.S. equities.

The purpose of this study is to examine in detail events in the stock, futures, and options markets during the week of October 14 to October 20, and to focus in particular on the actions and motivations of market participants.

The five trading sessions beginning October 14 were among the most tumultuous and volatile in history. From the closing level of 2,505 recorded on Tuesday, October 13, the DJIA declined by 30.6 percent to 1,738 by the close on the following Monday. On Tuesday, October 20, the DJIA, after a series of wild swings, rallied by over 100 points to

---

* The Brady Report dealt with the market break twice: first in chapter four of the main body of the report, and then more extensively in Study III of the appendix. The more extensive treatment from Study III of the appendix is here substituted for chapter four.

1,841. This pattern was followed by major equity markets around the world.

The prominence during this period of new derivative instruments, such as futures and options on stock market indices, increased investor uncertainty because of their interaction with the stock market. Trading strategies which relied on these new products, coupled with a deteriorating environment for stocks, helped compress trading activity into a few hyperactive days, as equities were revalued on an unprecedented scale. Trading volume on the New York Stock Exchange and in the Standard and Poor's 500 futures pit on the Chicago Mercantile Exchange remained at record levels during these five days as a relatively small group of major institutions intensified their selling activity.

The catalyst for this abrupt shift in market direction was a series of economic and political events which served to reinforce concerns that had developed in the late summer about the market's overvaluation. Fueled by weak currency and bond markets in late August and early September, the DJIA had slid to 2,480. Although the total return on stocks continued to outstrip that of bonds, by August the relative yield on stocks was at an historic low to the yield on bonds, which sent a warning to investors. In addition, investors were being asked to absorb, domestically and internationally, a record amount of new equity issues.

A rally in late September—including a one-day advance of more than 75 points in the DJIA—erased these concerns for many investors. They became convinced that the recent decline was simply a correction in the bull market and that new highs in the DJIA were likely in the near future.

Events in early October proved how wrong these convictions were. Bond yields were steadily approaching the pyschologically important ten percent level, while the dollar remained near its record lows. Word circulated in the markets of possible tax law changes that would make takeovers less attractive, sending a chill into a market that had fed on takeover speculation. At the close on Tuesday, October 13, the DJIA had dropped back near its September low, and market participants waited nervously overnight for Wednesday's release of the September U.S. merchandise trade figures—an important economic barometer.

What follows is a day-by-day account of the major events and the actions of investors that moved the markets from Wednesday, October 14 through Tuesday, October 20.

Wednesday, October 14. Several events which occurred from Wednesday, October 14 through Friday, October 16 appear to have been

FIGURE BRADY-S1
Takeover Stock Index vs S&P 500 Index
Normalized Price Series
December 1986 to October 21, 1987

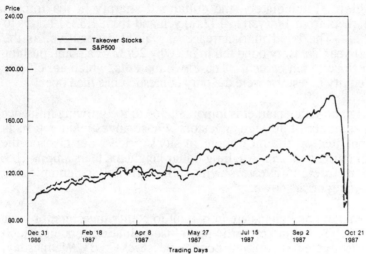

Takeover Stock Index:
Allegis, USG Corp., Tenneco, Gillette, Newmont Mining, GAF Corp., Irving Bank, Kansas City
Southern Industries, Telex, Sante Fe Southern Pacific, Dayton Hudson

FIGURE BRADY-S2
Takeover Stock Index vs S&P 500 Index
Normalized Price Series
October 9, 1987 to October 23, 1987

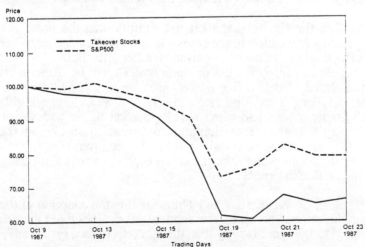

Takeover Stock Index:
Allegis, USG Corp., Tenneco, Gillette, Newmont Mining, GAF Corp., Irving Bank, Kansas City
Southern Industries, Telex, Sante Fe Southern Pacific, Dayton Hudson

the catalysts for the October 19 market crash. On Wednesday morning at 8:30 a.m. (all time references are to Eastern Time), the Commerce Department announced that the U.S. merchandise trade deficit for August amounted to $15.7 billion, compared to a market expectation of $14 billion to $14.5 billion. Immediately, the dollar fell sharply in the foreign exchange markets from 144 yen to 142.50 yen and from 1.8231 marks to 1.8050 marks. The bond market reaction was also negative, as the bellwether 30-year Treasury bond fell in price by 20/32 of a point, pushing the yield up close to ten percent These two markets, which are closely watched by equity investors, were the only domestic ones then open.

The foreign currency market is important due to the growing influence in the U.S. markets of foreign investors whose investment return is dependent not just on the movement in stock prices, but also on the movement in currency rates. A falling dollar heightens fears among U.S. investors that foreign investors will sell their dollar-denominated securities, forcing prices down.

Movements in bond yields are important to equity investors for three reasons. First, many market participants use valuation models which compare the expected returns on bonds and stocks. By Wednesday, October 14, most of these models were indicating that stocks were overvalued relative to bonds. A further decline that morning in bond prices exaccrbated this valuation discrepancy. Second, a rise in interest rates can slow the growth of the economy and thereby slow corporate earnings. Finally, higher interest rates would make the financing of leveraged buyouts more costly. That, in turn, could reduce corporate takeover activity, which had helped fuel the bull market in stocks.

Compounding the financial market uncertainty was the news late Tuesday of pending legislation in the House Ways and Means Committee that would effectively eliminate the current tax benefits associated with leveraged buyouts and impose a tax on "greenmail" profits. Rumors of this news had already led to a five percent decline in selected takeover stocks since October 9 (see Figures Brady-S1 and S2). These highly visible and volatile stocks had often led the market up as widespread takeover activity led market participants to invest in stocks on the expectation that they might be acquired at handsome premiums to their market value. Such investment began to take place across the board, pushing up the market in general.

As fears spread on Wednesday and Thursday that the adoption of the proposed legislation was possible, the suddenly less attractive takeover stocks continued to fall more rapidly than the market. In fact, on Tuesday,

October 20, the takeover stocks fell an additional five percent to their lows for this period, while the DJIA registered a one-day record advance of more than 100 points. In part, this underperformance by the takeover stocks may also have been tied to rumors beginning on Friday, October 16, that a number of firms, known as risk arbitrageurs, that invest in the securities of potential takeover candidates had to meet large margin calls. When prices started to fall these firms were left with two choices: putting up additional capital or selling their shares. The firms' inability or reluctance to meet these margin calls contributed to the selling of takeover stocks.

An additional alternative for the risk arbitageurs was to hedge their positions by selling in-the-money call options on their takeover stocks. The premium received for the calls would protect the risk arbitrageurs from a moderate decline in the market. However, as the market tumbled and the stocks declined through the strike price of these calls, the existence of short call positions did not provide downside price protection. This served to concentrate the selling pressure in these stocks and, at times, the takeover stocks led the market down. By 9:00 a.m. Wednesday morning, trading oriented investors were faced with the news of both the trade deficit figure and proposed House Ways & Means Committee tax bill and braced themselves for a tough market opening (see Chart Brady-S1).

Although the stock market opens at 9:30 a.m. each morning, one futures contract, the Major Market Index, opens on the Chicago Board of Trade at 9:15 a.m. The MMI is comprised of 20 major stocks and is used by market participants as a leading indicator of the stock market's opening level, even though the MMI market is relatively small, with a low open interest level and minor trading volume. As the MMI opened on Wednesday 30-year Treasury bond yields had just traded about ten percent for the first time since November 1985. The reaction in the futures pit was to open the MMI contract at 492.50, a substantial drop of 5.15 points below the Tuesday afternoon closing price.[1] Other futures and equity markets opened down sharply at 9:30 a.m. The most widely followed stock index futures contract at the time was the S&P 500 December futures contract ("Contract") which trades primarily on the Chicago Mercantile Exchange. The Contract declined 3.3 points to 312.35 at the opening (it would trade as low as 181.00 by Tuesday, October 20). The DJIA dropped 35 points at the opening of trading to the 2,473 point level, falling below the lows of September. Many trading-oriented investors believe

---

[1] Although various indices do not necessarily track each other perfectly, there is a reasonably high correlation among them. Thus, generally speaking, a one point move of the MMI futures index translates into a move of about 4.8 points on the DJIA; a move of one point on the S&P futures contract is equal to a move of about eight points on the DJIA.

that once a market has declined and then risen again as the stock market had in September, the lowest point of the move provides a support level in the future. If this support level is subsequently violated, it represents a sign of weakness. Therefore, when the DJIA broke through its September low point of 2,480, many technical trading-oriented investors, who use a variety of stock price movement theories to guide their investments reacted by selling stock and stock index futures.

On the Chicago Mercantile Exchange, the negative market expectations resulted in selling by trading-oriented investors, who were betting on the direction of the market. During the first hour of trading, these investors accounted for 18 percent of trading activity. The price of the Contract fell below the technically important 311 level. Due to the sharp downward opening of the Contract, the difference in price, or the spread, between the Contract and the S&P 500 stock index ("Index"), on which the Contract is based, caused a group of trading-oriented investors known as index arbitrageurs to begin buying the Contract and selling stocks that make up the Index.[2]

This index arbitrage can be done by utilizing many different stocks and derivative securities. In addition to using the Contract and the Index, arbitrageurs commonly use the MMI and the 20 stocks it represents as well as Chicago Board Options Exchange's option on the S&P 100 ("OEX") and the 100 stocks which it represents.

The buying of futures by the index arbitrageurs caused the Contract to rally to the 313.40 level, its high for the day. The arbitrage activity resulted in the sale of at least $200 million in baskets of stock, 16 percent of the first half hour's volume. By 10:00 a.m., the futures discount had disappeared, largely because of arbitrage activity.

After the first hour of trading, the DJIA had fallen to 2,464, down 44 points on the day. Between 10:30 a.m. and noon, the stock market drifted

---

[2] Index arbitrage is a trading strategy by which investors purchase or sell stocks comprising an index and establish offsetting positions in derivative stock index futures or options, when the difference or spread between the price of the index and the price of the derivative is greater or less than fair value. At fair value, the spread equals the difference between a risk-free rate of return (i.e., Treasury bills) and the dividend yield of the stocks comprising the index. In other words, at fair market value an investor would be indifferent to owning risk-free securities or engaging in index arbitrage. In essence, the arbitrageurs take advantage of the spreads that periodically open up between equities, futures and options markets by buying in the lowest-priced market and selling in the highest-priced market. While an attempt is made to execute simultaneously both sides of the arbitrage, the trader runs some risk in both marketplaces in attempting to carry out his strategy.

sideways with the DJIA unchanged. There was little index arbitrage activity during this period.

The price of the Contract dropped sharply from 312.25 to 308.00 between 12:15 p.m. and 1:15 p.m., largely as a result of selling by portfolio insurers. This selling pressure pushed the Contract back to a discount to the Index and, as in the morning, index arbitrageurs entered the market to bring the prices back into line. Index arbitrageurs bought futures and sold stock worth approximately $300 million, or a striking 30 percent of the total stock volume this hour. By 1:15 p.m., the DJIA had dropped 75 points to a level approximately ten percent below the August peak. This important technical level helped to support the market psychologically for much of the afternoon, and the DJIA changed little from 1:15 p.m. to 3:30 p.m. But the market's inability to rally from this support level began to create selling pressure late in the afternoon. The volume of block trades of 100,000 shares or more increased during the afternoon, suggesting that institutional investors were beginning to reevaluate their equity positions. Between 3:30 p..m. and 4:00 p.m. index arbitrageurs were again active, selling $120 million in stocks or 14 percent of the volume. During this time period, the DJIA fell 17 points.

The DJIA closed at 2,412, down 95 points—then its largest-ever one-day point decline—on volume of 207 million shares. Index arbitrage stock selling activity accounted for $1.4 billion, 17 percent of total activity. Of the 207 million shares traded on the New York Stock Exchange, block trades of 10,000 shares or more accounted for 47.6 percent, which is slightly larger than normal. The 20 largest NYSE member firms sold as principal approximately $689 million net of stocks, or eight percent of total volume, a signal that the members were lightening their inventory positions because of an unfavorable market outlook (see Figure Brady-S3). Down volume was nine times greater than up volume during the day, which was indicative of a broad base of selling (see Figures Brady-S4 and S5).

While the stock market closes every day at 4:00 p.m., the futures market remains open until 4:15 p.m. On Wednesday afternoon, the Contract continued to sell off after 4:00 p.m., suggesting the possibility of heavy arbitrage activity at the opening on Thursday. Overall, trading-oriented accounts in the futures markets sold $2 billion on Wednesday, which on a gross basis represents 12 percent of the total selling volume. This was nearly four times the activity of any other category except for the market makers in the futures pit at the CME, who are known as locals (see Figures Brady-S6 to S11).

Thursday, October 15. After achieving a record-high close in Tokyo on Wednesday, the Nikkei stock average, Japan's equivalent of the DJIA, fell 218 points to the 26,428 level, in reaction to the weakening U.S. bond, currency, and stock markets. In London, the Financial Times index of 100 stock, fell 22 points to the 1.812 level for the same reasons. The performance of these international markets prior to the daily opening of the U.S. markets sends important signals to investors for several reasons. For one, many securities are traded in several international markets, achieving different price levels in each time zone. Moreover, investors, both domestic and foreign, have become major participants in a variety of international markets. Price changes in one market may cause investors to alter their investment decisions in another market. In addition, global investors must decide to which market they will allocate new investment funds. During the month of October, for example, public offerings for British Petroleum and Nippon Telephone & Telegraph absorbed approximately $50 billion of investors' capital. Several trading-oriented investors have stated that they saw foreign capital withdrawn from the U.S. market because of these two offerings. In addition to these two large foreign offerings, the new issue calendar in the U.S. was extraordinarily heavy, with 285 public stock offerings in registration.

On the foreign exchange markets Thursday morning, the dollar threatened to break through the 1.80 level against the Deutschemark. This approached the bottom of the presumed trading range established under the Louvre accord, reached in February 1987 in Paris by the finance ministers of seven major industrial nations. Consequently, the dollar firmed as trading-oriented investors expected central bank intervention.

Trading in the U.S bond market was exceptionally weak in the morning, given the market's expectation of an imminent increase in the discount rate by the Federal Reserve Board. The 30-year Treasury bond opened at a 10.25 percent yield and by 10:30 a.m. was trading at 10.37 percent, when the Federal Reserve Bank of New York surprised the market by announcing overnight system repurchase agreements. This represented an injection of liquidity into the banking system and led bond investors to question their assumption of a discount rate increase. Because of the early time of the announcement (repurchase activity is normally announced between 11:30 a.m. and 11:45 a.m.), as well as the general perception that the Federal Reserve had been tightening credit to support the dollar, the view spread that the Federal Reserve was caught between two conflicting objectives: to provide liquidity to a falling stock market at the same time it restricted credit to protect the dollar's value and to extinguish inflationary expectations. Through the rest of Thursday and Friday, 90-day Treasury bill rates fell, reflecting the easier money stance, while longer term rates continued to rise in expectation of tighter credit in the future.

Given the market weakness at Wednesday afternoon's close and during Thursday's Far Eastern and European trading, the S&P 500 futures contract opened down 1.85 points to 303.15 at 9:30 a.m. At 9:45 a.m. the DJIA was at 2,392, 19 points below Wednesday's closing level. During the first half hour, volume on the NYSE was an extremely heavy 48 million shares, with approximately 60 percent of the trading in the form of blocks of 10,000 shares or more. This unusually heavy institutional activity came from foreign investors who were large buyers of stock (see Chart Brady S2).

Portfolio insurers were heavy sellers early in the day on Thursday in response to Wednesday's market decline. The portfolio insurance vendors use different trading strategies in reacting to volatility in the market. While some investors employing portfolio insurance constantly reevaluate their correct hedge ratios during trading hours, others believe it is less costly to run their models only at the end of the trading day. By lagging the market, these insurers hope to avoid the hedging costs created by intraday volatility. This lagging strategy works well in choppy, trendless markets but can be very expensive when the market moves in the same direction for several trading sessions in a row.

On Thursday morning, this reactive selling of futures contracts by portfolio insurers led to an initial spread between the Contract and the Index of negative 1.50 points compared to fair value of positive 1.75 points. (The spread is the difference between the price of the contract and the underlying index.) In the first half hour of trading, two large foreign speculative accounts and three portfolio insurers sold approximately 2,900 contracts or 15 percent of the total for that period. Much of the futures buying was related to short covering and activity by index arbitrageurs. Index arbitrage selling of stock during this period amounted to $231 million or 12 percent of total volume. That level of activity is normal for index arbitrage which indicates, given the market weakness, that there were other significant sellers of stock.

The stock and bond markets both rallied between 10:30 a.m. and noon, in part because the activity of the Federal Reserve indicated that there would not be an immediate rise in the discount rate. Many of the large buyers of stock were such non-trading-oriented institutions as pension funds and bank trust departments. These institutions are sometimes referred to as "fundamental buyers." Short coverings in the futures market also helped to fuel the rally. However, at 12:30 p.m., market expectations were disrupted by disappointing news regarding the budget deficit when the Administration stated "that simple prudence should make it possible to meet the 1988 Gramm-Rudman-Hollings deficit reduction target." This statement indicated the Administration was not planning any special deficit cutting effort, and activity in the equity markets slowed immediately as investors analyzed the impact of potentially larger-than-expected domestic deficits. The bond market rally fizzled as well.

Still, by 3:30 p.m., the DJIA was only down four points. Over the last 30 minutes of trading, it would fall another 53 points, as an announcement by the Administration that the dollar could fall further, coupled with increased uncertainty in the bond market about the dollar's already weak condition, led to some equity selling. Broad-based selling in the futures market quickly drove the spread between the stock and futures to a discount, and index arbitrageurs stepped in and started to buy futures and sell stocks. Their activity led to the sale of $192 million of stock in the last half hour, which accounted for 19 percent of trading activity during this period.

Also active was the selling of baskets of stocks representing the S&P 500 through the NYSE's Designated Order Turnaround automated execution system. This practice, often unrelated to index arbitrage activity, is know as straight program selling.[3] This selling accounted for $100 million of shares sold or ten percent of total volume. Therefore, total index arbitrage and straight program activity accounted for 29 percent of the last half hour's total volume. By 4:00 p.m. the Dow was down 57 points and the Contract closed even with the underlying Index. This broad, rapid sell-off late in the trading session in the absence of substantive fundamental news confused trading-oriented investors, and many turned negative on the market.

Thursday's volume was heavy at 263 million shares with block volume accounting for 51 percent. Overall, arbitrage-related stock sales were a low seven percent of total volume, while total program sales accounted for nine percent of the volume. Both activities were concentrated at the beginning and the end of the trading session. Seven trading-oriented institutions sold a total of $834 million of stocks,

---

[3] Straight program trading occurs when a large portfolio of stocks is bought or sold as a basket either through the DOT system or manually on the floor of the NYSE. There are no offsetting trades in the futures market, which differentiates this trading from index arbitrage. A typical program trade involves the sale or purchase of one portfolio of stocks weighted in certain industry groups. Program trading is used for its speed and efficiency of execution, lower commission costs and reduced market impact.

representing approximately nine percent of total volume for the day. Two Japanese investment advisors bought $284 million of stock, or three percent of total volume. The ten largest sellers together accounted for $1.049 billion, or 11.3 percent of the day's volume of transactions. The ten largest buyers accounted for $1.013 billion, or 10.9 percent (see Figure Brady-S12).

Illustrating the concentration in the market, the fourth largest seller and the second largest buyer of stock was the same institutional investor. This investor was also the third largest buyer and fourth largest seller in the futures market, and was also active in the options market. This shows that a relatively small number of institutional investors tend to account for a significant amount of trading volume in all three markets. In fact, they often turn up on both sides of the market.

In the futures market, total volume for the day was 125,000 contracts worth $19 billion. A high concentration of activity was evident, as just five portfolio insurers sold $968 million contracts, which accounted for nine percent of non-local volume.

Another factor in turning some fundamental investors bearish was a signal flashed at Thursday's close by the Dow Theory, one of the oldest and most widely-watched technical indicators. The Dow theory holds that a bear market will begin when the stocks of the companies that make goods—those comprising the Dow Jones Industrial Average—and the stocks of the companies that move goods—those comprising the Dow Jones Transportation Index—both begin to break through certain critical levels. On Thursday, the Transportation Index suffered its second largest one-day decline in history, falling 31 points to 980—breaking through its September 21 low of 1,005. At the same time, the DJIA was already trading well below its October 9 low of 2,482. (It finished the day at 2,355.) Complicating the decline of the Transportation Index, many of the stocks of the companies that comprise that index were themselves takeover candidates, and takeover stocks had been adversely affected by Wednesday's Ways and Means announcement. These stock were especially hard hit on Thursday.

Friday, October 16.   Despite the quick sell off at Thursday's close in New York, trading in Tokyo was relatively quiet with the Nikkei down just 62 points to 26,366 on Friday morning. Because of a hurricane, the London markets were essentially closed, as most market participants were unable to get to their offices.

At 8:00 a.m., reports of an Iranian attack on a U.S.-flagged oil tanker crossed the Dow Jones new wire. The U.S. government announced it was weighing its response to this incident. The growing tension in the Persian Gulf added to the general feeling of uncertainty and at times there were rumors of a war between the U.S. and Iran.

At 9:15 a.m., the MMI opened at 467 to 468, up from 465 the day before. The DJIA opened up 12 points to 2,367. The slightly firmer tone in the first few minutes of trading quickly gave way to selling pressure on the CME. (see Chart Brady-S3).

One key factor behind this selling pressure was the expiration at the close of trading on Friday of options on the MMI, S&P 500, and OEX indices as well as futures on the MMI. Due to the expiration, investors must either roll their holdings into a new contract month, or unwind their positions by selling or buying the appropriate security prior to the expiration or at the closing bell.

Because of difficulties in the options market, several firms noted for trading heavily in options markets became major participants on both sides of the futures markets. Options trading-oriented investors accounted for seven percent of the gross selling and six percent of gross buying in the futures market during the day; they were net sellers of $150 million in the futures market.

Normally, options trading-oriented investors are far less active in the futures market. This spillover of trading activity was especially eliminated all at-the-money options, which meant that investors could not roll their positions into a new contract month. Most listed option strike prices were above the prevailing market levels. Since it became difficult to establish, or to maintain, efficiently hedged positions using options, many options trading-oriented investors shifted their hedging activity to the futures market.

By 11:00 a.m., the DJIA was down seven points. Then, new selling entered the futures market as three portfolio insurers sold the equivalent of $265 million of futures. Futures led the stock market down because, despite the apparent lack of a significant discount between the Contract and the Index, some index arbitrageurs took the other side of the portfolio insurance sellers, buying futures and selling $183 million of stock, 18 percent of total New York Stock Exchange volume from 11:00 a.m. to 11:30 a.m. The DJIA fell 30 points during that half hour, then subsequently bounced partially back, aided by index arbitrageurs who reversed their positions, selling futures and buying baskets of stock. The DJIA stood at 2,340 at noon, down 15 points for the day.

The market then plummeted. Between 12:00 p.m. and 2:00 p.m., the DJIA declined by another 70 points to 2,271, or a total drop of 85 points thus far during the day. Index arbitrage activity accounted for sales of $334 million in stock, or 13 percent of NYSE volume over this period, which indicates significant selling pressure from sources other than index arbitrageurs.

Total index arbitrage and straight program selling over this period accounted for 15 percent of NYSE volume. In addition, the number of large block transactions in the DJIA stocks accounted for approximately half the volume in those stocks. This suggests that large institutions had begun to sell their blocks of stock. A rally caused by investors covering short positions, as well as index arbitrage and straight program buying by technicians responding to what was believed to be a key support level, brought the DJIA back to 2,311.

This technical rally died swiftly, however, and by 2:30 p.m. the spread between the contract and the Index had widened to its largest discount of the day. Between 2:30 and 3:30 p.m., $271 million of stock was sold by index arbitrageurs, representing 18 percent of the total volume during that hour. An additional $31 million of program selling unrelated to arbitrage accounted for another two percent of the volume. At 3:30 p.m., the DJIA level had fallen back to 2,274, 81 points below the previous day's close.

Given the extreme weakness in the stock market thus far that week, trading-oriented investors felt more comfortable establishing short positions before the weekend. Additionally, institutional investors that had been fully invested in equities began to lighten their exposure to the stock market. Specially, just four investors believed to be fully invested sold $482 million of stocks during the day.

Between 3:30 p.m. and 3:50 p.m., the DJIA fell another 50 points. Then, in the last ten minutes of trading, it regained 22 points, demonstrating extreme volatility. During this half hour, index arbitrageurs sold $580 million of stock and portfolio insurers sold $151 million of stock for a total of $731 million, accounting for a striking 43 percent of the total NYSE volume. The buy side was made up primarily of trading-oriented investors who were unwinding options hedges.

The extreme volatility experienced in the last half hour of trading capped the largest one-week decline in the DJIA to date. The DJIA was now 475 points below its August 25 high, and this 17.5 percent decline represented the Dow's largest correction since the low of 777, registered in August 1982 at the start of the bull market.

FIGURE BRADY-S3
NYSE Member Principal Position
Twenty Largest Members

Date	Net principal positions	Net (selling)/buying activity
October 13	$183,885,000	....
October 14	(505,116,000)	($689,001,000)
October 15	(26,405,000)	478,711,000
October 16	(185,267,000)	(158,862,000)
October 19	(188,528,000)	(3,261,000)
October 20	(233,584,000)	(45,056,000)

Source: NYSE.

FIGURE BRADY-S4
NYSE Large Institutional Dollar
Volume-Sales[1]

[In millions of dollars]

	October 15	October 16	October 19	October 20
SELL				
Portfolio insurers	$257	$566	$1,748	$698
Other pension	190	794	875	334
Trading-oriented investors	1,156	1,446	1,751	1,740
Mutual funds	1,419	1,339	2,168	1,726
Other financial	516	959	1,416	1,579
Total	3,538	5,104	7,598	6,077
Index arbitrage (included in above)	717	1,592	1,774	128

[1] Sample does not include: (1) individual investors, (2) institutional accounts with purchases and sales less than $10 million per day and (3) certain sizable broker/dealer trades.

FIGURE BRADY-S5
NYSE Large Institutional Dollar
Volume-Purchases[1]

[In millions of dollars]

	October 15	October 16	October 19	October 20
BUY				
Portfolio insurers	$201	$161	$449	$863
Other pension	368	773	1,481	920
Trading-oriented investors	1,026	1,081	1,316	1,495
Mutual funds	998	1,485	1,947	1,858
Other financial	798	1,221	2,691	2,154
Total	3,391	4,721	7,884	7,290
Index arbitrage (included in above)	407	394	110	32

[1] Sample does not include: (1) individual investors, (2) institutional accounts with purchases and sales less than $10 million per day and (3) certain sizable broker/dealer trades.

FIGURE BRADY-S6
CME Large Trader Sales
(Dollar amounts in millions)

	October 14	October 15	October 16	October 19	October 20
SELL					
Portfolio insurers	$534	$968	$2,123	$4,037	$2,818
Arbitrageurs	$108	$407	$392	$129	$31
Options	$554	$998	$1,399	$898	$635
Locals	$7,325	$7,509	$7,088	$5,479	$2,718
Other pension	$37	$169	$234	$631	$514
Trading-oriented investors	$1,993	$2,050	$3,373	$2,590	$2,765
Foreign	$398	$442	$479	$494	$329
Mutual funds	$46	$3	$11	$19	$40
Other financial	$49	$109	$247	$525	$303
Published total	$16,949	$18,830	$19,640	$18,987	$13,641
Volume accounted for	$11,045	$12,655	$15,347	$14,801	$10,152
Percent accounted for	65.2	67.2	78.1	78.0	74.4
Portfolio insurance: Percent of publicly accounted for volume	14.37	18.80	25.70	43.30	37.91

FIGURE BRADY-S7
CME Large Trader Purchases
(Dollar amounts in millions)

	October 14	October 15	October 16	October 19	October 20
BUY					
Portfolio insurers	$71	$171	$109	$113	$505
Arbitrageurs	$1,313	$717	$1,705	$1,582	$119
Options	$594	$864	$1,254	$915	$544
Locals	$7,301	$7,530	$7,125	$5,682	$2,689
Other pension	$90	$76	$294	$447	$1,070
Trading-oriented investors	$1,494	$2,236	$3,634	$4,510	$4,004
Foreign	$240	$298	$443	$609	$418
Mutual funds	$0	$27	$73	$143	$51
Other financial	$155	$57	$126	$320	$517
Published total	$16,949	$18,830	$19,640	$18,987	$13,641
Volume accounted for	$11,259	$11,976	$14,763	$14,320	$9,915
Percent accounted for	66.4	63.6	75.2	75.4	72.7
Portfolio insurance: Percent of publicly accounted for volume	1.80	3.86	1.43	1.31	6.98

FIGURE BRADY-S8
CME Large Trader Contract Volume (Sales)
(In number of contracts)

	October 14	October 15	October 16	October 19	October 20
SELL					
Portfolio insurers	3,460	6,413	14,627	34,446	26,146
Arbitrageurs	700	2,700	2,700	1,100	285
Options	3,589	6,618	9,643	7,667	5,890
Locals	47,426	49,773	48,847	46,753	25,214
Other pension	238	1,122	1,615	5,387	4,770
Trading-oriented investors	12,906	13,587	23,246	22,098	25,651
Foreign	2,575	2,927	3,301	4,212	3,050
Mutual funds	300	19	77	160	375
Other financial	317	720	1,705	4,478	2,808
Published total	109,740	124,810	135,344	162,022	126,562
Contracts accounted for	71,511	83,879	105,761	126,301	94,189
Percent accounted for	65	67	78	78	74

FIGURE BRADY-S9
CME Large Trader Contract Volume (Purchases)
(In number of contracts)

	October 14	October 15	October 16	October 19	October 20
BUY					
Portfolio insurers	461	1,136	751	964	4,682
Arbitrageurs	8,500	4,750	11,750	13,500	1,100
Options	3,848	5,725	8,639	7,804	5,049
Locals	47,272	49,911	49,098	48,487	24,945
Other pension	582	504	2,029	3,816	9,931
Trading-oriented investors	9,673	14,823	25,043	38,482	37,149
Foreign	1,553	1,972	3,051	5,199	3,874
Mutual funds	0	179	505	1,217	473
Other financial	1,006	378	867	2,727	4,793
Published total	109,740	124,810	135,344	162,022	126.562
Contracts accounted for	72,895	79,378	101,733	122,196	91,996
Percent accounted for	66	64	75	75	73

FIGURE BRADY-S10
Gross Futures Sales Volume
(In percent)

	October 14	October 15	October 16	October 19	October 20
SELL					
Portfolio insurers	3.2	5.1	10.8	21.3	20.7
Arbitrageurs	0.6	2.2	2.0	0.7	0.2
Options	3.3	5.3	7.1	4.7	4.7
Locals	43.2	39.9	36.1	28.9	19.9
Other pension	0.2	0.9	1.2	3.3	3.8
Trading-oriented investors	11.8	10.9	17.2	13.6	20.3
Foreign	2.3	2.3	2.4	2.6	2.4
Mutual funds	0.3	0.0	0.1	0.1	0.3
Other financial	0.3	0.6	1.3	2.8	2.2
Accounted for	65.2	67.2	78.1	78.0	74.4

FIGURE BRADY-S11
Gross Futures Purchase Volume
(In percent)

	October 14	October 15	October 16	October 19	October 20
BUY					
Portfolio insurers	0.4	0.9	0.6	0.6	3.7
Arbitrageurs	7.7	3.8	8.7	8.3	0.9
Options	3.5	4.6	6.4	4.8	4.0
Locals	43.1	40.0	36.3	29.9	19.7
Other pension	0.5	0.4	1.5	2.4	7.8
Trading-oriented investors	8.8	11.9	18.5	23.8	29.4
Foreign	1.4	1.6	2.3	3.2	3.1
Mutual funds	0.0	0.1	0.4	0.8	0.4
Other financial	0.9	0.3	0.6	1.7	3.8
Accounted for	66.4	63.6	75.2	75.4	72.7

CHART BRADY-S1
Dow Jones Industrial One Minute Chart
Wednesday, October 14, 1987

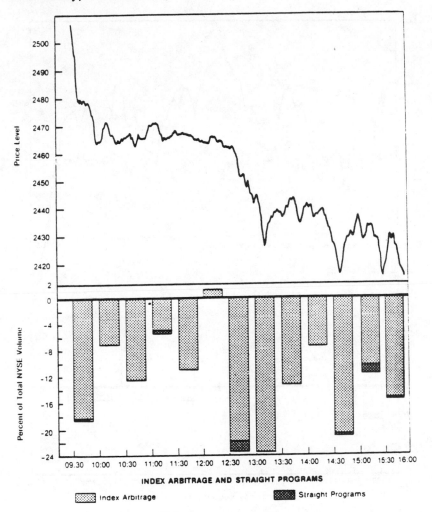

CHART BRADY-S2
Dow Jones Industrial One Minute Chart
Thursday, October 15, 1987

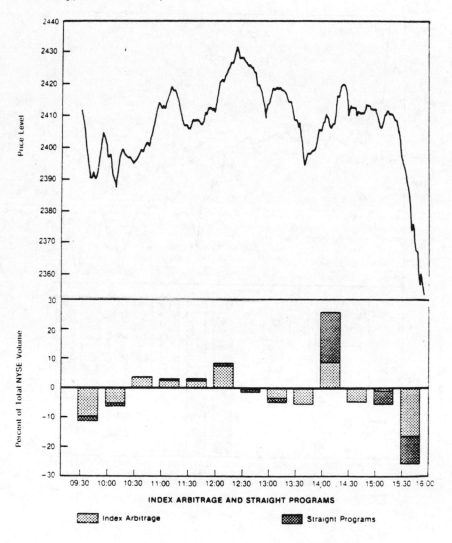

INDEX ARBITRAGE AND STRAIGHT PROGRAMS

Index Arbitrage   Straight Programs

CHART BRADY-S3
Dow Jones Industrial One Minute Chart
Friday, October 16, 1987

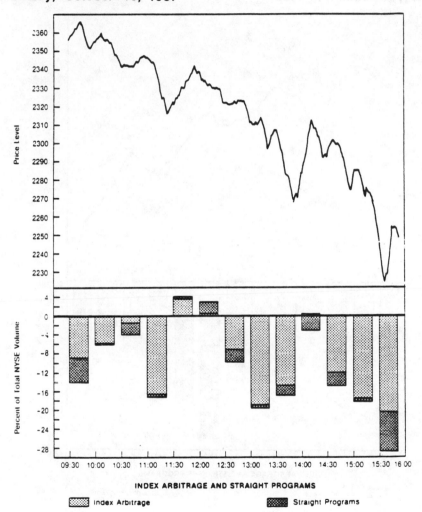

INDEX ARBITRAGE AND STRAIGHT PROGRAMS

Index Arbitrage   Straight Programs

CHART BRADY-S4
Dow Jones Industrial One Minute Chart
Monday, October 19, 1987

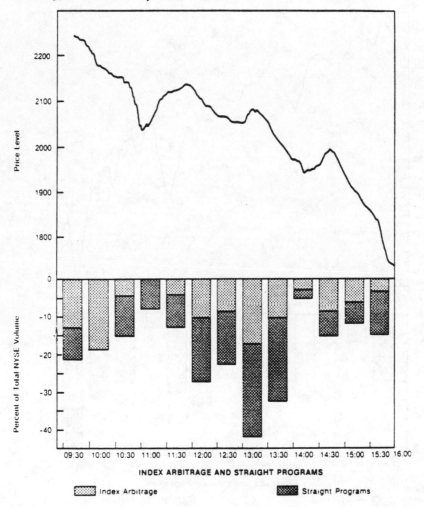

INDEX ARBITRAGE AND STRAIGHT PROGRAMS

Index Arbitrage   Straight Programs

CHART BRADY-S5
S&P Index and Futures Contract
Tuesday, October 20, 1987

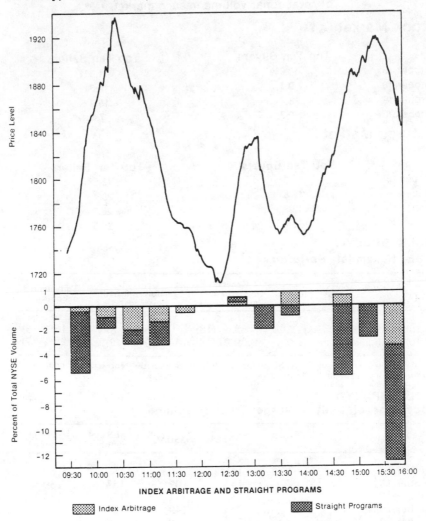

FIGURE BRADY-S12
Trading Concentration in the Futures and Stock Markets
The top ten buyers and sellers as a percentage
of total dollar volume in each market.

Stock Market

	Top Ten Buyers	Top Ten Sellers
October 15	10.9%	11.3%
October 16	9.7	12.3
October 19	8.7	15.2
October 20	9.7	7.1

Futures Market

	Top Ten Buyers	Top Ten Sellers
October 15	13.0%	15.5%
October 16	17.6	23.4
October 19	18.7	26.7
October 20	25.7	25.3

TABLE BRADY-2
NYSE Specialist Performance[1]

	Generally counterbalanced market trends	Generally reinforced market trends	Took limited net positions
October 19	58% (18)	26% (8)	16% (5)
October 20	39% (12)	39% (12)	22% (7)

[1] Based on a sample of 31 NYSE stocks. Figures in parentheses represent the number of stocks from the sample in each category.

TABLE BRADY-1
Percentage of Daily Average Trading Volume

	NYSE[1]	NASDAQ[1]	S&P 500 futures[2]	S&P 100 option[2]
October 14	115	97	135	162
October 15	145	107	153	180
October 16	188	131	166	133
October 19	335	149	199	72
October 20	337	189	156	42

[1] Based on daily average trading volume from January 1 to September 30, 1987.
[2] Based on daily average trading volume from January 1 to October 31, 1987.

Stock-selling activity, while generally broad, was often quite large and concentrated. The top ten stock sellers accounted for $1.545 billion worth of stock sales—12.3 percent of total NYSE volume for the day. The top ten buyers brought $1.216 billion of stock or 9.7 percent of total volume, but much of this buying represented short covering and was concentrated during large market movements.

The selling in the futures market was partially due to the use of portfolio insurance and other strategies designed to reduce stock market exposure. Five of the top seven net sellers in the futures market were portfolio insurance vendors. Portfolio protection strategies accounted for 11 percent of total selling in the futures market Friday—or about $2.1 billion—but as a group, portfolio insurers reduced their selling in the early afternoon.

Monday, October 19. Heading into Monday's trading a number of unsettling signs hung over the market. Over the weekend, numerous news stories had dissected the fragile condition of the U.S. and international capital markets. In its October 17 edition, the influential *Barron's* noted that the Dow had suffered its worst week since May 18, 1940, when a 15 percent fall was brought on by the French armies' crumbling resistance to the German advance. Another important article appeared in the Sunday edition of *The New York Times* quoting Treasury Secretary James Baker as exhorting the West German central bank to ease credit conditions and stimulate that country's economy. He appeared to warn the Bundesbank that if monetary easing in Germany was not forthcoming, the U.S. would feel less inclined to support the dollar in the foreign currency markets. Reacting to press accounts, Japanese and European investors would sell the dollar in early Monday trading.

Moreover, the clear market perception over the weekend was that the portfolio insurers had sold fewer futures contracts than their models had dictated. Therefore, there was the potential for great selling pressure on Monday morning.

In Tokyo overnight, the Nikkei Index dropped 620 points to 25,746. There were sharp declines in Hong Kong and Sydney. Near midday in London, stocks had declined ten percent, with the FTSE Index down 224 points to 2,077. Trading hours on the London Stock Exchange and the New York Stock Exchange normally overlap for approximately two hours each day. One explanation for the particularly heavy decline in London was that because that market had been closed on Friday, investors were only now able to fully react to New York's plummeting markets of Thursday and Friday.

Thus, prices of U.S. stocks and bonds trading in London were falling sharply lower on heavy volume early Monday morning New York time. Some U.S. portfolio managers tried to beat the expected selling on the New York Stock Exchange by dumping U.S. shares in the London market. In particular, one mutual fund complex sold $95 million of its equity portfolio on London prior to New York's opening.

At 8:05 a.m. New York time, sources reported that U. S. forces had responded to Friday's attack by the Iranians on a U. S.-flagged Kuwaiti tanker by bombing Iranian oil platforms in the Persian Gulf. Though a flight by night to dollar securities in the wake of Gulf tensions might have been expected, fears of the demise of the Louvre currency accord proved stronger, causing the dollar to weaken substantially as foreign currency trading began in New York. The Treasury bond market opened with yields higher, the 30-year bond rising to 10.50 percent, and orders to sell shares of stock flooded the floor of the New York Stock Exchange.

By 9:00 a.m., large sell order imbalances were reported on the NYSE. Prior to 9:30 a.m., there was approximately $500 million, or 14 million shares, waiting to be sold through the DOT system. Between 9:30 a.m. and 10 a.m., another $475 million to sell was loaded into DOT. This represented approximately 25 percent of the first half hour's record volume of 51 million shares. Over the next hour, new orders to sell another $1.1 billion of shares were entered into DOT. This massive selling pressure was accumulating while many major stocks remained closed for trading due to the order imbalances. (See Chart Brady-S4).

In Chicago, the MMI opened at a price of 430.00, dropping 11 points, or 2.5 percent, from Friday afternoon's already weak close. On the CME, the portfolio insurers that had fallen behind in their selling programs on Friday, reacted quickly, selling in excess of 3,000 Contracts in the first half hour. This activity was 18 percent of the total volume traded in the time period and 24 percent of the non-local volume.

At 9:45 a.m. the DJIA was off 21 points. Because most of the DJIA stocks did not open on time, the average was based in part on Friday's closing prices. Selling pressure was intense from mutual funds and index arbitrage trading-oriented investors. One mutual fund complex sold $500 million in the first half hour, representing 25 percent of the volume. At least 6.2 million shares, or 12 percent of total volume, were sold by index arbitrageurs in the first half hour. At this point on Monday, the apparent discount between the Contract and the Index varied between ten and 17 points. For the day, a premium of one point would have represented fair value. The size of the discount or premium had become one of the most widely followed indicators of the direction of the stock market even by investors who do not use the futures exchanges as a trading vehicle. The potential arbitrage profits which could be earned by selling the Index and simultaneously buying the Contract amounted to an annualized return of 47 percent at these price levels.

Ironically, the large discount on Monday morning was illusory. Since many of the stocks in the Index had not yet opened, the Index was calculated from their Friday closing prices. Although the index arbitrageurs clearly knew that many stocks had not yet opened, they nevertheless believed that a large discount existed. This belief led the index arbitrageurs to conclude that the market was headed much lower and instead of simultaneously selling the index and buying the Contract, many merely sold the Index and waited to buy what they believed would be a cheaper Contract. Aside from encouraging the index arbitrageurs to hold back on buying the futures half of the arbitrages, the apparent discount also discouraged buyers of stock from entering what appeared to be a relatively overpriced stock market.

By 10:30 a.m., the DJIA was down 104 points to the 2,080 level. Volume at 11 a.m. had already reached 154 million shares, a record pace. At 10:33 a.m., a portfolio insurer with the ability to sell either stock or futures for its clients sold the first of thirteen $100 million dollar baskets of stock it would unload during the day. This institution sold stock rather than futures because the size of the discount in the futures market made selling stocks seem relatively more attractive. This alternative of selling stock was not available to most of the other large portfolio insurers because they do not have the authority to sell clients' stocks. Therefore, they continued to sell futures throughout the morning and early afternoon at tremendous discounts to the prices in the stock market.

By approximately 11:00 a.m., most stocks had finally opened sharply lower on the New York Stock Exchange and the index arbitrageurs who had not yet completed their arbitrage by buying futures suddenly realized that the spread between the Contract and the Index was virtually nonexistent. Caught in a short squeeze, they rushed into the market to buy the Contract and it rallied from 254 at 10:50 a.m. to 265.5 at 11:40 a.m. During this period portfolio insurance selling temporarily abated, and short covering by one large foreign investor—which bought $218 million of futures—caused the Contract to trade at a premium to the Index for the only time of the day. Between 11:00 a.m. and 11:40 a.m., index arbitrageurs bought approximately $110 million of stocks while selling futures. Non-trading oriented investors, believing that the market might have reached a support level, also began to purchase stock.

The market, however, began a dramatic reversal at 11:40 a.m., with the Contract plunging from 265.5 to 251.5 by 12:40 a..m., while the DJIA fell from 2,140 at 11:46 a.m. to 2,053 at 12:55 p.m., as 36 million shares, or $1.3 billion, were routed through the DOT system. The price declines were caused by the lack of significant buyers and the resumption of large selling by the portfolio insurance providers. Between 11:30 a.m. and 1:30 p.m., the portfolio insurers sold over 10,000 futures contracts, the equivalent of $1.3 billion. These contracts amounted to 28 percent of total futures volume traded and 41 percent of public volume. Index arbitrageurs during this period sold approximately $350 million in stock. More significantly, straight program selling of stocks totaled $560 million, of which one portfolio insurer alone sold $400 million of stocks.

At 1:09 p.m., the Dow Jones news wire reported that the Chairman of the Securities and Exchange Commission said that he had not discussed halting trading on the NYSE with The New York Stock Exchange or President Reagan, although "anything is possible." He continued, "...there is some point, and I don't know what that point is, that I would be interested in talking to the NYSE about a temporary halt in trading." Between 1:15 p.m. and 2:05 p.m., the Contract plunged from 255 to 227; the Index fell from 258 to 246, and the DJIA dropped from 2,081 to 1,969, breaking through the 2,000 level for the first time since January 7, 1987.

By 1:25 p.m., the Dow Jones news wire quoted the SEC as stating that it was not discussing closing the stock markets. However, the uncertainty created by the possible inability to sell may have exacerbated the dramatic selling pressure. In fact, between 1:30 p.m. and 2:00 p.m., one portfolio insurer sold 1,762 Contracts, worth $200 million, which represented 20 percent of the total volume during that half hour. In addition, during this same time period, this portfolio insurer sold $500 million of stocks. Between 1:00 p.m. and 1:30 p.m., index arbitrageurs sold $216 million of stocks, and straight program selling totalled $305 million of stocks. Together these two selling interests accounted for 39 percent of total share volume during this period.

A short-lived rally, the last one of the day, began at 2:05 p.m. and was led by the futures market. The Contract rallied from 227 to 239 at 2:35 p.m. The buying interest was concentrated in the futures market and the Index only rallied 4.00 points. The DJIA rose approximately 50 points to the 2,000 level.

By about 2:00 p.m., many index arbitrageurs had discontinued their activity because they could not be assured of timely execution of their orders. This removed a significant buyer in the futures market and, combined with the continued selling by portfolio insurers, caused the spread between the Contract and the Index to widen to a huge discount. Trading-oriented accounts that were not fully invested and were active in both the futures and stock markets, chose to buy futures because of their belief that this discount represented a good trading opportunity. Most of the buying in the stock market by trading-oriented investors was short covering. Most non-trading oriented investors that were fully invested sold stocks throughout the day to lighten their exposure to the equity market. The only non-trading-oriented accounts that were significant buyers were pension funds and financial institutions, such as bank departments, that perceived bargain prices to exist on many blue chip stocks.

By 4:00 p.m. the Contract had declined to 200 and the DJIA had fallen from 2,000 to 1,738, a closing level last reached on April 7, 1986.

While the stock and stock index futures markets were collapsing, flight to safety began in the fixed income markets. Over the next twenty-four hours, 90-day Treasury bill yields would fall from 6.75 percent to just above 5 percent and the 30-year Treasury bond would rally from a price of 85 to 96 1/2 as the focus of market participants abruptly changed from fears of inflation and tight money to worries about deflation, recession and potential stock market failure.

The falling stock market was stopped only by the 4:00 p.m. close. The DJIA had fallen 508 points, or 23 percent, on volume of 604 million shares. On the day, the Contract had dropped from 282.25 on Friday to 201 at the close, a decline of 29 percent on volume of 162,000 contracts.

The record volume on the New York Stock Exchange had overwhelmed the data processing and communications systems of the exchange. Execution of stock trades were at times reported more than an hour late which created confusion for traders and investors. One major problem on the floor of the NYSE was the breakdown of the computerized DOT system because of inadequate capacity. A total of 396 million shares were routed through DOT, but 112 million shares were not executed, of which 92 million were limit orders. Because timely information was scarce, investors did not know if their limit orders had been executed and therefore did not know to set new limits. Of the 284 million shares which were executed on DOT, 33 million were market orders to buy and 148 million were market orders to sell. Limit orders which were executed included 69 million shares to buy and 24 million to sell. Of the 396 million shares routed through DOT, 89 million shares were related to program and arbitrage activity, representing 15 percent of total NYSE volume for the day. By the close of trading, specialist firms on the NYSE were carrying approximately $1.3 billion of inventory, up from $900 million on Friday, October 16. This heavy inventory was a major factor in their inability to make orderly markets the following day.

The options markets were unable to keep pace with the rapid price changes occurring in the equity markets on October 19. While both futures and stock volume increased dramatically from Friday, the volume of trading in the OEX market was only 35 percent of Friday's level. Options did not trade freely for most of the day due to lengthy and unwieldy rotations. As a result, options trading-oriented investors turned to the futures and equity markets to reduce their equity exposure and to hedge positions. In options, many short put strategies require the sale of the underlying security when the market declines. Because of the inability to close option positions, there may have been more selling in the futures and equity markets than there otherwise would have been had the options markets been operating normally.

In many options markets, retail investors are the major component. When a broker places emergency margin calls, the retail investor with exposed option positions is the first to be called. In the absence of additional margin, these positions are liquidated. Discussions with many brokers revealed that forced liquidations contributed to the enormous downward pressure in the market throughout the day.

At the same time, the cost of using the options market increased dramatically as normal levels of volatility increased at least fourfold— beyond all precedent. Some options investors thus turned to the futures or equity markets to hedge positions, because the cost of using those markets was significantly lower. This created additional selling pressure in those markets.

Two commonly used options strategies that went awry Monday were so-called "dividend capture" and "buy-write" strategies. Both involve buying stock and selling a call on that stock. The premium received for writing the call options provides a measure of protection in a falling market, but when the market falls more than the amount of the premium received, the investor is long stock which is declining in value. On October 19 and again on October 20, investors employing these option-based strategies found themselves in just this long position and many sold stock.

The dominant sellers in the futures market on October 19 were portfolio insurance providers. Total portfolio insurance-related selling amounted to approximately 33,000 contracts, 21 percent of total volume and 43 percent of public volume. Significantly, even though these insurers were the largest group of sellers, they remained far behind the hedge ratio dictated by their computer programs. In addition, those portfolio insurance vendors who react to market changes with a one day lag, sold only enough on Monday to hedge Friday's market move. The 23 percent decline in the market on Monday implied, then, that the portfolio insurers would inevitably need to sell more on Tuesday if they continued to follow their models. In addition to the $4 billion of futures contracts sold by the portfolio insurers, most of the $2.2 billion of straight sell programs in the stock market appears to be related to portfolio insurance. One portfolio insurer alone sold $1.3 billion in stock. The buying in the futures market was largely related to index arbitrage and short covering.

The ten largest sellers in the stock market sold equities worth $3.2 billion or 15.2 percent of total volume. The ten largest buyers bought $1.8 billion, 8.7 percent of the total market volume. The largest individual sellers of stocks were mutual funds and portfolio insurers, while the largest individual buyers were pension funds and financial institutions. One mutual fund complex sold over $800 million of stock. Block trades of stock of 10,000 shares represented 51 percent of the NYSE share volume and 31 percent of the dollar volume.

Tuesday, October 20. The Monday break of the U.S. equity markets affected all international markets. The Nikkei Index was down Tuesday by 3,336 points to 21,910, a fall of 13.2 percent. Because Tokyo has a limit on daily price movements of 15 percent, trading was light as all but three stocks hit their lower daily trading limits and ceased to trade. At mid day in London, the FTSE Index was down 296 points to 1,755, a drop of 14 percent. In Hong Kong, the stock exchange was closed for the remainder of the week, and there were considerable questions about the viability of the Hong Kong Futures Exchange.

Comments by the Bank of Japan early Tuesday morning indicated that Japan would continue to support the Louvre accord, and helped to calm currency markets in early morning trading.

At 8:41 a.m., Federal Reserve Chairman Alan Greenspan released a one line statement: "The Federal Reserve, consistent with its responsibilities as the nation's central bank, affirmed today its readiness to serve as a source of liquidity to support the economic and financial system." This statement rallied the bond market because it was interpreted as an indication of the credit strains being seen by the Federal Reserve. The bond market rally thus demonstrated a flight to quality by investors.

At 9:30 a.m., the New York Stock Exchange announced that it had asked its members to refrain from using the DOT system to execute "program trades." Doing so would effectively eliminate index arbitrage, severing the trading link between the Contract and the Index. There was, however, a great deal of confusion among market participants as to whether or not arbitrage could be manually executed and whether straight program activity could be routed through DOT.

In New York, a startling reversal from Monday's activity was apparent from the start of trading as many stocks did not open due to buy side imbalances. Although some corporations had announced stock buybacks programs on Monday and early on Tuesday, the order imbalances at the open could not have resulted from buyback activity as corporations are prohibited from opening the market in their own stocks.

The vast majority of orders to buy at the market's open were market "orders," enabling the NYSE specialists to open stocks significantly higher than Monday's close. From 9:30 a.m. to 10:27 a.m., the DJIA rallied from 1,739 to 1,936 as specialists opened stocks higher, in many cases on large volume.

On the CME, the Contract opened at 223, up 21.5 points from Monday's close. The tremendous opening increase was due to trading-oriented investors who believed that the NYSE's higher opening levels could be sustained. Buying pressure also stemmed from nervous investors closing out short positions due to rumors circulating about the financial condition of the CME and its clearing members, as well as the exchange's ability to clear trades from the previous day. These rumors would keep certain investors out of the futures market for the entire day.

The Contract continued to recover until 9:50 a.m., at which time catch-up portfolio insurance selling and some renewed short selling drove it to lower levels. In the first hour of trading, portfolio insurance selling amounted to 4,500 contracts or 16 percent of total volume.

The Contract now began to trade at a significant discount to the Index. However, because of the restrictions placed on the use of DOT, index arbitrageurs were unable to perform their function of keeping the two markets in line. The futures markets plummeted from 10:00 a.m. to 12:15 p.m. During this time the Contract fell from a high of 246 to a low of 181—a decline of almost 27 percent. By comparison, that drop was equivalent to a move of more than 500 points in the DJIA. At 12:15 p.m., the CME decided to close the market temporarily.

While market volatility this extreme made investment decisions difficult, some trading-oriented investors were able to use it to their advantage. One example of the profit potential of short selling on Tuesday was that of a large investor which sold 500 Contracts at an average price of 229 and covered the short within 40 minutes at an average price of 210. The profit on this trade amounted to $7 million.

On the NYSE, many stocks of major corporations opened late and closed at various times during the day. For instance, between 1:00 p.m. and 1:30 p.m., 49 stocks stopped trading. Yet there was heavy volume for each half hour trading period. During the first two hours alone, total volume was 259 million shares.

Once the buying was absorbed and the futures market had begun to fall, the stock market started a sustained and dramatic reversal as the DJIA declined from 1,936 at 10:27 a.m. to 1,711 at 12:29 p.m. Selling pressure was broad-based due to fears of index arbitrage activity, mutual fund redemptions and portfolio insurance. Although no DOT orders were being executed for index arbitrage on the NYSE, the appearance of large and unprecedented discounts in the futures markets led many participants to believe that additional selling pressure in the equity markets was imminent as the size of the discount itself had become a market indicator. The process became self-reinforcing. Large discounts fed selling expectations, and these expectations, in turn, inspired selling in anticipation of further declines. Thus, while the inability to carry out arbitrage via the DOT system severed the trading link between the equity and futures markets, the flow in information emanating from the respective markets continued to exert a strong influence on trading decisions.

With many stocks having closed as order imbalances on the sell side built up, and with price information from the NYSE exceedingly difficult to obtain, the CBOE and the CME suspended trading of their derivative products at 11:45 a.m. and and 12:15 p.m., respectively. At the time of the CME closing, the futures discount was more than than 46 points, the largest ever experienced. With the CME closed, the last in the circuitous relationship between the futures and stock markets—pricing information—was severed.

Some specialists took this opportunity to reopen stocks at higher levels. Non-trading-oriented investors who had been leery of the apparent discount between the Contract and the Index also began to buy. However, this buying was not sustainable and the rally was soon extinguished. During the 49 minute period that the futures market was closed, the DJIA rallied from 1,711 to 1,835.

The Contract reopened at 1:04 p.m. at 213, up from 183 at the temporary 12:15 p.m. closing. At this price, the Contract was at a 17 point discount to the stock market. Even though no arbitrage took place, renewed perception of a discount was enough to discourage buyers. The initial trading in the futures market was characterized by buying by speculative accounts and moderate selling by portfolio insurers. Volume in the first half hour after the reopening was a relatively heavy 7,500 Contracts, worth $800 million.

In the following hour, major investment bank buying activity dominated the futures market and narrowed the discount to approximately eight points.

Another force affecting the stock market at this time was the growing list of U. S. corporations announcing that they were willing to buy their stock from investors. On Monday and Tuesday, corporations announced approximately $6.2 billion in stock buybacks. This, combined with the narrowing of the discount between the Contract and the Index, may have led market participants to belive that the buybacks were going to maintain a solid floor price. Bargain hunters rushed in to buy and sellers finally could unload large blocks of stock directly to corporate buyers. As prices started to rally, short covering began and the DJIA rose toward the close when some profit taking, additional uncertainty concerning overnight activity, and portfolio insurance selling resulted in a rapid decline. The DJIA, which was trading at a level of 1,712 at 12:30 p.m., had rallied back to 1,919 at 3:33 p.m., before dropping back to 1,841 at the close.

Tuesday can at best be characterized as confusing and uncertain. The absence of any clear relationship between the stock, futures and options markets led many trading-oriented investors to exit the market altogether. Many trading-oriented investors that would have bought, postponed their buying until a better understanding of the linkages could be developed. One of the factors that was prevalent from Thursday through Tuesday was the concentration of buying and selling activity by a small number of large investors. This concentration peaked on Monday when the top ten buyers and sellers accounted for nine and 15 percent of stock market activity, respectively, despite the record volume. In the futures market the top ten trading-oriented buyers and sellers comprised between 25 and 26 percent of the total volume. In both markets, these top ten institutions were net sellers of securities on Friday and Monday and became net buyers on Tuesday (see Figure Brady-S12).

During the course of the day on Tuesday, the ten largest buyers bought $2.1 billion of stocks and the ten largest sellers sold $1.6 billion of stocks. The largest buying institutions were portfolio insurers, pension funds, corporations and foreign investors. The largest selling institutions were portfolio insurers, foreign investors, and risk arbitrageurs. The largest buyer and seller on Tuesday was the same portfolio insurer.

CHAPTER FIVE: MARKET PERFORMANCE

Market performance can be measured against a variety of quantitative and qualitative criteria, including the availability of the market, the liquidity and depth provided by the market makers, the orderliness and fairness of the market and the strength of the clearing and credit systems that support the market. The events of October 19 and 20 tested the capacity of the equity market to a degree that was not widely anticipated.

Availability of Market. The most immediately striking fact about the performance of the equity market during the market break is that, in the face of selling pressure of unprecedented severity, it handled a record volume of transactions. A summary of the volumes traded in each marketplace is described in Table Brady-1.

The extent to which trading in listed stocks and the S&P 500 futures contract was suspended during the critical days of October 19 and 20 was, in light of the pressures brought to bear, surprisingly limited. On the morning of October 19, eight percent of NYSE issues, or a total of 187 stocks, failed to open for trading at or near 9:30 a.m. By 11:30 a.m. 41 of these stocks remained unopened, and by noon all but 25 were trading. During the course of October 19, trading was halted in seven stocks. On the morning of October 20, 90 stocks failed to open promptly and by 11:30 a.m., all but 15 of these were trading. However, during the course of October 20, trading was halted in 175 stocks, including some of the most actively traded issues on the exchange. The S&P 500 futures market was open throughout the day on Monday and halted trading only between 12:15 p.m. and 1:05 pm. on Tuesday.

While the NASDAQ trading volume increased during the market break, it declined dramatically as a percentage of NYSE volume. From a level of 83 percent of NYSE volume prior to the break, NASDAQ volume dropped to 37 percent of NYSE levels on October 19, and 47 percent on October 20.

The options market had great difficulty trading on both Monday and Tuesday. On October 19, the S&P 100 option went through two rotations before opening for free trading at 12:36 p.m. On October 20, the S&P 100 option again required two rotations to open and the CBOE halted trading for about one and one half hours. Thus, free trading did not begin until 3:30 p.m., which allowed just 52 minutes of free trading.

Thus, all marketplaces, except the options market and, to some extent, the over-the-counter market, remained reasonably available for trading on October 19 and October 20.

However, the performance of financial markets cannot be judged solely in terms of volumes traded. The terms on which trades were executed are equally important. Effective market making mechanisms should sustain fair and orderly trading in several critical respects. At best, market mechanisms should smooth out temporary fluctuations in market prices. At a minimum, they should not exacerbate price fluctuations. Also, trading should be conducted on an equitable basis. Similar orders entered under equal conditions should not be executed on widely different terms. In neither of these respects did market mechanisms perform effectively during the critical days of the October market break.

Price Behavior. Throughout the week of October 12 to 16, market mechanisms for equity-related instruments coped reasonably well with heavy and gradually increasing selling pressure. Even on Friday, October 16, the major stock markets handled a record volume and a substantial selling imbalance without the kinds of extreme price deviations that occurred on the 19th and 20th. Compared to the events of the 19th and 20th, the stock indices also tracked their respective futures contracts reasonably.

In contrast, the price performance of market mechanisms on the 19th, the Dow fell by 220 points or 11.2 percent. At the open on Tuesday, October 20, most of these losses were made up as the Dow opened 12.1 percent higher, to just below the levels that had been in effect an hour before the close on Monday. By noon on Tuesday, the Dow had dropped back 11.4 percent almost exactly to the level of the close on Monday. When the Dow finally stabilized on subsequent trading days between 1,900 and 2,000, it had recovered all of these additional losses.

Price fluctuation in the futures market were often more violent. For example, in a period of one hour, beginning around 1:30 p.m. on Monday, October 19, the price of an S&P 500 futures contract fell by 12 percent despite a drop of only seven percent in that hour in the S&P 500 Index. Similarly, on Tuesday, October 20, price fluctuations in the futures market were often more extreme than those of the underlying stock indices. Thus, the S&P 500 contract, which fell about 17 percent in the final two hours of Monday's trading, opened up ten percent on Tuesday and quickly recovered the full 17 percent loss of the final hours of Monday. At the same time, the S&P 500 Index rallied nine percent. However, in the next two hours, this entire gain, and more, disappeared as the S&P 500 futures contract fell by 25 percent until trading was halted. The Index dropped 12 percent in the same period. After several more gyrations during the week, the futures market finally stabilized in subsequent weeks near the level it had reached before the sharp midday decline on Monday, October 19.

This pattern of large, but transitory, price changes also characterized trading in individual stocks. For example, two large capitalization NYSE-listed stocks that failed to open on Monday morning until about 10:30 a.m., opened down 17 percent and 19 percent. Within the next hour, the Dow moved down 1.4 percent, and these two stocks rose by 13 percent and 16 percent respectively, recovering roughly 80 percent of their opening losses. On Tuesday morning four stocks (out of a sample of 50 large capitalization stocks studied in detail) opened at prices more than 25 percent higher than at their close on Monday. These openings occurred at various times between 9:50 a.m. and 10:50 a.m. and the four stocks opened up by an average of 27.8 percent. By 11:30 a.m., their prices had declined an average of 15.1 percent from the opening levels, eliminating about 55 percent of their opening gains. Patterns of sharp movements in individual stocks, which were rapidly reversed, were common on Tuesday, October 20.

Based on an examination of the average prices at which NASDAQ stocks traded within 15 minutes intervals, the setting of prices by a large number of market makers appears to have smoothed out price trends. However, extreme disparities in prices at which individual trades were executed during these intervals were not uncommon. On Monday, October 19, and Tuesday, October 20, the highest reported prices at which particular stocks changed hands was sometimes more than ten percent higher than the lowest reported price of those stocks in the same 15 minute interval. In certain instances, price disparities of more than 20 percent occurred in essentially contemporaneous trades.

Price behavior in the S&P 100 market is more difficult to assess. In contrast to the stock and futures markets, which handled volumes well in excess of normal, volume in the S&P 100 options market was down significantly on October 19 and 20. Also, as noted above, the S&P 100 option did not trade freely for extended periods of time, especially on Tuesday. Nevertheless, prices at which the S&P 100 options did trade exhibited discontinuous jumps. For a typical example, the S&P 100 November 305 put option traded at $66 in the first rotation on Monday and $58 in the second rotation, a 12 percent difference with no intervening trades (although the second rotation occurred roughly an hour later). Some prices were also disorderly. For example, on Tuesday, the S&P 100 November 250 put opened at 11:31 a.m. at a price of $75. The S&P 100 November 185 put, which should have been substantially less valuable, opened at 11:54 a.m. with a price of $81. In the intervening 13 minute period, the actual level of the S&P 100 Index had changed by less than two percent and the S&P 500 futures contract was unchanged.

Equal Access to Trading Opportunities. The extreme volatility of market prices on October 19 and 20 subjected all market participants, and particularly small investors, to capriciously different treatment.

Price variations as large and erratic as those that occurred on October 19 and 20 can be inherently discriminatory. An investor selling stock, or futures contracts, near the close on Monday suffered a loss of ten to 12 percent compared to investors who sold either an hour earlier or the next morning. In contrast, an investor who sold either an hour earlier or the next morning paid from ten to 20 percent more than one who bought either at the previous afternoon's close or two hours later.

In addition to these discrepancies, small investors were at an apparent disadvantage in speed of order execution. Part of the disadvantage stemmed from an understandable difficulty experienced by small investors in reaching retail brokers, which was widely reported but impossible to quantify after the fact. Another part of the problem was, however, attributable to delays and failures of the automated, small-order-oriented processing systems of both the NYSE and the OTC market. The orders of small investor are generally executed through these systems, and small investors tend to have less access to other means of executing orders than do larger investors.

Although the NYSE DOT system was originally designed for small orders, the permitted order size has increased to 30,099 shares for market orders and 99,999 shares for limit orders. Nevertheless, the DOT system remains the most important means of processing small investor orders.

On Monday, October 19, orders for 396 million shares were entered into the NYSE's DOT system. This unprecedented traffic at times overwhelmed the mechanical printers that print DOT orders at certain trading posts, resulting in significant delays in executing market orders and in entering limit orders. These delays meant that market orders were executed at prices often very different from those in effect when the orders were entered. The delays also meant that limit orders may not have been executed because of their limits having been passed by the time the order reached the trading post.

The SOES system, designed to execute trades in the OTC market of 1,000 shares or less, typically handles 12 to 15 percent of trades in OTC stocks traded in the National Market System—although less than two percent of share volume. In addition to SOES, some large full-service brokers and wholesalers have comparable proprietary computer systems, which typically execute more than one half of their orders.

On October 19 and 20, two factors limited execution of trades through the SOES and other automated execution systems. First, some large firms—four of the 50 largest on October 19 and 18 of the 50 largest on October 20—did not participate in the SOES system at all during those days, even though they had previously participated. Other firms withdrew for a portion of those days. Second, automatic protection features, designed to protect market makers against potential losses from executing orders where the ask price in the quotation system is not higher than the bid price, shut down trading in many stocks on SOES and the proprietary systems during much of the 19th and 20th. On October 19, these systems were incapable, on average, of trading each of the top 50 NASDAQ stocks 43 percent of the time. On Tuesday, October 20, this figure rose to about 53 percent.

During these shutdown periods, small orders in some of the proprietary systems backed up and, in some instances, were automatically executed in batches when the system again began to function. Others were executed even later in the day.

These system failures, coupled with natural delays in processing orders at the retail level, meant that small investor orders were executed at random times and, therefore, at prices that varied widely from those in existence when purchase or sale decisions were made. The unequal speed at which trades were executed did not necessarily disadvantage small investors. In some cases, delays in execution—for example, of buy orders entered prior to the opening on Monday—might have been substantially beneficial to some small investors. However, the existence of unequal access would almost necessarily have created at least an appearance of unfairness.

In futures and options marketplaces, differing levels of access to trading have a significantly different impact than in the various stock marketplaces. Non-institutional participants play only a limited role in the S&P 500 stock index futures market but play a significant role in the S&P 100 options market. The problem of the different treatment of large and small investors in these markets was a consequence of differences in response speeds and access to information. Non-professional participants, who lack access to continuous market information, expect to have continuous opportunities to withdraw from investments in a timely way. Obviously, on October 19 and 20, these expectations were unfulfilled. In the S&P 100 options market on October 19 and 20, everyone suffered from some inability to trade. Individual participants who wrote put options before October 19 and 20 often found themselves either locked into their positions or involuntarily liquidated during these critical two days. Individual participants in the futures market may have suffered substantial losses before becoming aware of what had happened, and even "normal" delays in executing retail orders may have exacerbated these losses.

Market Maker Performance. The active market makers whose performance was analyzed based upon information available to the Task Force include the NYSE specialists, OTC and options market makers, and the "local" traders in the futures market, who play the analogous market maker role. Data was not available to enable the Task Force to analyze the performance of NYSE block traders, who also play an important market making role.

New York Stock Exchange Specialists. The performance of NYSE specialists during the October market break period varied over time and from specialist to specialist. From October 14 through October 16, while the Dow was falling by 10.6 percent, specialists, on balance, purchased approximately $286 million in stock. On October 19, specialists as a whole purchased just under $486 million worth of stock. During the first hour and one half on October 19, specialists bought heavily in the face of unprecedented selling pressure. At this critical time, specialists were willing to lean against the dominant downward trend in the market at a significant cost to themselves. Also, in the price collapse which characterized the final hour of trading on October 19, most specialists again appear to have been net purchasers of stock, although their participation at this time was significantly less extensive, in the face of a greater price decline, than their intervention at the October 19 opening.

These figures, however, conceal marked differences in behavior among specialists. Fully 30 percent of specialists in a sample of 50 large capitalization stocks were net sellers of those stocks on October 19. Further, ten percent of specialists in that sample finished the day with net short positions in those stocks. Finally, about ten percent of the openings on October 19 that were down sharply from the closing prices on October 16 were followed by sharp rebounds that eliminated much of those initial losses.

On October 20, roughly one third of the specialists in the 50 stock sample set opening prices which were substantially higher than closing prices on October 19 and which declined rapidly to levels at or near their October 19 closes. These apparent misjudgments of opening prices may have aggravated an already uncertain atmosphere on Tuesday, October 20.

On the whole, specialists sold over $450 million in stock, and, in the sample of 50 large capitalization stocks, fully 82 percent of the specialists were net sellers on October 20.

An examination was made of the 331 stocks for which detailed trade data for October 19 and 20 were available. These stocks were classified into three groups: those for which specialists purchased stock in a way that generally tended to counterbalance market trends and smooth price fluctuations (even if they were not always successful); those for which specialists acted in a way that generally reinforced market trends; and those for which specialists took only limited net positions. [The classification was done by the Task Force and differs from the tests used by the NYSE to evaluate specialist performance (see Study VI).] The results of this examination are described in Table Brady-2.

The limited nature of some specialists' contributions to price stability may have been due to the exhaustion of their purchasing power following attempts to stabilize markets at the open on October 19.

However, for other specialists, lack of purchasing power appears not to have been the determining factor in their behavior. It is understandable that specialists would not sacrifice large amounts of capital in what must have seemed a hopeless attempt to stem overwhelming waves of selling pressure. Nevertheless, from the final hours of trading on October 19 through October 20, a substantial number of NYSE specialists appear not to have been a significant force in counterbalancing market trends.

OTC Market Makers. Unlike shares on the NYSE, each NASDAQ stock is served by a number of market makers, none of which has either an express or implied commitment to maintain an orderly market. Under these conditions, it is difficult to relate the performance of this market as a whole to the performance of individual market maker.

During the week of October 19, some market makers formally withdrew from making markets. In addition, some market makers ceased performing their function, merely by not answering their telephones during this period. However, it is impossible, on the basis of information available to the Task Force, to assess the extent and impact of this form of non-participation. Other market makers who were willing to trade were unreachable when they were overwhelmed by the volume of telephone orders, many of which normally would have been executed by the automated systems. There were also widespread reports that many market makers, who normally stand ready to buy and sell hundreds and sometimes thousands of shares at their quoted prices, were only willing to fulfill their minimum obligation by buying and selling 100 shares at the quoted price. Another indication of deterioration in market making performance is the withdrawal by some market makers from the SOES system, thus reducing from 1,000 to 100 the number of shares they were obligated to buy or sell.

In addition, bid-offer spreads also widened during this period. For example, On October 20, the larger NASDAQ securities, for which real-time quotations are disseminated, had quoted spreads of 1/8 or 3/8 only 32.6 percent of the time, compared to such quoted spreads 42.8 percent of the time during the three weeks ending October 16.

"Locals" in the Futures Market. Locals in the futures market, who, like OTC traders, have no formal commitment to stabilize prices, were as a group somewhat more aggressive than normal in taking net positions on October 19.

During the three day market decline from Wednesday, October 14, to Friday, October 16, gross purchases by locals averaged about 48,000 contracts per day or about 46 percent of total volume. The best available data indicates that locals were not sellers on October 14 and small net buyers on the subsequent two days. Over the three day decline, local net buys were 235 contracts worth about $34 million or less than 0.1 percent of total volume. Thus, locals did not help offset the market decline during those days.

On Monday, October 19, locals purchased 48,487 contracts or 31.4 percent of total volume. Net buys were 1,743 contracts, worth $221 million, representing about one percent of total volume. These net buys were generally concentrated in time periods when prices were falling. Only after 2:30 p.m. did locals not enter the market as net buyers during periods of declining prices.

Moreover, like the stock market, the willingness of locals to lean against prevailing price trends was largely exhausted by the middle of the afternoon on October 19. From 2:30 p.m. to the close of business on October 20, gross local buys amounted to 35,325 contracts or 24.1 percent of total volume. Net buys were a negative 530 contracts, worth $59 million.

In sum, while the locals as a group absorbed some selling pressure, they did not act uniformly and were not able to counterbalance the public selling pressure.

Since the locals do not, and have no responsibility to, absorb significant imbalances in order flow, the futures market functions as an efficient risk transfer mechanism only when the activity of locals is supplemented by market participants, such as speculators and index arbitrageurs. This is especially true with respect to imbalances of the magnitude exhibited during the October market break.

Options Market Makers. The structure of the options marketplace is more important to an assessment of the performance of the options marketplace than is the performance of the options market makers. Options market makers were constrained from maintaining a stable, orderly market because options are inherently susceptible to the largest percentage price changes of all equity products; reliable data about underlying indices was not always available; the exchanges failed to add new strike prices in a timely fashion; extraordinary demands for additional margin were made, even on market makers with hedged positions; and the truncated periods of free trading may have justifiably affected the willingness of market makers to establish positions that they were unsure of being able to liquidate readily. Although the lack of free trading inhibited reasonable price continuity on October 19 and 20, the bid-ask spread in the S&P 100 market shifted frequently but generally remained reasonable during periods of free trading. However, there were numerous price disparities in the options market (see Study VI). On the whole, options market makers did not play an important role in stabilizing their own market, and through their hedging activities may have marginally added to the pressure in other markets.

Clearing and Credit. Difficulties with the clearing and credit systems further exacerbated the difficulties of market makers and other market participants during the market break. Because of the five day settlement rule for stocks, these concerns were less immediate in the stock markets than in the futures and options markets, where settlement is made the next day. However, in the stock markets, the unprecedented volume led to an unusually large number of questioned trades. Questioned trades affected 67,673 NYSE trades on October 19 and 62,564 NYSE trades on October 20. That represented 4.02 percent and 4.25 percent of transaction sides; these latter figures were 202 and 220 percent above normal, respectively. Uncertainties concerning the ultimate disposition of questioned trades added to other uncertainties regarding the financial condition of specialists and other broker-dealers on October 19 and 20.

Settlement problems in the futures and options markets also contributed to these uncertainties. During the day of October 19, the CME clearinghouse, which is responsible for setting margins on futures contracts, responded to the sharp price decline by making intraday variation margin calls for $1.6 billion. Cash and cash-equivalents covering these margin calls were paid in by "losing" clearinghouse members during the day. According to clearinghouse rules, these funds were not paid out to the "winners" until the next day. In addition, variation margin calls, which had been made on Monday morning to cover settlements of Friday's closing positions, were unusually high. Total variation margin calls on Monday morning and during the day on Monday were $2.0 billion.

At the same time, OCC members also faced substantial morning and intraday margin calls to cover the deterioration in the positions of put options sellers, both proprietary and customer. On October 19, the OCC issued four intraday margin calls that collected $1.0 billion from clearinghouse members. In many cases, the OCC clearing members, such as large investment banks, also belong to the CME. Like the CME clearinghouse, the OCC does not pay out excess margin funds on an intraday basis. Thus, OCC and CME clearing members were required to deposit $3.0 billion on Monday, October 19. Some of these deposits were to cover options losses that were offset by futures profits, which resulted in further strains on liquidity.

After giving credit for Monday's intraday margin calls, Tuesday morning margin calls for Monday's trading activity were $2.1 billion for the CME clearinghouse and $0.9 billion for the OCC. Because clearinghouse members are required to meet these calls even before any compensating deposits are received either from customers or clearinghouses, the clearing members were compelled to increase their reliance on intraday credit from their commercial bankers. However, the bankers in question were already concerned about potential losses that their clearing member customers might have suffered in other lines of activity, such as risk arbitrage, block trading or foreign exchange trading. Bankers were also concerned that the clearinghouses would be unable to collect all their margin calls and would be unable to pay in full the balances owed to their clearinghouse members. These concerns apparently resulted in the withdrawal of uncommitted lines of credit to some market participants, restrictions on new loans to some clearinghouse members and a general concern on the part of bankers over extending credit to cover Tuesday morning margin calls.

In this atmosphere of uncertainty, the mere possibility that commercial banks might curtail lending to clearinghouse members was enough to raise questions and feed rumors about the viability of those firms and the clearinghouses. However, timely intervention by the Federal Reserve helped assure a continuing supply of credit to the clearinghouse members. At 8:15 a.m. on Tuesday morning, it was announced that:

The Federal Reserve Bank affirms its readiness to serve as a source of liquidity to support the economic and financial system.

Notwithstanding these assurances, there were continued difficulties on Tuesday. For example, because of delays in the CME clearing process, two major clearinghouse members with margin collections of $1.5 billion due them on Tuesday did not receive their funds until after 3:00 p.m., many hours later than normal. Meanwhile, these clearinghouse members had already credited customers with balances from their profitable trades and, in many cases, the customers had already withdrawn these balances from the clearinghouse members. OCC's clearing process was also delayed on Tuesday and one of its major clearing members required an immediate capital infusion to meet margin calls.

Although the cash, credit and the timing demands of the current clearinghouse system raised the possibility of a default, none occurred. On the other hand, the mere possibility that a clearinghouse might default, or that liquidity would disappear, contributed to volatility on Tuesday in two important ways.

First, some market makers did curtail their market making activities, especially in the case of block trading where temporary commitments of capital were required, because they feared that loans or credit lines from their commercial bankers might be exhausted or withdrawn. Second, uncertainties about the activities and viability of the clearinghouses, as well as major broker-dealers, appear to have increased investor uncertainty in the already turbulent atmosphere of October 20.

These uncertainties intensified market fluctuations and the sense of panic evident that day. Had decisive action not been taken by the Federal Reserve, it appears that far worse consequences would have been a very real possibility.

Summary. The degree to which existing market mechanisms can be held responsible for what occurred during the October break depends upon the standards by which these mechanisms are measured. Ideally, the full transition from a Dow level of 2,500 on Wednesday, October 14, to a range between 1,900 and 2,000, where equity markets settled in late 1987, should have occurred in a rational way without sharp, transitory declines or rises.

From October 14 to 16, price movements, trading activity and market maker performance were generally consistent with any reasonable notion of orderly markets, despite a decline of about seven percent in the major market indices. However, as the rate of decline accelerated on October 19, the efficiency with which the equity market functioned deteriorated markedly. By the late afternoon of October 19, market makers on the major stock exchanges appear to have largely abandoned serious attempts to stem the downward movement in prices. In the futures and options markets, market makers were not a significant factor during that time. As Study VI indicates, price changes and trading activity were highly erratic from late Monday afternoon through most of the day on Tuesday, October 20, as market makers were overwhelmed by selling.

Realistically, in the face of October's violent shifts in selling demand for equity-related securities, a rational downward transition in stock prices was not possible. Market makers possessed neither the resources nor the willingness to absorb the extraordinary volume of selling demand that materialized. Even under conceivable alternative arrangements, market makers would still face limited incentives and resources to manage an absolutely smooth transition in the face of the kind of demand fluctuations which confronted them on October 19 and 20.

The violence of the market movements, both upward and downward, threatened to undermine the integrity of the markets and may have substantially inhibited buyers' participation. At the same time, these market shifts created uncertainty about the solvency of major market making institutions, both directly and through the impact of these rapid price changes on the clearing and settlement systems of the futures and options markets. These factors, in turn, threatened the availability of credit to market makers which could have forced them, at a minimum, to curtail their market making activities and, at worst, to fail. By midday Tuesday, October 20, it appeared possible that a continuing steep decline could have reduced the capital of certain market makers to a level at which they could not obtain sufficient additional funds to continue their participation in the markets. At that point, the major exchanges might have decided to halt trading. The consequences of such a sequence of events, even without a failure of a major broker-dealer or a clearinghouse, could have been severe. Yet, at one point on October 20, such an outcome appeared to be conceivable.

CHAPTER SIX: ONE MARKET–
STOCKS, STOCK INDEX FUTURES, AND STOCK OPTIONS

Analysis of market behavior during the crucial days in mid-October makes clear an important conclusion. From an economic viewpoint, what have been traditionally seen as separate markets—the markets for stocks, stock index futures, and stock options—are in fact one market. Under ordinary circumstances these marketplaces move sympathetically, linked by a number of forces. The pathology which resulted when the linkages among these market segments failed underlay the market break of October.

Many mechanisms link these marketplaces. The instruments—stocks, stock index futures, and stock options—are fundamentally driven by the same economic forces. The same major investment banks dominate the trading among all three segments, both in executing orders for others and for their own accounts. In addition, many of the same institutions are responsible for a large amount of the trading in all three instruments, and particularly in stocks and index futures.

Many of the trading strategies discussed in this Report also serve to link these marketplaces. Index arbitrage provides a direct linkage between the stock and index futures markets. Faced with increasingly chaotic markets in October, portfolio insurers, to the extent possible, abandoned their reliance on the futures markets to execute their strategies and switched to selling stocks directly, underlining the commonality among market function. Another link is the routine use of the futures markets by institutions investing in index funds as a fast and low-cost entry and exit vehicle to the stock market. And, of course, a host of hedging strategies for individual stock positions employ counterbalancing purchases and sales by market makers in these marketplaces.

Market makers in these markets routinely hedge their positions by trading in two markets. For example, market makers in the S&P 100 option hedge by using the S&P 500 futures contract, and some NYSE specialists also hedge their market making activities with futures contracts. Specialists and market makers in futures and options constantly monitor up-to-the-minute prices in other markets on electronic screens. Market makers tend to carry minimal positions from day-to-day, providing liquidity for normal market moves but not for the kind of abnormally large swings experienced in October 1987.

Clearing procedures in the several market segments produce further inter-twining. While it is not yet possible to cross-margin positions, proceeds from sales in one market segment may provide funds needed to pay for purchases in another. Fears that a clearinghouse in one market segment might be unable to deliver funds owed to investors can ignite concern throughout the system, as it did in October.

In sum, what may appear superficially to be three separate markets–for stocks, stock options, and stock index futures–in fact behaves as one market.

   As the data in Chapter Four makes clear, the market's break was exacerbated by the failure of institutions employing portfolio insurance strategies to understand that the markets in which the various instruments trade are economically linked into one equity market. Portfolio insurance theory assumes that it would be infeasible to sell huge volumes of stock on the exchange in short periods of time with only a small price impact. These institutions came to believe that the futures market offered a separate haven of liquidity sufficient to allow them to liquidate huge positions over short periods of time with minimal price displacement.

   In October, this belief proved to be unrealistic. The futures market simply could not absorb such selling pressure without dramatic price declines. Moreover, reflecting the natural linkages among markets, the selling pressure washed across to the stock market, both through index arbitrage and direct portfolio insurance stock sales. Large amounts of selling, and the demand for liquidity associated with it, cannot be contained in a single market segment. It necessarily overflows into the other market segments, which are naturally linked. There are, however, natural limits to intermarket liquidity which were made evident on October 19 and 20.

   Just as the failure of sellers to understand that they were trading in a single equity market exacerbated the market break, so too did the breakdown of certain structural mechanisms linking these separate market segments.   Unopened stocks inhibited trading in the derivative instruments. The CME's temporary closing, and the difficulties the CBOE had in opening options trading, interfered with intermarket transactions. Transactions delayed through the NYSE's DOT system, and the subsequent decision to prohibit proprietary index arbitrage through the system, also disconnected the market segments.

   Under normal circumstances, index arbitrage acts as one of the primary bridges between stock and futures markets. By midday October 19, this arbitrage became difficult. First, transactions backed up in the DOT system, and then, on subsequent days, access to the system was denied to these traders. However, had the system functioned more effectively, this linkage would have been incapable of transmitting the full weight of the estimated $25 billion of selling dictated by portfolio insurance strategies.

   Even as direct arbitrage between stocks and futures failed, portfolio insurers provided some indirect arbitrage when they switched from selling futures to selling stocks. The amount of such indirect arbitrage was limited by, among other things, structural and regulatory rigidities. Many insurers were authorized to sell only futures, not stocks, for their clients, and so they continued to sell futures despite the large discount which confronted them. Many institutional stock investors are not authorized to purchase futures contracts, and therefore they could not supply buying support to the market despite the discount.

Differences in margin and clearing house mechanisms contributed further to the failure of linkages within the single equity market. Many investors, not fully understanding margin and clearing mechanisms in futures, responded to rumors of payment failures, and the reality of late payments by the CME clearinghouse, by refusing to buy in the futures market.

The decisions of lenders were also influenced by concerns over inconsistencies among the several markets. The complexity of clearing massive volumes of stocks, options, and futures through separate clearinghouses caused some lenders to hesitate in extending credit. The consequent threat of financial gridlock posed the prospect of major financial system breakdown on October 20, prompting the Federal Reserve to boost investor confidence by promising to inject liquidity into the market.

A number of factors ultimately contributed to the failure of the stock and futures markets to function as one market. As the markets became disengaged, a near freefall developed in both markets. Sellers put direct downward pressure on both markets. As large discounts developed between futures and stocks, those investors who could, switched from selling futures to selling stocks. Those unable to switch continued to sell futures, driving these prices down further. Stock investors not authorized to purchase futures, or fearful of buying them, provided no off-setting buying support in the futures market.

The enormous futures discounts signalled to prospective stock buyers that further declines were imminent. At one point on October 20, for example, the stock index futures price was "forecasting" a Dow of 1,400. This "billboard effect" inhibited some stock purchases. Moreover, the futures discount made stocks appear expensive, inhibiting buying support for the market.

The pathology of disconnected markets fed on itself. Faced with a surfeit of sellers and a scarcity of buyers, both markets—futures and stock—were at times on October 19 and 20 nearly in freefall.

The ability of the equity market to absorb the huge selling pressure to which it was subjected in mid-October depended on its liquidity. During periods of normal volume, the liquidity provided by market makers and participants in the entire equity market. The ability to sell futures is linked to stock market liquidity and vice versa.

The liquidity apparent during periods of normal volume provided by the activities of market makers and active traders on both sides of the market is something of an illusion. Liquidity sufficient to absorb the selling demands of a limited number of investors becomes an illusion of liquidity when confronted by massive selling, as everyone shows up on the same side of the market at once. As with people in a theatre when someone yells "Fire!," these sellers all ran for the exit in October, but it was large enough to accommodate only a few. For these sellers, it takes time to find buyers on the other side of the market. Potential buyers, such as value investors, do not operate by formula and must have adequate time to assemble data and make evaluations before they will commit to buy.

Certain important conclusions should be drawn from the behavior of the markets for stocks, stock index futures, and options in mid-October. First and foremost, these apparently separate markets are in an economic sense one market. They are linked by instruments, and regulatory structures interfere with linkages among them and hinder their smooth and efficient operation.

The illusion of liquidity in the futures, options and stock markets contrasts with the reality of the overall equity markets to absorb major selling or buying demands. Ironically, it was this illusion of liquidity which led some similarly motivated investors, such as portfolio insurers, to adopt strategies which call for liquidity far in excess of what the market could supply.

A number of failures of the one market system contributed to the violent break of the separate market segments in October and pushed the country to the brink of the financial system's limits. It is not possible to prevent investors from being misinformed about the capabilities of markets or to prevent markets from adjusting to the demands put upon them. But it is only prudent to design mechanisms to protect investors, the market's infrastructures, the financial system and the economy from the destructive consequence of violent market breaks.

CHAPTER SEVEN: REGULATORY IMPLICATIONS

Stocks, stock index futures and stock options constitute one market, mandating a regulatory structure designed to be consistent with this economic reality.

The failure of these market segments to perform as one market contributed to the violence of the market break in October 1987, which brought the financial system near to a breakdown. To a large extent, the failure was rooted in institutional and regulatory rigidities as well as misconceptions of market participants. That this crisis was precipitated to a large extent by the activity of a few active institutions, illustrates the vulnerability of the financial system and the need for remedial action.

This failure is amenable to reform. To prevent future damage this inextricably interrelated system of markets needs to work smoothly and in harmony. The growth of intermarket trading activities is a phenomenon of the 1980's. The October experience illustrates that regulatory changes, derived from the one-market concept, are necessary both to reduce the possibility of destructive market breaks and to deal effectively with such episodes should they occur. The guiding objective should be to enhance the integrity and competitiveness of U.S. financial markets

ONE MARKET MANDATES ONE AGENCY FOR INTERMARKET ISSUES

The analysis of the October market break demonstrates that one agency must have the authority to coordinate a few but critical intermarket regulatory issues, monitor intermarket activities and mediate intermarket concerns.

This "intermarket"—across-markets-agency need not take responsibility for all "intramarket"—within one market—regulatory issues. Such matters as securities registration, tender offer rules, and regulation of stock and option trading practices should be be left to the SEC, which has the required expertise in these areas. Intramarket issues in futures markets should remain within the purview of the CFTC, which has expertise in the design and regulation of futures contracts and markets.

However, there are a few important intermarket regulatory issues which must be considered jointly and simultaneously across market segments to ensure that the intermarket systems operate harmoniously. These are issues which cannot be decided from the perspective of a single marketplace. Doing so imposes pervasive, unavoidable and possibly destabilizing influences on other related market places and   on the interrelated market system as a whole.

Intermarket reform raises two fundamental questions. Who should have the responsibility for intermarket coordination? What are the few crucial inter–market issues which must be assigned to the intermarket agency? The choice of the agency follows from the requirements of the intermarket task.

The October experience demonstrates that the issues which have an impact across related markets, and throughout the financial system, include clearing and credit mechanisms, margins requirements, circuit breaker mechanisms, such as price limits and trading halts, and information systems for monitoring intermarket activities.

It is important to recognize that this approach does not involve imposing substantial new regulatory burdens. For the most part, it involves the reallocation of existing regulatory tasks in a manner designed to conform to the fundamental economic reality that stock, stock index futures and options are one market.

The Intermarket Agency. The October episode gives a clear view of the characteristics and expertise required to coordinate intermarket issues relating to stocks, stock index futures and options. The most fundamental requirement is broad and deep expertise in these market segments and instruments. However, expertise in individual instruments and market segments is not sufficient. The key requirement is expertise in the interaction of instruments and marketplaces as an integrated system.

Moreover, the October break illustrates that difficulties in stocks and derivative market segments produce dislocations in other financial markets. These, in turn, exacerbate the problem in stocks and derivative market segments. The market break profoundly affected bond and foreign exchange markets as well as the extension of credit by the banking system. Indeed, the confidence and liquidity of the entire financial system were at risk in October.

In addition, global markets were involved. The precipitous decline in the U.S. market was accompanied by a concurrent break in equity markets around the world. Cross-listing of stocks and cross-border investment have strengthened the linkages among global equity markets. During the October break, U.S. market participants were sellers of foreign stocks and U.S. stocks listed on foreign markets. Specialized transactions in U.S. securities and stock index futures were executed in London. United States bond futures markets in London were influenced by the Federal Reserve's injection of liquidity, as were foreign exchange markets. In short, the October market break had ramifications in a wide variety of global financial markets.

Expertise in individual market segments is, therefore, not sufficient for effective response to intermarket crises. The October experience demonstrates that the intermarket agency must consider the interactions among a wide variety of markets encompassing stocks, stock index futures, stock options, bonds, foreign exchange and the credit and banking system, in both domestic and foreign markets.

The critical requirement for the intermarket agency is broad expertise in the financial system as a whole because the greatest potential risk of intermarket failure is to the financial system as a whole, rather than to individual market segments. Financial system expertise is required to deal with a financial system crisis. This expertise is also critical for monitoring and responding to intermarket problems and thus avoiding a financial crisis.

Because of its broad constituency, this agency needs the independence to resist demands of partisan political and economic interests, particularly those of active market participants. The stakes are simply too high; the potential adverse consequence of market failure too pervasive.

Independence Must Be Balanced by Responsivesness. The intermarket agency must respond to evolving needs of financial market participants. Competitive financial markets are a valuable national asset and the competition for their services is worldwide. Intermarket coodination must be sufficiently flexible to accommodate the innovation in instruments and markets necessary to maintain and strengthen the competitiveness of U.S. financial markets.

Therefore, an analysis of the October experience demonstrates the need for one regulatory body with responsibility for rationalizing intermarket issues. The task requires broad expertise in the interaction of domestic and global financial markets, financial strength, prestige, independence and responsiveness. The Task Force compared these requirements with alternative regulatory structures.

Self Regulatory Organizations. Self Regulatory Organizations ("SROs"), such as securities and commodities exchanges, are uniquely qualified to regulate intramarket activities. Since they are closest to the action, SROs have the best view of the regulatory needs of their individual market segments. Furthermore, they are motivated by self-interest to preserve the integrity of their marketplace.

Nonetheless, SROs are not well suited for intermarket tasks. They lack the authority to coordinate issues across markets and the resources to deal with intermarket issues. Finally, it is not apparent that they possess either the expertise or the incentive to represent the broader constituencies within the domestic and global financial system.

The Securities and Exchange Commission. Centralizing responsibility for stocks, stock index futures and options within the SEC is attractive on several grounds. The SEC has responsibility for regulating stocks and stock options. Thus, it might seem logical to assign the SEC the responsibility for stocks and all derivative instruments. Moreover, the SEC is structured as an independent agency and has the prestige and influence required for effective regulation.

There are drawbacks to this solution to intermarket regulation. Extending SEC authority to stock index futures might require an investment in expertise necessary to regulate complex instruments new to its regulatory purview. This was necessary for the SEC's regulation of stock options. The expertise needed to regulate stock index futures could be acquired by transferring personnel from the CFTC. Doing so might deplete the CFTC's resources and interfere with its capacity to carry out its other regulatory duties.

Moreover, the SEC's experience and expertise is focused primarily on regulating intramarket activities, not on rationalizing the interactions among markets. To be effective as an intermarket regulator the SEC might have to fund the acquisition of expertise in a wide variety of financial markets, in the credit and banking system, and in international markets.

Joint SEC-CFTC Responsibility. A single regulator, created through joint SEC-CFTC responsibility, could be achieved through a merger of the two agencies, a formal joint committee arrangement, or strict requirements for coordination of intermarket regulatory issues. This alternative would bring together the expertise of the SEC and CFTC with respect to specific types of instruments and intramarket regulatory issues. Nonetheless, combining two agencies with intramarket expertise in their respective market segments would not necessarily produce effective intermarket regulation.

This alternative might not provide the broad financial system expertise needed to oversee the interaction of domestic and global markets as well as the banking system.

Finally, the need for coordinating the few critical intermarket issues does not diminish the importance of detailed supervision of the much wider range of intramarket activities. The addition of intermarket responsibility risks draining resources from the important regulatory tasks that the SEC and CFTC must administer within their respective market segments.

Joint Federal Reserve-SEC-CFTC Committee. The addition of the Federal Reserve would supplement the intramarket expertise of the SEC and CFTC with the broad financial system expertise of the Federal Reserve.

Although this alternative has attractive aspects, there are drawbacks. The committee's effectiveness depends upon resisting the intramarket perspective and constituencies of committee representatives.

Moreover, the most important objective of intermarket regulation is to avoid an intermarket crisis. This requires clear responsibility for ongoing monitoring of intermarket activities and clear authority to act to avoid a crisis. A joint agency committee may not be well-suited for this task. Within a joint agency committee, responsibility and authority could become diffuse. In times of crisis, a committee structure could prove cumbersome, when immediate action would be imperative.

Although there are relatively few intermarket issues to be coordinated, the health of the financial system depends upon effective intermarket regulation. This argues for investing the responsibility in a single responsive agency with the authority to act promptly, rather than assembling a committee representing several agencies.

The Federal Reserve. In most countries, the central bank, as part of broader responsibility for the health of a nation's financial system, is the intermarket regulator. The Federal Reserve has a primary responsibility for the health of the U.S. financial system. The Federal Reserve works closely with the Department of the Treasury to achieve this goal. This responsibility, and the Federal Reserve's accumulated expertise in discharging this responsibility, are arguments in its favor as the appropriate intermarket agency.

The intermarket crisis in October ultimately required the Federal Reserve to step in to inject liquidity and boost confidence. This rescue imposed costs and constraints on other economic policy objectives. Since intermarket failure and damage to the financial system ultimately fall upon the Federal Reserve, it could be argued that the Federal Reserve should possess the authority to prevent such an intermarket crisis.

Further, in a crisis, the liquidity of the financial system in general, and the banking system in particular, is affected. This is the Federal Reserve's central area of expertise.

The Federal Reserve, with its view of money flows, is experienced in assessing interactions and imbalances among marketplaces, as opposed to intramarket concerns. It has experience in international financial market coordination. The importance of these attributes is illustrated by the October break which involved not only stocks, futures and options but bonds, foreign exchange and international markets.

The Federal Reserve also possesses the other characteristics required of an effective intermarket agency. It has the ability, standing and influence to establish and coordinate consistent intermarket requirements and to inspire intermarket confidence.

Finally, there are precedents for the Federal Reserve as an intermarket agency. The Federal Reserve already has formal responsibility for margin requirements on stocks and stock options. Adding futures margins to the Federal Reserve's purview would be logical extension of its current responsibilities and is not a major change. Also, the Federal Reserve regulates bank lending to securities market participants.

Despite these advantages, there are drawbacks to the Federal Reserve as the intermarket agency. Intermarket coordination would be a new responsibility, involving the burden of additional tasks. The Federal Reserve might need to build expertise in intramarket issues in order to carry out its intermarket oversight.

Another problem with the Federal Reserve as the intermarket agency is the danger that market participants may take on more risk in the expectation that the Federal Reserve will bail them out in a crisis. Intermarket responsibility could give the Federal Reserve a role to play before financial system crises develop. However, it would still have no requirement to guarantee the actions of any particular firm.

Balancing the advantage of independence is the need for responsiveness. Of all the major regulatory agencies, the Federal Reserve is perhaps the most independent. Therein lies the potential for a lack of responsiveness to legitimate needs for financial market evolution and innovation. If unresponsive, the Federal Reserve could impair the competitiveness of U.S. financial markets.

The Department of the Treasury. The Treasury Department possesses most of the advantages of the Federal Reserve. It has broad financial system perspective and expertise, international standing in a variety of markets, financial strength, prestige and influence.

However, unlike the Federal Reserve, the SEC, and the CFTC, which are structured as independent agencies, the Treasury is part of the executive branch. Because of the President, it has less independence as a regulatory agency.

A New Regulatory Body. It would be possible to establish a new regulatory body designed to coordinate intermarket issues. This alternative appears to be more expensive than, and inferior to, harnessing the accumulated expertise and standing of an existing agency.

Guided by the October experience, an analysis of the requirements for effective intermarket coordination demonstrates that expertise in the interaction of markets is the critical requirement. This does not require major restructuring of intramarket regulatory responsibilities. Instead, a few important intermarket issues need to be coordinated by one agency possessing intermarket perspective and expertise.

INTERMARKET ISSUES

Intermarket issues are those which systematically and unavoidably impose influences on all markets. The few important intermarket issues which need to be harmonized by a single body include clearing and credit mechanisms, margin requirements, circuit breaker mechanisms such as price limits and trading halts, and information systems for monitoring intermarket activities.

These issues are not the separate concern of individual market segments.

The October break illustrates that decisions in one marketplace profoundly affect other marketplaces and the financial system as a whole.

Clearing and Credit Mechanisms. Clearing and credit mechanisms need to be unified. With separate clearing houses for each market segment, no single clearing corporation has an over-view of the intermarket positions of market participants. No clearinghouse is able to assess accurately intermarket exposure among its clearing members and among their customers. Separate clearing also hampers lenders in assessing the risk exposure of market participants and interferes with collateralization of intermarket positions. In the current system, margin flows differs across clearinghouses. For the sort of intermarket transactions which are the mainstay of these markets, funds must be shuttled from clearinghouse to clearinghouse in the margin settlement process. This process creates imbalances in financing needs and increases demand for bank credit.

The complexity and fragmentation of the separate clearing mechanisms in stocks, futures and options—in conjunction with massive volume, violent price volatility, and staggering demands on bank credit—brought the financial system to the brink on Tuesday, October 20. Some clearinghouses were late in making payments. There were rumors concerning the viability of clearinghouses and market participants. This in turn affected the willingness of lenders to finance market participants under the uncommitted lending arrangements common in the industry. This crisis of confidence raised the spectre of a full-scale financial system breakdown and required the Federal Reserve to provide liquidity and confidence. The complexity of the clearing and credit mechanisms, rather than a substantive problem of solvency, was at fault.

What is needed is unified clearing with stocks, stock index futures and stock options, all cleared through a single mechanism. Unified clearing facilitates the smooth settlement of intermarket transactions, which is the linchpin of these markets. It clarifies the credit risk of lending to participants engaged in intermarket transactions. This would reduce the chance of financial gridlock and the attendant risk to the financial system.

Margin Requirements. Since stocks, stock index futures and stock options compose in an economic sense, one market, margins need to be rationalized across markets. While margins on stocks and options are already within the Federal Reserve's regulatory purview, futures margins are currently determined by futures exchanges, and thus are not subject to intermarket oversight. Futures margins should be consistent with effective stock margins for professional market participants such as broker-dealers, and cross-margining should be implemented.

Margins have two fundamental characteristics. First, margin requirements affect intramarket performance risk. Margins serve as a performance bond to secure the ability of market participants to meet their obligations. Second, margins represent collateral; thus, margin requirements control the leverage possible in the investment in any financial instrument.

On the first point—the intramarket financial performance control aspect of margin requirements—the concept of margins on futures differs fundamentally from that of margins on stock investments.[5] The daily process of marking-to-market the value of investments, in which futures losers must advance margin to pay futures winners, differ fundamentally from the stock market margin process of advancing payments against a lending formula. Despite low margin requirements, the financial performance control aspect of futures margins has operated in a sound and effective manner on an intramarket basis.

However, margins are more than a financial performance control mechanism. All margin requirements have one aspect in common; margins are collateral and control the effective economic leverage achievable in any financial instrument.

Because margins on futures are lower than those on stocks, market participants can achieve much greater leverage by investing through futures. With a given initial investment, a market participant can control a much greater equity investment indirectly through futures than through a direct investment in stocks.[6]

The differing level of financial leverage inherent in differing margin requirements warrants concern for two reasons. First, constraints on leverage control the volume of speculative investment activity. Second, leverage translates into financial risk, which extends beyond the performance obligation of a specific transaction and a specific market place.

It has been long recognized that margin requirements, through leverage, affect the volume of speculative activity. Controlling speculative behavior is one approach to inhibiting overvaluation in stocks and reducing the potential for a precipitate price decline fueled by the involuntary selling that stems, for example, for margin calls.

---

[5] For simplicity, margins on stock options are not considered in detail in this section.

[6] For example, on October 19, a professional market participant, who is classified as a hedger, could have taken a position in the equity market by purchasing an index futures contract with an underlying value of $130,000 (500 times the index value of 260) by making an initial investment of $7,500, or approximately 5.8 percent of the contract's value. In order to purchase $130,000 worth of stock, such a participant would have to make an initial investment of about $354,000, or about 25 percent of the value of the stock. Although the futures investor only has to come up with $7,500, the entire $130,000 stock equivalent may be transmitted into the stock market through index arbitrage. Similar leverage is possible on the short side of the market.

The equity action achievable with low margin investment in futures has potential to increase intermarket leverage for market participants. The resulting financial risk may affect their ability to meet obligations in other market segments. Because of the potentially wide-ranging consequences, the level of leverage within the financial system is a legitimate intermarket concern, rather that the narrow concern of a particular market segment.

The October experience illustrates how a relatively few, aggressive, professional market participants can produce dramatic swings in market prices. Moreover, the mid-October episode demonstrates that such pressures are transmitted from marketplace to marketplace and, at times, pressures concentrated in one market segment can have traumatic effects on the whole system. Low futures margins allow investors to control large positions with low initial investments. The clear implication is that margin requirements affect intermarket risk and are not the private concern of a single marketplace.

Nonetheless, it does not make sense to impose on all futures investors the stock margin requirement for individual investors. The stock index futures market is a professional market. Speculation by individual investors appears not to have been a serious problem in the October decline.

Speculation by professional market participants is, however, a realistic concern. In the stock market, professionals are not subject to the 50 percent margin requirement applicable to individuals. Professionals such as broker dealers, can invest in stocks on 20 percent to 25 percent margin. The same professionals can take equivalent positions in stock through the futures market on much lower margin.

To protect the intermarket system, margins on stock index futures need to be consistent with margins for professional market participants in the stock market. Such requirements need not produce equal margins on futures and stocks but should reflect the different structure of the two related market segments. However, similar margins resulting in roughly equivalent risk and leverage between the two market segments are necessary to enforce consistent intermarket public policy objectives concerning leverage and speculation.

Higher futures margins (in line with equivalent stock margins for professionals) need not hamper futures market makers and hedged futures participants. Consistent with the one-market concept, cross-margining should be allowed. Market participants with an investment in futures should be allowed to receive credit for an offsetting, or held, investment in stocks or options. Cross-margining allows margin regulations to focus on the true intermarket risk exposure of participants, rather than focusing myopically on a single market segment.

In view of the October experience, the underlying logic of consistent margins for professional market participants in the one market system is compelling. If, from a public policy viewpoint, a given margin level for investment in stocks makes sense, should lower margins and the potential for more financial leverage and speculative investment be allowed for market participants investing in stocks via derivative instruments? Should two margin requirements apply to what is, in effect, one market.

Circuit Breaker Mechanisms. Circuit breaker mechanisms involve trading halts in the various market segments. Examples include price limits, position limits, volume limits, trading halts reflecting order imbalances, trading halts in derivatives associated with conditions in the primary marketplaces, and the like. To be effective, such mechanisms need to be coordinated across the markets for stocks, stock index futures and options. Circuit breakers need to be in place prior to a market crisis, and they need to be part of the economic and contractual landscape. The need for circuit breaker mechanisms reflects the natural limit to intermarket liquidity, the inherently limited capacity of markets to absorb massive, one sided volume.

Circuit breakers have three benefits. First, they limit credit risks and loss of financial confidence by providing a "time-out" amid frenetic trading to settle up and ensure that everyone is solvent. Second, they facilitate price discovery by providing a "time-out" to pause, evaluate, inhibit panic, and publicize order imbalances to attract value traders to cushion violent movements in the market.

Finally, circuit breaker mechanisms counter the illusion of liquidity by formalizing the economic fact of life, so apparent in October, that markets have a limited capacity to absorb massive one-sided volume. Making circuit breakers part of the contractual landscape makes it far more difficult for some market participants—pension portfolio insurers, aggressive mutual funds—to mislead themselves into believing that it is possible to sell huge amounts in short time periods. This makes it less likely in the future that flawed trading strategies will be pursued to the point of disrupting markets and threatening the financial system. Thus, circuit breakers cushion the impact of market movements, which would otherwise damage market infrastructures. They protect markets and investors.

There are perceived disadvantages to circuit breaker mechanisms. They may hinder trading and hedging strategies. Trading halts may lock investors in, preventing them from exiting the market. However, circuit breakers in a violent market are inevitable. The October market break produced its own circuit breakers: the clogging of the DOT system for NYSE order processing and OTC trading systems; ad hoc trading halts in individual stocks, in options and stock index futures; jammed communication systems; and some less than responsive specialists and market makers throughout markets.

These market disorders became, in effect, ad hoc circuit breakers, reflecting the natural limits to market liquidity. The October 1987 market break demonstrates that it is far better to design and implement coherent, coordinated circuit breaker mechanisms in advance, than to be left at the mercy of the unavoidable circuit breakers of chaos and system failure.

To be effective, circuit breaker mechanisms need to be rationalized across stocks, stock index futures and options markets. Coordination is necessary to prevent intermarket failure of the kind experienced in October. The intermarket impact of trading halts was vividly illustrated in October. When the NYSE's automated stock order system, DOT, was rendered ineffective, index arbitrage became infeasible, robbing the index futures of much needed buying power. From the narrow perspective of the stock market, an inactive DOT system may have appeared beneficial, since it made program selling difficult. However, this contributed to the development of a futures discount which, in turn, put downward pressure on stock prices. Also, trading halts in NYSE stocks interfered with options and futures trading. Indeed, there are numerous examples in the October break of the impact of trading constraints in one marketplace on conditions in other marketplaces.

Trading halts such as price limits are not the private concerns of individual market segments. Because they affect trading throughout the intermarket system, circuit breakers need to be coordinated from a broader intermarket perspective. In a crisis, the need for intermarket information and coordination of trading halts is imperative to avoid intermarket failure. Closing one market segment can have a destabilizing impact throughout the market system. An intermarket perspective facilitates a timely and effective response to crisis.

Information Systems. Intermarket information systems are currently insufficient to monitor the intermarket trading strategies that are so significant to the one-market system. Intermarket monitoring systems are necessary to assess market conditions and to diagnose developing problems.

The October experience illustrates the need for a trading information system incorporating the trade, time of the trade and the name of the ultimate customer in every major market segment. This is critical to assess the nature and cause of a market crisis to determine who bought and who sold. This information can be used to diagnose developing problems as well as to uncover potentially damaging abuses.

The futures clearinghouse and large trader information systems currently allow assessment of trading time by trading customers. The stock exchanges have no systems which detail trades and trading times by customer. Stock systems include only the broker-dealers involved and whether the broker dealer acted as principal or agent. Customer information for all market segments is critical to assessing threats to the intermarket system, and all major exchanges should be required to maintain such an information system. The October experience illustrates the need for information systems capable of monitoring conditions throughout the one-market system.

Conclusions. One intermarket system mandates one agency to coordinate the few critical intermarket regulatory issues—clearing and credit arrangements, margins, circuit breakers and information systems. This intermarket agency need not be involved in detailed intramarket regulatory issues in which the SEC, the CFTC and the self regulatory organizations have expertise. The expertise required of the intermarket agency is evident from the nature of the task.

In many respects, the problems associated with the October market break can be traced to intermarket failure. Institutional and regulatory structures designed for separate marketplaces were incapable of dealing with a precipitate intermarket decline which brought the financial system to the brink. Although exchanges may not be pleased with the prospect of intermarket regulation, the Task Force has concluded it is essential to ensure the integrity of financial markets.

It is important to note that, for the most part, this proposal does not involve substantial additional regulatory burdens. Rather, it involves the reallocation of existing responsibility to conform to new economic realities. Intermarket trading activities are an important innovation and contribute to the competitiveness of the U.S. markets. These activities have evolved and grown rapidly during the past five years. The regulatory structure has not evolved in a corresponding manner and remains primarily an intramarket activity. This needs to be changed.

The pressing need for coordination of intermarket issues is the chief lesson to be learned from the October experience. Rationalizing intermarket issues is the key to avoiding future market crises and ensuring the efficiency and competitiveness of U.S. markets.

CHAPTER EIGHT: CONCLUSIONS

On Thursday, October 22, following the stock market break earlier that week, the President announced the formation of the Task Force on Market Mechanisms. Its mandate was, in 60 days, to determine what happened and why, and to provide guidance in helping to prevent such a break from occurring again.

The Task Force concludes that the precipitous decline in the stock market was characterized by large sales by a limited number of institutional investors throughout the interrelated system of markets—stocks, futures and stock options. The massive volume, violent price volatility, and staggering demands on clearing and credit raised the possibility of a full scale financial system breakdown.

The Task Force also concludes that stocks, stock index futures and options constitute one market linked by financial instruments, trading strategies, market participants and clearing and credit mechanisms. To a large extent, the problems in mid-October can be traced to the failure of these market segments to act as one. Institutional and regulatory structures designed for separate marketplaces were incapable of effectively responding to intermarket pressures. The activities of some market participants, such as portfolio insurers, were driven by the misperception that they were trading in separate, not linked, marketplaces.

The simple conclusion is that the system grew geometrically with the technological and financial revolution of the 1980's. Many in government, industry and academia failed to understand fully that these separate marketplaces are in fact one market.

Nonetheless, that the market break was intensified by the activities of a few institutions illustrates the vulnerability of a market in which individuals directly own 60 percent of the equities. The experience underscores the need for immediate action to protect the equity market and financial system from the destructive consequences of violent market breaks.

Our understanding of these events leads directly to our recommendations. To help prevent a repetition of the events of mid-October and to provide an effective and coordinated response in the face of market disorder, we recommend that:

1. One agency should coordinate the few, but critical regulatory issues which have an impact across the related market segments and throughout the financial system.

2. Clearing systems should be unified to reduce financial risk.

3. Margins should be made consistent to control speculation and financial leverage.

4. Circuit breaker mechanisms (such as price limits and coordinated trading halts) should be formulated and implemented to protect the market system.

5. Information systems should be established to monitor transactions and conditions in related markets.

Analysis of the October episode also gives a clear view of the attributes required of an effective intermarket agency. These are: expertise in the interaction of markets, not simply experience in regulating distinct market segments; a broad perspective on the financial system as a whole, both foreign and domestic; independence; and responsiveness.

The Task Force has neither the mandate nor the time to consider the full range of issues necessary to support a definitive recommendation of the choice of the intermarket agency. We are, nevertheless, aware that the weight of the evidence suggests that the Federal Reserve is well qualified to fill the role of the intermarket agency.

MILLER

"Miller," the selections from the reports of the Committee of Inquiry that examined performance of the Chicago Mercantile Exchange and its S&P 500 contract during the crash, consists of two parts. First is the Committee's final report, which addresses key policy issues such as margins, "circuit breakers," and regulatory obstacles to market efficiency. Second is the preliminary report, which examines in detail evidence regarding CME performance.

Final Report of the Committee of Inquiry

Appointed by the Chicago Mercantile Exchange to Examine the Events Surrounding October 19, 1987

Committee of Inquiry Members:
Merton Miller, Chairman
Myron Scholes
Burton Malkeil
John Hawke, Jr.

INTRODUCTION

On October 29, 1987, the Chicago Mercantile Exchange appointed the authors of this report as an independent Committee of Inquiry to study the role of CME's futures market during the extraordinary stock market decline of mid-October 1987. The Committee was also expected to recommend any changes in the CME's contracts or procedures that might improve the functioning of the markets, especially under conditions of great stress. The three academic members of the Committee have each conducted research studies on issues relating to the stock market, the futures and options markets, and the interrelations between the markets; and they have written extensively on these subjects. The fourth panel member is a practicing attorney with substantial experience in financial regulatory matters, including service as General Counsel to the Board of Governors of the Federal Reserve System.

COMMITTEE'S PRELIMINARY REPORT

The Role of Futures During the Crash

On December 22, 1987, we submitted to the CME a Preliminary Report of our findings and our suggestions. Our study of trading and open interest in CME stock index futures contracts had led us to three tentative conclusions about the role of index futures in the market fall of October 19-20:

First, the crash of October 19 did not originate in Chicago and flow from there by means of index arbitrage, carried out by program trading, to an otherwise calm and unsuspecting market in New York.

Although this charge was made at the time and has been repeated frequently since then, the evidence shows clearly that the selling wave hit both markets simultaneously. The perception that a price decline in the futures market led the decline in the stock market was an illusion traceable mainly to the different procedures followed in the two markets at their openings. At the New York Stock Exchange the huge overnight imbalance of sell orders had delayed the opening of many of the leading stocks in the Standard & Poors 500 index. The prices for these stocks used in calculating the publicly reported index value on Monday morning were, therefore, the last available quotes from the previous Friday's close. By contrast, the futures price at the CME reflected the Monday morning information. Thus, while it may have appeared to some that a tidal wave was on the way from Chicago, delayed openings at the NYSE showed that it had already arrived there, even before the opening bell had sounded.

Second, on Monday, October 19, the futures market in Chicago appears actually to have absorbed selling pressure on balance. While some pressure from the selling of futures contracts by portfolio insurers and other institutional investors was indeed transmitted back to the NYSE by index arbitrage, the equivalent of 85 million shares—about 14 percent of the day's volume on the NYSE and 57 percent of CME S&P 500 volume—was absorbed by the market makers, day traders, anticipatory hedgers, institutional buyers, and speculative position holders in Chicago.

Third, the futures markets in Chicago were no more responsible for the turnaround in the market on Tuesday, October 20, than for the initial downturn on Monday, October 19. The dramatic recovery of Tuesday afternoon is more plausibly traced to the announcement of large corporate buyback programs and the promise of Federal Reserve support for bank liquidity, than to any manipulations in the Major Market Index futures contract at the Chicago Board of Trade or to the rupture of the linkage between the stock market and the main futures market during the 40-minute period that the CME had suspended trading.

In the two months or so since our Preliminary Report presented these tentative conclusions, at least five other investigative commissions and regulatory agencies have submitted reports on the crash and several academic studies of the trading record have been completed. These reports and studies have filled in many pieces of the puzzle that were still missing when we first wrote and they have offered new insights and perspectives on the way the markets functioned. After examining these studies in detail, however, we find no compelling reason to retreat from or to alter the analysis or the conclusions presented in our Preliminary Report. In fact, some of the conclusions we put forth somewhat tentatively at the time, can now be considered as having been strongly supported by the data that subsequently became available.[1] In later sections of this report, we shall note some of the important new findings, particularly where they have a bearing on our policy recommendations.

PRELIMINARY POLICY RECOMMENDATIONS: PORTFOLIO INSURANCE AND INDEX ARBITRAGE PROGRAM TRADING

Although our Preliminary Report sought mainly to establish what had happened, we tried also to give a preliminary assessment of some of the main proposals for change in market structure that had surfaced in the

---

[1] An Example is the study, "Nonsynchronous Trading and the S&P 500 Stock-Futures Basis in October 1987," by Lawrence Harris, University of Southern California, manuscript, December 1987. Harris constructs a measure for the S&P 500 index that adjusts for delayed openings and trading halts on the NYSE. The revised series strongly confirms our view that the opening discount on October 19 was an illusion. An index adjustment by the Commodity and Futures Trading Commission similar to that of Harris also supports our interpretation of the seeming discount at the opening. See Commodity and Futures Trading Commission, Divisions of Economic Analysis and Trading and Markets, "Final Report on Stock Index Futures and Cash Market Activity During October 1987," pp. 15-18, January 1988. Although most severe at the openings, similar distortions in the normal relation between futures and cash market prices arose at several points during the critical two days in response to trading delays, reporting lags and the efforts of some NYSE specialists to fill in any large gaps between prices on successive trades.

wake of the crash. For some of these proposals, we felt the evidence was already strong enough for us to take a clear stand. In particular, we recommended against any attempts to ban either portfolio insurance or index arbitrage carried out through program trading.

Portfolio Insurance and the Crash

Our recommendation against legislative or regulatory restrictions on portfolio insurance does not mean that we believe portfolio insurance selling played no role in the events of the 19th. Certainly, as we showed, substantial portfolio insurance selling did occur. But it is important to keep the portfolio insurance sales in perspective. On the 19th, portfolio insurance sales of futures represented somewhere between 20 and 30 percent of the share equivalent of total sales on the NYSE. The pressure of selling on the NYSE by other investors—mutual funds, security dealers and individual shareholders—was thus three to five times greater than that of the portfolio insurers. Price falls as large, and market conditions as chaotic, as those in the U.S. occurred in many countries on the 19th, even in those with no portfolio insurance or index futures markets.

Nor are we persuaded by the view expressed in both the Report of the Presidential Task Force on Market Mechanisms ("Brady Report") and the Report of the Securities and Exchange Commission's Division of Market Regulation[2] that the timing of the portfolio insurance sales magnified their impact. The SEC Report notes that portfolio insurance and index arbitrage, though accounting for no more than 20 percent of S&P 500 volume during the entire day of the 19th, and no more than 40 percent in the fateful 1:00-2:00 PM EST hour, did account for "more than 60 percent of S&P 500 stock volume in three 10-minute intervals within that hour" (SEC Report, p. xiii). But since transactions are recorded sequentially, there must surely have been shorter intervals in which the portfolio insurance trades approached 100 percent of total market trades!

No reliable methods exist for relating observed price changes in active, competitive markets to the actions of particular sellers or buyers. Hence we chose not to attempt the detailed, almost tick-by-tick account of trading presented in the Brady and SEC Reports. We did provide a rough visual sketch in our Figures Miller-P3 to P6 of net trading activity by major groups for fifteen-minute intervals during the 19th and 20th, but we could

---

[2] Securities and Exchange Commission, Division of Market Regulation, "The October 1987 Market Break," February 1988. The SEC Report carries the caveat that although the Commission authorized publication of the Report, it has expressed no view on the Report's analysis, findings or recommendations.

find no consistent patterns of association with price changes. Because visual scanning can be deceptive, however, and because both the Brady and SEC Reports claim they do see such patterns, we asked the CME staff to carry out a formal statistical analysis of the degree of association between the transactions by pension funds or broker/dealers and price changes in both the stock and futures markets. That study finds no consistent or statistically reliable relation between price changes in either market and trading activity by pension funds and broker/dealers.

Some accounts of events on the 19th suggest that the fear of further portfolio insurance selling to come may have been as much or more responsible for frantic selling by the public, and especially by the large trading firms, as the actual portfolio insurance selling that did occur. Such perceptions, of course, are difficult to document; but to the extent that they did arise on the 19th, they point up the need not for restrictions on portfolio insurance, but for better and quicker dissemination of information about the flow of insurance transactions waiting in the wings.[3]

Portfolio Insurance and the Pre-Crash Buildup

Concern has also been expressed that portfolio insurance may have contributed to the crash by pushing prices in the U.S. stock market to higher pre-crash levels than might have been the case without the comfort that such insurance programs seem to offer.[4] Once again, however, it is important to keep a sense of proportion about the relevant magnitudes. The U.S. market rose between January and August 1987 by 30 percent, an increase in value of about $600 billion. The total value of pension fund assets under formal portfolio insurance plans at that point may have reached as much as $100 billion. Not all of this total was in equities, of course; pension funds typically also have substantial holdings of fixed income securities to reduce the downside vulnerability of the fund's assets. Believing that portfolio insurance could now play a similar risk reduction

---

[3] Some of these information-related problems of conducting portfolio insurance might have been avoided had the insurance been carried out with traded options, rather than with the synthetic options created by dynamic hedging with futures. See, e.g., Sanford J. Grossman, "An Analysis of the Implications for Stock and Futures Price Volatility of Program Trading and Dynamic Hedging Strategies," *Journal of Business,* July 1988. The much more restrictive position limits on options than on futures, however, have tended to discourage the use of options by the portfolio insurers.

[4] In testimony before the Senate Committee on Banking, Housing and Urban Affairs on February 2, 1988, Federal Reserve Board Chairman Alan Greenspan said: "To the degree that derivative instruments facilitate a better redistribution of price risk to those most willing and able to bear it, they can add to the appeal of cash equity investments to investors, encouraging them to hold larger permanent equity positions."

role for their equity component, some pension fund managers may well have decided to increase the equity portion relative to the fixed income portion of their asset mix. But even if this shift in proportion away from debt and toward equity amounted to as much as $30 billion and even if it had all come in 1987, it would still have amounted to less than five percent of the increase in the value of U.S. equities between January and the time of the crash.

In the months since the submission of our Preliminary Report, the amount of portfolio insurance in force has, by all accounts, been dropping steadily and substantially. The programs have been modified to admit a wider and more flexible range of response by the managers when futures are selling at what appears to be a substantial discount to the cash market, as occurred often on the 19th and the days thereafter.[5] In short, the problems posed by portfolio insurance—if indeed they were problems—appear to have been largely self-correcting. Recognizing that fact, the calls for restricting portfolio insurance, so frequently voiced in the aftermath of the crash (and again after the presentation of the Brady and SEC Reports) have also largely subsided. Such has not proved to be the case, however, for index arbitrage program trading.

Index Arbitrage Program Trading

In our Preliminary Report, we took the position, amply documented in extensive previous academic research on the subject (and apparently fully concurred in by the Brady Commission) that, given an index futures market, inter-market arbitrage was a benign rather than a malignant influence.[6] Index arbitrage carried out through trading is merely one among a large number of examples in economic life of how financial

---

[5] See, e.g., Hayne Leland, "Dynamic Asset Allocation: After the Crash," *Investment Management Review*, January/February 1988, pp. 13-19. Leland is one of the inventors of portfolio insurance and a co-founder of Leland, O'Brien and Rubinstein, the leading purveyor firm.

[6] Among the many statistical studies of index arbitrage program trading, two recent ones are perhaps worth special notice. In their study "The Dynamics of Stock Index and Stock Index Futures Returns" (Working Paper Series 88-101, Fuqua School of Business, Durham, NC, January 21, 1988), Hans Stoll and Robert Whaley can find no evidence that futures tend to "overshoot" their true values and hence to cause whipsawing of the kind pictured in the popular press. In a paper entitled "Report on Program Trading: An Analysis of Interday Relationships" and prepared for the Katzenbach study, Sanford Grossman could find no relation "between any measure of volatility or any measure of program trading. The days in which volatility was high were not, systematically, the days in which program trading intensity was high" (p. 2). The CFTC Report also notes, aptly, that during the immediate post-crash period of October 21-23, volatility was extremely high but program trading had virtually ceased (CFTC Report, pp. 107-136).

intermediaries, in this case the arbitragers, serve to lower the costs of transacting. Their presence links, and hence increases, the effective market-making capacity in both markets.

Nonetheless, while logic and the evidence of virtually every academic investigation of the subject suggest that index arbitrage program trading really affects only the route by which selling or buying orders reach the NYSE, such trading has come under increasing attack from legislators, as well as many in the investment community including some of the largest brokerage concerns. In part, this hostility may reflect a fear on the part of some mutual funds and other institutional investors of "front running" against them by the brokerage firms with which they do business—that is, trading in futures to profit on the knowledge of the customer's impending order in the stock market. In part, it may reflect a populist concern that sophisticated traders may be profiting by "locking in" profits without risk through techniques beyond the reach of the average investor. In part, it may also be a response to the strains that such trading sometimes imposes on the transaction processing capacities of the NYSE. Finally, some members of the brokerage community seem to believe, on the basis, however, of no foundation in evidence that we have been able to discover, that ending program trading will somehow reduce market volatility, increase investor confidence and restore trading volume to its pre-crash levels.

To deal in detail with each of these misconceptions about arbitrage program trading, some of very long standing, is a task best left to the educational arms of the futures and options exchanges themselves. The focus of our Committee is the narrower one of market performance in the crash and its immediate aftermath. Here perhaps we need only call attention once again to the key point emphasized throughout the Brady Report: the markets performed most chaotically precisely when the arbitrage link between them was broken. Breaking the link knocked out market-making capacity both on the floor at the futures markets at Chicago and at the upstairs, block-trading desks in New York. The specialists at the NYSE were then left to face the avalanche on their own.

THE CRITICAL POLICY ISSUE: WHO SHOULD SET FUTURES MARGINS?

An issue that has dominated policy discussions since the crash has been that of index futures margins. Because percentage margins on futures are smaller than some margins required on purchases of stocks, the concern has been voiced that greater leverage can be achieved in the futures market than in the stock market, thus encouraging "speculation" and promoting greater volatility. Further, because stock margins are set by the

Federal Reserve, while futures margins are set "privately" by the futures exchanges, it has been argued, in the wake of the crash, that not only equalization, but governmental control of futures margins is necessary.

In our Preliminary Report we stated that we found no evidence that the level or method of setting futures margins had intensified the crash; and we cautioned that imposing fundamental changes in the setting of futures margins could easily have unintended and unpredictable consequences for the continued viability of the U.S. futures markets. None of the studies of the crash published since our Preliminary Report has caused us to alter those views. None of the studies, in fact, attempted any detailed or quantitative appraisal of the role of futures margins. Absent such documentation, we fear that the frequent references to margins in the summaries and in the policy sections of those Reports have only tended to reinforce widely-held misconceptions about margins and crashes, past as well as present.

Sixty years of academic research, for example, plus a thorough study by the staff of the Federal Reserve Board, have not succeeded in dispelling the misconception that stock market margins on the eve of the crash of 1929 were only ten percent; or that the vast bulk of shares on the NYSE were held in these low-margined accounts; or that the forced liquidation of those accounts under the pressure of margin calls was mainly responsible for the severity of the crash. As noted, however, not in the text, but only, alas, in an Appendix to the Brady Report:

> Beginning in the Summer of 1929, brokers began to increase margin requirements and by the time of the crash, actual margins were about 50 percent. Total outstanding margin debt at the time of the 1929 crash was equal to only about ten percent of the value of outstanding stocks. It is difficult, therefore, to imagine that margin calls were sufficient to account by themselves for any significant fraction of the secular decline in the stock market following the 1929 crash (Brady Report, Appendix A, Analytical Study VIII, p. VIII-2).[7]

Similarly, while many may have come to believe that the level of margins on index futures was a cause of the 1987 crash, the facts are that the entire open interest in margined index futures in October 1987 came to the share equivalent of only two percent of the value of shares listed on the NYSE; that so far from contracting in a liquidation panic under the

---

[7] Essentially similar findings were in *A Review and Evaluation of Federal Margin Regulation*, Board of Governors of the Federal Reserve System, December 1984

pressure of margin calls, the open interest in futures actually expanded slightly during the 19th; and that futures traders whose margin accounts were classified as "speculative" were, as noted earlier, substantial net buyers of futures, not sellers on the 19th.

Misconceptions about the role of futures margins, if translated improvidently into legislative or governmental policy decisions, could have significant consequences for the efficiency of markets. It is crucial, therefore, that the margin issue be addressed with a clear understanding both of the facts and of the valid purposes and functions of margins.

Futures Margins As Guarantees Of Contract Performance

Participants in futures markets buy and sell "contracts" that embody promises to make payments of a fixed sum at some future "delivery" date. The value of such a contract depends upon the relation between the fixed price and the value of some specified "spot" price at the maturity date of the contract. The credibility of such promises to pay in the future is maintained in part by requiring the parties, both the buyer and the seller of the obligation—and not just the buyer, as in stock market margins—to post collateral in the form of a cash margin with their brokers. Brokers in turn post margins with a clearing house member when they undertake a trade. For further protection, the margin account is marked to market daily. If the price movement during a day is favorable, and more margin is on deposit than needed, the excess is credited to the customer; but additional margin must be posted whenever prices move adversely and the value of the collateral on deposit falls below a specified maintenance margin level. Thus, knowing that continually updated margins will be required—and knowing also that the members of the clearing house, and ultimately the membership of the entire exchange, are committed to make good any failures—a trader may take a position in futures with no concern about the other party's ability to perform as promised because the clearing house is, in effect, substituted for the other party.

How Futures Margins Are Set By The Exchanges

Futures exchanges currently set their margins by economic standards comparable to those in any other private sector business. Exchanges have the institutional concern of protecting the financial integrity of their clearing system, and they are naturally aware of the basic economic importance of trading volume to their members' operations. They must, therefore, try to balance the gains to their members from a reduced risk of customer default against the higher costs that the extra degree of protection demanded might impose on the users of the system. Of course, individual members can, and do, elect on their own to increase customer margins on deposit with them to protect further their own obligations to meet exchange requirements. The margins required to meet the exchange's goals are not set arbitrarily, but depend, among other things, on the price volatility of the contract and the speed and assurance with which additional margin can be collected. Since the futures exchanges make their cash settlements daily, the margins they set have typically approximated the maximum price move likely in a single day, plus an added safety factor that can be further increased whenever the underlying price volatility suddenly increases. Margins are also lower for "hedgers" and spreaders than for speculators, since the hedger's position in the underlying commodity, or the spreader's in the offsetting contract, is itself an implicit guarantor of the resources required to fulfill the promise in the futures contract.

Performance of the margin process during the October crash

That the U.S. futures exchanges have in fact succeeded in finding an appropriate balance of costs and benefits in their margin policies—and that they have not short-sightedly sought to build up trading volume with margins set too low—is clear from their survival. On October 19, a day that saw the largest one-day price change ever recorded in the S&P 500 futures market, no trader suffered losses because of a contract default by a counterparty, no clearing house failed, and no futures clearing firm failed to meet its obligations to its customers, despite the unprecedented volume of margin-related cash flows and the intra-day margin calls.

This is not to suggest, of course, that no problems or difficulties with the clearing and margining process were encountered on October 19 and 20. Serious strains occurred, particularly in the options markets, where the setting of margins for writers of options, or for combinations of option positions, is technically more difficult than setting margins for futures. Even in the more experienced futures markets, however, rumors of impending collapse of particular brokers and clearing firms appear to have circulated at various times during the two days, unquestionably intensifying a sense of panic. Such apprehension can become important because margin accounts at clearing firms and the retail futures commission merchants have some of the characteristics of demand deposits in banks—not including federal deposit insurance. If rumors start that a brokerage firm is failing or that holders of under-margined accounts are not posting more cash because their banks are refusing to transfer funds, every holder of a margined futures position has an incentive to withdraw any free cash balance as quickly as possible and to refrain from further , even stabilizing ones.

Fortunately, the banking system, with the normal liquidity support to be expected from the Federal Reserve in a threatened crisis, was able to avert a financial collapse in October. Steps for further strengthening the liquidity support system, based in part on the experience gained during the crash, are already being taken by clearing firms and their banking connections. Whether this strengthening should aim for a unified clearing system covering stocks, options and futures as recommended in the Brady Report is far from clear, however. Competition in providing clearing services, like competition generally, can be a spur to innovation and improved efficiency. Some of the presumed gains from unified clearing, moreover, can be accomplished simply by better sharing of information between banks and clearing houses along lines already being implemented. We believe that if the economic advantages of unified clearing are as large and as unambiguous as the Brady Report suggests, the various exchanges will find ways in their mutual interest to bring about such a consolidation without specific legislative intervention.

The Costs Of Changing The Present System Of Setting Futures Margins

The demonstrated success of the margin policies of the private-sector futures exchanges carries with it a direct implication for public policy, albeit one that many who recognize that success seem reluctant to accept. If private-sector margin policies are currently being set on rational, economic grounds, and if they are passing the survivorship test, not only routinely, but in the face of the most dramatic market collapse in our history, then, absent clear evidence of what economists call "externalities," the adoption by a public sector regulator of any different set of policies can be presumed to be socially inefficient. In particular, the frequently heard call for 50-percent performance margins on index futures contracts—far higher than experience has shown necessary to protect the clearing process—would amount, in effect, to the imposition of a tax on futures transactions, although not a tax, of course, from which any government revenues would be collected. All the negative effects of an excise tax would be present, however, including in particular the reduction in sales volume. That higher margins, arbitrarily imposed, are effectively a tax on futures transactions must be emphasized. The tax is reduced, but not eliminated, by the interest paid on the account either directly by the broker or by the return on any U.S. Treasury bills deposited in lieu of cash. Funds tied up in such low-yield uses usurp other, more productive, opportunities for employing the resources.

The argument is sometimes made—indeed, we made the point in our Preliminary Report—that even a 50 percent margin requirements might not be onerous for true hedgers because they could, in principle, meet the margin requirement by depositing the assets against which they are selling the futures contract. Quite apart from the fact that 50 percent margins might leave no one in the market to take the other side of the hedgers' trades, the argument that high margins do not deter hedgers overlooks the small, perhaps, but still nontrivial, risk of banking large sums without insurance coverage.   Margin deposits, although segregated, are still ultimately at risk in the event of a catastrophic crash.   Therefore, a pension fund hoping to hedge 25 percent of a $1 billion portfolio of equities would, if faced with a 50 percent margin requirement, surely be reluctant to deposit as much as $125 million in cash or Treasury bills with an outside broker.   It would be even less likely to turn over custody of any substantial fraction of its $1 billion in shares merely to reduce the interest loss for pledging low-yield liquid assets. The most prudent strategy for such a fund for reducing its equity proportion thus may well be to avoid exchange-traded futures altogether and turn to substitutes—either selling $250 million of stocks and investing the proceeds in Treasury bills directly, or perhaps undertaking an equivalent hedging transaction on an overseas exchange or in an off-exchange dealer market.

Driving major classes of users to seek alternatives to futures exchanges not only reduces the revenues of those exchanges but undermines the liquidity and market depth that is, after all, the very reason for their existence.   Some of the calls for higher margins on futures appear, in fact, to have just such an undermining of the market's liquidity as an objective. The fear is that thanks in part to the development of index futures, the market for equities has become too sensitive to news and hence too volatile.   Whatever the merits of those arguments—and we, at least, do not find them persuasive—they do not appear to recognize the alternatives to futures transaction that pension funds and other large institutional investors already have at their disposal, let alone the alternatives not yet on stream, but that will surely be developed if the U.S. index futures markets can no longer function efficiently.

One of the alternatives to an index futures transaction is, of course, a transaction directly in the stocks that make up the index.   Some of the clamor for higher margins on index futures notably that in the Brady Report, appears to be less a call for killing the futures markets or reducing their liquidity than an appeal for restoring competitive equality between these two specific alternatives.

The point is made that whatever may be the original motivating differences between futures margins and stock market margins—good faith deposits in the case of futures, and down-payments on a purchase in the case of stocks—the margins are functionally equivalent for important classes of traders.   Many speculators, and even some longer-term investors, have a choice between buying futures on the one hand, and borrowing to buy stocks on the other, as a means of establishing a leveraged position in equities. If they invest on the stock side they must, of course, comply with the 50-percent initial cash margin requirement imposed under the Federal Reserve's margin regulations.   That requirement is far higher than the margin currently required by the futures exchanges for initial speculative positions in index futures—about 15 percent.

Futures Margins And Sock Market Margin: Some Misconceptions

In evaluating this competitive equality argument, however, it is important to avoid a number of widely-held misconceptions about current stock market margin rules.

First, very few stock market margins are currently at 50 percent. Market professionals, such as specialists and member broker-dealers are exempted from the regular margin rules. They must comply instead with certain minimum net capital requirements. The Brady Report puts these requirements as the effective equivalent of initial margins of 20 to 25 percent.

Second, not all stock market margins, or their equivalents, are set by the Federal Reserve System. The Federal Reserve sets only the initial margins. The critical maintenance margins—the requirements that trigger margin calls and any inter-market spillovers—are set by the stock exchanges. The maintenance margin for stocks, currently 25 percent, is as much a private sector responsibility as the maintenance margin for futures. Furthermore, it is not the Federal Reserve that sets the capital requirement for market professionals, a subject that was a concern to the Brady Commission. Those requirements arc set by the exchanges and self-regulatory bodies such as the National Association of Securities Dealers.

Third, rules on extensions of credit as well as the risk exposure to exchange member firms are very different in the two markets. Futures contracts, unlike stock, are marked to market daily, and in times of rapid price change are subject to intra-day margin calls. The objective of the futures margin system is to avoid the accumulation of credit obligations. An initial stock purchase, by contrast, need not be settled for five days, and if clearing house funds are used for payment, one additional business day may lapse. Maintenance margin calls, moreover, particularly for good customers, are much less peremptory for stocks than for futures. In other words, larger cash buffers are substituted by stock brokers for the quicker speed of collection approach adopted by the futures industry.

Finally, the 50-percent initial margin requirement applicable in the cash market applies to individual stocks, while index futures contracts relate to portfolios of stocks. It is a well-accepted principle of finance that the price volatility of a portfolio of stocks is less than that of any of its particular components. Hence, if the function of margins is to protect the integrity of the clearing process, margins on baskets of stocks *should* be lower than on individual stocks—and if margins on stock baskets were to be set in the private sector, like those on futures, they presumably *would* be lower. The problem of competitive inequality would disappear.

Federal Reserve Margin Rules And Speculative Excesses: A Skeptical View

That so simple a solution to making margins consistent as removing the Federal Reserve altogether has not so far been seriously proposed is testimony to the lingering power of the notion that control over stock market margins plays an important role in controlling excessive leverage and speculation. The conventional wisdom, echoed repeatedly in the Brady Report, is that the control of leveraged investment in stocks through the Federal Reserve margin rules is necessary to curb speculative excesses. It is worth noting, however, that the Federal Reserve itself, in its 1984 staff study and evaluation of margin rules, was far less confident than the Brady Report about the role of stock market margins in this respect. The Fed's detailed historical review of market volatility turned up no discernible relation between stock margin levels, or margin changes, and market movements, either in the aggregate or for particular, highly speculative stocks. In the report's words, the evidence pointed up "the lack of any positive demonstration that margin regulation has served to dampen stock price fluctuation" (FRB Study, p. 163).

Certainly the Board's actual decisions on margins over the years suggest no great confidence in that agency's ability to affect speculation. The current initial margin of 50 percent was set in 1974 and has been kept unchanged at that level ever since. Nor is the Federal Reserve justly to be censured for this passive policy. Neither economics nor legislation offers any clear guidelines to the Federal Reserve as to when speculative "excess" is in fact occurring. Absent any universally accepted indicator that the stock market is at, or approaching, a level that is unsustainably high, can the Federal Reserve Board reasonably be expected to take dramatic steps to curb stock market credit, and thus risk precipitating a panic that might, like the crash of 1987, reduce national wealth by half a trillion dollars? Or, if trading volume is languishing, can the Federal Reserve reasonably be expected to lower appreciably a margin rate that has remained unchanged for almost 15 years, particularly with a recent major crash still so vividly in memory?

The political setting in which the Fed necessarily operates will inevitably cause it to act with great caution—particularly against the backdrop of its own 1984 study, which reflects strong misgivings about the utility and effectiveness of margins as a tool for curbing "speculative" investment and market volatility. In short, public sector controllers of margins—whether the Fed, the SEC, or the CFTC, and whether directly responsible or merely exercising final review powers—bear only the political costs of being charged with setting margins too "low" should another crash occur. The natural tendency, therefore, will be to avoid setting margin levels that might subject the agency in the future to public criticism and political pressures. Margins set in the private sector, by contrast, can go up and down as economic circumstances change because the exchanges themselves both bear the costs and get the benefits of setting margins too high or too low.

Margin Rules As A Private-Sector Responsibility

We recommend, therefore, that the equalization of margins called for by the Brady Report be undertaken in the most direct way possible, namely by turning over to the private sector those remaining parts of the stock margin process still administered by the Federal Reserve System. We recognize, of course, that in an important sense the issue of competitive equality of initial speculative margins may already have become academic, although some in New York may believe futures margins are still inadequate. The Board of Governors of the CME has recently voted to raise initial speculative margins to 15 percent—a level that may be higher than would originally have been set in the past for the day-to-day volatility currently being experienced. Margin levels higher than needed to protect the settlement process may perhaps serve to deflect political pressure from the futures markets in the short run; but if long maintained they are also likely to add impetus to the kind of search for cheaper methods of portfolio adjustment that led to the development of index futures in the first place.

Trading Halts And Circuit Breakers

The tidal wave of selling on October 19 had effects on both the New York and Chicago exchanges that were similar in all essential respects to those that afflict an electric power utility when all its customers turn on their air conditioners at once. The demand for service then exceeds the systems' capacity to supply it at normal cost and a variety of formal and informal rationing and "peak-load pricing" mechanisms come into play. In the equity markets these peak-load pricing and rationing adjustments took the form of widened bid-ask spreads, large gaps between successive prices, over-loaded printer buffers, crossed markets, lost orders, unanswered telephones, bans on program trading, and so on, as described in great detail in the Brady Report, and the SEC Report, as well as in the report of the General Accounting Office.[8]   Under such conditions of system overload, the Brady Report's call for the installation of circuit breakers is certainly understandable, and the possible need for circuit breakers has been a concern of the exchanges themselves, as well.

Shortly before our Committee was formed, the CME had, in fact, instituted temporary 30-point per day price limits for its S&P 500 contact—a limit of approximately 15 percent. Daily price limits had, of course, long been a feature of commodity futures contracts and even financial futures contracts, notably Treasury bond futures, but had been dropped from stock index futures shortly after their introduction. We summarized in our Preliminary Report the main arguments for and against making those temporary limits a permanent feature of the contract and we need not repeat them here. Since a 15-percent limit would be reached only very rarely, our inclination was toward keeping the 15-percent limits in place on stock index contracts, particularly if the consequences of reaching the price limit were to trigger only a brief pause, rather than a halt in trading activity until the next trading day.

In the several months since we submitted our Preliminary Report, however, the CME has reduced the daily price limits to 15 points—roughly seven percent—and has instituted a smaller five-point limit—about 2.5 percent—at the opening. We have no great concern with the new limit at the opening since the delay before trading may be resumed in only ten minutes. All of the studies of the crash have shown that congestion and confusion on October 19 and 20—and even later in the week—was greatest at the open and, as we suggested in our Preliminary Report, some rethinking of opening procedures in all of the markets was clearly needed. The new 15-point daily limit, however, is only half that of the initial margin and hence appears narrower than needed to protect the integrity of the clearing process. Limits that narrow are likely to slow the return to equilibrium. If so, they serve only to reduce the value of the market to hedgers, to exacerbate problems at the resumption of trading and, over the longer run, to weaken the case for maintaining futures exchanges— particularly U.S. futures exchanges—as a primary medium for portfolio transactions by large institutional investors.

The same concerns apply with equal or greater force to the price limits recently proposed by the NYSE that would deny access to the Exchange's

---

[8] General Accounting Office, "Financial Markets: Preliminary Observations on the October 1987 Crash," January 1988 (GAO/GGD-88-38).

Designated Order Turnaround ("DOT") system for program trading once a price movement of 50 points on the Dow Jones Industrial Average—about three percent—is experienced on any given trading day. Rationing access to the DOT system does not, of course, completely sever the link between the cash and futures markets. Theoretically, index arbitrage could still be carried out manually, as it was before DOT was available, but only at a slower pace and subject to more uncertainty.[9] The higher costs of program trading in New York widen the arbitrage bounds around the index and hence raise the effective costs of trading index futures in Chicago as well. Moreover, the higher cost of hedging positions in Chicago reduces the ability of the block-trading desks in New York to take positions, which in turn reduces the market-making capacity of the NYSE's specialists, thus raising the cost of trading for everyone.

Removing Regulatory Obstacles To Market Efficiency

The exchanges are privately-owned business organizations, and as outside observers with no investments at stake, we are reluctant to offer advice about specific methods for making or processing transactions, or about other details of running those businesses. We understand that the NYSE is currently planning computer capacity for a one-billion share day. In fact, we suspect that if the orders were to come in large enough lots and at a steady enough pace, the NYSE could handle a load that size even with its present capacity.

The challenge, however, as we see it, is not one of meeting maximum processing targets for a few rare peak days, but of developing market mechanisms that can, over the longer run, better accommodate the trading needs of the public, and especially the portfolio-based trading of large, institutional investors. None of the reports on the crash, we believe, has faced up to this critical issue. The main preoccupation of the Brady Commission has not been with the needs of the users, but with the lack of a unified regulatory structure. This focus, we believe, is misdirected. The chaos and confusion of October 19 and 20 may well have been compounded by regulatory failure, but if so it was not so much a failure to coordinate policies across agency lines, as a failure of the policies themselves.

---

[9] Under a NYSE rule adopted in February, member firms are prohibited from using the DOT system for index arbitrage program trading on any day during which the Dow Jones Industrial Average moves more than 50 points. The first such movement after adoption of the rule occurred on April 6, 1988. According to a press report, sophisticated traders who were prepared for a shutdown of DOT simply switched to manual execution to perform index arbitrage. One floor broker stated "It made things slightly less efficient, but they could still do the trades." *The Wall Street Journal*, April 8, 1988, p. 3.

We propose to call attention here to some of these long-standing regulatory policies that, we believe, served to weaken market structure and performance on October 19 and 20, and that will continue to inhibit the expansion of market capacity, at least in the U.S., for institutional trading.

The "Uptick" Rule

The SEC's so-called "uptick" rule[10] governing short sales of registered stock on a securities exchange allows short sales to be executed only at a price higher than the price of the last different trade price preceding it. Hence when prices are falling, as they were through much of October 19 and 20, short sales by public traders are effectively ruled out. The rule was introduced originally, and is still defended by some today, as a way of preventing "bear raids" against the shares of thinly-traded corporations.

An unintended consequence of the uptick rule, however, has been to keep selling pressures from being spread efficiently between the index futures market and the stock market. When selling pressures happen to hit the futures market first, the market makers on and around the floor absorb the initial shock into inventory, hoping this will be a temporary condition. Should still more selling orders arrive before these initial positions have been offset, increasingly large price concessions must be offered to the market makers to induce them to commit what may still remain of their available capital resources. Additional capacity can be made available from the stock market, however, if index arbitragers can take over some of the market makers' inventory of futures contracts and simultaneously sell shares to market makers and other buyers in the cash markets.

By blocking short sales of stock markets, the uptick rule limits index arbitrage to the smaller number of players who happen to be long in those of the underlying stocks that are not trading above previous trades at different prices. If the access of futures traders to the additional market-making capacity of the stock market is reduced, price concessions in the futures market, and hence the effective cost of transacting there, must increase. Some transactors who might otherwise have preferred to sell futures are then driven to sell stock directly; and some who might have preferred to buy stock are driven to buy futures. Distortions in normal trading patterns of precisely this kind, representing substantial increases in the effective costs of trading to all market participants, were a conspicuous feature of the markets throughout the entire week of October 19.

---

[10] Rule 10a-1(a) (1) of the SEC's General Rules and Regulations under the Securities Exchange Act of 1934.

The 30-Percent "Short-Short" Rule

The pernicious effects of the SEC's uptick rule in weakening inter-market linkage have long been known both to academic researchers and to market professionals. However, the adverse consequences, particularly on October 19 and 20, of an important provision of the Internal Revenue Code, section 851(b) (3), have so far gone largely unremarked. Under this section, often dubbed the "30-percent" or "short-short" rule, a regulated investment company, such as a mutual fund, may derive no more than 30 percent of its earnings for any taxable year from the sale of securities held for less than three months. Profits from a futures or options transaction, even when resulting merely from the closing out of a successful futures or options hedge, fall under the rule, and when the market falls as far as it did on October 19, even partial hedges can quickly exceed the rule's limits, with the result that the fund's entire earnings, not just its profit on the futures component of the hedge, become subject to full income taxation. It is not surprising, in view of this rule, that mutual funds in the U.S. have virtually shunned the futures markets.

The effects of the 30-percent rule in keeping mutual funds and the effects of many state insurance statutes in keeping insurance companies from employing futures or options are particularly significant in the light of the substantial and persistent discounts of futures under the cash index on October 19 and thereafter. Mutual funds and insurance companies seeking "yield enhancement" are natural buyers of underpriced futures; to the extent that they can anticipate regular inflows of cash subscriptions, they are, in effect, precisely the kind of potential institutional "sellers" of portfolio insurance whose absence has caused major concern over the possibly destabilizing effects of portfolio insurance.

Position Limits And Sunshine Trading

Position limits raise issues that are similar in many respects to those discussed earlier in the setting of futures margins. When the position limits are set by the exchanges and their clearing firms they give little ground for concern. The incentives to balance costs and benefits are appropriate, exactly as with margins. But when the limits are set by outside regulators, the emphasis of the regulators is inevitably less on strict economic efficiency than on avoiding being seen as too soft on "manipulation" or "speculation." The position limits are thus likely to be set below those that the exchanges would consider reasonable on their own, and in the process to introduce unintended market distortions and imbalances.

We noted earlier, for example, the effect of the SEC-mandated position limits on exchange-traded options as a factor in keeping institutions out of the option market, and, in particular, in inducing many portfolio insurers to turn to constructing synthetic puts with futures. At the same time, the CFTC's position limits on "speculative" holdings of futures were intensifying the seller-buyer imbalance in the futures market, because the limits on the speculator buyers are much smaller than those on the portfolio-insurer hedger sellers.

We recommend, therefore, that both the SEC and the CFTC undertake a thorough re-examination of their policies on position limits for index options and futures. Whether or not there is a rationale for traditional position limits in thinly-traded markets, where there may be some threat of cornering, mandated position limits appear to be pointless, at best, in the index markets, and quite possibly destabilizing.

We believe also that the CFTC should give urgent priority to a review of what has come to be called "sunshine trading." Under sunshine trading, a pension fund or portfolio insurer intending to sell a large number of futures contracts announces that intention in advance. The possible buyers, having been notified of what is being put up for sale, can then develop purchase plans in the spirit of an announced public auction. Under current CFTC rules, however, such an announcement might be construed as "prearranged trading"—although even now it is far from clear how the CFTC would have responded to a selling announcement by a large portfolio insurer on October 19. In the face of that uncertainty no one, apparently, was willing to try. Instead, some big selling orders were sent directly to the pit where they strained the capacity of the locals.

Open-outcry futures markets are remarkably efficient trading facilities, but they cannot be expected to do everything. They tend to be most effective when the order flow is continual and heavy, but the typical order is small relative to the combined capital of the market makers in and around the pit. The agricultural futures pits, in their heyday, could offer deep and liquid markets because the industry's heavy capacity was all on the floor. The NYSE, by contrast, adopted the franchised specialist system long ago, not for any unique advantages that that system of market-making possesses, but simply because the order flow for the typical stock was too small and too irregular to support a pit of competing market makers. When the fixed commission was finally eliminated in the early 1970s, and block trading by institutional investors surged, the effective trading market for many big customers moved off the trading floor altogether and on to the trading desks and screens of the large broker-dealers.

The relation of institutional trading to financial futures markets has been subject to a quite different evolution. The first financial futures were in foreign exchange, where a huge, dealer-based "upstairs" forward market already existed—and, along with the off-exchange "swap" market still, in fact, dominates the transaction flow. The upstairs dealer markets in U.S. Treasury securities were also well-established long before futures trading was opened in those instruments. But for stock index futures, there was, and still is, no functioning, alternative dealer-based market in the baskets of stocks that are now the relevant trading unit for so many institutional investors. Institutional investors have become the main force in equity futures; but they are not on the floor and the rules governing their dealings off the floor are far from clear.

We do not mean to suggest, of course, that allowing upstairs block trading of futures or of stock baskets would be an unmixed blessing and that regulation should encourage it. There are important social benefits in centralized, competitive public markets, especially for "price discovery." Off-exchange trading also raises serious concerns about regulatory "free-riding." Clearly, many delicate trade-offs must be studied and appraised before a coherent regulatory policy can be developed. But we fear that the delays may be retarding development of new ways of adapting futures markets to the needs of traders, particularly large institutional traders.

A FINAL NOTE

In the face of so many commissions and studies inspired by the October 1987 crash, we are reluctant to recommend the formation of still another study group. There is a clear need, however, to examine the capital markets and their regulation from a perspective broader than that of a single day or week and with a concern beyond that of the individual investor. In the wake of an event as dramatic as the crash there is a great tendency to look for easy or politically appealing remedies, "fixes" that can be put in place quickly. It is this spirit, we believe, that has caused such clamor for changes in margin rules, despite the absence of evidence that margins had any relation to October's events, let alone evidence that variable margin requirements can be effectively administered by a public body to dampen "excessive" speculation or curb volatility. Any new study group should include—as principals, not merely as support staff— professional economists who are knowledgeable about futures markets and especially some who have contributed to the revolution in the economics profession's thinking about market regulation that has taken place over the last 50 years. The time for an in-depth study of market mechanisms—a study focusing on means for removing impediments and restrictions that inhibit the efficient functioning of the market—has indeed arrived.

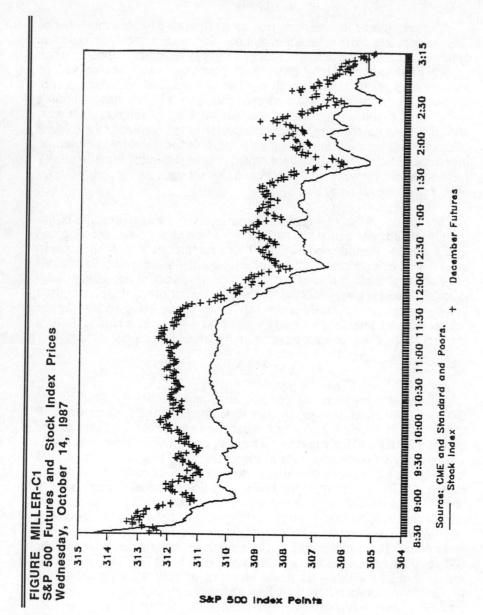

FIGURE MILLER-C1
S&P 500 Futures and Stock Index Prices
Wednesday, October 14, 1987

Source: CME and Standard and Poors. + December Futures

—— Stock Index

S&P 500 Index Points

FIGURE MILLER-C2
S&P 500 Futures Value Minus Fair Value
Wednesday, October 14, 1987

Source: CME and Standard and Poors.

FIGURE MILLER-C3
S&P 500 Futures and Stock Index Prices
Thursday, October 15, 1987

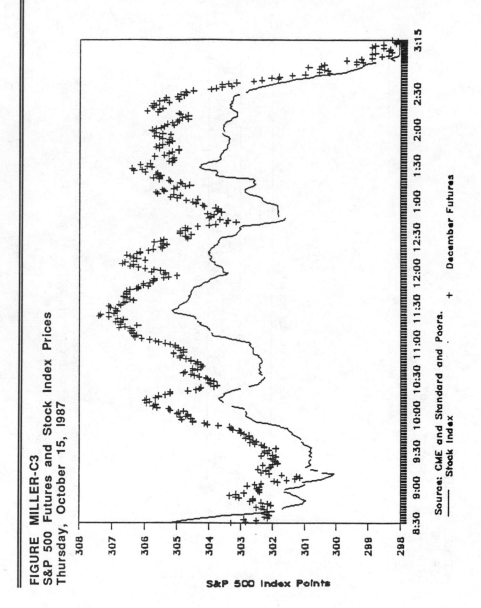

Source: CME and Standard and Poors.

—— Stock Index   + December Futures

S&P 500 Index Points

FIGURE MILLER-C4
S&P 500 Futures Value Minus Fair Value
Thursday, October 15, 1987

Source: CME and Standard and Poors.

FIGURE MILLER-C5
S&P 500 Futures and Stock Index Prices
Friday, October 16, 1987

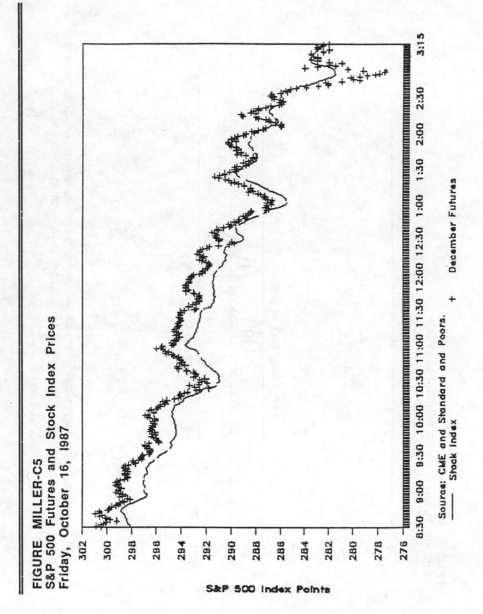

S&P 500 Index Points

Source: CME and Standard and Poors.   +   December Futures
——— Stock Index

FIGURE MILLER-C6
S&P 500 Futures Value Minus Fair Value
Friday, October 16, 1987

Source: CME and Standard and Poors.

FIGURE MILLER-C7
S&P 500 Futures and Stock Index Prices
Monday, October 19, 1987

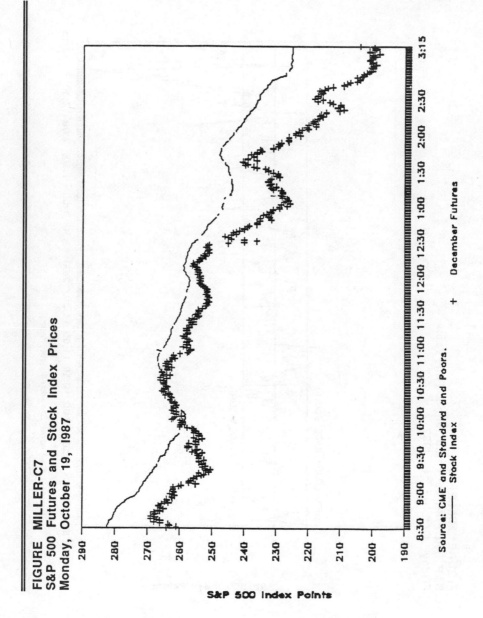

S&P 500 Index Points

Source: CME and Standard and Poors.
—— Stock Index   +   December Futures

FIGURE MILLER-C8
S&P 500 Futures Value Minus Fair Value
Monday, October 19, 1987

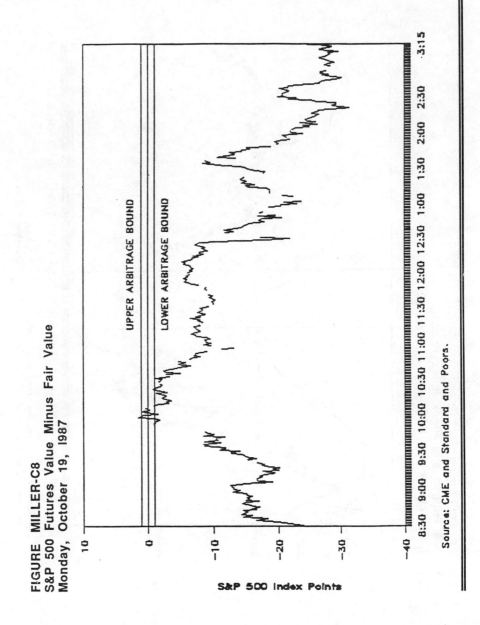

Source: CME and Standard and Poors.

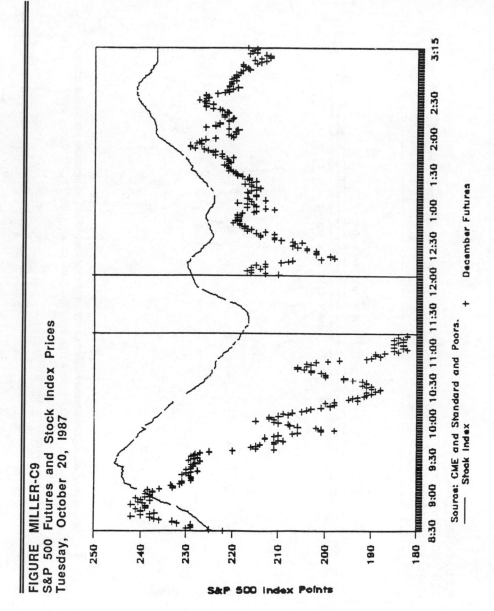

FIGURE MILLER-C9
S&P 500 Futures and Stock Index Prices
Tuesday, October 20, 1987

Source: CME and Standard and Poors.
— Stock Index   +   December Futures

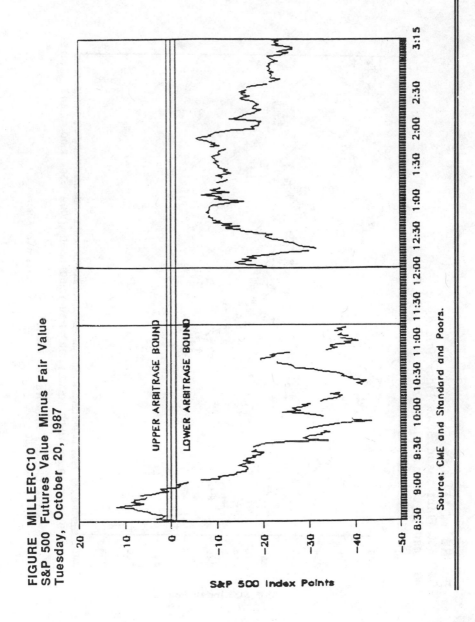

FIGURE MILLER-C10
S&P 500 Futures Value Minus Fair Value
Tuesday, October 20, 1987

Source: CME and Standard and Poors.

FIGURE MILLER-C11
S&P 500 Futures and Stock Index Prices
Wednesday, October 21, 1987

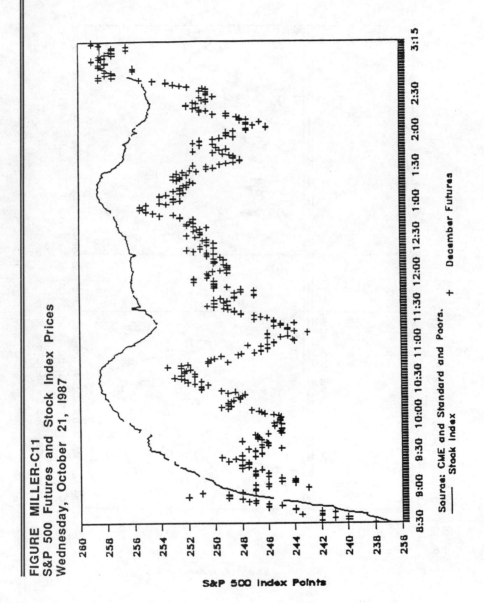

S&P 500 Index Points

Source: CME and Standard and Poors.   +   December Futures
                                       ——   Stock Index

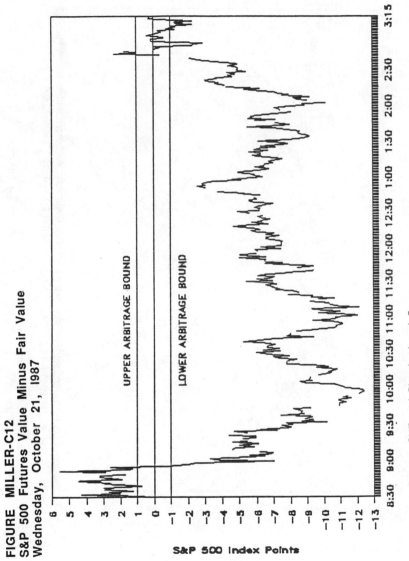

FIGURE MILLER-C12
S&P 500 Futures Value Minus Fair Value
Wednesday, October 21, 1987

S&P 500 Index Points

UPPER ARBITRAGE BOUND

LOWER ARBITRAGE BOUND

Sources: CME and Standard and Poors.

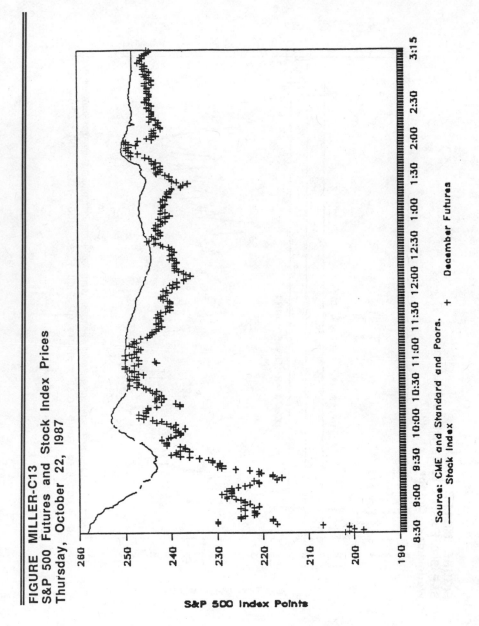

FIGURE MILLER-C13
S&P 500 Futures and Stock Index Prices
Thursday, October 22, 1987

Source: CME and Standard and Poors.   +   December Futures
     —— Stock Index

S&P 500 Index Points

FIGURE MILLER-C14
S&P 500 Futures Value Minus Fair Value
Thursday, October 22, 1987

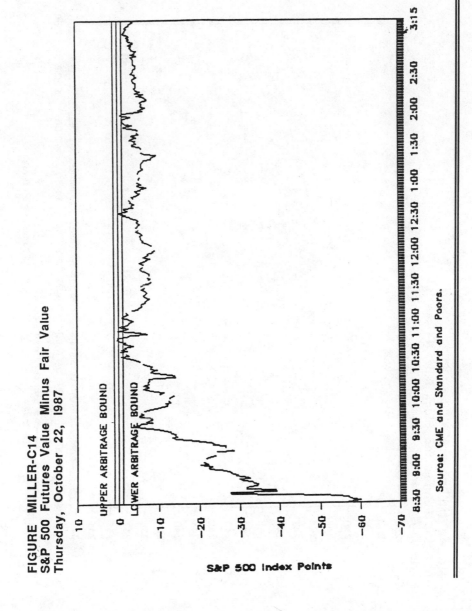

Source: CME and Standard and Poors.

FIGURE MILLER-C15
S&P 500 Futures and Stock Index Prices
Friday, October 23, 1987

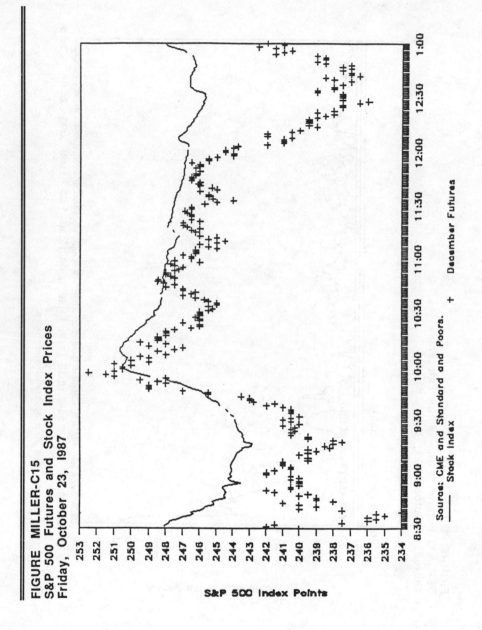

Source: CME and Standard and Poors.   +   December Futures
——— Stock Index

S&P 500 Index Points

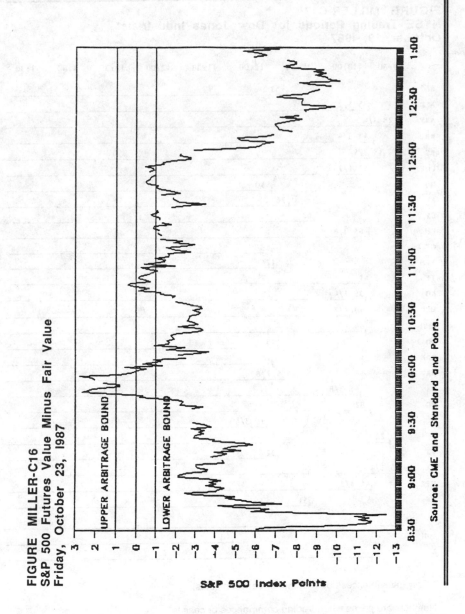

FIGURE MILLER-C16
S&P 500 Futures Value Minus Fair Value
Friday, October 23, 1987

Sources: CME and Standard and Poors.

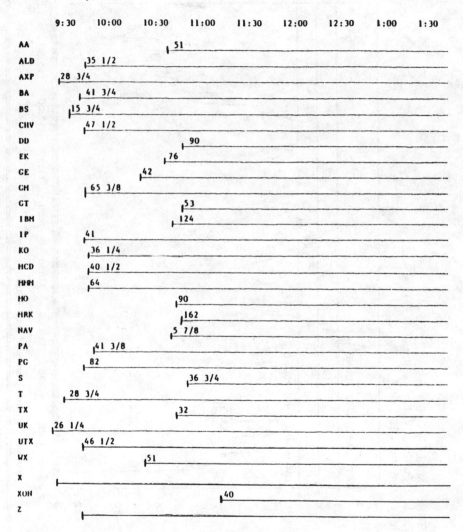

FIGURE MILLER-C17
NYSE Trading Periods for Dow Jones Industrials*
October 19, 1987

* Only gaps in excess of 10 minutes between sales.

Numbers are prices when trading commences or ceases.
Source F.E. Fitch, Inc. (New York Stock Exchange)

FIGURE MILLER-C18
NYSE Trading Periods for Dow Jones Industrials*
October 20, 1987

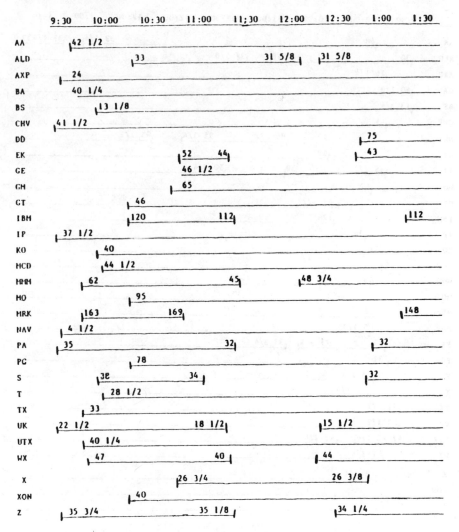

* Only gaps in excess of 10 minutes between sales.

Numbers are prices when trading commences or ceases.
Source F.E. Fitch, Inc. (New York Stock Exchange)

FIGURE MILLER-C19
NYSE Trading Periods for Dow Jones Industrials*
October 21, 1987

| | 9:30 | 10:00 | 10:30 | 11:00 | 11:30 | 12:00 | 12:30 | 1:00 | 1:30 |

AA — 40 ... 39 1/4 ... 39 1/4 39
ALD — 36 ... 37 5/8 ... 37 5/8
AXP — 26 1/4
BA — 40 1/8
BS — 13 3/4
CHV — 46
DD — 86 1/2 ... 85 3/4 ... 85 1/2
EK — 59
GE — 49 1/2 ... 50 ... 50 3/4
GM — 62
GT — 47 1/2
IBM — 124
IP — 38
KO — 41
MCD — 42
MMM — 63
MO — 95
MRK — 167
NAV — 5 1/2
PA — 33 ... 33 3/4 ... 33 3/4
PG — 81
S — 37 3/4
T — 29 1/4
TX — 31 1/2
UK — 23 1/2
UTX — 42 43 1/4 ... 43 1/4
WX — 52 3/4
X — 28 3/4
XON — 43
Z — 35 1/2

* Only gaps in excess of 10 minutes between sales.

Numbers are prices when trading commences or ceases.
Source F.E. Fitch, Inc. (New York Stock Exchange)

Preliminary Report of the Committee of Inquiry

Appointed by the Chicago Mercantile Exchange

Introduction

The extraordinary decline in world equity markets that occurred in October 1987, has significantly affected investors and created widespread concern among members of Congress, regulatory bodies and the public. There is little consensus concerning the causes of the events or the steps required to prevent a reoccurrence. There is, however, widespread agreement that it is important to develop an understanding of the relevant facts, so that any proposed remedial steps will not increase the risks inherent in investment activities.

The focus of this Committee's inquiry is not upon the underlying macroeconomic events and circumstances surrounding the decline. Nor is our Preliminary Report intended as a treatise on how futures markets work. We are not advocates for any particular institution or point of view. Rather, we have seen our task as requiring a careful and specific look at the performance of the market provided by the Chicago Mercantile Exchange for trading in a futures contract based upon the Standard and Poor's 500 stock price index in mid-October 1987.

Our inquiry was driven by one principal question: Did index futures markets cause, accelerate, alleviate, or have some other impact on the precipitous market decline of October 19?

Our focus is upon the activities in the markets during October: The impact of the trading "mechanics," futures-related strategies, and the relation between activity on the CME and on the stock exchanges. We then review and evaluate actions taken by the CME during this period.

The Committee had broad authority to investigate CME operations and to recommend possible modification to CME policies. The Committee has met with senior officers and staff of the CME, and at the direction of the Committee, the staff compiled and analyzed various statistical information.

The Committee has received complete cooperation from the CME and its staff.

The Comittee believes it appropriate to issue a Preliminary Report so that the information compiled can be made available to regulators and other interested persons.

There are a number of points that the reader should bear in mind in reviewing this Preliminary Report: The Committee to date has focused on empirical data concerning market transactions, and has not attempted to assemble a large body of interview data. While anecdotal evidence is significant and must be considered, the Committee believes that caution must be used in evaluating such evidence, since individual traders are rarely positioned to have a good overall perspective on market events. The Committee is aware that others are in the process of analyzing the events of October and that hearings will be held by various regulatory bodies and by committees of the Congress. Our contribution lies in evaluating the empirical record.

We did not review developments in other markets, except to the extent their actions directly affected or related to trading in the index futures market at the CME. Others undoubtedly will be looking, in depth, at the performance of the stock and options markets and will evaluate various possible remedial steps, such as improving and expanding the capability of the New York Stock Exchange's Designated Order Turnaround system for computerized order-taking, revising the NYSE "specialist" system, and strengthening the capital of market intermediaries. That review is beyond the scope of this Preliminary Report. We believe that the October price shock, as any dramatic event, must serve as a catalyst for constructive review. We hope that this review will prompt careful thinking about the markets and result in further and better coordination among the CME, the NYSE, and other markets.

We fear that uninformed demands for a quick fix could compel policymakers to look to the government as the arbiter for "correcting" the markets. We anticipate that the events of October will spur the exchanges themselves to review their own procedures and to work toward an even higher level of cooperation. Government oversight should encourage this review, but because of the complicated and highly sensitive nature of these markets, we think it would not be wise for government to attempt to mandate specific changes.

The capital markets are increasingly complex and experts commonly disagree about the effect of proposed changes in economic policy or regulation. Even "noncontroversial" changes in a stable economic environment can lead to unanticipated and far-reaching results. While we must strive to understand the events of October and to make changes that are warranted, we must take equal care to avoid damaging a market system that has fostered unprecedented economic prosperity.

Prelude to the Crash

Stock market prices peaked in August, and then declined gradually through September. The decline accelerated in early October, with a total drop of over five percent during the week of October 5, and with further large losses on October 14 and 15. Finally, the pre-crash decline culminated with a five percent drop on October 16, the largest one-day point move on record at that time. In total, the index declined by about 14 percent between the open on October 5 and the close on October 16.

The price move on October 16 provides a useful backdrop to the events of the next week. Figure Miller-C5 shows both the price of the S&P 500 futures contract, and the value of the S&P 500 "cash index," which represents the weighted average prices of the 500 index stocks. As is evident, the futures price maintained a reasonably consistent spread above the index price. The correct or "fair" value of this spread reflects the slightly different characteristics of the futures and the stocks, and depends both on the average dividend rate of the stocks, and on short-term interest rates.

Under normal conditions, the futures price is held close to the level consistent with interest rates and expected dividends ("fair value") by the activity of index arbitrage, also called program trading. When a sharp change in demand or supply on one market pushes its price away from fair value, arbitrage traders step in to buy the cheaper instrument, while simultaneously selling the more expensive one. This trading keeps the markets in line, and diffuses supply and demand shocks across related markets, thereby moderating the impact on any one market. Arbitrage locks in a profit when properly executed, but arbitrage programs always create the risk of losses for the trader if not precisely executed. This problem becomes especially acute when prices are changing rapidly, or when execution in one of the markets becomes difficult or slow.

Despite the sharp price decline and volatile market on October 16 the spread remained close to fair value throughout the day, reflecting continued, successful arbitrage trading. Toward the end of the day, however, and particularly between 2:30 p.m. and 3:00 p.m. Central Standard Time, the spread dropped sharply below fair value, as illustrated in Figure Miller-C6.[1] Figure Miller-P1, which shows the net activity of broker-dealers by 15-minutes intervals, verifies that trading by these firms, which generally conduct a substantial fraction of total arbitrage activity, slowed after 1:45 p.m.[2] The absence of arbitrage allowed the futures price to fall to a discount below the cash index, although the size of the discount was small compared to those that were to follow over the next few days.

The activity on October 16 also provides an introductory view of another widely discussed strategy—portfolio insurance. Portfolio insurance provides institutions with a means of placing a lower bound on their return, at least under normal conditions. An institution that requires a seven percent minimum return for its beneficiaries, for example, can afford to take a reasonable amount of risk when its current portfolio is earning 12 percent. Such an institution might want to increase its exposure to the stock market, thereby increasing the returns its investors can expect. However, a stock price decline that lowered the portfolio's return to nine percent would place the fund much closer to its minimum acceptable return. Under these conditions, the institution might seek to reduce its risk by selling some of its stock, and substituting cash or bonds. This strategy, generically know as portfolio insurance, generates stock purchases after a price increase and sales after a decline. These purchases and sales often occur in futures rather than directly in stock, because transaction costs for baskets of stocks are normally lower in futures.

Portfolio insurance is only one of many futures-related strategies used by institutions to manage their risk. Most hedging strategies, however, do not generate the kind of concentrated buying and selling associated with portfolio insurance.

---

[1] The price of an S&P 500 contract on the CME is $500 times the index, so at 282, for example, each contract is worth $500 X 282, or $141,000. Accordingly, a move of one point in the index will reflect a change of $500 value in the contract. The discount from fair value of almost five points that occurred just before 3:00 p.m. is thus worth about $2,500 per contract. Since the transaction costs of arbitrage are about $500 per contract—arising largely from brokerage costs on the stock side of the arbitrage—arbitrage will usually eliminate any deviation larger than one S&P point away from fair value.

[2] This analysis was constructed from CME trade data, and includes those accounts in each 15 minute period that had net position changes of more than 40 contracts. This methodology will generate somewhat different totals than an analysis based on daily position change data, although the results are broadly consistent.

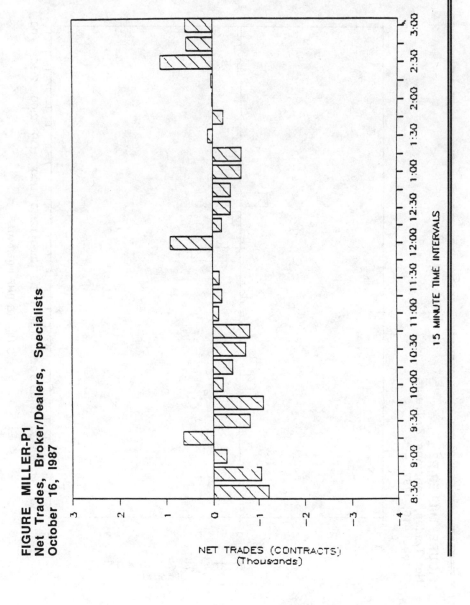

FIGURE MILLER-P1
Net Trades, Broker/Dealers, Specialists
October 16, 1987

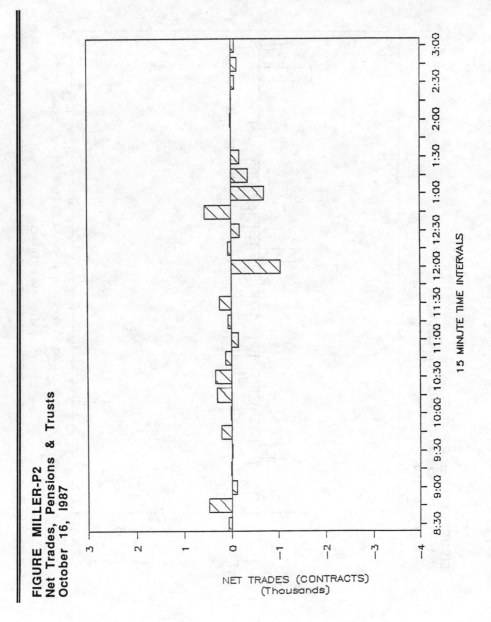

FIGURE MILLER-P2
Net Trades, Pensions & Trusts
October 16, 1987

Figure Miller-P2 shows net activity by pension funds and trusts by 15 minute intervals on October 16. This group includes the major portfolio insurers, although not all activity in this category represents insurance. As we would expect, following the substantial declines of October 14 and 15, these institutions were net sellers throughout most of the day on October 16, although they stopped selling after 1:30 p.m. CST. Insurance sales thus contributed selling pressure throughout the day, but probably did not participate in the final 700 points of the 1500 point S&P decline.

In summary, the futures market functioned normally through a week of heavy selling pressure prior to the crash, without any important loss of liquidity, and without falling away from its correct relation to the underlying stocks. However, a more difficult test lay ahead.

Events of the Week of October 19

With this brief look back at how the markets fared prior to October 19, we turn now to the events on the critical days of October 19 and 20. We will first present a factual review of events, and will then return to provide a deeper analysis. The relation between the S&P 500 cash and futures prices throughout Monday, October 19 is shown in Figure Miller-C7. Figure Miller-C8 graphs the spread between the two price series along with the estimated arbitrage boundaries.

The difference between these charts and those of the previous Wednesday or Friday is striking. Note first the enormous gap between the opening futures price on Monday at 264 and the reported index cash value at 283. This discount of the futures price below the cash price of some 19 points (about seven percent) was unprecedented.[3]   The largest discount seen even in the previous week of somewhat hectic trading had been the gap noted earlier of some four points (about 1.4 percent) shortly before the close on Friday. Since the lower arbitrage trigger point is normally only about one point below fair value, a discount of as much as 19 points might well have suggested that a tidal wave of sell programs was likely to come. Perhaps no single event over the entire two-day span was more responsible than this 19 point gap at the opening for creating the impression that the futures market had initiated the collapse (presumably under the pressures of portfolio insurance selling) and had dragged the cash market down inexorably in its wake. We will return to re-examine this issue in the next few pages.

---

[3] A point gap is worth $500 X 19 = $9,500 per contract, far above the normal arbitrage "trigger points" of about $500 above or below fair value.

That some arbitrage-driven program trading or portfolio insurance selling did indeed take place immediately after the opening will be documented later. Whatever the reason, it is certainly clear from Figure Miller-C8 that the discount had closed steadily to little more than half its opening value by 9:00 a.m. CST. Although it had widened again by 9:30 a.m. CST, something very close to the normal relations between the two series had been reestablished. To be sure, volume in both markets had been heavy to that point and the new downward price movement of about seven percent was large by past standards. But the markets were functioning normally at that point and seemed successfully to have absorbed what we will hereafter call the "Opening Shock."

Somewhere shortly before 11:00 a.m. CST, however, a new phase in the market evolution clearly commenced. The futures price slipped below the cash price again, with the discount steadily between four and eight points (two to four percent) over the next 90 minutes, and with downward jumps in the futures price series carrying the discount on occasion to as much as 12 points (five percent). At around 12:30 p.m. CST, a large drop of about 15 points (six percent) over the space of a few minutes showed up in the futures price series. The phase we shall call the "Mid-day Plunge" then proceeded rapidly. Gaps and discontinuities in the price series appeared frequently and, despite some occasional temporary rallies, the trend in the futures price was sharply down to the close. Admittedly, examination of the evidence reflected in Figure Miller-C8 seems to suggest that the futures were not only down, but had led the way throughout the collapse. Again, we will return to re-examine this issue.

At the opening on Tuesday, October 20, a semblance of stability had been restored. As Figures Miller-C9 and C10 show, the futures contract opened in its normal positon above the cash price, although the positive spread of ten points (four percent) reached at 9:00 a.m. CST would seem abnormally high by past "cost-of-carry" standards.[4]

The apparent stability did not endure, however. By shortly after 9:00 CST, the futures market entered a new phase, which may be called the "Tuesday Morning Collapse." Prices fell even more rapidly over the next two hours than they had during Monday afternoon. By 11:00 a.m. CST, the discount of futures below the cash prices had reached 37 points (a gap of 17 percent, given the then current index value of about 221). Shortly after 11:15 a.m. CST, trading in the S&P 500 contract was halted on the CME.

---

[4] As explained above, expected stock dividends and short-term interest rates interact to create a "cost-of-carry" relation that determines the "fair" value of the futures price.

Trading was resumed on the CME about 40 minutes later and with that resumption the market entered still another phase, the "Tuesday Turnaround." The S&P 500 contract reopened about 15 percent above its last recorded value before the halt. The discount remained substantial, however, reaching 46 points (20 percent) just after noon CST, recovering to about 12 points (five percent) at 1:00 p.m. CST, and widening again steadily thereafter to about 20 points (8.5 percent) at the close. Despite the conventional view that a discount in the futures price to the cash index forecasts (or causes) a market drop, the index cash value itself rose more or less steadily over this interval reaching 327 at the Tuesday close, an increase of about three percent over its value at the reopening of the CME at noon.

By Tuesday close the worst was over, although aftershocks of varying severity continued to be felt throughout the rest of the week. The normal positive spread of futures over cash had not been restored by the end of the week; in fact, the discount to cash on occasions, such as at the Friday close, reached as much as ten points (about 2.5 percent).[5]

The Opening Shock. We have divided the week's history into several distinct phases because we believe the episodes served as specific "stress tests" of somewhat different parts of the structure of the two markets and of their connecting links. The opening-shock phase, for example, provided simply the most dramatic illustration to date of what both informed academic and industry observers had long realized was the fundamentally different way the two markets deal with any overnight accumulation of order imbalances.[6]

It is apparent that prior to the openings on October 19, the accumulations of sell orders in both cash and futures markets were extremely heavy. The previous week had been unsettling both in terms of news and price movements. The London market had already experienced heavy selling both of U.K. company shares and shares of the internationally-known U.S. companies listed there. The large U.S. brokerage firms with overseas branches knew that further selling by

---

[5] At the opening on Thursday, October 22, the discount reached an astonishing 60 points (23 percent). But as the day developed, this discount was not followed by any major downward price move. The details of prices and spreads on the post-crash days are reflected in Figures Miller-C1 to C16 .

[6] It was, in fact, precisely the recognition of these differences in opening mechanisms that had led to what appeared to be a successful resolution of the so-called "triple witching day" problem—the problem that prior to the October market collapse had seemed to be a leading source of differences between the cash and futures exchanges.

foreign investors was on the way to both the cash and the futures markets in the U.S.

Confronted with these pre-opening selling order imbalances, each market responded according to its own long-standing, but quite different, opening procedures. The rules of the NYSE permit—indeed encourage— specialists to delay opening when the overnight accumulation of orders for a particular stock is too far out of balance to allow market clearing at a price near the previous close. The delayed opening is intended to give the specialist time to search for balancing orders on the other side. Under ordinary conditions, when most other stocks have opened and are trading normally, that search is completed successfully and trading resumed— though, typically, with a somewhat larger than usual price gap—in a few minutes. On the morning of October 19, however, the order imbalances at opening were apparently so widespread and so large that no immediate help was available to the specialists in many of the stocks most heavily represented in the S&P 500 index. In fact, one hour after the opening bell more than one-third of the stocks in the Dow Jones Industrial Average, including such large capitalization companies as IBM, Sears and Exxon, had yet to start trading.[7]

By contrast, futures markets seek not to stabilize prices, but to provide a setting in which prices can best and most speedily reflect current information. If the outcry at the opening bell on a futures exchange shows the overnight accumulation of orders to be heavily unbalanced, the price will jump directly to a level at which trading can take place. The previous closing price plays no explicit role in setting that level or the path to reach it. This is clearly demonstrated by the October 19 experience at the CME with respect to the S&P 500 contract, as Figure Miller-C7 illustrates, when the opening price had to fall some seven percent—an enormous jump by recent past standards—before trading could begin.

Normally the differences in the opening procedures of the two markets are mostly of academic interest, but on October 19 the unusually large size of the price drop in the futures market, viewed without regard to the methodology used in constructing the published cash index, presented a fundamentally misleading picture of where the selling pressure was localized. The cash index, which is recalculated and reported by various services at intervals of only a few seconds, is computed from the last transaction price of each component stock. When a stock included in the index does not open, the price used in the calculation is the previous day's

---

[7] The record of delayed openings and major trading halts of the stocks is presented in figures Miller-C17 through C19.

close for that stock. Since so many stocks, including those of some of the largest companies included in the index, did not open on October 19, the reported value of the NYSE cash index, which was relying in substantial measure on October 26 closing prices, was substantially in excess of what it would later be when actual opening prices were available. Thus, it is clear that the discount of the futures price to the cash price reported around the world was excessively large.

To an experienced observer, gaps between cash and futures prices at the open are hardly noteworthy. But given the magnitudes involved on October 19, it is understandable how an observer not fully aware of the events occurring at the NYSE, and not cognizant of the method by which the cash index is constructed, might imagine that Chicago was causing or leading the selling that subsequently occurred on the NYSE. Instead, the gap indicated that large sell imbalances existed in New York as well as Chicago.

This is not to deny, of course, that even after correcting for the stale quotes in the cash index, some discount might have still remained. No one can say with certainty what the prices of the non-trading stocks might have been had they been allowed to open freely.

We do know that several of the stocks included in the Dow Jones Industrial index that opened after the official open did so at price gaps down from their previous close. These gaps were roughly in line with the futures price drop from the previous close to that point.[8] Moreover, had the NYSE opened, the CME might not have exhibited as large a discount. It absorbed pressure from the NYSE failure to open. In fact, as we have seen earlier, by 10:23 a.m. CST, when the last of the Dow Jones stocks had finally opened, the futures price and the index were back in line. The ominous discount that existed at the opening had vanished.

The Monday Mid-Day Plunge. Although the two markets appeared to have righted themselves between 10:00 and 11:00 a.m. CST, discounts emerged again shortly thereafter, small at first, but larger and larger as the session wore on.

Stale prices in the index once again undoubtedly accounted for part of the discount, because the specialists were repeatedly forced to delay

---

[8] For example, Hewlett-Packard opened at $53.50 at 8:54 a.m. CST down about ten percent from its Friday close at $59.75; Minesota Manufacturing opened a minute later at $64.00, down about nine percent from the Friday close; Exxon the last of the Dow stocks to open opened 10:23 a.m. CST, down about nine percent from the Friday close.

transactions as they searched for offsetting orders. These delays, however, cannot be the sole explanation. The index never fell as far as the futures had dropped—although it might have if the trading day had been longer. In part the discount may have been only a reflection of the oft-noted asymmetry in the index arbitrage process introduced by the NYSE's so-called "up-tick" rule. When the futures price rises above its upper arbitrage bound, the warranted cost-of-carry relation between the cash and futures markets is restored as arbitragers sell futures contracts and buy stocks. In principle, anyone can participate in that process, whether or not they actually hold stocks. When the futures price falls to its lower bound, however, arbitrage requires a sale of stock and a purchase of futures. Any arbitrager who actually holds the stocks can sell them—and some institutional investors and index funds did—but under the "up-tick" rule, short sales cannot be undertaken in any NYSE stock except at a price higher than that of the previous transaction. Thus, theoretically arbitrageable gaps on the down side might tend to be larger and to persist longer than those on the upside.

Since there were few up-ticks during the crash, and even fewer that occurred simultaneously for many of the major stocks in the S&P 500 index basket, the lower-bound asymmetry was undoubtedly larger and more persistent than usual.

But again, this cannot be the entire explanation. Even if the persistence of a discount can be related to the difficulty of effecting arbitrage transactions through short sales in the cash market, this does not explain why so many transactions continued to be made in the futures market at what were seemingly such disadvantageous terms.

That the discounts shown in Figures Miller-C7 and C8 must be completely anomalous if taken literally becomes clear once the decision alternatives available to large investors are taken into account. Portfolio insurers and other institutinal traders can opt to reduce their equity exposure either by selling futures or by selling stocks from their portfolios. Their choice will depend on which route seems to offer the lower transaction costs, in the broad sense of that term. When the relation between the cash and futures markets is normal, as in Figures Miller-C1 to C4, and arbitrage program trading is able to keep the relative costs in line, the choice may well be futures. But if such investors should perceive that futures are at a very substantial discount to cash—as appeared to be the case, for example, at 1:00 p.m. CST on October 19, when a 22 point discount appeared—then they would almost certainly prefer to sell stocks, in order to avoid the extra selling charge of nine percent represented by the discount.

The logical explanation for the choice made by investors to sell futures on October 19 is that they did not believe that transaction costs, properly computed, really would be lower in the cash market, for the effective costs in the cash market were raised by the risks attendant to uncertain and delayed execution in a highly volatile market.

We deemed it not within the scope of this Committee's assignment to document the performance of the NYSE DOT system, or to establish why the cash market in New York experienced delays and uncertainties in execution during these critical days. The interaction between the futures and stock markets, however, must play a critical role in any analysis.

Estimating Net Absorption by the Futures Market of Selling Pressure. Estimates of the net absorption of selling pressure by the futures market on October 19 and 20 were first presented publicly by the officers of the CME in the immediate aftermath of the crash. Since evidence of spillovers to and from other markets from the practice of risk management strategies that employ futures may be important in weighing some of the policy options currently being suggested, the Committee believed it important to check the source of those earlier estimates. Accordingly, we have discussed the details of the caluculations at some length with the members of the CME's surveillance staff and economic research group. We have concluded that, while recognizing that complete accuracy in these matters cannot be assured, the main outlines of the earlier calculations of net pressure are essentially correct. Traders at the CME apparently did take into inventory a considerable volume of futures contracts sold by portfolio insurers and other hedgers, sales that might otherwise have been diverted to the cash market.

The basic data from which the calculations are constructed are shown in Table Miller-1. The numbers are tabulated from the reports filed under regulations of the Commodity Futures Trading Commission by large traders, defined for this purpose, as any account with a position change in excess of 50 contracts and a reportable net position of at least 100 contracts. Virtually all portfolio insurers and index arbitragers active on the critical days will qualify under those guidelines. The table shows breakdowns of purchases and sale of contracts by six broadly defined classes of traders over five separate days. The estimates of net absorption were made by associating particular sub-classes of traders with particular trading strategies.

Specifically, portfolio insurance and other hedging selling of futures on October 19 can be estimated conservatively as the sum of sales by institutional investors—that is, 43,209 contracts sold by pension funds and trusts and 4,410 contracts sold by endowments and other nonspeculative institutional accounts, or a total of 47,619 contracts. These are sales that might otherwise have gone to the cash market. This would have represented total selling pressure of 150 million shares or 15 percent to total stock market volume.

Index-related arbitrage buys represent the flow back to futures of sales in the cash market. They will show up in the data mainly in the proprietary buys of broker-dealers, but also in the buying by institutional investors. The most conservative estimate would be to assume that most of the buys in those categories, except for those known by market surveillance not to be such, are arbitrage-related, making the flow back to futures from the cash market 11,277 from broker-dealers, 12,802 from pension funds and trusts, and 10,204 from other institutions, for a total of 34,283 contracts. A lower bound on the flow back would be the 11,277 of the broker-dealer group alone. The best estimate of the surveillance staff, based on their knowledge of the individual accounts, puts the flow back at about 20,000 contracts, or about ten percent of NYSE volume.

Based on these calculations, the futures markets absorbed about 27,000 contracts from the total 47,000 contracts of institutional sales, and passed the remaining 20,000 on to the NYSE via arbitrage. The 27,000 contracts would have represented about 85 million shares of stock or 14 percent of NYSE volume had they reached New York instead of stopping in Chicago.

These estimates of the gross and net intermarket flows from portfolio insurance and index arbitrage trading on October 19 are shown in Tables Miller-2 and 3 both in units of contracts and of approximate share equivalents. The estimates of the index arbitrage have already been explained. The estimates of portfolio insurance activity are based on position data and on interviews conducted by CME market surveillance staff with portfolio managers. The lower bound of 27,264 contracts represents total insurance sales by those portfolio managers who represent slightly less than 90 percent of insured assets. The upper bound of 47,619 represent all institutional sales. The staff estimate of 32,000 is an average of these upper and lower bounds.

Timing of Net Position Changes. Although the futures market on balance appears to have absorbed selling pressure that might otherwise have been directed to the NYSE, many questions about the timing and sequencing of the intermarket flows remain to be considered. Figures Miller-P3 and P4 present a breakdown by 15 minute intervals during the day in the net position of large traders. The net selling by pension funds at the opening and again at about 10:00 a.m. CST undoubtedly reflects to a considerable extent the implementation of portfolio insurance programs.

The net buying by broker-dealers over the same interval is a likely indication of the backflow from index arbitrage. Note, however, that neither group appears to have been active in the critical period between 10:30 and 11:15 a.m. CST, when the sizable discounts of futures below cash again began to appear.[9]

Further net selling by pension funds and net buying by broker-dealers occurred in the period between 11:15 a.m. CST and 12:15 p.m. CST, but the discount remained roughly steady until shortly after 12:15 p.m. CST, when the futures price broke sharply below the then quoted cash value. No large positon changes, however, by either pension funds or broker-dealers coincide with this break. No specific bad news event appears to have shown up on the broad tape during this 15 minute interval, but rumors of an impending shutdown were circulating widely at the time. Both pension fund and broker-dealer activity resumed after the break, though on a smaller scale than in the pre-break hour. The price volatility had by then become substantially greater than was the case earlier in the day. Even the smaller net changes in position were associated with larger changes in prices.

The Tuesday Morning Collapse. Issues of sequencing become especially important on Tuesday, October 20. Recall that the two markets, after a brief recovery at the opening, slipped steadily downward at an accelerating pace, culminating in a trading halt at the CME at 11:19 a.m. CST. (See Figures Miller-C9 and C10.) We sought to determine whether the price break had been precipitated by the frantic dumping of big blocks of futures by portfolio insurers whose trigger points had been set off by the 23 percent drop in share prices of the day before. Our study of the data, however, suggests no such localization of the source of the selling pressure.

Figures Miller-P5 and P6 present summary data prepared by the surveillance staff of the CME on net position changes by brokers and dealers and by pensions and trust in 15 minutes intervals on Tuesday. As noted earlier, this analysis, which captures all trades of at least 50 contracts per 15 minute period, will reflect almost all significant index arbitrage and portfolio insurance trading.

From figure Miller-P6 it is clear that portfolio insurers in the pension/trust account grouping were not major net sellers in the pre-shutdown period. We know from Table Miller-1 that they were indeed net

---

[9] It is worth noting that the broad tape at 10:54 a.m. CST reported SEC Chairman Ruder's remark about a possible trading halt.

sellers for the entire day, though on a smaller scale than on the previous day. But in the critical morning period, pension funds and trusts were actually net buyers of futures, not sellers as they have been so widely pictured.

We also should note that the Value Line futures also were selling at a large discount on the Kansas City Board of Trade. Little, if any, portfolio insurance is carried out with this futures contract.

If no heavy portfolio insurance driven selling was occurring on the morning of October 20, what can account for the very large discounts of futures to cash that were opening up at that time? We believe that a significant part of the answer lies once again in the fact that the reported values for the S&P 500 index itself were not realistic. With prices moving down so fast, any index value based on the last transaction prices was obsolete before it even appeared on the quote screens. The obsolescence factor in the quotes became even more pronounced when trading halts of as much as several minutes began to occur for particular stocks, as they did with increasing frequency after 9:00 a.m. CST. In fact, so many stocks were not trading by 11:15 a.m. CST that the Chicago Board Options Exchange was required to suspend trading in its index options. The CME followed suit a few minutes later at a time when it was widely believed, wrongly as it turned out, that the NYSE was itself about to suspend trading.

In emphasizing the role of index lag and of trading delays in the reported discount, we are not suggesting, of course, that there were no corresponding unrealities in the quoted futures prices. Those prices, too, undoubtedly gave many traders a misleading picture of the executions that could actually be achieved when prices were falling rapidly. It must also be remembered that the market-making capacity in futures, both on the floor and among day traders, had been substantially reduced by the fall in prices of the day before. The extraordinary volatility and uncertainty present in the market meant that very sizeable price concessions had to be offered to induce anyone to take a long position.

Just reassembling the CME trading data from that chaotic day represents a major research effort, and this Committee does not have access to the stock data necessary to reconstruct in detail the stock side of various futures trades. From our perspective, the key policy issues remain largely the same regardless of the market in which the selling pressures originated or even if, as we suspect was often the case, these pressures were impacting both markets simultaneously.

The Tuesday Turnaround. Whatever may have been the role of the CME S&P 500 futures contract in leading or forecasting the fall in prices in the cash market, certainly no such leading role can be assigned to those futures in the sharp turnaround that occurred at about noon on Tuesday. By the time the CME had reopened for trading, the reported index value had already risen by nearly five percent above the value at the time of the halt. The leading role, however, had been attributed in press accounts to another index futures contract, the Major Market Index contract of the Chicago Board of Trade. Whatever current investigations may ultimately show in this regard, there was already evidence of a surge in real buying power coming into the cash market at about that time, and with no direct connection initially to any futures market.

One part of the surge was arranged by the investment banks and "upstairs" block trading firms who worked with their corporate clients in instituting share repurchase programs. The other part was initiated by the Federal Reserve System, which added liquidity by increasing bank reserves and by encouraging banks to make the added liquidity available to the market through loans to brokers and dealers for financing their inventory positions in securities.

That such liquidity infusions from outside regular market channels had to be invoked to turn the tide of selling should not be regarded as a sign of fatal flaws in the market structures of either the cash or the futures markets. Those markets were never designed to absorb order imbalances of the size and persistence actually experienced; and it is far from clear that any market system could successfully absorb selling of that magnitude over a time interval as short as an ordinary seven-hour trading day.

The market-making structures of the exchange, whether of the open-outcry or the specialist or the upstairs dealer form, are intended primarily for temporary imbalances of orders, reflecting the lack of perfect synchronization between the arrival of customer buy orders and customer sell orders. The market makers take these trading overflows into their own inventory positions hoping, of course, that the positions they are assuming are temporary and can be turned over quickly when offsetting orders come in on the other side. Most of the time they are successful and the markets can function well despite heavy volume, as was the case on the pre-crash Wednesday, Thursday, and Friday, pictured in Figures Miller-C1 to C6.

But if a second surge of sell orders should come in before the first offsetting wave of buy orders has arrived, the market makers are put in a difficult position. Much of their capital has already been committed, and larger inducements in the form of price concessions have to be offered to lead them to increase their positions by committing more of their remaining capital. Some of the market makers in New York may be able to restore their market-making capacity by hedging their inventories with futures— that is, by shifting some of their inventory overload to other market makers who may still have some uncommitted capacity. But if a third wave and then a fourth wave of sell orders pour in, the capacity of even the best capitalized market makers can be exhausted. The sellers must look then, not to market makers or other short-term inventory holders, but to ultimate long term buyers on the other side of the trade.

There were many such instances of a desperate search for the buy side of trades during the two sell off days in October. The delays at the opening and the trading halts during the day were only the most visible evidence. The corporate buyback programs and the actions of the Federal Reserve Board may ultimately have been the most effective.

The Aftermath. Although no further episodes of cumulative panic occurred after the Tuesday turnaround, conditions during the rest of the week of October 19 can hardly be said to have returned to normal. The diminished capacity of the futures market to supply liquidity to transactions is evident in many ways throughout the period as, for example, in the large reversal in the futures price at the opening on Thursday and again shortly after the opening on Friday. These reversals represent the market's reaction to the imbalances of sell-at-market orders at the open. The imbalances were large even by previous standards. But with the capital resources of market makers reduced by the events of Monday and Tuesday, with volatility so great and with hedging ability reduced by the restrictions on program trading at the NYSE, the price concessions needed to induce market makers to position the orders had to be extremely large by past standards. The discount, which can be considered the effective implicit cost that the sellers of futures on Friday morning had to pay, was about five percent. For sellers at the Thursday opening, the implicit cost was a startling 23 percent.

Transaction costs this high normally, and quite rightly, are regarded as evidence of market inefficiency. In fact, they virtually define it. It is disquieting to realize, therefore, that some of the policy proposals currently being advanced, however well intentioned, would make these inefficiencies of the after-shock days a permanent part of U.S. capital markets. The further irony is that some of these well intentioned policy proposals, had they already been in place, might actually have intensified, rather than alleviated the panic.

CHANGE IN POSITION OF LARGE TRADERS*
Dec S&P 500 Futures

	BROKER DEALERS			INSTITUTIONAL INVESTORS						MARKET MAKERS			SPECULATIVE					
	Broker Dealers (Proprietary)			Pensions/Trusts			Endowments, Corporate Entities, and Other Non-speculative Institutions			Option Market Makers and "Locals"			Retail Speculative, Partnership Trading and Managed Accounts			Foreign Speculative		
	Bot	Sold	Net	Bot	Sold	Net	Bot	Sold	Net	Bot	Sold	Net	Bot	Sold	Net	Bot	Sold	Net
16-Oct	4,630	2,148	-2,482	5,197	19,598	-14,404	7,374	2,187	4,187	6,559	1,653	4,906	2,026	1,730	296	2,038	3,172	-1,134
19-Oct	11,277	2,411	-8,866	17,802	43,209	-25,407	17,204	4,410	12,794	5,844	10,904	-5,060	4,398	1,273	3,125	3,381	5,000	-1,619
20-Oct	13,876	3,028	-10,848	24,144	35,333	-11,189	8,536	3,328	5,208	8,278	6,893	1,385	2,647	3,708	-1,133	4,520	3,541	979
21-Oct	2,905	6,136	-3,231	32,382	15,772	16,610	13,885	13,100	785	1,693	4,211	-2,518	1,148	1,779	-631	1,361	2,696	-1,335
22-Oct	7,391	6,878	513	15,744	8,348	7,396	2,898	6,561	-3,663	959	2,373	-1,414	2,091	1,434	657	437	1,799	-1,362

* Preliminary estimates based on large trader accounts with positions chazes in excess of 40 contracts

Note: Bot = Increase in long plus decrease in short positions
        Sold = Increase in short plus decrease in long positions

TABLE MILLER-2
Estimated CME Futures Market-Index Arbitrage and Portfolio
Insurance Activity on October 19, 1987
Number of Futures Contracts

	Estimated Index Arbitrage Bids		Estimated Portfolios Insurance Futures Sales	
	Number of Contracts	% of Total S&P Futures Volume	Number of Contracts	% of Total S&P Futures Volume
Upper Bound	34,283	21%	47,619	29%
Staff Estimate	20,000	12%	32,000	20%
Lower Bound	11,277	7%	27,264	17%

TABLE MILLER-3
Estimated CME Futures Market-Index Arbitrage and Portfolio
Insurance Activity on October 19, 1987
In Terms of Equivalent Number of Stock Shares[1]

	Estimated Index Arbitrage Bids		Estimated Portfolios Insurance Futures Sales	
	Number of Shares	% of Total S&P Market Volume	Number of Shares	% of Total S&P Market Volume
Upper Bound	106,651,343	18%	149,375,453	25%
Staff Estimate	62,736,486	10%	100,380,540	17%
Lower Bound	35,356,138	6%	85,519,734	14%

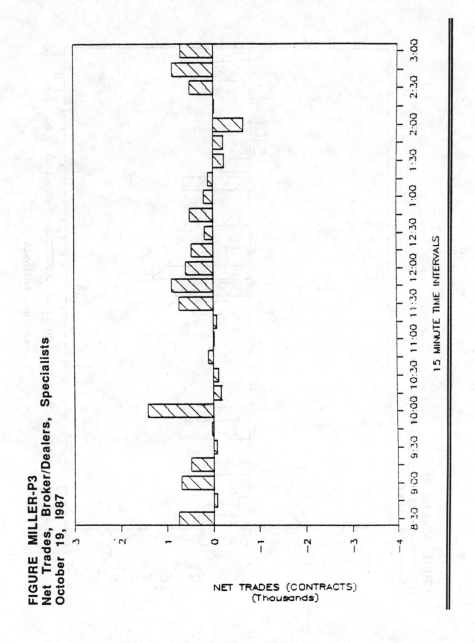

FIGURE MILLER-P3
Net Trades, Broker/Dealers, Specialists
October 19, 1987

NET TRADES (CONTRACTS)
(Thousands)

15 MINUTE TIME INTERVALS

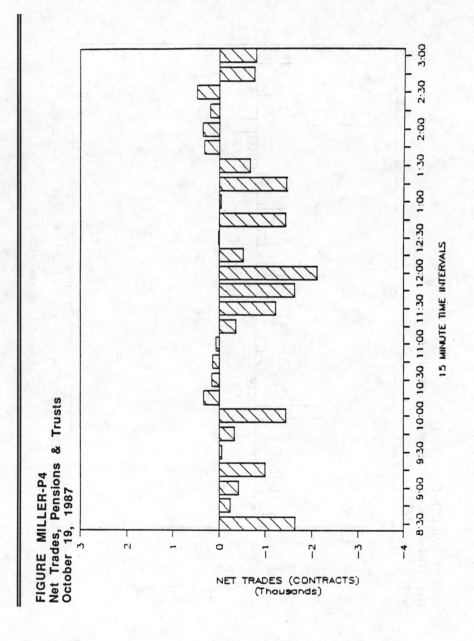

FIGURE MILLER-P4
Net Trades, Pensions & Trusts
October 19, 1987

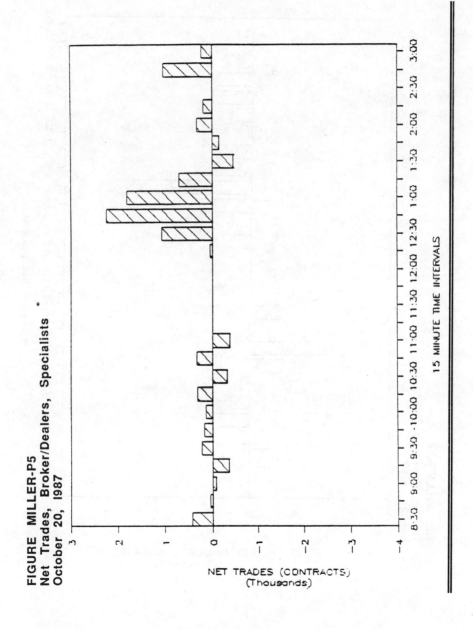

FIGURE MILLER-P5
Net Trades, Broker/Dealers, Specialists
October 20, 1987

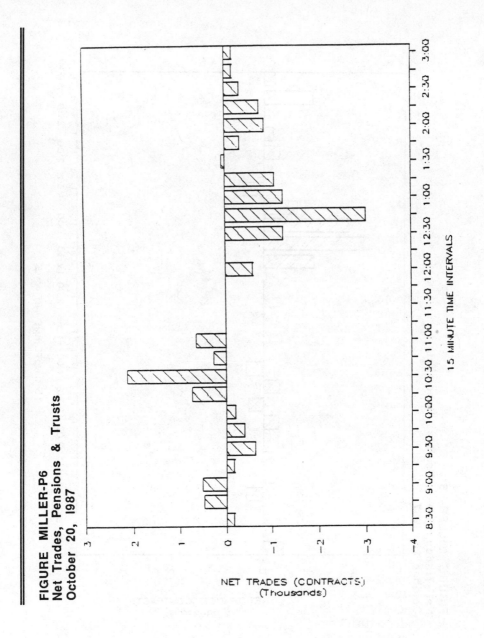

FIGURE MILLER-P6
Net Trades, Pensions & Trusts
October 20, 1987

BRITAIN

The International Stock Exchange of Great Britain*

Summary of Key Points

UK Equity Markets

- The market crash in the week October 19th saw a fall of 22 percent in the FTSE 100 Index. It ushered in a period of far greater price volatility than had existed previously.

- Volumes in the week of the crash reached unprecedented levels. Customer transactions peaked at over 100,000 bargains per day on October 21st and 22nd. Customer value exceeded £3.5bn on October 20th.

- Intra-market turnover was proportionately lower during the three week period from October 19th to November 6th. However, equity IDBs gained and have retained a considerably higher proportion of intra-market business.

- The pattern of customer business during this three week period suggests that individual investors were substantial net buyers.

- Market makers performed a valuable stabilization function on October 19th when they were net purchasers of UK equities to the tune of £250m. In subsequent days, market makers were able substantially to reduce their positions.

- Despite the declaration of "fast markets" for limited periods and despite the difficulties of keeping pace in a rapidly moving market, there is strong evidence to show that customer business was generally executed at close to SEAQ screen quotes. There is no evidence that market makers screen prices were significantly away from the market for anything but short periods.

---

* From *The Quality of Markets Report*, Winter 1987/1988.

- Fears that the high level of visibility of the market may have caused panic among market makers and thus precipitated price cuts appear to have been unfounded. Results show that price falls were associated with selling pressure.

Foreign Equity Markets

- During the week of October 19th, over 50 percent more customer bargains per day were transacted compared with September's daily average. Average daily customer turnover value during the week of the crash was £890 million, 69 percent higher than September's daily average.

- Customer turnover in Japanese equities peaked on October 23rd at £331 million, compared to about £60 million per day normally.

- Over 70 percent more customer bargains per day transacted in US equities during the week of the crash.

- Average daily customer turnover in French equities during the week of October 19th was more than two and a half times the September average.

Inter-Relationships Between Markets

- All three markets (cash, traded options and futures) saw record volumes during the crash; traded options traded a record 121,000 contracts on October 21st while LIFFE traded over 9,000 FTSE contracts daily on Monday 19th and Tuesday 20th.

- All three markets traded continuously throughout the week of the crash. Spreads increased significantly in all markets as trading risk increased. In general, the size in which deals could be made decreased. Market quality has recovered in all three markets though equity spreads and option premia are still higher than pre-October levels.

- A significant number of investors were short of FTSE puts at the start of the week. Limited trading on October 16th (due to storms) meant that these investors had no opportunity to close positions before substantial losses had been incurred. These investors were seeking to close positions at almost any price on the Monday and Tuesday.

- Margins were raised in the options market on Tuesday 20th, and also at various times during the week for FTSE futures. This, together with the principle of marking to market, ensured the robustness of the markets by limiting the credit risk associated with highly leveraged instruments.

- Index arbitrage and portfolio insurance trading are not yet well developed in the UK. Trading difficulties, largely relating to access to the cash market, restricted index arbitrage even further than usual during October 19th and 20th.

- The absence of effective index arbitrage, combined with the perceived difficulties of access to market markers in the equity market, allowed FTSE to trade at a significant discount.

1. INTRODUCTION

The events of Monday 19th and Tuesday 20th October 1987, more likely to be remembered as "Black Monday" and "Terrible Tuesday," marked the beginning of a new reality. Over the course of those two days, stock markets world wide experienced dramatic price falls, in many cases by as much as 25 percent. Accompanying these sharp price movements, exchanges around the world, particularly UK and US exchanges, experienced unprecedented trading volumes. Significantly increased volatility is now the norm and investor confidence is greatly reduced. Why did it happen? And how did it happen so quickly?

These are questions which many are asking. In the US, several Congressional committees have been set up to investigate what happened, why, how, and what can be done to prevent similar occurrences. Most major exchanges have also initiated studies to understand the events of those two days. Here in the UK, the ISE is also vitally concerned at establishing the facts— what happened exactly? How did our systems and markets perform in light of such extraordinary events.

As an exchange, at the end of the day, it is the efficient way in which business is conducted—that is, the expedient execution and settlement of investors' decisions to buy or sell securities—which determines just how good a market is. That prices in London fell more quickly or less quickly than other exchanges is merely a reflection of the speed and reaction of our market makers to new information. Prices and price levels are the messages, albeit very important messages, which arise from investor pressure and changes in expectations or perceptions.

The principal tasks of the Quality of Markets Committee of the ISE is to provide a continuous evaluation of the quality of the Exchange's markets. In this Quarterly, we report on the results of several studies which focus on the activities of October 19th and 20th. As can be appreciated, when one is in the midst of a maelstrom of frenetic activity (as virtually every dealing room in the City will no doubt remember) just trying to understand what was going on would prove difficult enough, let alone understanding why.

During the last three months, with studies conducted by the ISE using ISE's comprehensive transaction database and supplemented by numerous detailed interviews and discussions with market practitioners and a broad range of investors, the events of October 19th and 20th were pieced together. Work was also carried out in association with the London International Financial Futures Exchange (LIFFE) to examine the interrelationship between the futures, cash and traded options market. Detailed analyses into the size of transactions, timing of transactions, the inter-play between the cash and derivative markets, the flow of buying and selling orders, and the quality of price quotations made by market makers in the underlying cash and derivative markets, are just a few of the areas covered by our investigations.

The results of our studies have been structured as follows: Section Two concentrates on the performance of the UK equity market during the period of the crash. As well as examining trading activity on a minute by minute basis on October 19th and 20th, a much wider view and longer period is taken so that the events of the crash can be seen in perspective.

Much of the price movements in major international stocks followed price changes on their home market, and since a number of overseas exchanges experienced considerable problems in maintaining a continuous market, it was not surprising to see record trading on the ISE's foreign equity market. Details of the performance of this market are outlined in Section Three of this Quarterly, and particular attention is paid to specific country sectors which experienced very high levels of activity.

The inter-relationships of the underlying cash and derivative markets is a topic which has attracted much attention, particularly in the US and especially since the release of "The Report of the US Presidential Task Force on Market Mechanisms" (the Brady report). In the UK, there is also much interest, especially in light of very significant discounts between the price of FTSE futures and the actual FTSE 100 Index and the sharp rise in options' implied volatility. Why did such pricing anomalies exist? This question, and other related issues, are the subject of Section Four.

Summary and Conclusions

In general, results indicate that given the record increases in activity and the extent of price movements, trading systems coped remarkably well. The resulting decline in market quality, in terms of much wider price spreads and touches and much lower quotation sizes, is only to be expected given the extraordinary circumstances. While the decline in market quality involves increased costs of dealing, the cost of closing or halting trading would be far greater.

It seems clear that market makers, with their increased capital backing as a result of the Big Bang restructuring of firms, were able to perform a valuable stabilisation role, especially on October 19th when they took on net long positions of around £250 million.

It also appears that, for most of the time during the Monday and Tuesday, screen quotations fairly represented the level at which the market was trading.

One of the major conclusions arising from our study is that the discount persisted in the futures market because of the lack of techniques, such as index arbitrage, which help to provide convergence between interconnected markets. In addition the futures market is an "open outcry" market and thus is more accessible during volatile periods.

The issue of accessibility to market makers essentially rests with decisions relating to capacity. It is only realistic to expect systems to cope with normal activity levels; as with most industries, the degree of excess capacity to be built into a system depends on a firm's commercial outlook. The introduction of the ISE's automated execution service, SAEF (SEAQ Automated Execution Facility) next year, should release considerable resources within firms to handle a much greater proportion of higher value transactions. SAEF will enable member firms to execute client orders of up to 1,000 shares at the touch of a button, thus reducing the time of execution and settlement of small transactions.

Finally, a note must be made of the lack of certain information which would have greatly assisted in determining exactly from where the selling pressure was coming. While the ISE has records of every transaction conducted on its markets by its members, one piece of information which is not captured is the type of client who is dealing. Readers of past Quality of Markets Reports will recall the results of detailed surveys of transactions which provide analyses of business by a number of parameters, one being client type. Such information, which is considered vital for marketing and planning within the industry, can only be gained with the co-operation of firms who submit coded returns of a sample of transactions over a period of time.

This information could be captured in the same way as other bargain details are collected using the Central Checking System. This requires member firms to record details relating to each transaction—e.g., time and date of deal, issue traded, buy or sell, number of shares dealt, dealing price, etc.—which are entered into the Checking System to be matched. If Checking details were to include an indicator for client type, then we would have a most invaluable tool from which to provide many more answers.

2. UK EQUITY MARKET

- The market crash in the week October 19th saw a fall of 22 percent in the FTSE 100 Index. It ushered in a period of far greater price volatility than has existed previously.

- Volumes in the week of the crash reached unprecedented levels. Customer transactions peaked at over 100,000 bargains per day on October 20th.

- Intra-market turnover was proportionately lower during the three week period from October 19th to November 6th. However, equity IDBs gained and have retained a considerably higher proportion of intra-market business.

- The pattern of customer business during this three week period suggests that individual investors were substantial net buyers.

- Market makers performed a valuable stabilising function on October 19th when they were net purchasers of UK equities to the tune of £250m. In subsequent days, market makers were able substantially to reduce their positions.

- Despite the declaration of "fast markets" for limited periods and the difficulties of keeping pace in a rapidly moving market, there is strong evidence to show that customer business was generally executed at close to SEAQ screen quotes. There is no evidence that market makers screen prices were significantly away from the market for anything but short periods.

- Fears that the high level of visibility of the market may have caused panic among market makers and thus precipitated price cuts appear to have been unfounded. Results show that price falls were associated with selling pressure.

- We are left with an open verdict on the impact of foreign selling of UK stocks. Evidence from depositories of ADRs suggest that US investors were not disproportionately heavy sellers of UK stocks. It is not possible to reach firm conclusions on actions by investors from other countries.

- The weeks since the crash have seen a gradual but steady recovery in market quality. Market makers' spreads are generally narrowing and the depth of the market is generally increasing. However, continued volatility makes the market more risky than before and until this volatility declines, market quality will remain lower than before the crash.

Introduction

The market events of October 19th and 20th were the first occasion for the new market system, then almost one year old, to be subjected to significant and substantial selling pressure. By any standards, the extreme levels of activity and conditions produced the most bracing experience which a market could face. Like most major markets which are conducting research into the performance of their market mechanisms during this period, we are particularly concerned with certain features of our own market.

Our concerns relate less to the interaction between cash and derivative markets, in which many US researchers have focused, (though the possibilities for interaction exist and these are studied in Section Four of this Quarterly)—we are more interested in the impact of market visibility on the stability of our market. What are the effects of a continuous, highly visible display of market makers' price quotations, combined with a high level of trade publication on market activity? Do these features bring a tendency for market participants to over-react?

This study is structured to cover these issues. Beginning with a look at the price movements experienced during and immediately after the crash, we shall examine the structural features of the UK equity market during that period. The next two sections examine market quality, analysing market depth and price quality respectively. This is followed by a discussion of the impact of visibility and internationalisation, followed by a look at how market quality has recovered in the period after the crash.

Generally speaking, our investigations cover the period from October 12th to November 13th, 1987, with particular attention paid to the events of October 19th and 20th.

Market Price Movements

Equity prices world wide experienced sharp falls as a result of the mid-October crash. Over the one week period, Wednesday 14th to Tuesday 20th October, the FTSE 100 index fell 22 percent, the Dow Jones Industrial dropped 24 percent, the Nikkei-Dow 18 percent, Germany 15 percent, and France 14 percent. The next two weeks saw some recovery in New York and Tokyo but prices continued to decline in London. In this two week period, European exchanges, which had to some extent been shielded from the slump of the first week, fell significantly and continued declining to the year end. The recovery experienced in Tokyo was reversed as the Nikkei-Dow fell significantly further to the year end, while both New York and London stabilised.

With hindsight, a downward trend is now apparent in most markets since peaking around July and August. Market indices world wide have been moving down more or less gently since then. There have been some significant announcements (e.g., the publication of worse than expected trade figures which moved FTSE down 56 points on August 6th), but nothing to compare with the movement experienced on October 19th and 20th.

New York had fallen sharply in the week of October 16th, the biggest fall coming on Friday 16th when trading in London was nominal due to extreme, adverse weather conditions. On Monday 19th, FTSE opened 137 points (six percent) down on the previous trading day's close (Thursday 15th October) and fell a further 113 points (five percent) during the day. On Tuesday 20th, FTSE opened another 186 points (nine percent) down, falling a further 65 points (three percent) during the day. Wednesday 21st saw FTSE open 113 points up and a further 29 points rise during the day, but this recovery in London and elsewhere was shortlived.

As well as the decline in prices, extreme volatility became a feature of the market. To illustrate, on October 20th, FTSE saw a high of 1985.1 and a low of 1748.2— a movement of 237 points (though the net open to close change at 65 points was far less). Figure Britain-2.1 illustrates the daily FTSE range for the last six months of 1987. The sharp rise in volatility is very obvious in the post-crash period compared to earlier months.

More recently, the level of volatility appears to have eased somewhat; however, one day movements are still frequently larger than on even the most volatile days before the crash. During November and December, there were six days when the closed to closed movement was more than 50 points. This increase in volatility has important implications for market quality since it represents a higher level of risk. Higher risk raises the cost of risk transference, shown most clearly in wider spreads made by market makers and the higher premiums for traded options. Both features are discussed in detail later on.

There have also been suggestions that both the extent of the fall in London and the ensuing volatility are a direct result of specific features of the London market— in particular, the high visibility of the market and the high level of overseas holders of UK stocks. These features are also examined in detail later in this report.

It is true that there were special features in the UK market which may have exacerbated the fall and certain features elsewhere which might have softened the crash:

- UK institutions may have been less willing and less able to take on further equity after the crash even though, in valuation terms, equities may have seemed good value. This possible reluctance was a likely result of two factors. Firstly, UK institutions already hold a higher proportion of equity in their portfolio compared to US or Japanese funds. Over the past year, while the market has risen substantially, UK institutions continued to invest particularly heavily in equities (see Table Britain-2.1). Secondly, considerable institutional cash has been absorbed in recent underwritings (including BP) and this may have left them short of liquid funds.

- Reports from the US suggest that listed companies have taken the opportunity to reduce their takeover vulnerability by buying back stock when the price falls sufficiently. As this practice is not widely used in the UK, although it has become more popular (especially among Property Companies and Investment Trusts), this type of support was not present in the London securities market.

- Use of derivative products (futures and options) is less highly developed in the UK than in the US. Discussions continue as to whether the impact of these markets in the US exacerbated or softened the crash. Either way, the possible destabilising impact of derivative markets has been less of an issue here in the UK than in the US.

STRUCTURE OF TRADING ACTIVITY

During the weeks following October 19th, significant changes in trading patterns occurred. Three features stand out: the massive volume of trading, the significant increase in the proportion of customer purchase orders to customer sales orders, and the changing pattern of intra-market trading.

Trading Volumes and Liquidity

Despite the sharp falls in prices, volumes reached unprecedented levels in the week of October 19th, peaking at over 100,000 bargains daily on two days. Figures Britain-2.2 and 2.3 show daily customer and intra-market turnover as bargains and value over the period October 12th to November 11th.

Much of the higher turnover experienced during the week of the crash was in alpha stocks. Trading of alphas accounted for an average of 68 percent of turnover value in the three weeks from October 19th to November 6th, compared to 50 percent before October. The levels of trading in betas, gammas, and deltas (despite being a lower proportion of total turnover) rose in the week of October 19th, but declined during the following two weeks.

The emphasis on alpha stocks is to be expected given these circumstances. Since alphas represent the greater proportion of institutional UK equity portfolios and are also the most liquid equities, investors wanting to reduce equity exposure could do so quite easily by selling large blocks of alpha stocks.

Intra-Market Business

On average, intra-market turnover accounts for half of total turnover (customer plus intra-market) by value. In the period from October 19th to November 6th, intra-market turnover accounted for only 40 percent, much lower than usual

Of more interest perhaps is the fact that intra-market business conducted via equity IDBs increased substantially during the week of the crash and has continued at a higher level than before. The number of intra-market bargains being dealt via IDBs increased three fold after October 20th.

It is worth noting that wider touches and spreads, which as we shall see have prevailed since the crash, make it easier to transact IDB business.

This is because IDB deals are conducted using one price to match the buyer with the seller. Wider touches mean there is more room to "negotiate" a price which is acceptable.

To explain the growth in IDB business, it has been said that the very high level of uncertainty has discouraged market makers from trading amongst themselves directly. This is particularly true during "fast market" periods when price quotations are indicative only. Market makers have been able to avoid being "hit" by other market makers if their price moved out of line. However, the growth in IDB business has been sustained which would indicate that this type of service is now more widely appreciated by market makers.

The "fast market" indicator is used when the volume of market activity is such that market makers are unable to keep their quotes up to date. When the "fast market" status indicator appears on the screens, all prices shown on SEAQ are regarded as indicative only and must be confirmed prior to dealing with market makers.

It is widely felt that during highly volatile periods, declaring a "fast market" actually improves the quality of the market since this is considered to be the only realistic option when prices are moving too fast for screens to be updated. In fact, as we shall see, during "fast market" periods, the bulk of customer business is done at prices very close to the markets best quotations as displayed on the screens.

Because prices are not firm during "fast market" periods, market makers are able to avoid being "hit" for large trades by other market makers if they are slightly slow in updating, or if delays within systems prevent them from updating immediately. Without the fast market "safety valve," in such circumstances a market maker would have three options, any of which would be more detrimental to the market. These options are:

- To reduce his quotation size to avoid large "hits."

- To ensure that his bid quote was below the current market bid quote (since a bid price below the market bid would not be hit by other market makers).

- To cease dealing. This is an extreme decision since a market maker opting to de-register in a stock is not allowed to re-register for three months.

Fast markets" were declared at the following times during the week of October 19th:

	Fast Markets Declared
Monday 19th October	09.10—09.23
	11.00—12.00
Tuesday 20th October	09.00—11.00
	14.32—16.00
Wednesday 21st October	09.00—09.30
Thursday 22nd October	09.08—10.00
	11.47—12.40

Buying and Selling Pressure

In recent years, which have seen an upsurge in individual investor business, there has been a fairly even balance of small and large bargains among buyers and seers. In the three weeks after the crash, the pattern changed significantly. There was a consistent and marked pattern of many more small buy orders to a much lower number of larger sell orders.

While the split of customer turnover by money value between purchase and sale orders was roughly 50:50 as usual, in terms of the number of orders transacted, between October 21st and November 3rd, purchases accounted for up to 80 percent of all customer bargains. Subsequently, the split has returned to normal levels. Figure Britain-2.4 shows the daily split of buy and sell transactions.

The clear implication is that individuals were net buyers in that period. This is borne out both by comments from member firms and by independent surveys of investor attitudes.

Resilience of Market Maker System

Net customer sales were very substantial on October 19th, amounting to over £250 million. This represented additional inventory for market makers who, in general, were already long of stock. On subsequent days, the net positions were much smaller until the week ending November 6th when substantial customer buying re-emerged.

Figure Britain-2.5 shows the accumulative net purchases over the October 12th to November 11th period. One can conclude that in the period from October 19th to November 3rd, market makers were judging their price quotations with a reasonable degree of success. They managed to modify selling pressure, thus allowing them to unwind their position.

It is important to note that the ISE's Account trading system, where deals can be closed within the ten working day period without any transfer of funds, might tend to exacerbate selling pressures because of investors' ability to close sales within the Account. Most brokers would, of course, discourage short selling within the Account since they as firms are ultimately liable if a client is unable to meet his obligations.

There is little doubt from our results that the ability of market makers to hold substantial long positions is a reflection of their valuable stabilising role in absorbing the weight of selling pressure. Commentators have argued that without the increased capital inflow and restructuring of firms as a result of Big Bang, market makers may not have been able to "weather the storm" as well as they did.

Obviously, most if not all market makers lost money, and it has been widely publicized that some lost very large amounts. Market maker positions were monitored extremely closely by the Surveillance Division of the Exchange during this period. A measure of the strength of the system can be gleaned from the fact that despite these very extreme trading conditions, there were no doubts about the ability of market makers to meet their obligations and no market maker left the market during this period.

MARKET DEPTH

A key test of the effectiveness of a market is how well liquidity is maintained under pressure. We have commented in previous Quarterly reports on the improvement in liquidity—as measured by depth and touch—over the past year. How then did liquidity hold up under the extreme conditions during the period of the crash? There are actually three aspects to this question:

1. How did the usual measures of liquidity (based on the size of quotations) behave?

2. To what extent were the prices of quotations a fair reflection of actual dealing prices?

3. To what extent did liquidity in less active stocks suffer in comparison to the more active stocks?

Measures of Depth and Touch

We have seen that on October 19th market makers provided a high level of support in a falling market. Their net purchases of UK equities exceeded a quarter of a billion pounds on that one day (to put this in context, this is equivalent to the total throughput of the equity market on an average day in 1986). Market makers generally maintained their screen sizes and spreads at pre-crash levels until well into Monday afternoon, or even Tuesday morning. After that time, the liquidity of the market started to deteriorate quite rapidly.

To illustrate the extent of the deterioration, we looked in detail at the quotations of three alpha stocks during the two day period. The three were chosen to cover a range of circumstances:

- SHELL TRANSPORT & TRADING CO. — an internationally traded stock which over a three week period, October 12th to 30th, outperformed the FT All Share Index.

- AMSTRAD — a stock with limited international interest which moved roughly in line with the FT All Share Index.

- JAGUAR — stock which is heavily traded in the US, has a large dollar exposure and substantially underperformed the FT All Share Index.

Our results are illustrated in Figures Britain-2.6 to 2.8. Firstly looking at Figure Britain-2.6, the top portion shows the average quoted spread and the touch (in pence) throughout October 19th and 20th for Shell. As can be seen, the spread remained unchanged throughout the Monday but increased to a 20 pence spread on the Tuesday, four times higher than the day before.

Fast markets were declared for two periods during the Tuesday: from 09.00 to 11.00 and from 14.32 to 16.00. During these periods of very rapid price changes, screen quotations actually produced negative touches.

The mid-section of Figure Britain-2.6 shows the mid-price for the best bid and offer quotes for Shell. Quotes declined only slowly during the Monday, but were marked down dramatically at the market opening on Tuesday. The increasing price trend throughout the morning continued until 14.30 (opening of the NYSE) when the price began to fall, but by less than the fall experienced across the whole market (as measured by FTSE).

The bottom portion of Figure Britain-2.6 shows the total market size for Shell as expressed in terms of the total of all bid quotation sizes made by registered market makers in Shell. Market size was reduced by about a half by Monday afternoon after NYSE opened, and reduced even further on the Tuesday.

Figure Britain-2.7 illustrates the similar factors for Amstrad, while Figure Britain-2.8 shows the effect on Jaguar shares.

In all three stocks (though to a lesser degree for Shell) total market size fell sharply in the late morning of October 19th. This coincided with the start of the fast market period from 11.00 to 12.00 on that day. There was little change in market size for each of the three stocks despite very substantial (though temporary) price recoveries in the early afternoon.

These examples reflect the extent to which market makers on October 19th were attempting to hold the market at a steady level, by tending to treat the events of the day as a temporary phenomena and holding prices. Not only did they maintain their spreads and sizes, they also took on very substantial inventories during the course of the day given the weight of selling pressure. By the next morning perceptions had changed due largely to the dramatic 509 point fall in the Dow Jones Industrial Average Index on the NYSE overnight.

Looking at a wider picture and longer time period, Figures Britain-2.9 to 2.13 show measures of the touch, average quotation spreads, market size, maximum quote size and size premia for each group of alpha, beta and gamma stocks. The graphs cover the period October 12th to November 13th and were taken at 10:30 a.m. each day. The observation for October 16th has been omitted as the market was closed due to severe storms.

Key features are outlined below:

ALPHAS

- Average alpha spreads, which were running at 1.2 percent prior to October 19th had, by the morning of the 20th, more than doubled to three percent. They continued to rise for the rest of the period, peaking at over 3.4 percent. (The percentage spread, of course, reflects the widening in absolute terms, together with the fall in the price of shares in general during the period.)

- Average alpha touches increased more slowly than spreads in other stocks. Prior to the crash, alpha touch averaged 0.8 percent.

Towards the end of the period, the average touch settled at around two percent.

- The total size of the market reduced from an average per stock of 650,000 shares to 300,000 shares on October 20th (in value terms, the fall was steeper). At the same time, market makers substantially reduced the maximum size offered. In the week before October 19th, many alphas had quotes in L x L (100,000 shares) or at least 50,000 shares, giving an average maximum quote size of 64,000 shares. On the 19th and 20th, the number of L x L quotes was reduced so that the average size of the maximum quote fell to 34,000 shares. In the week to October 30th both the total market size and the maximum quote size began a slow recovery, and this recovery has continued to the present.

- A significant size premium emerged for alphas. Normally the difference between the yellow strip quote and the quote at maximum quote size is very small, averaging only 0.05 percent across all alphas. After a peak on the 20th, the premium settled at 0.25 percent for the rest of the week and fell in the succeeding week (see Figure Britain-2.13).

BETAS

- Average beta touches and spreads showed a profile similar to that of alphas. Spreads which had averaged about 2.5 percent prior to the crash moved up sharply by Tuesday 20th to over five percent. Average touches, from a pre-crash level of around 1.8 percent, rose more slowly than spreads to over four percent by October 30th. (The observation for October 20th is clearly something of a quirk. In the fast moving conditions on that Tuesday there were many occasions when stocks had negative touches).

- The total size of the market for betas contracted from an average of around 120,000 shares to around 40,000 shares per stock—a 66 percent reduction. There is an indication of a recovery by October 30th but this recovery had not led to an increase in the average maximum quote size. The maximum quote size languished around 12,000 shares compared to 50,000 shares before October 19th.

- The average premium for dealing in the maximum available size (the maximum size being much smaller as we have seen) rose from about 0.1 percent to about 0.5 percent (the spike on October 20th reflects the abnormal negative touches on that day.)

GAMMAS

*   Average spreads for gammas rose proportionately less than other SEAQ stocks but from an already higher level. Touches widened throughout the period from around three percent to about six percent.

*   Total market size for the average gamma stock dropped sharply from around 20,000 shares to 6,000 shares and the average maximum quote size came down from 7,000 shares to around 2,500 shares. Since quotes of above 1,000 shares for gammas are deemed to be firm, this reduction means there were very few firm quotes in gammas on days following October 19th; the situation had not recovered by October 30th.

*   The size premium for dealing at larger sizes rose approximately threefold, despite the fact that the maximum available size had been reduced considerably.

Price Quality

There are two distinct aspects to the question of price quality. Firstly, did quoted prices move "sensibly" in relation to each other and secondly, were the quoted prices available anyway?

The first was a particular concern in alpha stocks where there were obvious, substantial differences in relative price movement. For example, Cable and Wireless fell 40 percent while BT fell only 17 percent over the same period.

The results of an analysis of the price movements of each FTSE stock (relative to the movement in the market as measured by the FT All Share Index), against each stock's US dollar exposure, (a company's share of profits arising in the US) shows that stocks (such as RTZ, Welcome, BOC, Jaguar) with high dollar exposure performed much worse than stocks with a lesser dollar exposure e.g., Marks and Spencer, BT, ASDA, etc.

While one should be aware that this relatively simple measure of dollar exposure may not provide a total picture since apparent exposures may be more or less hedged, it is apparent from the results that there is a clear relationship: stocks which were most vulnerable in terms of dollar exposure have fared worse. Obviously other factors influence individual stocks differently but there is nothing here to suggest that price relativities have moved in an inconsistent way.

The second question concerning price quality is the extent to which price quotes displayed on the screen were actually available for trading. We have noted that "fast markets" were declared on both October 19th and 20th. It is also well known that getting access to market makers was extremely difficult at many times on those days.

Let us look at the access difficulties first. The two day period saw an unprecedented level of business, an unprecedented number of quote changes and an unprecedented level of information flows. Like any industry, the securities industry is staffed and equipped for something like a "normal" level of business with some spare capacity for peak periods. There was substantial growth in activity during the first nine months of 1987 and some strains were beginning to show—not only in the settlement area but also in dealing systems where there were a number of plans afoot to expand or upgrade system capacities. Given this, it is unsurprising that with turnover of 100,000 bargains per day compared to an average level of around 60,000 per day, there were delays which, occurring while prices were moving very fast, must have been particularly vexatious.

Moving to the more general question of the availability and reliability of quotations for trading, some commentators have argued that quotations were substantially different from actual dealing prices obtained in the market for long periods during Monday 19th and Tuesday 20th. If this was true, then one would expect to see marked divergences between quotation and transaction prices. The major continuous market indicator, the FTSE 100 Index, is in fact calculated on the basis of mid price quotations of the best bid and best offer for each of the Index's 100 constituents and weighted by each constituent 's market capitalisation. In order to examine how reliable quotations were compared to actual transaction prices, we recalculated FTSE minute by minute for the two days using trade of dealing prices of customer transactions and compared this index to the official FTSE 100 Index.

Figure Britain-2.14 shows the results of the newly calculated FTSE using transaction prices against the official FTSE which uses quotations. As can be seen, apart from brief divergences—particularly around noon on the Monday—the two indices moved closely in step.

The brief divergences which occurred just past 12.00 on Monday and around 15.00 on the Tuesday could be simply a result of one or more technicalities which arise from this particular type of analysis.

Firstly, recall that the official FTSE is calculated using the mid-price of the best bid and best offer quotations. In using transaction prices to recalculate FTSE, these prices will almost always be away from the mid-price: customer buy orders being executed at the offer price whilst customer sell orders are executed at the bid price.

Secondly, actual transaction prices may be further away from the mid-price quotation if the transaction involved a very large order. As discussed earlier, a significant size premium emerged for alpha stocks during this time.

Thirdly, the divergences between the two FTSE calculations may be a result of inaccurately time-stamped transactions. Stray observations well away from the market could result from such inaccurate timings.

The closeness of the fit between these two indices is particularly encouraging especially in light of these technicalities. The results provide substantial evidence to suggest that for most of the two days, screen quotations (from which the official FTSE is calculated) were indeed a fair representation of where the market was.

Impact of Visibility and Internationalisation

We now focus our attention on two further issues concerning the effect of the high degree of visibility of the ISE's trading system on volatility, and the impact of foreign investors' activity on the UK market.

Visibility of the UK Market. It has been argued that the high level of visibility of SEAQ causes jumpiness among market makers which, in a volatile phase, generates "excessive" (and possibly spurious) price movements. Market makers may over-react, cutting prices more than is justified in order to protect themselves and possibly generating a domino-type effect as other market makers leapfrog downwards.

If this was true we would expect that stocks with higher visibility, (i.e., alphas), would be more susceptible to greater volatility than less visible stocks such as betas, gammas and deltas. Conversely, it could also be argued that because alphas make up a significant share of trading, visibility of the alpha market may exert some influence on the perceived visibility of the market as a whole. If this was the case, then one would expect similar levels of volatility across all sectors of the market and not just in alphas.

While conclusive results on volatility will require more research, a study of a sample of stocks from each of the four groups (international stocks, major ADR stock, other alphas, betas and gammas) has been conducted.

Obviously volatility increased for all types of stock during the crash period. We compared price volatility in the 15 business days before October 19th and the 15 business days after. The measure of volatility was the standard deviation of closing price changes. Changes in volatility are illustrated in Table Britain-2.2.

The results show some differences—volatility of international stocks and gammas apparently increased more than in alphas and betas. However, given that volatility of all types of stocks had increased enormously, these differences in volatility between different types of security can only be considered comparatively minor. In particular, the differential increase in volatility between alphas and betas is very small indeed. This is particularly significant given the fact that it is between alphas and betas that the main difference in visibility exists: transactions in alphas require instantaneous trade publication, whereas betas transactions are not published until the following day.

Our results indicate that there is no significant evidence that volatility has been stimulated by visibility. Nor do they indicate that a domino-type collapse of prices occurred—prices fell as selling pressure developed. Our results suggest that the enhanced visibility of ISE markets has meant price sensitive information and changes in market sentiment can be and are, much more quickly reflected in prices. The more quickly information is relayed to the market and absorbed into prices then the more efficient and (and fairer) is the market —"the stock exchange is the messenger, not the message."

On examining the statistical data there is no evidence to suggest that market makers responded irrationally, or that they panicked and over-reacted by making arbitrary or spurious price cuts. Indeed, our results suggests that prices moved to reflect trading pressure.

To recap, key results indicate that transaction prices and quotations show a very close relationship and there was no evidence of any domino-type effect movement in prices. Generally speaking, trends in price movements reflect the net customer trading activity: when there was net selling pressure, prices moved down as one would expect; when buying orders dominated, prices moved up.

EFFECT OF INTERNATIONALISATION

It might be that London, with a higher representation of international stocks, overseas securities houses and overseas client base, is more exposed to changes in global sentiment. London is a major centre for trading foreign stocks but, more importantly for the UK equity market, many major UK equities have a significant number of foreign holders. It is widely considered that shareholdings in the UK companies by overseas investors are likely to be more volatile than holdings by domestic institutions.

London, since it remained open with a high level of liquidity, would have been the easiest market in which foreign investors could raise cash. Investors wanting to reduce the equity content of their portfolios would have found it easier to trade into London.

The question which concerns us is whether foreign investors were more inclined to liquidate their holdings of UK stocks and if so, whether this was a factor which caused the UK market to fall more than it might otherwise have done?

It is unlikely that we will ever be able to answer this question with absolute certainty. There is no requirement for foreign investors to declare themselves to the ISE. Brokers may know but in very many cases transactions are dealt through nominees without any identification of the ultimate beneficial owner. However, we are able to examine the trading pattern of one particular group of foreign investors, namely holders of American Depositary Receipts of UK stocks. These holders are mainly American investors who have bought or sold UK equities in ADR form because of the relative ease in trading and settlement, especially when dealing outside of the UK.

First, looking at the volume of trading in UK ADRs during the period of the crash, we found that in London volumes had increased significantly from about one million ADRs per day before October to over 2.5 million per day during the week of October 19th.

The question that arises then is 'how much of this trading activity was a result of ADR holders selling into London?' Actual flowback, or the converting of ADRs back into equity form as a result of net selling pressure, was in fact limited; most of the turnover activity in ADRs represented transfers within the ADR holding community, and not sales of ADRs back into the UK market.

This result is born out by our analysis outlined in Table Britian 2.3 Column (a) which shows the ADR turnover in the U.S for each UK stock during the period from October 15th to November 6th. The next two columns show the percentage of each company's shares which were held in ADR form as at October 15th and November 6th. Column (d) is simply the percentage change in ADR holdings during these two dates. The final column calculates the net change in ADR holdings as a percentage of the ADRs traded over that period in the US.

For example, looking at British Gas, there were 3,216,000 ADRs traded in the US, or 32.1 million shares since there are ten British Gas shares to one ADR, during the period. Data from US depositaries show there was a 0.2 percent reduction in British Gas shares held in ADR form between October 15th and November 6th. Since there are 4,150 million shares in British Gas, 0.2 percent is equal to 8.3 million shares. This implies then that 8.3 million British Gas shares (or 0.2 percent of total British Gas holdings) had been sold by ADR holders and converted back into equity form, and this "flowback" is equivalent to only 25 percent of the total turnover of British Gas stock (in ADR form) in New York.

The two key points to note from the table are:

• The flowback as a percentage of the total market was relatively modest in most cases. Of the four cases in which flow back exceeded one percent, two, Jaguar and Reuters, were particularly hard hit by the crash (Jaguar because of the high proportion of its earnings originating in the US and Reuters because of its heavy involvement in the financial sector which was being hit hardest by the crash).

• The proportion of US turnover which was flowback varied markedly from company to company (from four percent for Hanson through to 38 percent for Glaxo). From this, while it is clear the US investors were heavy sellers of ADRs (as they were of all types of equity), trading was by no means all one way— there were buyers as well as sellers in the US market for UK shares.

There is nothing here to suggest that US investors were panicking to get out of UK equities. This result is supported by a comparison of trading and net selling of alpha stocks during the crash week with the week prior to the crash. Since the degree of foreign involvement varies among alpha stocks, we would expect to see a systematic bias towards higher trading in those with higher foreign involvement if the argument that foreign investors were dumping UK equities into London was to hold.

In a comparison for the 126 alphas, plotting comparative turnover in the pre-crash week and the week of October 19th, no obvious pattern emerges, implying little support for the hypothesis that UK stocks were being dumped by the US investors.

It is important to stress that our knowledge in this area is extremely sketchy, and ISE has very little solid information on investors from overseas. What we do know about US investors arises solely from their holdings of UK stocks in depositary receipt form. It is important to bear in mind that some US investors may choose to hold stock in non-depositary form while others may have opted not to sell the depositary receipt (which would result in a stamp duty should they decide to repurchase at a later date) but instead may trade in a derivative product to hedge their exposure.

Recovery

This section updates the liquidity situation to the year end. The most apparent change between the pre-crash and crash period is the decline in turnover. The number of transactions has been particularly affected, with current levels running at between 40 percent to 50 percent of pre-October levels. The value of transactions has fallen less sharply, suggesting some change in the client profile. We saw that during the latter part of October, there was an upsurge of small business, which is usually indicative of individual investors. The implication now is that the market is more the preserve of professional investors.

The continued volatility of markets represents increased risk which has brought an unwelcome rise in the cost of dealing and a reduction in market depth. Prior to mid October, the largest daily movement of FTSE was 56 points. Since then daily movements of 50 points and more have become more commonplace (six daily movements of 50 points or more in November and December 1987). Only when price movements become less extreme can we expect spreads to return to something like the lower levels which prevailed before the crash.

Spreads and touches have narrowed somewhat for alphas and betas but still remain much higher than before October. Alpha and beta touches at the year end were about double the pre-crash level. Gamma touches remained at their high levels with little recovery.

The continuing lack of liquidity (measured by the touch) in gammas suggests that the market for less active securities is not as robust as the alpha and beta markets in times of stress. It is said that because gamma prices are only firm for quotes in over 1000 shares or at the option of the market makers, gamma quotations on SEAQ screens were frequently and persistently unavailable for trading (contrast to our results for alphas).

While it is not feasible to insist that market makers quote firm prices for gammas in 1000 shares, there is a need to tighten the commitment of market makers in gammas to improve price quality. Perhaps a requirement to make firm prices in a significantly smaller size would be more appropriate. This would avoid the risk to market makers from making firm prices in inactive stocks (market makers who trade in gammas experienced substantial losses on gamma positions which they could not trade out) while ensuring that screen prices were available for dealing.

However, while spreads and touches have recovered only slightly there has been a greater improvement in market quality as measured by market depth, as Figures Britain-2.16 and 2.17 illustrate. In each group of securities—alphas, betas and gammas, the graphs show:

•   A recovery of total market size (Figure Britain-2.16).

•   A recovery in the maximum size of quote (Figure Britain-2.17).

•   A decline in the size premium for dealing at that maximum size.

FIGURE BRITAIN-2.1
FTSE Daily High-Low - Open-Close
July to December 1987

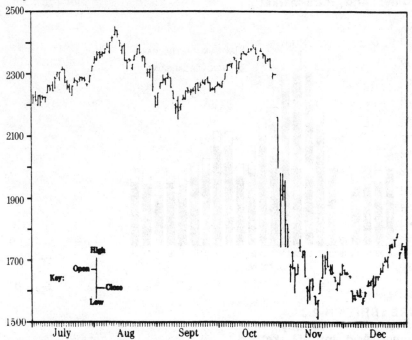

TABLE BRITAIN-2.1
Proportion of UK Insurance Companies'
And Pension Funds'
Portfolios Invested In Equities

Invested in:	1982 (end period)	1983	1984	1985	1986	1987 Q3(e)
UK Equities	34%	35%	39%	39%	41%	44%
Overseas Equities	8%	10%	10%	11%	12%	14%

(e) = estimated
Source — Bank of England

FIGURE   BRITAIN-2.2
Bargains Traded Per Day
Customer And Intra-Market

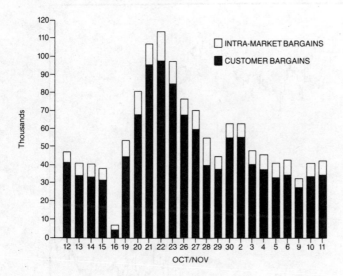

FIGURE   BRITAIN-2.3
TurnOver Value Per Day
Customer And Intra-Market

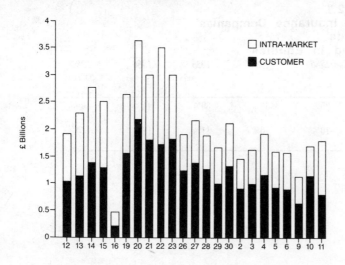

FIGURE BRITAIN-2.4
Daily Customer Bargains
Purchases And Sales

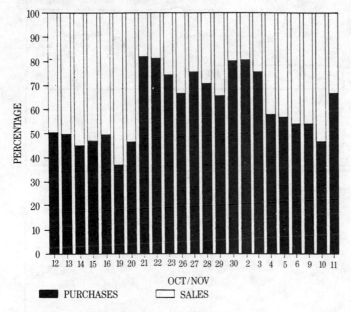

PURCHASES   SALES

FIGURE BRITAIN-2.5
Net Customer Purchases-UK Equity
Daily: October 12-November 11

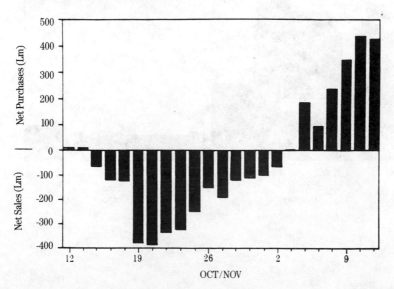

FIGURE BRITAIN-2.6:   Shell T&T
19th and 20th October

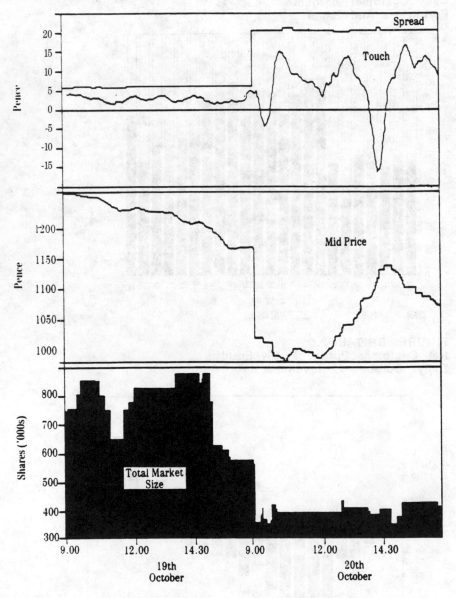

FIGURE BRITAIN-2.7: Amstrad
19th & 20th October

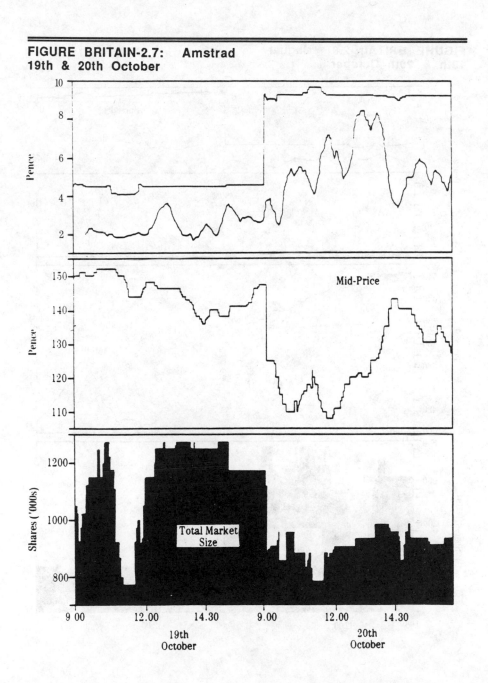

FIGURE BRITAIN-2.8:   Jaguar
19th & 20th October

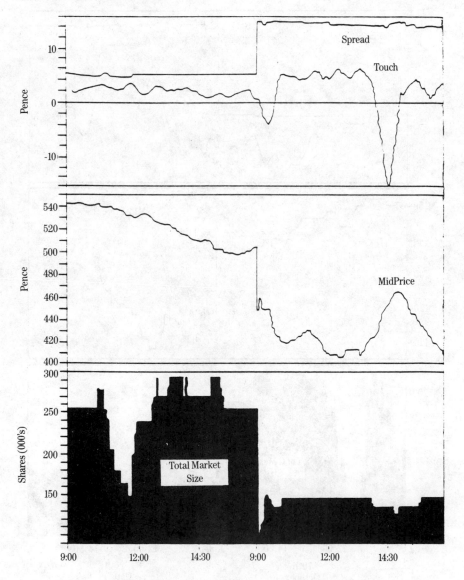

FIGURE BRITAIN-2.9
Percentage Touch-October 12, 1987
Alpha, Beta and Gamma Stocks

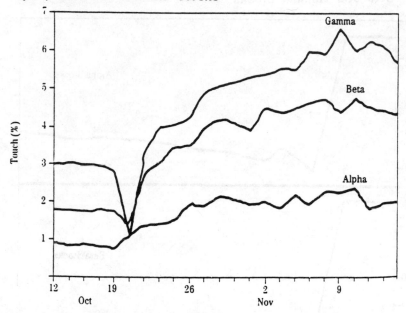

FIGURE BRITAIN-2.10: Average
Percentage Spread-October 12 to November 13
Alpha, Beta and Gamma Stocks

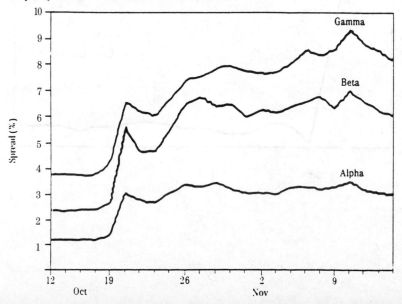

FIGURE   BRITAIN-2.11
Total Market Size-October 12 to November 13
Alpha, Beta and Gamma Stocks

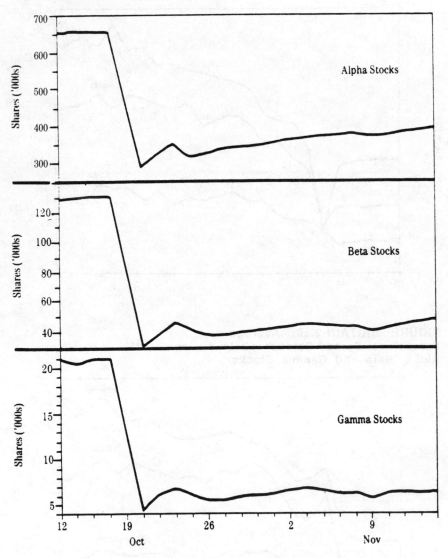

FIGURE BRITAIN-2.12
Maximum Quote Size-October 12 to November 13
Alpha, Beta and Gamma Stocks

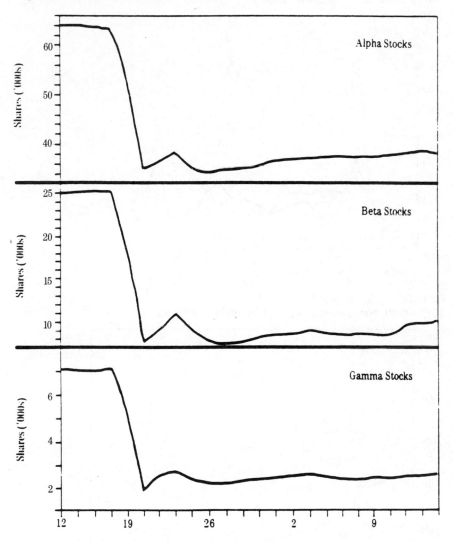

FIGURE   BRITAIN-2.13
Size   Premium-October   12   to   November   13
Alpha,   Beta   and   Gamma   Stocks

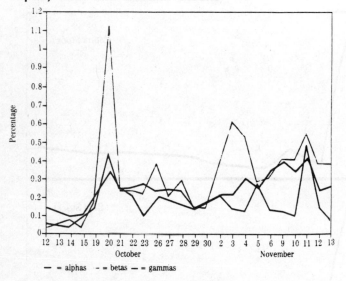

FIGURE   BRITAIN-2.14:   FTSE
19th   October-Quotes   v.   Transaction   Prices

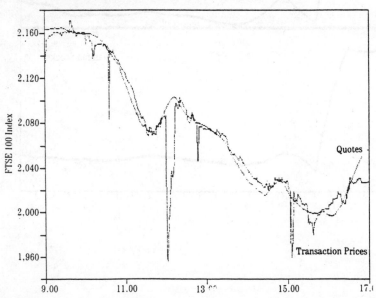

TABLE BRITAIN-2.2
Volatility In Four Groups Of Stocks

Stock Group	Standard Deviation of Daily % Price Movements:		Relative Volatility
	(a) before	(b) after	(b/a)*100 %
International	.050	.220	437.5
Alphas	.063	.218	345.2
Betas	.070	.239	340.6
Gammas	.062	.272	415.9
All Stocks	.062	.237	383.1

TABLE BRITAIN-2.3
Trading and Holdings of UK ADR's in USA:
October 15-November 6

	US Trading of UK ADRs	Holdings in US Depositories as % of Total Shareholding as at:			Flowback as % of Trading
	('000s ADRs) (a)	Oct 15 % (b)	Nov 6 % (c)	Flowback % (d)	% (e)
Beecham	2,867	1.3	1.6	+ 0.3	n.a.
British Gas	3,216	3.8	3.6	− 0.2	25
BP (F/P)	5,846	5.2	5.1	− 0.1	9
Brit Tel	788	0.8	0.8	0	0
Glaxo	19,147	14.6	13.6	− 1.0	38
Hanson	16,192	18.2	18.1	− 0.1	4
ICI	4,111	11.2	10.4	− 0.8	31
Jaguar	19,049	37.6	34.9	− 2.7	26
NatWest	952	1.9	1.8	− 0.1	15
Reuters	7,074	45.7	44.6	− 1.1	8
Saatchi	2,065	20.9	19.4	− 1.5	32
Shell	2,145	3.0	2.9	− 0.1	17

(Source: Kleinwort Grieveson)

FIGURE   BRITAIN-2.16:
Total Market Size-October 12 to December 29
Alpha, Beta and Gamma Stocks

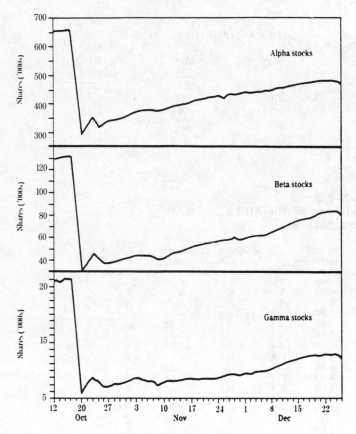

FIGURE BRITAIN-2.17:
Maximum Quote Size-October 12 to December 29
Alpha, Beta and Gamma Stock

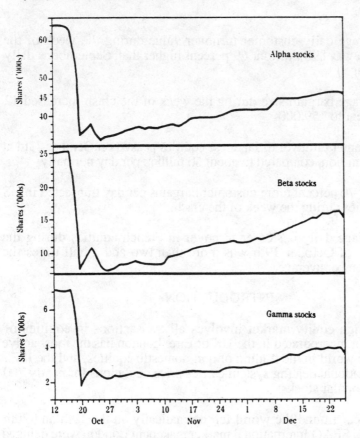

3. FOREIGN EQUITY MARKET

- During the week of October 19th, over 50 percent more customer bargains per day were transacted compared with September's daily average.

- Average daily customer turnover value during the week of the crash was 890 million, 69 percent higher than September's daily average.

- Average bargain size during the week of the crash increased 12 percent to 159.000.

- Customer turnover in Japanese equities peaked on October 23rd at 331 million, compared to about 60 million per day normally.

- Over 70 percent more customer bargains per day transacted in US equities during the week of the crash.

- Average daily customer turnover in French equities during the week of October 19th was more than two and a half times the September average.

INTRODUCTION

The foreign equity market involves all transactions in equities of companies not incorporated in the UK or Eire. London has the most active market in the world in the trading of non-domestic equities, and the ISE's SEAQ International dealing system carries price quotations for nearly 700 of the most popular stocks.

As markets around the world fell dramatically on the 19th and 20th October 1987, SEAQ International market makers in London were deluged with sell orders. While the debate about the reasons for the sudden change in mood of investors will no doubt continue for many months, this article concentrates on an examination of how the London market in foreign equities performed under the extreme pressures of the week of the crash, and to what extent turnover volume has held up subsequently.

The analysis of transactions for the foreign equity market is considerably more difficult than for the UK equity market. The principal problem in analysing the foreign equity market is the fact that many of the large international houses who account for a considerable proportion of turnover in London are not currently members of the International Stock Exchange, although is expected that they will become members when the Financial Services Act is fully implemented late this year. As only member firms of the ISE are required to report their transactions to the Checking System, a substantial proportion of trading in London is not included in checking statistics. In addition, as all non-members are by definition 'customers', a trade between a SEAQ International market maker who is a member and one who is not, for example, is recorded as a customer bargain rather than an intra market bargain.

All market makers including non-members do now voluntarily report their trading in most of the major stocks displayed on SEAQ International, and this has been a useful addition to trading statistics, as well as enhancing market visibility. However, these figures are far less detailed than those from checking, and do not include many of the bargains transacted in London by private investors. The statistics we used in this report are taken from the checking system because it provides a much richer source of data. It is important to note that the general turnover trends from Checking statistics are conformed by those obtained from SEAQ International trade reports.

TRADING ACTIVITY

Turnover in foreign equities almost doubled in the year following Big Bang, growing steadily from a daily average of about 300 million in November 1986 to the October 1987 peak of over 600 million daily. Since October turnover has fallen, and by December turnover was showing a year on year decline of 22 percent by value against December 1986.

The exceptionally high daily average customer turnover in October is due primarily to the very high volume of business during the week of the crash. More detailed analysis of trading in different country sectors is outlined later in this report.

Activity on SEAQ International

As share prices tumbled around would, especially on Monday 19th and Tuesday 20th October, it was clear that the sheer number of sellers trying to contact market makers and the unprecedented speed of price movements overwhelmed both human and technological resources. As a result of these conditions, SEAQ International price quotes were declared officially 'indicative only' at 09.14 on Monday 19th and remained so until 14.50 adding to the foreign equity market's problem were long delays on other information systems such a Reuters, which normally carry up-to-date prices from overseas' markets and, of course, the chaos on the overseas' exchanges themselves.

Nevertheless, trading in London continued effectively by telephone. On Monday 19th, member firms transacted over 40 percent more bargains with customers with a value over 60 percent greater than the previous month's average trading levels (see Figure Britain-3.1).

Following the record overnight falls in world markets on Monday 19th and Tuesday 20th—the Dow Jones Industrial Average Index dropped 508 points (23 percent) and the Nikkei-Dow rapidly reached its maximum permitted daily decline of 15 percent—some overseas houses were ordered by their Head Offices not to quote prices on SEAQ International on Tuesday 20th.

In addition, the Hong Kong sector of SEAQ International was officially closed for the week in line with the closure of the Hong Kong Stock Exchange and market makers in Japanese stocks were not obliged to quote prices in view of the Tokyo Stock Exchange's rules limiting price falls. Despite this, trading on the basis of telephone negotiation not only continued, but once again did so at considerably higher levels than before the crash, in almost all sectors (although not, of course, the Hong Kong sector).

There was, unfortunately, often great difficulty contacting market makers to trade. Some inestors suggested that they were deliberately not answering telephones. However, given the fact that there was a 40 percent increase in the number of bargains actually transacted, this suggests that market makers simply did not have the human resources available to answer any more calls than they in fact did. While it would be unreasonable and uneconomic to expect firms to gear up for such unprecedented levels of activity, it is recognised that the efficiency and capacity of the trading system will need to be improved and expanded, and plans to do so are already well underway.

Wall Street staged a record rally on Tuesday night, and this led to much calmer conditions in London for the rest of the week. From Wednesday SEAQ International screen prices were generally once again the basis for trading in the quoted stocks, and turnover volumes continued to increase. Over the week as a whole, the average daily turnover was more that 50 percent higher than in September, in both volume and value terms.

FIGURE   BRITAIN-3.1
Daily Customer Turnover
Total Foreign Equities

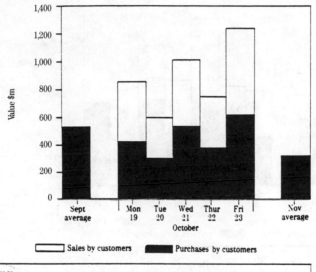

Average Bargain (£000's) Size	142	S P	160 165	115 125	196 171	149 105	239 175	86

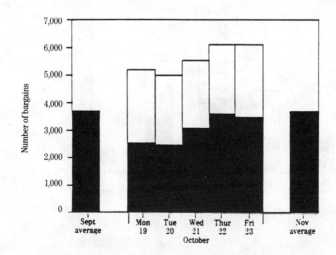

FIGURE   BRITAIN-3.2
Daily Customer Turnover
French Equities

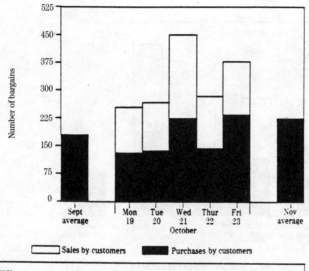

Average Bargain (£000's) Size	499	S P	951 861	502 481	910 947	155 167	1.083 659	304

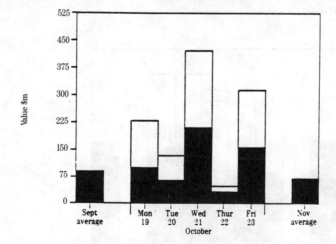

FIGURE   BRITAIN-3.3
Daily Customer Turnover
German Equities

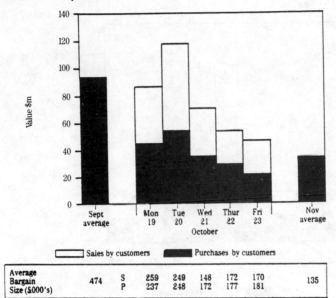

Average Bargain Size ($000's)	474	S	259	249	148	172	170	135
		P	237	248	172	177	181	

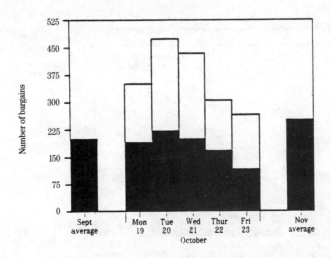

FIGURE BRITAIN-3.4
Daily Customer Turnover
Japanese Equities

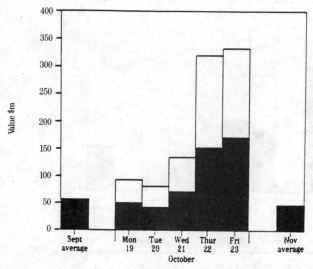

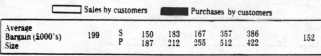

Average Bargain (£000's) Size	199	S P	150 187	183 212	167 255	357 512	386 422	152

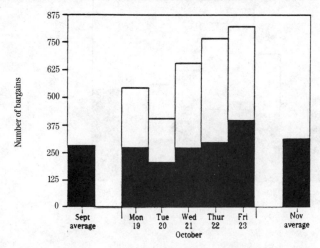

FIGURE BRITAIN-3.5
Daily Customer Turnover
Australian Equities

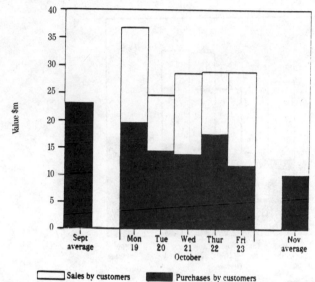

Average Bargain (£000's) Size	29	S	35	25	41	36	39	13
		P	38	31	18	16	13	

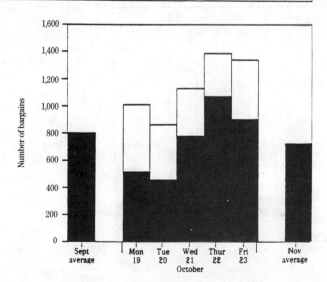

FIGURE BRITAIN-3.6
Daily Customer Turnover
US Equities

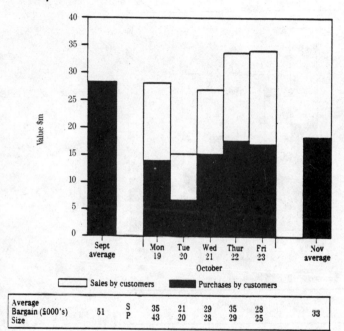

Average Bargain (£000's) Size	51	S	35	21	29	35	28	33
		P	43	20	28	29	25	

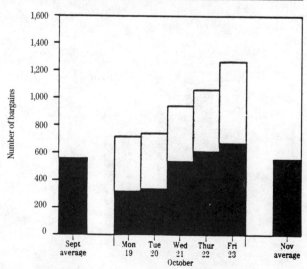

It is generally agreed that virtually all major investors' orders on Monday and Tuesday were to sell, and to sell any shares that they could. Indeed, gold shares were being sold at the same time as the gold price was rising. It may appear odd, therefore, that the Checking statistics on these days show an even split of customer sales and purchases through member firms both in volume and value terms. While this is usually the case in normal market conditions, it is not to be expected during a crash. In the UK equity market, market makers had to take a large amount of stock onto their books, especially on Monday. In order to try to explain this surprising balance, turnover in the equities of some individual countries is analysed in detail later.

Liquidity and Depth

During the initial period of heavy price falls, investors' appeared to differentiate little between different companies' stock, and were selling any equities that they could, in any market that they could. Some market makers claimed that they gained new customers, possibly due to a greater liquidity in London that in overseas' markets. However, liquidity between countries and individual stocks varied, and many smaller stocks became difficult to trade in size.

As figure Britain-3.1 shows, the average bargain size in foreign equities over the week actually incerased.

Not surprisingly price spreads widened dramatically, especially outside home market opening hours. Spreads of about three times pre-crash levels seems to have been the norm, although possibly less when reliable home market prices were available.

Both sizes and spreads have improved a great deal since October, but are still not back to pre-crash levels, reflecting the increased risk in making markets under volatile conditions.

INDIVIDUAL COUNTRY SECTIONS

The following sections provide more detailed analysis of different groups of foreign equities traded on the ISE.

French and German Equities

Turnover in European equities makes up some two-thirds of total foreign equity turnover value, but only about one-quarter of the number of bargain. The very large average bargain size characterises the professional nature of trading in London, with little private investor interest. Also important in the context of the crash is the considerable overlap of home market opening hours with trading hours in London.

Daily turnover in French and German equities for the week of October 19th are shown in Figures Britain-3.2 and 3.3. There are interesting similarities and differences between the two countries.

The most striking difference is that, whereas turnover value in French equities over the week averaged over two and a half times the September average, turnover value in German equities was 20 percent lower (despite an 85 percent increase in the number of bargains). The market in German equities was almost unique in this respect. A possible partial explanation for the increase in French equity turnover is that the vast majority of shares on the Paris bourse do not have their prices quoted continuously, unlike French equities on SEAQ International. In addition, the average bargain value indicates that investors were able to deal in very large sizes in London. Both of these factors may well have attracted business.

The decrease in turnover in German equities may have been partially due to investors being reluctant to deal in them in London outside the home market opening hours. The announcement in October by the West German Government of the new withholding tax on investments in Germany may also have had a depressing effect. Why there was such a distinct contrast in trading activity between the French and German sectors is still, however, unclear.

Overall trading in both French and German equities showed only a slightly greater value of customer sales than purchases over the week as a whole. European equities in total mirrored this trend, and as this sector makes up the bulk of trading by value in foreign equities, this balance is the principal reason for the overall balance of sales and purchases in the foreign equity market noted earlier.

The most likely reason for this, supported by our research, is that when London market makers were forced to buy stock from investors they rapidly sold it on to the home markets, which in Europe were open concurrently.

It is also interesting to note that the value of trading in French stocks in November held up considerably better than the average for the foreign equity market as a whole, whilst the value of trading in German stocks fell to only 36 percent of its September value.

JAPANESE EQUITIES

The Japanese equity market in London is, like the European markets, principally a professional one. There is no overlap of home market trading hours with those in London.

While the volume of trading in Japan itself fell during the crash, mainly because of the 'limit fall' rule for prices mentioned earlier, trading by ISE members in Japanese equities increased steadily through the week apart from a slight dip on Tuesday, when SEAQ International market makers were not obliged to quote prices following Tokyo's overnight limit fall. The statistics show average daily bargains for the week 127 percent higher than the September average, with value increased by 243 percent (see Figure Britain-3.4). On Friday, three times as many bargains, and six times as much value was transacted compared to the previous month's average. Averages bargain size rose to 400,000, compared to the September norm of about 200,000.

Although the London market was said to be more bearish in sentiment than the Japanese home market during the crash, it appears to have matched buyers and sellers well, and the volume of business transacted certainly supports the suggestion that new customers were attracted to the market at the time. It is also interesting to note that the daily turnover value for November, whilst 14 percent lower than in September, was considerably better in this respect than for the foreign equity market as a whole.

AUSTRALIAN EQUITIES

The market in Australian equities in London is considerably different in character from those in French, German and Japanese equities. This is most obviously apparent in the size, only 29,000 for example, in September (see Figure Britain-3.5). This indicates the importance of the individual investor in the market which, despite being much smaller in value than those already discussed, transacts about as many customer bargains as all three put together. Like Japan, there is no overlap of trading hours between the Australian home market and London.

Most interesting is that, just as for the UK equity market, there is strong evidence to suggest that private investors were net purchasers of

Australian equities during the second half of the week, whilst institutions continued to sell. This is suggested both by the significantly larger proportion of bargains that were purchases on Wednesday (69 percent), Thursday (77 percent) and Friday (68 percent); and even more strongly by the average bargain sizes, which fell to about 15,000 for purchases whilst rising to about 40,000 for sales. In contrast to most countries, the total value of customer purchases of Australian equities during the week was also ten percent higher than the value of sales.

The pattern of many more purchases than sales in fact continued in November, but whilst the daily number of bargains during the month was only ten percent lower than in September, the daily value fell 58 percent.

US EQUITIES

Trading on Wall Street begins early afternoon London time, but as the New York Stock Exchange forbids its members to trade in London whilst its own floor is open, trading activity in US equities in London is concentrated into the first half of the day.

With an average bargain size of 51,000 in September, this suggests a fair degree of private investor involvement in this sector (see Figure Britain-3.6).

Whilst trading on Wall Street soared over the week of 19th-23rd October, turnover value by ISE members in London was unchanged compared with the previous month's average. The number of bargains transacted however increased by 71 percent. This would suggest that professional trading was depressed over the week—many US securities houses were instructed by their head Offices not to quote prices on SEAQ International during the crash—whilst individual investors traded more actively than usual. The very low value of turnover on Tuesday (after the overnight fall of 508 points in the Dow Jones Index), is particularly striking.

The below-average proportion of customer purchases on Monday and Tuesday, and above-average proportion for the rest of the week, provides a little evidence to suggest that individuals may have been selling at first but the buying after Wall Street's Tuesday night rally, but this evidence is far less conclusive than in the UK and Australian equity markets.

The daily average number of bargains in November returned to the September level, but the daily value fell by just over a third.

Conclusion

In common with other markets around the world, there were a number of complaints during the period of the crash about the difficulties in trading and obtaining accurate price information in the London foreign equity market. However, in hindsight, despite their irritation at the time, many market participants now think that the market performed well, considering the circumstances—or at least that there was little more that could have been done to improve conditions at the time. The trading statistics certainly show London in a very good light.

That does not mean that there are no lessons to be learned form the experience. Whilst it is recognised that it would not be economic to build up systems and staffing levels to cope with enormous unpredictable surges in volume, there appears to be a strong feeling that computer system response times during peak periods require improvement. Long delays in the updating of prices not only lead to them being unrepresentative of the true market, but could also allow market makers to avoid trading. On the Monday and Tuesday of the week of the crash, lack of confidence in the systems caused some market makers to stop even trying to update their prices.

Although it may be coincidence, there is also evidence to suggest, in general, turnover in the equities of those countries which increased most during the week of the crash held up the best during November. The message could be that those who tried hardest to give the best quality of service during the crash will be rewarded with a greater share of business in the months to come. The others will have to try harder in the future. In general, however, the performance of the foreign equity market during the week of the crash should give us confidence in the future of foreign equities trading in London.

4. MARKET INTER-RELATIONSHIPS AND DERIVATIVE PRODUCTS

- All three markets (cash, traded options and futures) saw record volumes during the crash; traded options traded a record 121,000 contracts on October 21st while LEFFE traded over 9,000 FTSE contracts daily on Monday 19th and Tuesday 20th.

- All three markets traded continuously throughout the week of the crash. Spreads increased significantly in all markets as trading risk increased. In general, the size in which deals could be made decreased. Market quality has recovered in all three markets though equity spreads and option premia are still higher than pre-October levels.

- A significant number of investors were short of FTSE puts at the start of the week. The effective closure of the market on October 16th (due to storms) meant that these investors had no opportunity to close positions before substantial losses had been incurred. These investors were seeking to close positions at almost any price on the Monday and Tuesday.

- Margins were raised in the options market on Tuesday 20th, and also at various times during the week for FTSE futures. This, together with the principle of marking to market, ensured the robustness of the markets by limiting the credit risk associated highly leveraged instruments.

- Index arbitrage and portfolio insurance trading are not yet well developed in the UK. Trading difficulties, largely relating to access to the cash market, restricted index arbitrage even further than usual during October 19th and 20th.

- The absence of effective index arbitrage, combined with the preceived difficulties of access to market makers in the equity market, allowed the FTSE future to trade at a significant discount.

INTRODUCTION

This report explores the inter-relationship between three markets—the UK equity market, the London Traded Options Market (LTOM) and the London International Financial Futures Exchange (LIFFE)—during the October market crash. Undertaken as a joint exercise by the ISE and LIFFE, the study comments on the quality of the separate markets during the week of October 19th.

The quality of each market is assessed and compared to previous levels. Because of the diversity of the markets, no single information point is available (indeed, one of the lessons of the crash is the need for more, integrated information on these related markets). Our results are derived from information sources ranging from the exchanges themselves, the clearing houses and from discussions with practitioners.

During the week of the crash, both the UK equity market and the LIFFE market experienced unprecedented selling pressure. The traded options market experienced similar unprecedented levels of trading as investors, who earlier in the year had written put options, sought to reduce their exposure to falling equity prices by closing their short put positions or opening long put positions.

The existence of inter-relationships between the markets is well known to practitioners in those markets. More recently, particularly in light of "The Report of the US Presidential Task Force on Market Mechanisms" (the Brady Report), the interconnections have become a topic of much wider discussion.

The Brady Report concluded that the breakdown of normal feedback or information flows between the markets was a significant, perhaps crucial, element leading to the market break. Two factors particularly influenced their view. One was the breakdown of the use of index arbitrage strategies which maintain the price link between the cash or stock market and derivative markets (futures and options). The other was the lack of a centralized clearing system between the various exchanges. Because proceeds from a sale on one exchange may be required to meet a purchase on another, delays in the movement of such funds introduces risk and the possibility that the system may seize up, resulting in a form of "financial gridlock," not because of any real insolvency but because of temporary cash flow delays.

These problems are particularly acute in the US because of the relative size of the various markets. For example, the Chicago Mercantile Exchange's S & P 500 futures contract routinely trades twice as much in terms of underlying share value as the NYSE. Price consistency and ease of financial flows are clearly of paramount importance when the level of trading of interconnected exchanges are of similar orders of magnitude.

The position in the UK is markedly different. The derivative product markets,while they have grown rapidly, are still relatively small in relation to the underlying cash market. The combined trading in FTSE traded options and FTSE futures is equivalent to about 20 percent of UK equity turnover.

The considerable differences in size between the UK markets reduce the risk of a financial gridlock in payments, thus limiting the impact of any problems which may occur, as well as limiting the impact and extent of price anomalies between markets.

However, significant price anomalies did occur between the UK equity and derivative markets and these may have been contributory factors in the crash. This issue is examined in detail later on and results indicate that the way to limit the impact of price anomalies is to facilitate the connections which maintain price consistency between markets. It is hindering operations such an index arbitrage, which contribute to price consistency, is a solution to the problem of disconnected markets.

The structure of this report proceeds by examining in detail the type and scope of activity on each of the three markets. We begin by looking at the UK equity market. Much of this has already been covered extensively in Section Two of this Quarterly. Here, special attention is paid to the alpha stocks which represent the underlying securities on which individual stock options and futures products are based.

This is followed by an examination of the ISE's traded options market and its performance during the week of the crash. We then proceed to look at the LIFFE market, concentrating on the FTSE 100 index future and its relationship to the cash market. Key features of each market are highlighted, and events are pieced together from which we are able to draw certain conclusions relating to the impact of inter-relationships between these markets.

UK EQUITY MARKET

Because our interest is in the cash market in relation to futures and options, the focus is on the most active segment of the market, the alpha stocks. These 126 stocks, as well as being the most consistently active stocks, include the underlying equities for trade options in futures stocks and other derivative products based on the FTSE 100 index.

The features of the cash or stock market during the crash period which were of key importance in the relationship between that market and the derivative markets, come under three headings—volumes, volatility, market and price quality, and these are outlined in detail below.

Trading Volume

Volumes in the cash market have been growing during the course of 1987, paralleled by the growth of futures and options trading. The proportion represented by alphas has generally averaged between 50 percent to 60 percent of the total.

During the week of the crash, turnover reached unprecedented levels. Since sellers were keen to reduce their holdings, and since alphas represented the largest and most liquid stocks, the proportion of UK equity turnover accounted for by alphas was considerably higher at (68 percent) than usual. Figure Britain-4.1 shows the daily turnover in alpha stocks for the three week period 12th October to November 2nd (excluding October 16th when because of the storm, the figures are abnormally low).

VOLATILITY

Price volatility increased very substantially during the crash period and this had important implications for equity market liquidity, options premia and price spreads in derivative markets. Prior to October 19th, the largest close to close change in FTSE was the 56 point drop in August 1987 following the publication of particularly unfavorable trade figures. Figure Britain-2.1 shows daily highs/lows for FTSE in the month of October. Three key features are apparent and have significant impact on the derivative product markets and the relationship with the cash market:

- Large close-to-close daily movements.

- Very large movements between one day's closing and the next day's opening.

- Enormous movements within the day e.g., as Figure Britain-2.1 shows, October 20th saw an overall downward movement of 67 points but a difference between the high and low of the day of 236.9 points.

MARKET AND PRICE QUALITY

The market crash, since it marked a sharp change in market risk, had a serious impact on quality as measured by depth and cost of dealing. Figures Britain-2.9 to 2.12 illustrate four measures of market quality during the four week period, October 12th to November 6th. These results have already been discussed in detail in Section Two of this Quarterly; to recap, the key conclusions drawn were:

- Alpha spreads (the difference between each market makers bid and offer price quotation), more than doubled.

- Alpha touches (the difference between the best bid and offer) also increased but more slowly than spreads.

- Total size of the market (i.e., the sum of all market makers' bid sizes) was reduced by more than half.

- A significant size premium emerged.

More recently there has been a partial recovery in market quality for alphas. However, markets remain relatively volatile and the cost of market making remains correspondingly higher than before.

In looking at the question "to what extent were the quotations which were displayed on SEAQ screens actually available for trading?", our analysis comparing quotations and actual transaction prices in section 2 revealed very close correspondence between the two.

In summary, while market quality in terms of the widening of price spreads and touches and the reduction in quotation sizes fell, the cash or stock market continued to function at all times during the crash period. Trading was at unprecedented levels, and market makers' quotations provided a fair representation of the market.

LONDON TRADED OPTIONS MARKET

In this section we examine in more detail the level and pattern of trading in the traded options market. There has been a high rate of growth in the market since Big Bang. The growth has come part from the expanded product range—range traded options are now available on 59 equities, as well as two gilt options, two currency options and the FTSE 100 index option—but more from growing investor and professional use of traded options for hedging and investment purposes.

The period of the crash saw unprecedented volumes with over 121,000 contracts traded on October 21st. Volumes have since declined to an average of 36,000 contracts per day over the last quarter.

Patterns Of Trading

Two particular features of trading during the week of the crash were different from normal. One was the higher proportion of FTSE option contracts traded and secondly, the higher proportion of trading in FTSE put options. Figure Britain-4.2 shows the number of contracts traded for the pre-crash period and the crash period.

These figures are not surprising given the positions in the market before the crash. It has been a feature of the first part of 1987 that writing puts, particularly FTSE puts, was seen as a safe, easy way of enhancing the yield on a portfolio. Investors as a group had been writers (i.e., sellers) of out-of-the money FTSE puts. Premiums received on these puts had been very small, literally a few pence, but because the rise involved appeared low, the premiums were widely (but not universally) considered to be reasonable.

In the first half of October the situation was that investors as a group were short of FTSE puts, while options' market makers were generally long of (what seemed to be worthless) out-of-the money puts. This meant that investors were exposed to any significant price falls in the market as they, being writers of put options, had taken on the obligation to deliver should FTSE fall below a predetermined level and holders exercise their contracts. (In practice, since the FTSE option is a cash settled option, this means that the writer pays the holder an amount equal to the difference between the actual index and the strike value of the index option multiplied by 10.) This exposure of investors was to have significant, and for some very serious, implications in the week of the crash.

Clearly it is dangerous to be exposed in a falling market but what worsened the situation was the speed of the fall when it came and particularly the size of the fall from the close of Thursday 15th to the opening on Monday morning. Recall that Wall Street had fallen heavily on October 15th and and 16th. The fall on the 15th was not reflected in London as trading in London was nominal on Friday 16th because of severe weather conditions.

The first opportunity of writers of put options to get out or close their positions was Monday morning when FTSE opened 137 points down and carried on falling throughout the day. Inevitably this meant investors who had sold puts were in the market wanting to close at almost any price to stop their losses mounting further. This is confirmed by the relatively stable level of open interest during the crash period, despite very high volumes of trading.

The distribution of customer trading on October 19th in FTSE contracts is illustrated in Table Britain-4.1.

This shows clearly the emphasis on closing short put positions during the morning. However, by the afternoon, a more balanced pattern between puts and calls had emerged though still the emphasis was on buying, indicating a mixture of put closing and speculative activity in calls.

In individual stock options, a similar situation prevailed. Options' market makers were typically long of puts (i.e., they had bought put options, thus covering the possibility of a fall in the market) before the crash and were therefore exercising these puts at various times during the crash. The resulting purchases of stock by options' market makers was one of the few factors giving consistent support to the equity market during this period.

OPTIONS PRICE SPREADS

The FTSE option behaved very differently to individual stock options. This is a consequence of different client position (there were more investors or clients short of FTSE puts than of individual stock puts) and the greater uncertainty about prices as result of the discount of the FTSE futures on LIFFE.

Table Britain-4.2 shows the closing price spread for a sample of six options and the FTSE option, before the pre-crash and after the crash. The spreads are, as far as possible, those for at-the-money options. However, because it is only possible to introduce new series after the end of the trading day, the rapid movement of prices meant that there were often no at-the-money series at the close of business. This makes the movement in spreads more erratic than they would be if all observations were at-the-money. Despite this problem, the pattern of widening spreads is very clear. It is apparent that most of the widening of closing price spreads in individual stock option took place on the 20th.

Spreads on FTSE were especially volatile during the course of the 19th. Indeed, there has been some unfavorable comments about spreads. Table Britain-4.3, which is taken from trade records rather than quotations (spreads are measured by price differences between approximately simultaneous buy and sell trades), shows that spreads were volatile and very large at certain times in the day.

Two points are worth making when commenting on put spreads.

•   LTOM is an open outcry market so market makers, in very uncertain conditions, will quote wide prices. They are usually willing to deal inside their quotes. However, on the 19th, put buyers were not stopping to negotiate—in many cases they just wanted to trade at the quoted price.

•   There was some doubt about the true level of FTSE especially during fast market periods. This doubt was reinforced by the discount in the FTSE futures market (which we discuss later) where options market makers hedge their positions.

DISTRIBUTION OF TRADE SIZE

Based on an analysis of dealing slips during Monday 19th and Tuesday 20th October, size of trades reduced significantly during that time. Normally about 70 percent of transactions (as represented by dealing slips) are for ten or less contracts. This was the case of trades during Monday morning, but by Tuesday morning, almost 90 percent of trades in calls were for ten or less contracts and all put transactions were within this size.

MARGINING

The high levels of uncertainty during the crash prompted the LTOM to make intra-day margin calls on Tuesday 20th, and also to increase FTSE margins from 7.5 percent to 12.5 percent of the underlying value (plus for in-the-money contracts, minus for out-of-the-money contracts). Intra day margins were called between 1100 and 1300 on Tuesday 20th, and increased FTSE margins were implemented for closing client positions on Wednesday 21st onwards. Both measures were designed to increase the credit risk robustness of the market by ensuring investors were more able to cover potential losses from short (put) positions.

INTER-RELATIONSHIPS

The traded options market is highly dependent upon information feed. Trading in the crowd depends on information on options prices and the underlying asset prices. On October 19th and 20th, the volumes of transactions and number of quote changes on the UK equity market were such that there were significant delays in relaying such information to the screens on the LTOM floor. In fact, a separate, more robust, price and information feed for the floor of the LTOM is maintained but these feeds are still reliant on SEAQ for the data. The delays, together with the doubts about the quality of stock market prices and the fact that price movements were so large that all traded options' series were very considerably in or out-of-the money created very great uncertainty for the options traders. These factors are important in understanding the changes in market quality which the LTOM experienced in that period.

An additional factor which is relevant is the relatively low level of position taking by options' market makers, particularly those trading in the FTSE option. As a rule FTSE market makers will seek to lay-off their position in the LIFFE futures market. Options' market makers in individual stock options will similarly seek to open offsetting stock market positions. Therefore when, as was the case on October 19th and 20th, the level of the cash market was uncertain and when the FTSE future was trading at a discount to the apparent FTSE value on the cash market, it was difficult for options' market makers to hedge their positions, thus increasing their risk, resulting in them making wider price spreads and reducing their size.

LONDON FINANCIAL FUTURES MARKET

In the futures market we are interested in the market for the FTSE 100 Index future. FTSE futures account for only a minor part (three percent) of LIFFE's overall activity. We examine the trading pattern and level of activity. We examine the trading pattern and level of activity in this market and concentrate especially on the ensuing discount which arose between the price of the FTSE future and the actual index.

In discussing the FTSE 100 Index futures contract, we begin firstly by looking at normal operations and the typical type and amount of business transacted, before moving on to look at the week of 19th October 1987. It is important to set the scene because the contract has a number of characteristics which are quite distinct form those of US index futures contracts, e.g., expiry procedures, taxation and regulation. Without preempting any conclusions which may be drawn from this study, it is fair to say that these characteristics have direct bearing on the types of trading—programme, arbitrage, portfolio insurance—which are being closely scrutinized by US regulators as they seek to determine the effect of the interplay between cash and derivative markets during the crash.

As this is the first time we have discussed financial futures in this publication, it will be worthwhile to outline the major features of this particular financial instrument for readers who may be unfamiliar with this market. More detailed explanation of how the futures market operates can be obtained from LIFFE directly.

Like traded options, futures contracts are legally binding agreements made on the trading "pit," to buy or sell something in the future. This could be livestock, a foreign currency, or some other commodity.

A future on a stock index, like the FTSE 100 index, represents the equivalent of a stock portfolio of FTSE companies. It is a contract made between a seller (or writer of the contract) and a buyer (the holder of the contract), who have agreed on a price for the contract. That price reflects, in effect, the best expectation of the likely future value of the FTSE index.

When you buy a FTSE 100 Index futures contract you will gain if the stock market, as reflected in the index, is going up. If you sell a FTSE 100 Index futures contract you will gain if the stock market is going down.

The major difference between a future and a traded option is that with a futures contract, actual delivery must take place on the fixed date in the future at the price agreed today. Traded options give the holder the right to take delivery but he can choose not to. For this choice he pays a premium to the writer.

The London FTSE derivative market overall is shared more or less equally between FTSE options traded on the LTOM and futures traded on

LIFFE. One final point to note is that a one point movement in the FTSE futures price is equivalent to ten FTSE index points.

TRADING VOLUMES AND OPEN INTEREST

Since their inception on May 3rd 1984, FTSE futures have been slow in gaining depth and liquidity compared to index futures on overseas' exchanges. This relatively slow start contrasts with the popularity of other index futures contracts overseas such as the S& P 500 Index future in the US (where average daily volume was 77,000 contracts in 1986), and with more recent index future contracts in other overseas markets such as (pre-crash) Hong Kong's Hang Seng Index, Sydney Futures Exchange's Australian All Ordinaries Index future and Simex's Nikkei futures in Singapore.

Following Big Bang and during 1987, FTSE futures started to consolidate and grew considerably, both in the levels of volume and in open interest. Average daily volume for January to September 1987 (inclusive) was around 1600 contracts, a fourfold increase on 1986's daily average.

Open interest shows a similar pattern with over 6,000 contracts in the first nine months of 1987, compared with typical open interest level of about 2,000 contracts in 1986.

"Non-member" open interest in FTSE futures runs substantially higher than in any other contract traded on LIFFE. A distinction is made in recording "member" and "non-member" or client transactions. In the case of FTSE, "non-member" open interest runs at about the 75 percent to 80 percent level. This strongly suggests extensive outside interest in the contract, and, by contrast, relatively little market maker or LIFFE member participation. Other surveys confirm that this is institutional rather than retail business.

One final point that should be emphasized is that the FTSE futures market is a market for executing client orders rather than of principal to principal trading. There are some "locals," principal traders who are trading for their own account, but the major part of the business is client orders which are transacted in the pit.

ACTIVITY DURING THE CRASH

Total volume traded in FTSE futures in the week preceding the crash was 12,430 contracts, averaging 2,486 daily. This compares with an average daily volume in 1987 up to October of 1600. In the week of

October 19th, all volume records were broken. Total volume increased to 29,971 contracts (an average daily volume of 5,944). Both October 19th and 20th saw volumes over 9,00 contracts per day, with Tuesday standing as the record at 9,251. Trading was all in the December contracts, with no trading in the March contract or the spread.

Further volume records were established vis-a-vis the cash market. On Monday 19th and Tuesday 20th, FTSE futures turnover (in value terms) was 17 percent of equity market customer turnover, compared with an average for August and September of ten percent.

These figures indicate that futures were used more and not less over the week of October 19th. The trend in open interest showed a gradual increase from 7,371 contracts on 12th October to 9,317 on 23rd October. Although confidentiality forbids a detailed analysis of this figure, there are some observations which can be made.

- Although 9,000 contracts for open interest is the high end of the range up to October, it is not a new record. This suggests that if There was sudden opening of new positions—say by Portfolio Insurers adding to positions—there was also substantial closing of open positions.

- There was some change in the make up of open interest. Some short positions were closed, while some new ones were initiated and there is some indication of completely new business.

- Within the open interest cycle, open positions were relatively small. That is, following the September expiry, the portion of open interest which rolled off was only just beginning to be reinstated.

VOLATILITY

Volatility (expressed in terms of the daily range of the futures price, i.e., difference between the daily high and low) of the futures market increased significantly in the week ending the 23rd October.

In the week before the crash the daily range was between 20 and 45 index points. In the week of the crash, the daily range was between 95 and 595 index points.

October 20th was exceptionally volatile, with the opening range (difference between the high and low price during the the first two minutes of trading) accounting for 60 percent of the total day's range of 595 points.

This was exceptional, as the average movement of the opening range up to the 20th was only 19 percent of the daily range.

In the week before the crash the future closed between 22.5 and 43 index points over the cash index—that is, around or slightly over the fair value premium. This is typical of the cash futures relationship during the bull market of 1987. The week of October 19th saw greatly increased basis shifts (difference between cash index and future's price). Futures basis ranged between 60 points over and 350 points under the index. It is important to emphasize that this particularly large discount was only temporary, lasting three to four minutes on Tuesday morning. A more representative discount figure for the week was 60 points. Taking into account the fair value premium, this represents a five percent discount, i.e., people were willing to sell futures at a discount of five percent to the quoted index level.

PRICE AND MARKET QUALITY

The best way to analyse price quality is to look at the bid-ask spread and the movement between trades. In the week ending 16th October, the average bid ask spread was between one and two index points with spreads of up to, but not exceeding five index points 0.2 percent. The average move between trades was 0.5 index points with the most extreme movement of up to ten index points, or approximately 0.4 percent.

The following week saw the average bid-ask spread widen. The lowest average day's spread was on Monday 19th at three index points. The highest unsurprisingly, was Tuesday 20th at 11 index points. By Tuesday the market had fallen substantially, so this 11 index point spread equates to about 0.6 percent.

The average move between trades increased to four points (0.2 percent). The most extreme move was 100 index points (5.8 percent). All the six moves of this magnitude were experienced on the opening of the Tuesday morning. By far the widest bid-ask spread was on the morning of Tuesday 20th when spreads of up to 70 index points (four percent) were in the market and the volatility between trades was extreme. However, analysing the frequency of different spreads through the week of the crash reveals that, for the majority of the time, the bid-ask spread was under ten points—i.e., for most of the week there was a two way price with a spread not exceeding 0.5 percent.

MARGINING

The increased volatility and dramatic shift in prices resulted in increased margin requirements, both as initial margins were raised, and variation margins ("marking to market") were increased. A two-way market continued to be made and the average size of trades actually increased to eight contracts during the week of the crash compared to an average six of seven contracts in the previous week.

The initial margining system is based on the maximum price movement expected in a single day (the margin is derived from the standard deviation based on historical price movements). If the price moves by more than that covered by the initial margin then it is possible for an intra day margin call to have made to cover the price movement. These was no evidence of "forced closing" in London. Investors were generally able to meet margin calls without selling assets.

During the week of October 19th, several intra day margin calls and increases in initial margins were made:

- On 19th October, an intra day margin call was made on all long positions of £6,000 (representing 160 FTSE index points).

- On 20th October, an intra day margin call was made on all long positions of £7,500 (representing 300 index points).

- On 21st October, the initial margin was increased from £1,500 to £5,000 (representing an increase from 60 index points to 200 index points).

- On 22nd October, an intra day margin call was made on selected positions of £5,000 (representing 200 index points).

- On 2nd November, the initial margin was increased from £5,000 to £7,000 (an additional increase of 100 index points).

- On 16th November, the initial margin was reduced to £5,000 (representing a decrease of 100 index points).

- The current initial margin stands at £4,000 (representing 160 index points).

TYPES OF BUSINESS

We now move on to examine the different types of futures trading in general and how this changed during the period of the crash. It is important to note that several trading mechanisms commonly used in the US are not widespread in the UK because of the much smaller size of our derivative markets and the existence of certain structural features of our markets.

It is important to look at each type of trading before proceeding to examine the pattern of trading during the crash, because the breakdown of types of users of the FTSE futures differ from the breakdown of users of US futures. This becomes crucial in understanding the events that took pace during the week of October 19th.

ARBITRAGE

Arbitrage and index enhancement accounts for a major percentage of volume in the US index futures. Estimates of between 20 percent—30 percent of the volume in futures and individual stocks on any particular day have been ascribed to this form of "program" trading. The arbitrage is normally done by market traders who are running a flat or balanced book, trading on pricing anomalies between the futures and equity markets. Index enhancement is very much institutional based, and is similar to arbitraging except investors start from a long asset.

Use of both these types of transactions are very limited in FTSE futures in the UK. There are at most a handful of equity market makers who have dedicated systems set up to undertake arbitrage activities, and there is not index enhancement at all. The reasons for this are legion, but the key limitations relate to a number of structural factors of the UK market:

—Tax and Stamp Duty (plus Institutional worry about tax positions and added costs which transaction taxes imposed on trading).

—Cash settlement expiry procedures in the UK market which means that the arbitrage is not" locked in," i.e., it is not a perfectly risk free trade.

—Lack of automatic execution facilities for UK stocks prevent guaranteed execution and so introduces risk.

—Lack of credits for Index futures positions in the ISE capital adequacy requirements.

HEDGING

There is only limited hedging by the UK equity market makers. There are indications of a very small number of sizable hedges by institutionals, but portfolio insurance is at best embryonic in the UK. Traded options market makers use FTSE futures actively, as they are the only means of hedging the FTSE options book.

TRADING

There are a small number of locals who trade regularly, but nowhere near the legion number of local traders in the index futures pits of Chicago.

RETAIL

Before the crash a FTSE futures contract was worth about £60,000 (as opposed to about £24,000 for an LTOM FTSE option). This size discourages retail trade.

ACTIVITY DURING THE CRASH

Only a small amount of arbitrage activity took place during the week of October 19th and little of this was conducted by the normal arbitrageurs. Either they had "better things to do," or, in the case of the most sophisticated, were unable to use internal automated execution with their own market makers who were already very long of stock. Those who did arbitrage found particular difficulty executing small baskets of stock in the cash market; some complained that they could not contact market makers to deal.

Estimates indicate that arbitrage cannot have accounted for more than £50 -£70m at the outside. Taking 1700 as a representative futures price at that time, this means that perhaps 1200 to 1700 contracts can be attributed to arbitrage. It is estimated that about £100 dealt in FTSE futures was attributable to portfolio insurance strategies. This means that arbitrage and portfolio insurance strategies together cannot have accounted for more than ten percent of LIFFE's volume in the week of the crash. In relation to the cash market this represented a miniscule proportion (on a comparable basis, UK equity trading was £6.8 billion in that week).

Only a very limited amount of activity was seen by traded options market makers' hedging, since the volatility of the futures basis deterred them from doing so. On the other hand, equity market makers made increased use of futures. The uncertainty and risk of taking on stock may have been the main reason for equity market makers, who normally do not use futures as a hedge, to use them on this occasion.

There were still locals in the pit, and there seems to have been reasonable trading activity. However, some traders commented on the difficulties of trading associated with the volatility in basis. Equally, however, they noted that substantial business could still be executed.

In summary then, during the crash the balance of trade seems to have changed. There was less traded options hedging, but more equity market maker hedges and only a limited amount of arbitraging.

Inter-relationships and Concluding Remarks

We have examined in detail the types and levels of activity on the UK equity market and the two derivative markets, the LTOM and LIFFE. The inter-relationships which exists would tend to suggest that selling pressures of all three markets was exacerbated. Let us explain more fully.

Firstly, we have seen that the mechanisms which link the futures and cash markets in the US are not used to any significant level in the UK, and also the size of the futures market in relation to the underlying cash market is smaller than in the US. Portfolio insurance is in its infancy in the UK—insured funds are certainly less than £1/4 billion. While index arbitrage occurs in the UK, difficulties of executing complex trades in the cash market at guaranteed prices, together with special features of FTSE futures and UK taxation law, combine to limit its extent.

While the destabilizing impact of portfolio insurance and index arbitrage were not an issue in the UK, it is another thing to suggest that the discount to which FTSE futures went had no effect in the cash market. Clearly, the existence of very large discounts on FTSE futures, which were broadcast throughout equity dealing rooms of many member firms throughout the City, must have unnerved the cash market traders.

Normally some arbitrage would have been in operation to keep the markets in line, but during the crash period this was not the case. The normal arbitrageurs were not in evidence as it had ceased to be a "risk free" trade because of the pace of price changes and difficulties in executing orders. Of the handful of people who did undertake arbitrages buying the futures and selling the stocks, they found the futures slightly higher than was indicated on the screen, and the index some 30 to 40 points lower by the time they had dealt in sizes up to five million. A selling order of this size in the equity market may have taken much longer to execute given the reduction in market makers quotation sizes and difficulties of access.

It is important to stress that major futures strategies, particularly index arbitrage, was only in evidence in a very limited way. It is because they were limited (and thus not effective in erasing pricing anomalies) that the discount between FTSE futures and the cash index reached the proportions it did.

The question remains, "Why did the discount occur?" It is too simplistic to say that the heavy selling pressure in the futures market caused the discount without asking why sellers were willing to accept a discount of typically five percent to the quoted index. Two reasons may explain this.

It could be that sellers did not believe they could deal, especially sell, in the cash market immediately. Expecting further falls and unwilling to risk waiting, investors decided to liquidate their positions by selling the FTSE futures instead. Bearing in mind the size of the discount at certain times, such a rationale would imply that these sellers must have had extremely poor expectations of the time which would elapse before they could trade the underlying stocks.

Alternatively, sellers may not have believed the cash market prices were real and available for trading. Believing this to be the case, investors may have thought that the futures price was indeed the "real" market price, and thus continued selling the future.

In fact, as our research has shown, SEAQ prices were generally a good indicator of trading prices. On the question of accessibility to equity market makers to execute orders, we can only point to the record volumes of transactions, of which a higher proportion than normal were customer orders as opposed to intra-market business, which suggests that market makers were indeed providing a continuous market. However, the experience of those trading simultaneously in both the cash and futures markets suggests that, because of access difficulties in the cash market, some investors may have chosen to deal in a discounted market because it was more accessible and so provided certainty of execution.

What we do not know is how many orders did not reach the market makers for whatever reasons. We have already seen that record volumes of business was transacted on all markets. The issue of accessibility essentially rests with decisions regarding capacity levels. Like most industries, decisions need to be made concerning how much capacity to build into a system to cater to abnormal peak times.

If it is true that significant number of customer orders failed to be executed swiftly or executed at all because of capacity constraints—there is only a finite number of market makers, dealers and telephones—then it is a real concern for the ISE as this affects not only the immediate, but also much longer term, quality of its markets.

Given the present capacity of the trading system and the current size of the industry, our investigations into the efficiency and effectiveness of the ISE 's trading systems reveal that on the whole the systems coped well under the exceptionally high level of activity and pressures; despite the widening of price spreads and the reduction in size, a continuous two way market was maintained at all times during the trading day. Despite fast moving conditions, the SEAQ system provided quotations which fairly represented the market.

Decisions regarding individual member firms operating capacity in terms of human and technological resources are matters for firms themselves to make based on their own commercial outlook. From an exchange's point of view, it is essential that policies and plans are developed and implemented which aim to minimize adverse conditions which may impede the efficient execution of business for the investing community at large.

While it is not for an exchange to judge whether investors' decisions to buy, sell or hold securities is right or wrong, it is the function of a good quality exchange to provide the mechanism which can carry out investors' decisions in the most cost efficient and effective way. In doing so, the market mechanism should be able to accurately reflect such actions and sentiment via the prices which it transmits, and in addition to this, it should be able to absorb and reflect new information as quickly as possible.

Our studies into the efficiency and effectiveness of London's market mechanisms have revealed two distinct areas where development must take (and is already taking) place to help to minimize the difficulties experienced during the crash.

Firstly, it seems clear that the existence of wide pricing anomalies between the cash and derivative markets demonstrates the need for the London markets to encourage techniques, such as index arbitrage, which help to provide convergence in these markets so that an efficient means of risk transfer can be achieved.

Secondly, there is a need to provide more speedy execution services so as to increase the cash market's capabilities to execute (and settle) transactions more efficiently and, in turn, to increase its capacity overall via increased productivity. To this end, the ISE is well advanced in the development of its automatic execution service, SAEF (SEAQ Automated

Execution Facility), which is expected to be in operation by next year. SAEF will enable customer orders of up to 1,000 shares in SEAQ stocks, placed with member firms of the ISE, to be executed at a touch of a button. Since over half the transactions on the ISE are for 1,000 or less shares, the implementation of SAEF will considerably release resources within firms to handle a much greater proportion of higher value transactions.

To conclude, there can be no doubt that what we have now is not a group of separate markets with occasional overlapping but—since the links between markets are so strong—one, very complex market. This one market encompasses not only different assets within the UK but also covers international markets. This underlines the need to understand clearly the impact of changes—regulatory, procedural, technical and structural—in one area of the market on other areas. For example, while SAEF is seen mainly as an enhancement to the cash market, it may ultimately simplify arbitrage between interconnected markets and thus will have an impact on derivative markets. The results of our study, and studies from other exchanges and regulatory authorities, demonstrate that there is a long way to go before we fully understand and accept the implications of this single market phenomenon.

FIGURE   BRITAIN-4.1
Daily Turnover Value - Alpha Stocks
October 12 to November 16

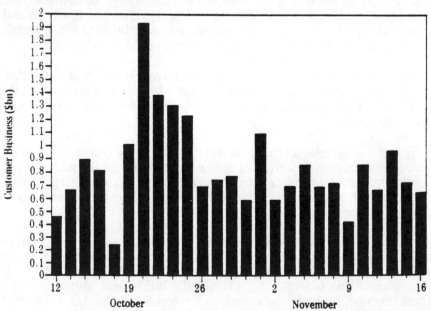

FIGURE BRITAIN-4.2
Turnover in Traded Options
October 1987

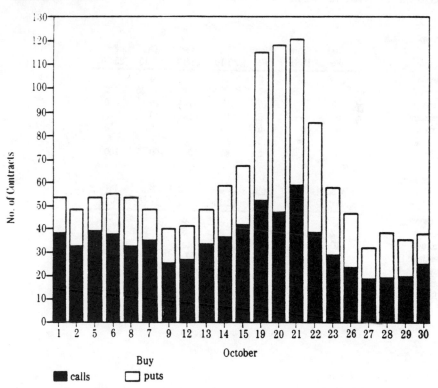

Buy

■ calls □ puts

TABLE BRITAIN-4.1
Distribution of Customer Trading
in FTSE Options on October 19

9.05 — 12.00 hours	Buy %	Sell %	Total %
Puts	59	15	74
Calls	22	4	26
	81	19	100

12.00 hours — Close	Buy %	Sell %	Total %
Puts	23	25	48
Calls	46	6	52
	69	31	100

TABLE BRITAIN-4.2
Closing Quote Spreads for
Sample of Traded Options (Pence)

December Calls

	Wed 9/9	Thu 15/10	Mon 19/10	Tue 20/10	Wed 21/10	Thu 22/10	Fri 23/10
Hanson	0.5	1	2	4	2	3	3
Sears	2	1.5	2	2	1	.25	2
Glaxo	10	7	10	15	15	10	40
Beecham	5	5	5	10	18	10	10
Circle	5	5	5	10	5	10	10
Amstrad	3	3	3	2	4	5	5
FTSE	5	5	6	80	65	100	100

December Puts

	Wed 9/9	Thu 15/10	Mon 19/10	Tue 20/10	Wed 21/10	Thu 22/10	Fri 23/10
Hanson	1	0.5	2	2	3	5	3
Sears	2	0.5	2	3	3	2	4
Glaxo	10	10	15	15	15	28	30
Beecham	3	5	5	10	8	10	20
Circle	5	3	5	10	10	7	10
Amstrad	3	2	3	3	4	8	7
FTSE	3	3	20	99	70	50	60

TABLE BRITAIN-4.3
Spreads on FTSE Puts: October 19 (Pence)

Time	Oct 2150	Oct 2250	Nov 2150
10.00	158	10	6
11.00	15	93	10
12.00	93	10	—
13.00	85	—	—
14.00	13	20	5
15.00	70	60	35

CFTC

Final Report on Stock Index Futures and Cash Market Activity During October 1987

to the U.S. Commodity Futures Trading Commisssion

Report Summary

During a few days in mid-October 1987—most notably October 19—U.S. and foreign stock exchanges experienced record declines in stock prices. The abruptness and magnitude of October's fall in stock value placed severe strains on the operational and financial control systems of securities and futures exchanges and created strains for the banking system as well. Although no system failed and no broader economic crisis has ensued, a number of regulatory and self-regulatory issues were raised that are receiving close scrutiny by the Congress, Federal authorities, and self-regulatory organizations in the futures and securities industries.

The Commission addressed several of the issues pertaining to trading on futures exchanges in its Interim Report and in two subsequent reports released by the Commission's Division of Trading and Markets. This final report primarily focuses on the futures and related stock market activity (including "program trading") of major commercial participants in the October 1987 markets, as well as the performance and floor activities of futures exchange members. In addition, this report contains recommendations for regulatory improvements in several areas.

A persistent assertion regarding the impact of stock index futures markets on stock prices concerns the "cascade theory." That theory suggests that short portfolio hedging and stock/futures market arbitrage activities can interact to cause a downward spiral in stock prices. A careful examination indicates certain inherent problems with the theory as an explanation of the October 19 market break. For one thing, the theory is dependent upon some assumptions that may not correspond to actual trading practices. More importantly, the cascade theory appears to describe at most a short-term and limited technical realignment of cash and futures prices that results from, rather than causes, an overall change in the equilibrium price level.

To ascertain the pattern of futures and related stock market trading in mid-October 1987, this report contains an extensive analysis of the timed daily trading data for the index arbitrage and portfolio insurance strategies of major broker/dealers and their institutional customers. Information on other forms of program trading in the stock market also is considered. The data were collected in a special survey that was conducted by the staffs of the CFTC and SEC.

As background to the trading activity of major market participants, Section II of this report summarizes a statistical analysis of the relationship between the S&P 500 index and the price of the December S&P 500 future for the period October 14 through 26. The focus of that analysis is a "trading proxy index," which was created for each day to minimize or eliminate the impact of delayed or stale stock market prices on reported values of the S&P 500 index. That analysis indicates that, during the periods when the reported futures discount was as extreme (e.g., the mornings of October 19 and 22), a significant portion of those discounts was illusory since a substantial number of stocks included in the S&P 500 index were not actively trading. Among other things, these findings cast substantial doubt upon both the cascade theory and the supposition that futures prices were leading the stock market as reasonable representations of what occurred during the morning of October 19.

Section III of this report provides an extensive analysis of the special intraday survey data. Index arbitrage programs in which futures contracts were bought and stocks were sold were largest on October 14, 16, and 19 but were insignificant thereafter as a result of the New York Stock Exchange's restrictions. The largest arbitrage trades accounted for sales of nearly 38 million shares on both October 16 and 19, representing about 11 percent and six percent respectively, of total NYSE volume. On a relative basis, reported index arbitrage sell programs were more significant on October 14, when they accounted for more than 13 percent of total NYSE sales.

Portfolio hedge sales in the Chicago Mercantile Exchange's S&P 500 futures market were at their highest levels on October 16, 19, and 20. Daily gross sales ranged from nearly 15,000 to nearly 34,000 S&P 500 futures contracts, amounting to from ten to 30 percent of total daily volume in that market. The largest reported net portfolio hedge sales occurred on

October 19, nearly 38,000 S&P 500 futures contracts. Since index arbitrage was only significant from October 14 through 19, and portfolio hedge selling was substantial only on October 16 through 20, a significant interaction of the two trading strategies most likely would have occurred on October 16 and 19. The analysis of the survey data on an intraday basis, however, does not support the contention that the two trading strategies interacted to cause the large fall in stock prices experienced on those days.

October 16 was the expiration date of a number of index option contracts as well as the Chicago Board of Trade's Major Market Index futures contract. Consequently, most index arbitrage activity that day occurred during the final hour of trading. Portfolio hedge selling, however, was dispersed throughout the day and was not particularly heavy during the periods when stock prices fell the most and when arbitrage sell programs were the largest. At times within the day and at the close, index arbitrage sell programs may be construed to have contributed to short-term, technical pressures on stock prices. It is noteworthy, however, that, at those times, futures prices were falling along with stock prices despite an equivalent magnitude of futures index arbitrage buying, thus indicating overall market weakness.

On Monday, October 19, the stock market opened with a massive wave of selling. Nearly 100 million shares of stock were sold in the first hour of trading on the NYSE even though a number of major stocks had delayed openings, and over 600 million shares were sold that day. One mutual fund group alone accounted for sale of 17.5 million shares (34 percent of volume) in the first half hour of trading, which was nearly three times the reported index arbitrage sell programs during that period. For the day, program selling of stocks not related to futures transactions was of a significantly greater magnitude than index arbitrage, totaling nearly 52 million shares. Clearly, index arbitrage was not the dominant selling force in the stock market that day. Also, the absolute amount as well as the percentage of arbitrage sell programs on October 19 were smaller than the stock sales associated with index arbitrage identified in prior studies that concluded that index arbitrage did not cause the significant stock price declines at other times.

Further, the intraday analysis of trading by major commercial firms does not support the interaction of index arbitrage and portfolio hedging strategies as an explanation for the extraordinarily large fall in stock prices on October 19. Although high levels of index arbitrage occurred early in the day, after 2:00 p.m. that activity diminished significantly. Moreover, for each half-hour interval after 10:00 a.m., other program selling in the stock market was larger than stock sales associated with index arbitrage.

Portfolio hedge sales of futures contracts were persistent throughout the day, but the highs and lows of that activity did not correspond with the periods of greatest weakness or recovery of futures prices.

Because of the imposition of NYSE restrictions on program trading, index arbitrage was insignificant on October 20. On that day, portfolio hedge selling in the futures market was large at times and was not offset by futures purchases from index arbitrage trading. Consequently, there were large futures price discounts relative to the underlying index that persisted throughout the day.

After October 20, stock prices continued to be volatile in the absence of significant index arbitrage and significant hedge selling of futures. For example, on October 22, when the Dow fell 78 points on volume of nearly 400 million shares, reported index arbitrage stock sales were less than three million shares. Similarly, on October 26, when the Dow fell 157 points on volume of over 300 million shares, no index arbitrage trades were reported. Furthermore, stock prices after October 19 did not recover to near the level of October 16, much less that of October 1. At the close on October 26, the Dow was only 55 points higher than at the close on October 19. This lack of recovery in the absence of index arbitrage reinforces the conclusion that futures-related program trading was not the principal cause of the collapse of stock prices. Instead, the wave of selling that engulfed both the stock and index futures markets, particularly on October 19, appears to have been precipitated by a massive change in investors' perceptions.

The SEC/CFTC survey data and interviews conducted by CFTC staff indicate that institutional hedging in futures markets was not uniform in nature during the mid-October period under review. In particular, while some firms employed portfolio insurance strategies, others pursued more varied hedging and market-timing strategies, including several who purchased futures during periods of declining stock prices in anticipation of later purchasing stocks. And, among those firms that earlier in October were adhering to portfolio insurance strategies, many abandoned or reduced the amount of futures or stock market sales implied by the plans. In addition, representatives of institutional investors indicated that, in the short run, they could use the stock market and stock index futures interchangeably for many portfolio management strategies. In particular, fund managers indicated that stocks would have been sold in the absence of the ability to hedge them in the futures market.

Section IV of this report examines trading in and the operational performance of the S&P 500 futures contract. Commission staff found that the operational systems of both the CME and its member firms functioned well, despite the high trading volume and price volatility in that market. Although a larger than usual number of out trades occurred on October 16 and 19, they largely were resolved before the opening of trading the next day because of two special trade checking sessions. In addition, a staff survey of 23 CME member firms found that their order-routing and execution systems required no substantial modifications. The order-execution times at one major wire house were reviewed in detail, revealing that those orders generally were executed expeditiously, with nearly half of all customer orders executed within a minute of their receipt on the trading floor.

CME audit trail data document broad participation in the market on October 19 and 20 by all major market groups, including members trading for their own accounts and brokers executing customer orders. CME members trading for their own accounts, absorbed customer sell orders on those days when the market was falling, including those times when the market fell the most. Further, the number of "primary" brokers executing customer trades in the S&P futures market increased on October 19 and 20 from the active trading day of October 16, indicating that experienced brokers remained available to execute customer orders.

Section V of this report describes the Commission's heightened trade-practice surveillance of stock index futures trading beginning on October 14. CFTC staff maintained an almost continual presence on the floors of the CME and the CBT during the week of October 19. Through the use of the CFTC's computer-assisted trade database and one-minute execution times required by CFTC audit trail regulation, staff reviewed large amounts of trading data on an expedited schedule. In addition, market participants were interviewed and exchange investigations of potential trading abuses were monitored. In particular, staff examined October 20 trading in the CBT's Major Market Index contract and trading in the S&P 500 futures contract by a CME clearing member that took place on the morning of October 22, as well as all exchanges of futures for cash executed in the S&P 500 contract during the mid-October period under review. To date, the staff has not discovered any pattern of trading activity in futures or options on futures that would indicate violative activity.

The final section of this report examines several pertinent aspects of the current regulatory system and suggests areas for improvement. Although the staff believes its current market surveillance system for stock index futures is sound, improved data collection capabilities in other markets, particularly regarding stock market trades of firms engaging in index arbitrage, would greatly expedite any subsequent studies of these markets.

The staff examined the traditional uses of daily price limits in futures markets, assessing the advantages and disadvantages of such limits. All but one of the smaller stock index futures contracts currently have rules providing for such limits. Any tightening of those limits, however, should take into account the potential impact on other markets.

Section VI also includes a brief review of interagency coordination, which describes the commission's establishment of surveillance liaison with the SEC and banking regulators. While the staff believes both interagency and interexchange coordination generally were excellent during October 1987, improvements are needed regarding access of futures exchanges to accurate information on delayed opening and trading halts of NYSE stocks. Coordination among exchanges with respect to emergency closings should be enhanced.

This report also summarizes the recommendations of its Financial Follow-Up Report. That report comprehensively analyzed the futures market financial systems and found that those systems withstood the stress placed upon them by the events of October.

Staff considered the concept of intermarket frontrunning as it may relate to trading between securities and futures markets. It was found that both securities and futures exchanges have rules that can be applied to such activity. The Intermarket Surveillance Group was identified as an appropriate forum for facilitating the communication of intermarket surveillance data needed to monitor such activities. CFTC staff also is considering the advisability of commission regulatory action on frontrunning.

TRADING ANALYSIS: REVIEW OF INTRADAY INDEX ARBITRAGE AND PORTFOLIO ACTIVITIES

SUMMARY AND CONCLUSIONS

Analysis of Commission and CME large-trader data indicates that, for the period October 14 to October 26, broker/dealers, institutional investors, and other commercial firms accounted for about two-thirds of total open interest in the CME S&P 500 futures contract. Special SEC/CFTC survey data further identify the activities of major firms with respect to those futures-related trading strategies that have been the object of specific concern. In particular, those data indicate that index arbitrage (including index substitution) was at relatively high levels on October 14, 16, and 19. On those dates, the total daily gross selling of component stocks for arbitrage purposes ranged between 28 and 38 million shares and between six and 13 percent of total NYSE volume, although substantially higher concentration of activity occurred during some intraday periods. Those daily amounts, however, are less than reported for September 11 and 12, 1986, a time period for which the SEC concluded that index arbitrage was not the cause of the magnitude of the market declines experienced on those days. Further, following actions by the NYSE on October 20 to discourage all forms of member program trading as well as other impediments to index arbitrage, such as trading halts in a number of major stocks, the amount of arbitrage activity declined significantly.

Portfolio hedging activities on the sell side (including portfolio insurance) were at relatively high levels on October 16, 19, and 20, when gross daily futures sales for those purposes by major institutions ranged between 15,000 and 34,000 S&P 500 futures contracts and amounted to between ten and 30 percent of total daily trading volume in that market. In contrast, on October 21, significant hedge selling in the S&P 500 futures market was more than offset by buying in that market on the part of institutional hedgers.

A detailed examination of the trading data by half-hour intervals from the SEC/CFTC survey does not provide empirical support for the theory that hedging in the futures market and index arbitrage activities interacted to cause a technical downward price spiral of stock prices. In those instances where it might be asserted that the stock market temporarily reacted to arbitrage selling, it is notable that futures prices were also declining despite offsetting arbitrage purchasing pressure in the futures market. Such a situation is more suggestive of a general weakness in the market than a stock market reaction to the selling side of arbitrage transactions.

CFTC interviews with institutional investors who held futures positions during October 1987, as well as the SEC/CFTC survey data, highlight certain facts that must be considered in analyzing the relationship of cash and futures activities and their impact on prices. In particular, while some may consider the stock market as a market for investing and the futures a market for hedging or initiating portfolio readjustments, major institutional investors and broker/dealers view the cash and futures markets as interchangeable for short-term implementation of their portfolio decisions, subject to considerations of relative transaction costs, market liquidity, and market value.

One indication of this is that, although futures normally have been used for portfolio hedging, on October 19, the firms surveyed indicated that about 40 million shares of stock were sold, via program trading, in implementing portfolio insurance strategies. This implies that firms may undertake certain trading objectives irrespective of the existence of futures markets. Another implication is that regulatory measures aimed at correcting market deficiencies perceived as a result of the October stock market decline should be designed to address a particularly identified problem and not harm other facets of the market.

ASSESSMENT OF REGULATORY AND SELF-REGULATORY PROGRAMS

The Commission's Market Surveillance Program

The Commission routinely conducts direct, daily market surveillance of all futures and options markets under its jurisdiction. The Commission receives, each day for each futures market, data detailing the total market activity, the aggregate positions and trading for each clearing member (separately for proprietary and customer accounts), and the positions of individual traders in excess of specified reporting levels. Those data are transmitted to the Commission via telecommunications or magnetic tape by exchanges, futures commission merchants, clearing members, and foreign brokers and are available for analysis on a next-day .

Preliminary computer processing subjects the data to an array of edit and cross checks among various data items for consistency. Displays of likely errors and inconsistencies allow Commission staff readily to identify and correct likely reporting errors. In addition, using specified identification items, individual trader's positions are combined for all reporting brokerage firms. A variety of computer analyses of large data are available, providing intra- and inter-commodity comparisons of traders by size of positions, trading activity, and deliveries on the underlying contract. Additionally, software systems combine options and futures data, immediately pinpointing those traders who may have exceeded Federal or exchange-sc. speculative positions limits. Other software systems are available for retrieving and analyzing historical data for single traders or groups of related traders.

Computer software also is available that provides analyses of prices and price relationships, open contracts, and trading volume, including comparisons with similar periods of time during previous months or years. These various data are useful both for detecting unusual trading patterns or price relationships that might indicate sources of potential market problems and for providing insights into changing market conditions. Analysts frequently contact major traders to discuss new trading strategies and to resolve potential market congestion. In addition, the Commission has broad inspection powers that permit immediate access to records of firms' and individuals' trading activities in futures and related option and cash markets.

Futures exchanges' market surveillance programs also rely heavily on large-trader reporting systems. Exchange surveillance programs periodically are reviewed by the Commission to determine, among other things, whether exchanges are obtaining and analyzing accurate and comprehensive data, whether traders' positions are identified properly and aggregated on the basis of common control or financial interest for speculative limits enforcement and general surveillance, and whether exchange analysts are receiving the information in a timely and usable manner.[96] The commission generally has found that exchanges' large-trader reporting systems meet CFTC standards, and Commission staff has provided, via its rule enforcement program, suggestions to each exchange for improving its systems.

CFTC and exchange surveillance of the four principal stock index futures and their associated option markets was intensified in early October 1987 as markets became more volatile. Emphasis was placed on the S&P 500 futures contract because it has much larger volume and open interest than the other stock index futures. The expiration of the CBOT's October MMI future on October 16, 1987, was monitored closely as well.

The results of the ongoing monitoring, analysis, and trade contacts were provided to the Commission and other regulatory agencies throughout the October period. As detailed in the Interim Report, the Commission's staff maintained particularly close contact and cooperation with staffs of the relevant futures exchanges, the SEC, and the Board of Governors of the Federal Reserve System (Federal Reserve Board). SEC staff, in particular, was provided detailed futures position data and, along with staff of the Federal Reserve Board, attended Commission surveillance briefings.[97]

Comparable data regarding NYSE activity by firms active in stock index futures, however, were not available on a timely basis as events unfolded. Detailed securities transaction data were not obtained by CFTC or SEC staffs until late November when firms responded to the previously discussed SEC/CFTC survey. While Section III of this report is based in large part of those survey data, the collection of those data was very labor intensive and difficult to standardize, and there was little opportunity to verify the accuracy of consistency of all of the survey information. At

---

[96] The results of such reviews routinely are published by the Commission's staff. See, for example, *Follow-up Rule Enforcement Review of the Chicago Mercantile Exchange*, Division of Trading and Markets, June 30, 1987.

[97] See Interim Report, *op. cit.*, pp. 25-29.

present, it is the deficiency in the rapid and accurate identification of timed stock transactions, by beneficial ownership, that is the principal weakness in implementing a comprehensive data system spanning stock and stock index futures transactions.

Commission staff believes a more routine and efficient means of compiling individual account data, for example on arbitrage related stock transactions, is needed.[98] In this context, Commission staff is analyzing alternative means and already has taken certain steps to improve the routine collection of futures market information to capture more specific stock index futures data by trading strategy. Such data will be particularly useful in conjunction with improved availability of cash market data. In particular, Commission staff has improved the timeliness of obtaining profiles of market participants by formalizing and automating what had been a manual method of classifying certain commercial traders' positions in stock index futures. In this context, the staff has flagged, in the account identification system, broker/dealers, whose futures trading if often associated with index arbitrage, and institutional investors, whose futures trading is often associated with portfolio insurance or other hedging strategies. Computer analysis of large-trader data using these profiles enable the staff to evaluate rapidly the aggregate size of certain types of trading strategies and, by reviewing the cumulative daily net position changes, to estimate the volume of those activities on specific dates.

The Commission's large-trader reporting system presently classifies traders, and from those trader classifications assumptions can be made about the trading strategies being employed. Nevertheless, a better way is needed to classify market strategies. For example, traders engaged in index arbitrage could be required to conduct all such activity through separately identified futures trading accounts. That trading could than be reconstructed rapidly on an execution-time basis through the futures exchanges' current audit trail systems. Similar procedures could be used to isolate other trading strategies of regulatory interest. Commission staff presently is exploring the most effective means of obtaining on a routine basis, such detailed data on the magnitude of stock index futures trading classified by principal trading strategies.

---

[98] See also the SEC's report regarding trading on September 11 and 12, 1986 *op.cit.*, Executive Summary.

DAILY PRICE LIMITS

Daily price fluctuation limits have long history on futures exchanges. Such rules prohibit trading at prices a specified level above or below the previous day's settlement price. The most often cited rationale for price limits is that they constrain the daily financial exposure of futures commission merchants and clearing members by providing a ceiling on the amount of margin calls due as a result of any day's trading. In addition, proponents of price limits believe they may serve to keep the market from overreacting to major market news or rumors, particularly during periods of significant uncertainty. The thought is that during such periods the market may temporarily move too far in one direction before reestablishing a less extreme equilibrium and that price limits will prevent participants from being "whipsawed" out of the market, for financial reasons, by the interim fluctuations. This latter argument typically is used with respect to futures markets that play a central role in pricing cash commodities, such as in the grains, and where the futures market is the major price-reference point.

The disadvantages of price limits are also quite straightforward in that they prevent the market from "clearing" on days they are in effect, *i.e.,* some traders will be unable to liquidate their positions, and new orders will go unfilled because the equilibrating price lies outside the daily price limit. This, for instance, makes it difficult or impossible to liquidate or establish hedging positions at those times when firms particularly may wish to do so.[99] In addition, of course, daily price limits directly impede the price discovery process and can result in intermarket distortions—and corresponding risks—when comparable limits do not exist for related markets.

Although price limits were at one time uniformly in effect on every actively traded futures contract,[100] there were none in effect for any of the actively traded stock index futures contracts on October 19, 1987. A trend toward liberalization or abandonment of price limits by futures exchanges

---

[99] In this regard, it has been argued that the fear of being "locked in" is an impediment to full commercial participation and liquidity in futures markets. It also has been suggested that the threat of being locked in may precipitate further limit moves on successive days as traders scramble to get out of the market.

[100] In May 1980, the Commission designated the first futures contracts to trade without daily price limits. These were the New York Futures Exchange's foreign currency contracts.

began in the early and mid-1970's in response to volatile conditions in the grain markets. In response to episodes of successive "lock limit days" that occurred at that time, exchanges first increased the levels of their price limits and then adopted rules for "variable" or "expanding" limits. Under such rules, the level of a price limit is increased automatically one or more times (and sometimes removed altogether) after a prespecified number of limit-move days, and the original levels are automatically restored once the limit moves have ceased. The rationale behind such variable limits is to provide the short-run advantages of price limits but to allow the market to adjust in a more orderly yet timely fashion to the new equilbrium in the event of continued unidirectional pressure.

Another trend in the liberalization of daily price limits has been their removal from the trading in the nearby (*i.e.*, next to expire) month and, in some cases, the two most nearby contracts. Often used in conjunction with variable limits, the rationale of this provision is to assure that there is always at least one segment of the market (*i.e.*, the lead month) available for trading. Even if trading in the more distant months is impeded by limits, traders can trade in the lead month, on a proxy basis, as a means of covering existing positions or establishing new ones.[101]

As initially designated by the Commission in 1982, several of the stock index futures contracts included price fluctuation limit rules and others did not. However, in many of those cases where price limits were initially in effect, amendments to remove them were subsequently approved. For instance, the CME S&P 500 futures contract had a maximum daily price fluctuation limit at the time of its designation in April 1982. The Commission subsequently approved an increase in those limits and, in January 1983, their deletion.[102]

On October 23, the CME, NYFE, and KCBT, by emergency actions, put into effect price fluctuation limits for their actively traded stock index contracts. The fourth exchange with stock index futures trading activity, the CBT, did not implement limits on an emergency basis. Subsequently, however, the Commission has approved permanent limits for the CBOT's,

---

[101] In this regard, there generally are no limits on the values for spread transactions, *i.e.*, transactions executed as the difference between a buy and a sell in different trading months. Under the conditions noted above, a spread transaction with one leg in the lead month may be executed as a means of rolling a more deferred position into the lead month where it can be liquidated in the absence of price limits.

[102] The CME also has removed all price limits from the Exchange's foreign currency futures (approved by the Commission in February 1985) and all other actively traded financial futures (approved by the Commission in December 1985).

CME's, and KCBT's actively traded stock index contracts. In each case, the exchanges' rules contain an expansion factor that increases the initial limit by amounts of between 30 and 50 percent after two days of limit moves. In addition, the limits do not apply on the last day of trading in an expiring contract.

Analysis of the recently approved price limits in terms of the 1986 and 1987 daily close-to-close prices of the nearby contracts in the three stock index futures contracts indicates that the limits would have been reached only on October 19, 1987. On that date the base limit level constituted from 37 to 74 percent of the close-to-close range for the spot future. For instance, the closing settlement price for the S&P 500 December future dropped nearly 81 points, between Friday, October 16, and Monday, October 19, while the recently approved price limit is 30 points (37 percent).[103] There were, however, other time periods when the intraday movement in some stock index futures markets exceeded the levels of the recently approved price limits, and there also were days when price changes approaching those levels were experienced. In submitting permanent price limit rules, two of the exchanges noted that they were continuing to consider alternative approaches or indicated that matters were still under review.[104] Further, in a January 19, 1988, letter to the Commission concerning price limits for its NYSE composite stock index futures contract, the NYFE stated that it was considering other alternatives.

The price limits imposed by the exchanges appear to strike a balance between the competing benefits and costs noted above. The magnitudes of the stock index futures limits now in place are outside the range of daily price movements typically experienced in the underlying index, yet these limits would have been reached during the trading day on October 19 in the case of each of the three stock index futures contracts that currently have price limits.[105]

---

[103] The base (non-expanded) limit levels for the other two actively traded stock index futures contracts with the October 16 to 19 change in closing prices in parenthesis are: CBT MMI, 40 points (108.50) and KCBT VLA, 35 points (46.90).

[104] Provisions of the Commodity Exchange Act pertaining to exchange emergency actions contain a 90-day limitation on the effective period of such rules. As noted, three of the exchanges implemented their emergency price rules on October 23, 1987, and permanent rules were approved by the Commission on January 21, 1988.

[105] In addition to price limits for the above-mentioned futures contracts, the CME also amended the terms of its option on the S&P 500 futures contract to provide that that contract will cease trading in the event that the underlying futures contract reaches its limits. These rules, which were approved by the Commission on January 21, 1988, on a permanent basis, also had been previously adopted as emergency rules. The option on the KCBT's VLA future is currently

One further observation is warranted. The discussion and analyses in previous sections of this report indicate that, when futures contracts are not accurately reflecting cash market prices, firms are likely to execute desired trades directly in the cash market. Accordingly, if the price fluctuation limits for stock index futures are reached, one effect may be to place additional pressures on the liquidity in the stock market.

INTERAGENCY COORDINATION

In today's complex, interrelated financial system the need for continued coordination among the Federal authorities responsible for regulating various segments of the system is undeniable. A significant failure in one segment can have serious repercussions for the other segments. Moreover, since the threat of a financial failure could take place in any segment all regulatory authorities need to be alert continuously to surrounding economic events.

The importance of interagency coordination became increasingly apparent to the Commission in the aftermath of the silver market crisis of 1979-80. Immediately following that situation, the Commission began to seek more formal liaison and information-sharing relationships with other financial market regulators. The Commission established regular interagency financial futures surveillance meeting involving staff representatives of the Commission, the Federal Reserve Board, the New York Federal Reserve Bank, and the Department of the Treasury. When stock index futures began trading in 1982, the Commission also invited Securities and Exchange Commission staff to participate in those quarterly surveillance meetings. At those meetings, which precede the expirations of the major fixed-income, foreign currency and stock index futures contracts, confidential surveillance information about those markets is exchanged. Designated staff members at each of the agencies also have been authorized to share confidential surveillance information more routinely when the need arises.

In recognition of the concerns of banking regulators, in 1982 the Commission also initiated a monthly report in which the reportable futures positions of all banks and savings and loan institutions are provided by CFTC staff to the appropriate regulatory authorities. The recipients of these data include the New York Federal Reserve Bank, the Federal

---

dormant within the meaning of Commission Rule 5.2, which provides that the option cannot be relisted without an opportunity for review by the CFTC. The CBT is not designated to trade an option on the MMI future, although the American Stock Exchange does trade an option on that index.

Reserve Board, the Comptroller of Currency, the Federal Deposit Insurance Corporation, and the Federal Home Loan Bank Board.

With these interagency liaison arrangements in place, when the events of mid-October unfolded, the Commission immediately began sharing extensive information with appropriate Federal counterparts, particularly the SEC and the Federal Reserve Board. Futures and securities exchanges also maintained close communications among themselves and with the CFTC, SEC, and Federal Reserve Board. The generally excellent information sharing and coordination among the futures and securities industry regulatory and self-regulatory organizations helped to confine the financial strains resulting from the October stock price decline and to avoid a broader, more serious financial crisis.

There is one area in which interindustry coordination could have been better during this period. That involves the closing of trading in individual stocks on the NYSE, especially on October 19 and 20, and, in particular, the confusion concerning the reported imminent closing of the entire NYSE at mid-day on Tuesday, October 20. Futures exchanges were not able to obtain accurate information from the NYSE about the number of stocks that were closed or had never opened. Consequently, the futures exchanges could not determine the exact extent to which trading was occuring in the stocks underlying the indices on which their respective futures contracts are based. Better sharing of accurate, timely information and coordinated interexchange responses to the situation at the NYSE clearly were needed; the unnecessary closing of any financial market should be avoided whenever possible.

The staff believes that the overall regulatory system worked effectively to help prevent a broader crisis. Staff evaluation of the events of mid-October has not revealed a basis for any major structural change in those systems. Complacency, however, is not in order. The strains placed on the nation's financial system as a result of the collapse of stock prices were sufficiently severe to warrant continuing efforts to identify further areas in which the market surveillance and financial control systems of futures and securities exchanges can be strengthened and to expand existing channels of coordination. In essence, additional emergency preparedness planning from an interindustry perspective is needed.

FINANCIAL SELF-REGULATORY PROGRAMS

As discussed previously, the staff's assessment of the operation of financial self-regulatory systems during the October stock market decline is contained in the Division of Trading and Market's Financial Follow-Up Report issued January 6, 1988. That report included recommendations with respect to aspects of financial self-regulatory systems that should be given further study to assure that they provide sufficient protection in periods of high market volatility. In particular, Commission staff made the following recommendations:

Clarification of legal relationships between clearing organizations and clearing banks. Based upon a review of the operation of futures clearing systems during the October 19-23 period, Commission staff concluded that the clearing and banking systems for the settlement of variation margin operated effectively in making daily and intraday margin settlements, which at the CME and CBT totaled nearly twice the number normally made in less volatile markets. However, to assure that variation margin transfers in volatile markets are not impeded by a lack of clearly defined relationships among key participants in the settlement process, the staff recommended that the legal relationships between clearing organizations and settlement banks be clarified to ensure that they adequately establish the finality of settlement bank confirmations of variation margin payments.

Availability of the Fedwire in Exigent Market Conditions. On October 19 and October 20, 1987, banks of the Federal Reserve System accommodated the increased margin flows generated by frequent intraday margin calls by keeping the Fedwire open later than usual. A number of market participants have cited potential benefits that might have accrued from early opening of the Fedwire during that period. The staff recommended that mechanisms for expanding the capacity of the system to transfer funds in periods of extreme volatility, (for example, a special procedure for opening for Fedwire early or extending its hours) be explored.

Settlement banks' access to financial data. The ability of settlement banks to evaluate the creditworthiness of holders of clearing firm accounts could be enhanced by measures to assure that such banks receive prompt notice of variation margin obligations and have access to data concerning other variation settlements with respect to their customer clearing member firms. The specific measures identified by the staff that could facilitate bank credit determinations and verifications of the availability of funds to satisfy variation obligations include: providing notice to settlement banks of clearing firm obligations on the evening preceding the daily morning settlement; fostering interbank communication concerning the aggregate variation payments and collects for individual clearing firms; and, with the consent of clearing firms, sharing actual clearing members position data among the banks with which the member maintains a banking relationship.

Intraday margin calls. Commission staff also recommended that the use of intraday margin settlements (both pays and collects) on a daily basis or with increased frequency be considered as a potential means to enhance the ability of the settlement system to function smoothly in times of extreme volatility.

FCM collection of customer margins. A staff survey of 23 FCMs concerning customer defaults and liquidations of customer positions in the S&P 500 futures contract elicited data on a sample basis reflecting that liquidations resulting in customer deficits represented a very low percentage of those FCMs' adjusted net capital and total customer equities. Those data also indicated a disproportionate incidence of such liquidations in accounts attributable to foreign-based traders. The staff therefore recommended that FCMs review their procedures to assure that they obtain adequate security from foreign customers to protect against aberrant price fluctuations and attendant high margin calls.

Financial adequacy of margin levels. While Commission staff's review indicated that applicable margin requirements afforded adequate financial security during the October 19-23 period, the staff recommended that the futures SROs review the adequacy of clearing and customer margin levels to protect against aberrant price spikes and extreme volatility. In particular, the staff recommended that consideration be given to the addition of a percentage "cushion" to margin levels derived from moving averages of historical volatility to establish greater protection against unexpected price spikes and that margin systems be reviewed to assure that they adequately address the increased risks created by undiversified or concentrated positions.[106]

Enhancement of financial surveillance data systems. Commission staff is exploring several ways in which existing data, particularly the large-trader and exchange clearing member position data currently collected and used by the commission and futures exchanges for market and financial surveillance, could be refined to conduct more effective financial surveillance. The staff is developing new formats to aggregate and analyze existing data to generate additional financial surveillance information of use to, but not generally immediately available to, the futures SROs. Such data also would be useful to the SEC and the securities SROs for dually-registered firms and could be made available in appropriate cases to foreign regulators.

---

[106] While the staff's recommendations focused on futures over-sight issues, the staff also recommended that the futures SROs carefully review the adequacy of option margin levels to assure their sufficiency in volatile markets.

The futures clearing organizations and the SRO audit and financial surveillance staffs now routinely conduct daily financial surveillance over their member FCMs. In this connection, they use large-trader, margin and debit/deficit data for positions held in their markets, and pay and collect daily margin settlement data for all markets that currently participate in the Board of Trade Clearing Corporation's data-sharing system, which provides data concerning clearing firms' pays and collects and risk projections based upon such data. Those data indicate circumstances where a firm's financial position may be in jeopardy, thereby facilitating identification of those firms that merit intensified surveillance, including on-site audit work or other intervention.

Use of Intermarket Trade Data For Financial Surveillance. Commission staff continues to believe that aggregated intermarket position data should be shared among regulators and self-regulators for fully effective financial surveillance of firms' position concentrations in related markets. In the past, the SROs have resisted attempting routinely to collect and share these data directly because of the sensitivity of position data generally and because of confidentiality concerns. As discussed below, the staff is pursuing several avenues to augment the availability of such intermarket data. In this connection, CFTC staff believes that the Commission to act as the repository for aggregate position data for financial surveillance purposes. Aggregate data could be made available to exchanges and other regulators during periods of volatile markets to identify concentrations of similar or related positions in futures held by customers and/or by clearing firms on multiple exchanges that may pose a possible financial threat to a clearing firm. Such intermarket position data would be useful not only to the futures SROs but, where firms or customers also are involved in the securities markets, to the SEC and the securities SROs. Additionally, once established, such a program could provide a model for routine compilation of data to permit ongoing, daily assessments of full intermarket exposures, including domestic and foreign securities as well as futures positions. Commission staff is taking steps to determine what systems changes or refinements would be necessary to produce aggregate intermarket position data for financial surveillance purposes for those regulated by the CFTC.

Continuous Input of Trade Data. The Financial Follow-Up Report discussed the feasibility of continuously inputting trade data from the trading floor and recommended making such data available on an on-line basis to financial surveillance personnel to facilitate financial surveillance of margins and open positions on a more current basis. At present, the most recent trading data available to financial surveillance personnel at most SROs is as of the close of business of the prior trading day. Enhancing computer systems to render such data available on a more current basis, consistent with exchange trade-data collection schedules, could enhance self-regulatory financial and clearance systems in several ways. For example, the availability of on-line information to financial surveillance personnel at SROs would assist them in identifying large traders with significant accumulated losses on positions established during a particular trading day. In addition, the continuous availability of such data may enhance the effectiveness of existing SRO systems for the identification and resolution of outtrades.

Development of Central Computerized financial data base. To facilitate financial surveillance and analysis of FCM financial positions, financial information should be maintained routinely on a computerized data base that would be accessible to the commission as well as to all SRO financial surveillance staff. The commission currently maintains financial information filed by FCMs in hard copy and computerizes a limited amount of such data. The staff is reviewing potential measures that may be taken by the Commission and futures SROs to establish a centralized data base for FCM financial data.

Ongoing Evaluation. The CFTC staff currently reviews the adequacy of the design and execution of financial compliance programs of the various SROs and recommends or requires adjustments as may be necessary.

INTERMARKET FRONTRUNNING

Frontrunning can be defined generally as conduct that entails trading while in possession of nonpublic information concerning orders or transactions that affect or could affect the market price of the instrument purchased or sold.[107] Historically, the concept of intermarket frontrunning has been deemed applicable to activity involving nonpublic information about securities or securities option "block orders and related trading in those markets."[108] Recently, however, a question has been raised as to the applicability of the concept of frontrunning to intermarket

---

[107] *See* A. Bromberg & L. Lowenfels, *Securities Fraud and Commodities Fraud,* vol. 3, § 7 .4 (135) - (136) (1986).

[108] See Poser, "Spotlight on Frontrunning," *Investment Dealers' Digest* 15 (1984). A block order generally is defined as an order for either 10,000 or more shares or a quantity of stock having a value of $200,000 or more. *See, e.g., New York Exchange Floor Official Manual,* p. 38.

activity between securities or securities option block orders and trading in stock index futures contracts or options thereon.[109]

What constitutes frontrunning under particular market circumstances is not always clear.[110] Although provisions of the federal securities laws and the Commodity Exchange Act may be applicable to particular instances of frontrunning,[111] no provision in either statutory scheme specifically addresses frontrunning. Similarly, the rules of securities, securities options, and futures exchange do not specifically address intermarket frontrunning.

Securities and securities options exchanges have sought to address frontrunning through issuance of circulars pursuant to exchange rules that generally prohibit acts in violation of "just and equitable principles of trade."[112] Significantly, futures exchanges have similar rules that, among other things, prohibit acts that are in violation of "just and equitable principles of trade" or are "substantially detrimental to the interest or welfare of the Exchange."[113] In fact, the CME, CBT, KCBT, and NYFE,

---

[109] See the Katzenbach Report, pp. 23-24   That report included reference to trading activity by a firm involving futures trading for a proprietary account and securities trading for customer and proprietary accounts on December 19, 1986. The firm in that case was a member of the securities exchange in question, had a discretionary order to trade securities for the customer (which it held during the day and did not disclose despite a request by the securities exchange that market-on-close orders be disclosed), and also traded securitities for its proprietary account on the close. Given these facts, such activity should be cognizable under securities laws. Notably, no allegations of frontrunning involving trading in stock index futures or options on futures during October 1987 have been brought to the attention of Commission Staff.

[110] The SEC has stated that "[t] he line which separates appropriate hedging and other legitimate activity and frontrunning is not always clear." Chicago Board Options Exchange Rule Proposal, Securities Exchange Act of 1934, Release No. 14156 (Nov 9, 1977).

[111] See e.g., Securities Exchange Act of 1934 §§ 10(b), and 14 (e); SEC Rule 10b-5; Commodity Exchange Act § 4b (1986); and Commodity Exchange Act § 9 (b) (1983). To date, the staff's research has not identified any cases brought by the SEC under the foregoing securities statutes and rule charging frontrunning as described above.

[112] American Stock Exchange Information Circular 82-37 (July 6, 1982); Chicago Board Options Exchange Information Circular No. 23 revised (Feb 21, 1986); NYSE Information Memo 85-36 (1985). The disciplinary actions that have been discussed in publications are few in number and focus on frontrunning of customer orders in favor of proprietary accounts.

[113] See, e.g., CME Rule 432 (q), CBT Rule 504.00, NYFE Rule 501 (a) (iv), and KCBT Rule 1173.00. Futures exchanges, in accordance with Commission Regulation 155.2 (a) and (b), also specifically prohibit trading in the futures and futures option markets ahead of a customer's order for purchase of sale of a futures or futures option contract. See, e.g., CBT Rule 350.05 and NYCE Rule 1.05 (a).

which trade stock index futures contracts, likewise take the position that frontrunning can constitute a violation of such exchange rules.[114] Accordingly, intermarket frontrunning activity involving stocks, stock options, and stock index futures and options thereon can be a violation of the rules of all relevant exchanges.[115] Notwithstanding the existence of futures exchanges' rules that address frontrunning activity under appropriate circumstances, the CFTC staff is continuing to consider this issue. In that regard, CFTC staff believes that it is necessary to establish standards for identifying potential intermarket frontrunning trading patterns and a mechanism for the timely and effective communication of market surveillance data related to possible frontrunning activity among all with common self-regulatory interests. The Intermarket Surveillance Group (ISG), of which all securities and securities options exchanges are members, appears to be an appropriate forum for facilitating the communication of such market surveillance data. The ISG has considered frontrunning issues in the past, and futures exchanges that trade stock index contracts have participated as observers in an ISG subcommittee. Currently, the ISG is considering the manner in which futures exchanges could be included more formally in its deliberations. The Commisssion believes that some manner of formal recognition of the futures exchanges by the ISG would contribute significantly to addressing common surveillance concerns of all exchanges. Lastly, CFTC staff also is consideraing whether it is advisable to recommend a regulation establishing a minumum futures industry standard for the prohibition of frontrunning activity involving transactions on futures exchanges.

---

[114] Letters from the CME, CBT, KCBT, and NYFE to the Division of Trading and Markets dated April 6, April 15, May 7, and May 1, 1987, respectively.

[115] Section 8c (1)(A) of the Commodity Exchange Act provides that, if an exchange fails to act, the Commission may take disciplinary action in accordance with the exchange's rules.

SEC

The October 1987 Market Break

A Report by the Division of Market Regulation
U.S. Securities and Exchange Commission[*]

Executive Summary

The following provides an overview of the subject areas covered in each of the chapters of the Report and summarizes the Division's findings.

CHAPTER ONE — BACKGROUND AND DESCRIPTION OF TRADING STRATEGIES

This chapter provides background information necessary to understand the market reconstruction discussed in the main body of the Report. The background information covers four areas. First, a description is provided of the various types of index-related trading strategies used during the market break: asset re-allocation and hedging, portfolio insurance, and index arbitrage (cash arbitrage and index substitution). Second, the use of automated stock order-routing systems for the above trading strategies, as well as for other forms of trading "baskets" of stocks, is discussed. Third, a summary is provided of the findings from earlier Commission studies of the impact of derivative index products on the securities markets. And fourth, the chapter outlines the scope of the Division's Report and the methodology employed in the staff's reconstruction of the markets during the market break.

CHAPTER TWO — CHRONOLOGY OF TRADING DURING OCTOBER MARKET

Chapter Two provides an overview of trading during the key days of the October market break, including an overall breakdown of trading into institutional, proprietary, and retail components, and a description of the interactions among the various types of index-related trading on the

---

[*] Although the Commission has authorized publication of this report, it has expressed no view regarding the analysis, findings or conclusions herein.

securities and index futures markets. More detailed chronologies of trading on these days are provide in Appendix A to the Report. Chapter Two also discusses significant Commission regulatory actions during the market break.

CHAPTER THREE— EFFECTS OF DERIVATIVE PRODUCTS

This chapter discusses a number of key issues raised by the effects of derivative index products on the securities markets in general, and on trading during the market break in particular. It includes background discussions of the continuing institutionalization of the securities markets, the recent increase in the use of passive asset allocation strategies and the level of trading of "baskets" of stocks, and a summary of the benefits derived from derivative index products, as well as their effects on the securities markets.

Chapter Three provides an overview of trading during the October market break. The staff's review of trading patterns during the period October 6 to October 22— including a detailed reconstruction of program trading activities (e.g., stock index arbitrage and portfolio insurance)— leads us to the conclusion that no single factor— economic, structural or psychological—was responsible for the size and breadth of the October 1987 market break. To the contrary, the staff believes that a variety of factors came into play during the key trading days that affected investment and trading decisions.

Analysis of trading suggests that the initial decline that immediately preceded the October 19 market break was triggered by changes in investor perceptions regarding investment fundamentals and economic conditions. With these changes as the "trigger," institutional stock selling was the largest single direct factor responsible for the initial opening declines on October 19. Finally, panic selling in a broad range of stocks— caused by a variety of factors— coupled with a complete absence of buyers (except at distressed levels), was primarily responsible for the free-fall decline that characterized the final hour of trading on the NYSE on October 19.

Accordingly, futures trading and strategies involving the use of futures were not the "sole cause" of the market break. Nevertheless, the existence of futures on stock indexes and use of the various strategies involving "program trading" were a significant factor in accelerating and exacerbating the declines. During certain critical trading periods, index arbitrage or portfolio insurance—or both—accounted for between 30 and 68 percent of total NYSE volume in the S&P 500 stocks. For example, on October 19, arbitrage and substitution programs sold 37.6 million shares, portfolio insurance strategies sold at least 39.9 million additional shares, and other programs sold an additional 11.8 million additional shares—together comprising 14.7 percent of total NYSE volume and 21.1 percent of S&P 500 stock volume. During crucial individual time periods, moreover, total program selling represented an even greater portion of total S&P 500 stock volume. Between 1:00 and 2:00 p.m. on October 19th, the combination of selling from portfolio insurance and index arbitrage totalled more than 40 percent of volume in the stocks comprising the S&P 500 index—and totalled more than 60 percent of S&P 500 stock volume in three different ten minute intervals within that hour. As indicated by these statistics, the Division also found that, in contrast to earlier periods of market volatility reviewed by the staff, portfolio insurance selling in stock and futures was significant during the market break, particularly during October 19th and 20th. Most of the program stock trading that occurred on October 19th and 20th that was not index arbitrage was accounted for by portfolio insurance selling. Much of that stock selling was done by a single large institutional investor that executed large portfolio insurance trades in both the stock and futures markets.

In addition to direct effects, the existence of futures trading and the use of derivative products in index-related trading strategies, in our view, had a significant indirect impact on the markets—particularly on October 19th —in the form of negative market psychology. The knowledge by market participants of the existence of active portfolio insurance strategies created, in our view, a market "overhang" effect in both the futures and stock markets; this resulted in the maintenance of futures discounts that discouraged institutional traders from participating in the stock market on the buy side, specialists from committing capital to maintain fair and orderly markets, and block positioning firms from maintaining normal levels of activity.

Finally, we note that the October market break did not result in merely a dramatic one-time re-valuation of securities markets. The after shocks of October 19 continue to affect the markets today. Quote spreads, liquidity and continuity on the NYSE continue to be substantially inferior to those indicators before the October market break, and actual market volatility has been substantially higher.

In summary, we believe that three dramatic trends have occurred as a result of trading in derivative index products. First, stock index futures have supplemented and often replaced the secondary stock market as the primary price discovery mechanism for stocks. Second, the availability of the futures market has spawned institutional trading strategies that have greatly increased the velocity and concentration of stock trading. Third, the resulting increase in index arbitrage and portfolio insurance trading in the stock market has increased the risks incurred by stock specialists and has strained and at time exceeded their ability to provide liquidity to the stock market.

We believe that these findings are significant and their implications need to be carefully reviewed by the Commission. We believe that the increased concentration and velocity of futures-related trading and resultant increases in stock market volatility can have long term, profound impacts on the participation of individual investors in the stock market. While many individual investors now participate in the stock market through institutional intermediaries, we believe individual participation remains important both for the additional liquidity it provides and for its contribution to consensus support for the U.S. economic system. We are not sanguine that such participation will remain if price volatility akin to October 19 occurs on even an occasional basis. We continue to believe, however, that derivative index markets provide valuable hedging and market timing benefits to institutions and, as a result, any changes to the regulation of those products must be effected with great care. Nevertheless, we believe a number of responses should be thoroughly explored.

Market Basket Trading. One of several alternatives that may be worthy of examination is the proposal to create one NYSE specialist post where the actual market baskets could be traded. A market basket post would alter the dynamics of program trading, in effect consolidating program trades back to a single order. The index specialist would have the informational advantage, not available to specialists in the individual stocks, of seeing the entire program order. Moreover, focusing institutional program trading at a single post might encourage additional block positioning activities, thereby potentially increasing the liquidity on the NYSE floor. While the feasibility and design of basket trading would require substantial analysis, we believe the concept of basket trading deserves the Commission's and the NYSE's attention.

Derivative Product Leverage. We believe thought should be given to steps to bring the available leverage of derivative products in line with the leverage of stock products. We believe this leverage derives from two sources—cash settlement and margin.

The availability of cash settlement eliminates the risk that a market participant must liquidate its position prior to the termination of the future or accept delivery (and make payment for) a market basket of stocks. The elimination of this risk increases the willingness of market participants to take larger positions with correspondingly tighter liquidation triggers. While a requirement for physical settlement of index futures raises a number of practical problems, the staff will continue to review the feasibility of physical settlement for index products.

The other primary difference in leverage between the stock and derivative product markets is margin. The Division recognizes the distinctions between futures and stock margin. Futures margin is, in effect, a performance bond that does not include an extension of credit. Moreover, futures positions are marked to the market daily and all futures margin has focused entirely on ensuring that both parties satisfy their respective obligations under the futures contract. Notwithstanding the absence of a debt relationship, however, the margin treatment for stock index futures and options provides significantly higher leverage for users of these products that can be achieved under stock margin requirements. Moreover, the increasing popularity of index substitution, index arbitrage, and portfolio insurance has resulted in an increasingly greater percentage of futures positions being taken precisely for the purpose of replicating cash market stock positions. Yet these positions require dramatically less cash to establish than would the equivalent position in the stock market.

The Division believes that the ease with which an institution or investment firm can increase or decrease the percentage of a portfolio invested in equities through the purchase or sale of derivative index products creates an environment in which investors buy and sell much larger positions than they might otherwise. Moreover, low margins contribute to increased speculative trading that, in normal market conditions, contributes to the illusion of almost unlimited liquidity in the futures market. During a market break, however, that liquidity disappears at a rate geometrically larger than does liquidity in the lower-leveraged stock market. For these reasons, the Division believes that relatively low margins may contribute to increased concentrated institutional trading and resulting greater price volatility.

Therefore, we believe the Commission should review carefully with the CFTC the impact on the stock market of present index futures and options margin levels. This review also should consider whether any benefits obtained from reducing the liquidity demands on the stock and derivative markets outweigh the costs and potentially lower derivative product liquidity resulting from higher margin requirements during periods of normal market activity.

Price Limits. Price limits historically have been employed in the futures markets to address extreme price volatility. While the Division believes that price limits, such as those recently imposed by the Chicago Mercantile Exchange may be a rational response to the present leverage levels in the index futures market, we nevertheless believe that there are substantial problems with their effectiveness. Setting price limits on index futures when there is an active alternative pricing mechanism in the stock market is somewhat self-defeating. The ability of institutions to shift their liquidations to the stock market was amply demonstrated on October 19th and 20th. Moreover, we do not believe, as a general matter, that price limits should be imposed on stock trading, although brief trading halts based on pre-set standards may warrant further consideration.

While we do not favor stock price limits, we do believe that greater coordination of stock and derivative index products trading warrants further review. We believe that the dominance of the futures as the price setting mechanism is most dramatic at the opening. The existence of a substantial futures price discount discourages specialists and other market participants from offsetting sell imbalances. Moreover, the ongoing trading in the futures may hinder the opening of the component stocks by encouraging additional waves of sell orders. Finally, the ability to trade futures before the component stocks have opened provides opportunities for firms to "front run" their customers' stock orders, possibly to the detriment of those customers. We believe further review should be made as to whether these concerns might be addressed by restricting the opening of index futures and options contracts until a set percentage (in value) of the stocks comprising the index commenced trading. Similarly, such a review should evaluate whether derivative products should stop trading when trading in an identified percentage of the stocks composing the index has been halted.

Short Sale Restrictions. The absence of short sale restrictions in the derivative markets, coupled with the greater leverage of futures, arguably presents the potential for greater speculative selling than could occur in the stock market. Moreover, through index arbitrage, that selling activity can be transferred to the stock market, often without being subject to Rule 10a-1 under the Securities Exchange Act of 1934 the short sale rule. Accordingly, the Division believes the Commission should review whether reducing price volatility should remain a goal of the short sale rule and, if so, whether steps should be taken to increase its effectiveness.

Reporting Requirements. In its Report on the Role of Index-Related Trading in the Market Decline on September 11 and 12, 1986, the Division noted the need to develop a "cost-effective, routine means of identifying and maintaining easily accessible records of index-related trading." Since then, the Division staff has worked with the staff of the NYSE to design such a reporting system. Despite recent improvements in this area, however, the Division still experienced substantial difficulties in reconstructing the October market break, impairing the ability of the staff to fulfill its oversight responsibilities and coordinate collection of trading information with the CFTC. Accordingly, the staff believes it would be appropriate to revisit the desirability of creating more specific recordkeeping rules at the broker-dealer level and to examine whether it would be feasible to develop a system, similar to the CFTC's large trader reporting system, for rapidly identifying large traders in the stock market.

As a separate matter, it also may be appropriate to consider how to integrate program trade reporting within the current systems of last sale reporting. In contrast to current systems to monitor and report block trades, there is no regularized reporting of program trades. The Division believes it would be appropriate to consider how to integrate program trading within the context of traditional transaction reporting. If, as some have suggested, program trading is the "block trading of the 1980s," then it seems appropriate to consider whether the more accurate and timely reporting of such trades can be made more readily available on a widespread basis.

Manipulation and Frontrunning. The Report provides a general description of concerns raised by the possibility of intermarket manipulation and frontrunning, as well as an overview of the findings of the reviews by the Division, the CFTC, and securities and futures self-regulatory organizations as to each of these areas during the October market break. While the Division found no evidence to question the CFTC's recently published determination that allegations of possible market manipulation on October 20 in the index futures markets were unfounded, the Division notes several instances of firms apparently trading in futures ahead of customer futures and stock programs, which raise significant concerns. Finally, Chapter Three contains a discussion of recent regulatory initiatives to address intermarket abuses. In this connection, the Division intends to work closely with the SROs and the CFTC to enhance futures and securities exchanges' routine access to each other's trading and surveillance data.

CHAPTER FOUR — EXCHANGE SPECIALISTS

Specialist Performance. The NYSE specialist system was placed under enormous strain during the market break period. Although there were some instances of questionable individual performance during this time, specialists as a whole met their market making obligations. They increased their aggregate buying activities and generally maintained markets in their stocks. Specialists often were the primary, and sometimes only, buyers during the morning and afternoon of October 19, with very little buying support from upstairs firms. Nevertheless, market quality deteriorated substantially on the 20th, as the market continued to strain under heavy volume and sell pressure. This is further evidenced by the significant number of delayed openings (92) and trading halts (167) on the 20th due to imbalances.

While specialists, in the aggregate, performed satisfactorily, there was a wide variation in individual specialist performance. In particular, a disturbing number of NYSE specialists on October 19 either were not sellers or did not take substantial positions. This inconsistent specialist performance deteriorated further during the afternoon of October 19 and throughout October 20. In addition, the Report identifies a number of instances throughout the market break where the appropriateness of the opening price set by specialists is questioned. While NYSE specialists' obligations to contribute to price continuity and depth must be viewed in the context of extraordinary price volatility, volume and futures discounts, the performance of certain specialists appears to have been unsatisfactory. The Division's analysis of Amex specialists performance during the market break period indicated a similar decline in overall specialist performance on October 19 and 20, and a disparity among individual specialists' performance. The Amex, however, also had several stocks that were halted for at least one day during the market break period.

In light of our findings, the Division believes that the Amex and the NYSE should examine carefully individual specialists performance during the market break. In this connection, the Division believes the Amex and NYSE must use their powers to reallocate stock pursuant to their rules where they identify specialists that exhibited a substantial or continued failure to maintain fair and orderly markets. Further, the Division believes the wide disparity in specialist performance underscores the need for the Amex and NYSE to develop relative, objective standards of performance for evaluating specialists.

Equity Specialists' Capital. During the market break, specialists at the NYSE increased their aggregate securities positions to at least twice that of their normal size with some individual specialist units increasing the size of their positions to four times that of their normal size. This increase in the size of positions resulted in the loss of approximately one-half of the buying power usually available to the specialists. At the end of trading on October 19, thirteen NYSE specialist units had no buying power.

The experience on October 19 and 20 demonstrates that the financial position of many specialist firms can become critically strained during a major market break. While specialist capital appears sufficient in normal trading situations, the staff is not confident that it will remain sufficient if the markets continue at their present volatility levels. Although the staff is not able to conclude that additional capital would have retarded to any great degree the market decline of October 16 and 19, the staff believes that additional capital might ensure that in any future down market specialists do not reach the limit of their buying power or become in jeopardy of failing.

In light of the above, the staff believes that further analysis of the specialist financial responsibility system should be conducted. In particular, the staff is concerned that the present minimum capital requirements imposed by the Amex, NYSE and the regional exchanges do not reflect the actual capital needed to ensure the maintenance of fair and orderly markets in different types of securities. Accordingly, the staff believes that the exchanges should consider revising the minimum financial requirements imposed on specialists to reflect more closely the requirements of today's markets. Moreover, the Division will review the appropriateness of applying the Commission's net capital rule to all specialists.

In this connection, the staff also has identified substantial limitations in the exchanges' present system of specialist surveillance. Accordingly, the Division will review with the exchanges possible modification by the exchanges of their existing specialist monitoring systems in order to increase the level of surveillance currently maintained.

Finally, the Division is concerned about potential difficulties specialists may have in obtaining financing during periods of market turbulence. Accordingly, we believe that the exchanges should explore the possibility of requiring all "self-clearing" specialists to maintain a line of credit with a bank or other lending institution or face higher capital requirements.

CHAPTER FIVE — ANALYSIS OF CAPITAL ADEQUACY

Upstairs Firms. In general, the large investment banking and retail firms suffered substantial losses in October as a direct result of the market crash. However, none fell below the net capital early warning levels. Of the approximately 6,700 firms dealing with customers and/or trading for their own account, about 60 were at some time in violation of the net capital rule. Of that number, only three carried customer accounts and only one of those had to be liquidated under the Securities Investor Protection Act. The remainder of the firms traded solely for their own accounts and/or introduced their customer business on a fully-disclosed basis to another broker-dealer.

In light of the increased volatility in the market, the Division believes that certain matters should be reviewed. First, the minimum net capital required of broker dealers that (1) carry customer accounts, (2) introduce customer accounts on a fully disclosed basis to another broker-dealer, and (3) are market-makers in OTC securities should be reexamined. Second, the net capital rule should be reviewed to determine whether to require broker-dealers to take haircuts for their securities-related futures positions that are independent of margin requirements and are related to the past volatility of the underlying securities. Third, the level and structure of haircuts for equity securities should be reexamined. In this connection, consideration should be given to establishing several levels of haircuts to differentiate among different types of securities. Moreover, attention should be devoted to whether equity haircuts alone are a sufficient leverage limiting device for firms that do not carry customer accounts, but either trade for their own accounts, act as market makers or clear through another firm. Finally, financial activities conducted in affiliates of a broker-dealer should be reviewed for their potential exposures to the broker-dealer and the financial markets generally.

Liquidity of Broker-Dealers. Bank lending to the brokerage community as a whole increased significantly during the week of the market break. While no precise measurement is available, data from the Board of Governors of the Federal Reserve System indicate that loans by banks to purchase and carry securities, including loans to broker-dealers as well as to mutual funds, increased by almost 50 percent during the week of the break.

Following the market break, the availability of credit to broker-dealers did not decrease on a generalized basis. Banks continued to make credit decisions on a client-by-client basis, taking into account the perceived creditworthiness of their customers, the value of securities pledged as collateral for secured loans, and the strength of their security interests. Most banks reported that their clients did not seek loans in excess of the banks' internal lending guidelines and that these loans were usually provided. It is not clear, however, if banks would have continued to provide liquidity to the same extent had the DJIA continued to drop significantly on October 20.

Banks were more cautious in making lending decisions during the market break. In response to the market decline, some banks made intra-day margin calls and lowered advance rates for particular borrowers. Specialists, risk arbitrageurs, and other firms rumored to be experiencing problems, including some major broker-dealers, were required by individual banks to provide additional collateral or to change the nature of their security arrangements. Finally, bank concerns over credit exposures contributed to some delays in futures and Options Clearing Corporation settlements, as well as settlements of foreign currency transactions.

While banks continued to provide broker-dealers necessary financing and settlement assistance, the market break underlined the critical importance of ensuring broker-dealer liquidity when the market system is under strain. The Division believes that the actions of the FRB and the Federal Reserve Bank of New York to encourage major banks to continue their prudent financing of securities firms were critical in avoiding any potential for a liquidity gridlock. In order to reduce risks of liquidity problems in any future market break, the Division believes that the self-regulatory organizations should review with broker-dealers the desirability of establishing diverse lending relationships with a number of banks, as well as the feasibility of obtaining more committed lines of credit than currently exist.

Options. Total market maker deficits at 11 options exchanges for those market makers that clear through the 16 clearing firms designated to the Chicago Board Options Exchange ("CBOE") for examination for compliance with financial responsibility requirements increased from approximately $6.2 million on October 14 to $137 million on October 23, a net increase of $130.8 million. On October 20, there were 164 market makers whose accounts were in deficit with an aggregate total deficit of approximately $217 million. During the October 14 through October 30 period, the market maker equity at all options exchanges for market makers carried by the 16 CBOE designated clearing firms decreased by approximately $287.5 million, from approximately $835.9 million on October 14 to approximately $548.4 million on October 30.

Aggregate net capital of CBOE designated clearing firms increased by approximately $178 million, from approximately $121.9 million on October 14 to approximately $300 million on October 30. The increase was due primarily to capital infusions and dramatic reductions in options market makers' positions. However, some clearing firms experienced severe liquidity problems. A number of factors contributed to the firms' liquidity problems, including: (1) intra-day variation margin calls; (2) difficulties in financing stock and options positions through banks; (3) problems with returned stock loans; and (4) market makers' withdrawals of equities from their accounts.

The liquidity problems experienced by clearing firms suggest that the following issues should be explored: (1) whether market makers should be required to maintain minimum equity in their accounts equal to the perceived risks in their positions; (2) whether there should be concentration haircuts for short options positions, either on a market maker by market maker basis or on a total clearing firm basis; (3) whether the net capital provision providing that aggregate market-maker haircuts cannot exceed ten times the clearing firm's net capital for a period exceeding five consecutive business days should be amended to reduce the five business day grace period; (4) whether the provision of the net capital rule that permits some options market makers that are not exempt from the net capital rule to avoid under certain circumstances the haircuts on their option positions should be eliminated; (5) whether self-clearing options market makers should be permitted to carry the accounts of independent market makers without having the net capital requirements of other firms; and (6) whether there should be limitations on the withdrawal of market makers' equity from their accounts.

In addition, the Division believes that the options clearing firms, options exchanges and the Options Clearing Corporation should enter into discussions with banks to encourage them to develop guidelines that would allow them to extend credit with confidence on in-the-money options positions.

CHAPTER SIX —ISSUER REPURCHASE ACTIVITY

In light of the significant number of issuer repurchase program announcements during the week of October 19 to 23, the staff conducted an analysis of repurchase activity of S&P 500 companies during this period. The staff analyzed the impact of repurchase volume and announcements on market price performance, and examined the operations of Rule 10b-18 under the Exchange Act.

The staff found that stock repurchases by many S&P 500 companies represented a significant proportion of the trading volume in their shares during the week. Purchasing activity had a favorable impact on price performance, and the effect of the announcement of a repurchase program also appeared to be positive.

While most issuers apparently followed the requirements of Rule 10b-18, the treatment of block purchases under the rule may effectively negate the volume limitation for many securities. As result, a number of issuers were the predominant buy force in their common stock after they commenced their repurchase activity. The staff expects to continue its review of the impact of issuer repurchases and the possible need for amendments to Rule 10b-18.

CHAPTER SEVEN— EXCHANGE OPERATIONAL PERFORMANCE

Market Information Systems. Market information systems were not subject to any major breakdowns or delays. The central processor for transaction and quotation information for listed equity securities, the Securities Industry Automation Corporation, experienced only two brief outages in reporting transaction information. The NASD experienced some delays on October 19 and October 20 in one of its services for providing transaction and quotation information to securities information vendors. Securities information vendors also did not experience many interruptions or delays in providing service. While the performance of equity information systems did not raise significant concerns, the Division believes that the NYSE should review whether it has adequate personnel and facilities to maintain accurate trade and quote reporting capabilities during periods of sustained high volume.

Although there were no system-wide interruptions or delays in disseminating options transaction and quotation information to securities information vendors, two problems did occur. First, as the value of underlying securities and indexes changed dramatically, the number of new options series that were created was much greater than usual. The addition of these new series to existing data bases strained the resources of several securities information vendors. The second problem relating to options information occurred when premiums reached three digits. Because three digit premiums previously had been a rarity, the options information message format only allowed two digit price information. Consequently, premiums with three digits were incorrectly reported.

Order Handling. The Division's review of order entry and routing procedures during the market break highlights at least two areas of concern. First, many broker-dealers appear to have been nearly overwhelmed by surge in order flow. Notwithstanding the fact that 600 million share days may not have been within the realm of reasonable expectations, some firms may not be routinely reviewing and assessing their capacities to accept orders from their clients and route the orders to the appropriate destination. Second, it is apparent that at least one major service bureau suffered operational problems that resulted in delays in order routing and execution reporting for a large number of firms. In light of the stress placed on firm order handling systems during the market break, the Division believes that firms should develop contingency plans to cope with unusual volume. These plans should include back-up computer systems, cross training of personnel and better communication with public customers. In order to ensure that these reviews regularly take place, the self-regulatory organizations and the Division should include a review of operational capacity in broker-dealer examinations. Moreover, because many firms rely on service bureaus to perform external order routing functions and these systems interlock and are dependent on the operations of the routing and executions systems of the exchanges, the entire network should be examined to determine the causes of inefficient operations during the market break. In this connection, the staff will review whether some degree of regulatory oversight of service bureaus is desirable.

Automated Order Routing and Execution Systems. Problems with the NYSE's Designated Order Turnaround system caused many delays in executing trades. Several components of DOT, which permits automated routing of small orders of up to 2,099 shares and the sending of orders in lists of securities, frequently were overburdened.

Moreover, all the small order routing and execution systems of the regional stock exchanges also experienced significant delays, particularly on October 19 and 20, in executing orders through their systems. The Pacific Stock Exchange ("PSE") SCOREX system encountered the most significant problems, losing both orders and trade reports, due to a system capacity overload. The Midwest Stock Exchange and Philadelphia Stock Exchange also had large queues for orders entering their respective systems. PHLX reverted to a manual execution system during most of the week of October 19 and, under manual mode, dispensed with sending execution reports to member firms until after trading hours. On the other hand, the MSE attempted to increase its system's capacity throughout the week of October 19 and by October 26 was able to add an additional computer to increase capacity.

The problems encountered during the week of October 19 highlight the critical need for all exchanges to implement quickly system improvements to enhance their ability to handle volume surges in the future. Moreover, the Division believes the Commission should consider whether to request that the PSE and PHLX refrain from adding new firms on their systems until they have made progress in increasing system capacity.

The problems during the week of October 19 also underscore the need for the markets to inform, in a timely fashion, member firms of any problems and delays in their systems in addition to any reductions in guarantee limits. Coordination among the markets, especially when systems are down and order flow may have to be sent to another market, also should be improved.

Finally, substantial delays occurred in routing orders through ITS. ITS is a communication system that links the seven major stock exchanges and the NASD. In addition, ITS suffered from the failure of the ITS plan to provide for a pre-opening notification routine after trading imbalance halts, as well as a general lack of communication among the participating exchanges. The staff determined, therefore, that modifications in the exchanges' order routing and support systems and improved communications between exchanges would result in a more efficient performance of ITS during periods of high volume.

CHAPTER EIGHT — PERFORMANCE OF THE OPTIONS MARKETS

The options exchanges experienced a number of problems throughout the week of October 19 due to the extreme price volatility in the market for the underlying securities, the absence at times of useful market information concerning conditions in the equity and futures markets, and the difficulty market makers faced in trying to hedge their options positions. The impact of these factors is reflected in the large number and protracted nature of trading halts called in individual equity options and index options; in the fact that prices, or "premiums," charged for option contracts, particularly put contracts, were inconsistent and often unrelated to price movements in the underlying index; and in the notable unwillingness of some options market makers to foster liquidity by trading on a continuous basis. In particular, the options market did not provide an effective, continuous market for the most actively traded index options classes at certain times on October 19 and for virtually all of October 20. Accordingly, the Division believes there are a number of areas that require review by the Commission and the options exchanges.

First, the Division and the exchanges may wish to reconsider the efficacy of rules that currently permit options on indexes of securities to open prior to the opening of all component securities in the underlying market and to continue trading for a certain time even though underlying component securities are not trading. Second, the options exchanges, particularly the CBOE, need to examine methods to speed up opening rotations. Index option opening rotations were excessively long on October 20, and, in the opinion of the Division, limited the ability of options customers to receive timely executions, and contributed to higher premiums being charged in some options series. Third, the Division believes there is a need for the options exchanges and market information vendors to develop a plan concerning what options series, if any, should be delisted from vendor quotation services when vendor data base capacity is outstripped. Fourth, the Division believes that the performance of small order execution systems during the week of October 19 evidences the need for the CBOE and the Amex to revisit their rules governing market maker participation in these systems. Fifth, the Division believes that the performance of index options market makers on both the CBOE and Amex, particularly on October 20, warrants close examination by these exchanges to determine whether they met their obligations to maintain, to the maximum extent possible, fair and orderly markets.

CHAPTER NINE —THE OTC MARKET

During the week of the market break, the prevalence of unreliable quotations, delayed transaction reports, reduced market maker participation, and increased manual order handling, coupled with greater telephone inquiries, undermined the liquidity and orderliness of the OTC market.

During the market break, the OTC market suffered from a combination of extreme downward volatility and unusually high share volume. An extraordinarily high number of locked and crossed markets disabled the NASD's automated Small Order Execution System ("SOES"), as well as similar systems operated by individual market makers, forcing market makers to execute transactions of small size manually. Because of the difficulty in reaching other market makers by telephone, customers' orders for securities whose markets were locked or crossed were often not executed in a timely manner, not executed at all, or executed at prices that reflected only a securities firm's best estimate of the prevailing market.

The NASD has responded to problems encountered during the market break by proposing a number of initiatives. These initiatives include raising the penalty for unexcused withdrawals by market makers from NASDAQ; requiring all NASDAQ market makers to participate in SOES; providing that SOES executions will continue in an OTC/National Market system security when quotes are locked or crossed; eliminating preferencing of market makers when a locked or crossed market exists; and establishing the Order Confirmation Transaction service that will permit firms to access market makers over the computer without voice contract. While the Division believes that these proposals demonstrate a willingness of the NASD to respond to the serious breakdowns that occurred during the market break, we believe there are a number of additional areas that merit attention.

First, the NASD, as part of its self-regulatory responsibility, should review the conduct of market makers during the market break to ascertain whether they complied with the NASD's rules. Second, the large number of transactions reported out-of-sequence by particular firms may be an indication of the firms' inability to comply with the transaction reporting rules. Third, the NASD and the Commission should reconsider, in light of the market break, the need to require market makers to include realistic sizes as part of their quotations. Fourth, the NASD should consider additional steps that would ensure the ability of market makers to execute electronically against other market makers' quotations during high volume periods.

CHAPTER TEN — CLEARANCE AND SETTLEMENT

During October 1987, clearing agencies, broker-dealers, and securities markets cooperated successfully to compare, clear and settle unprecedented sustained daily trading volume. Although the volume placed tremendous strain on personnel and systems, the vast majority of that trading volume was cleared and settled within routine time frames. Volume and record price volatility also increased dramatically the financial risk of loss to clearing agencies and their members. Although some losses were suffered, clearing agency safeguards were effective in preventing significant or widespread losses.

The record trading volume and securities price volatility experienced during October 1987 does suggest, however, the need for improvements in two primary aspects of the clearance and settlement process: (1) post-execution trade processing, and (2) clearing agency safeguards against member default.

The NYSE, NASD and Amex should consider accelerating efforts to compare all trades on trade date. Currently, over 50 percent of share volume is compared through two-sided trade input that results in compared trades several days or longer after trade date. The October 1987 experience indicates that current two-sided comparison process cannot be completed fully on a timely basis with sustained daily trading volume exceeding 600 million shares. Those considerations should include expansion of automated systems which permit comparison at or near the time of trade execution.

Clearing agencies also should consider a variety of enhancements to their risk management systems to reflect increased risks that result from increased price volatility and trading volume. Those considerations should include enhanced member monitoring systems to enable clearing agencies to obtain better and more up-to-date information about members' financial strength, activity in other markets, and customer activity. Clearing agencies also should consider whether risks posed by individual members require increased capital requirements or the deposit of additional assets with the clearing agency.

Options clearing systems and market participants also should reexamine safeguards and consider improvements in light of events in October 1987. As demonstrated in October, equity price volatility can generate geometric increases in options price volatility. The OCC should consider the same member monitoring improvements as equity clearing organizations as well as how those monitoring techniques can provide better early warning of risks and what increased measures should be taken to guard against those risks. Moreover, basic volatility assumptions and margin formulas should be reassessed in light of the record volatility in October. When OCC margin is insufficient to cover intra-day volatility OCC resorts to variation margin calls to protect itself. Events in October suggest that OCC should reassess the manner and timing of variation margin calls to determine whether it can obtain earlier warning of and protection from potential member insolvency, especially for volatility that occurs late in the trading day near the close of banking hours. Finally, OCC, the commodities industry, and regulators should discuss ways to coordinate margin requirements and settlements for entities involved in securities options and futures market activity.

CHAPTER ELEVEN —INTERNATIONALIZATION

The interdependency of the world's securities markets was never more apparent than during the market break. The commission staff's findings indicate that the major world markets responded quickly and dramatically to movements in other major world markets and that, for the most part, U.S. markets led foreign markets.

To some degree, the interdependency of the markets is the result of cross-border investing by market participants who are seeking new ways to diversify portfolios. Although there were rumors that foreign investors were abandoning U.S. markets when the DJIA turned sharply down, the staff has not found evidence to support this belief. Foreign investor activity does not appear to have had a disproportionate effect on U.S. market moves. U.S. investors also appear to have engaged in substantial trading in foreign markets during the break. Much of this trading, however, was probably prenegotiated crosses, arranged in the U.S. and executed abroad for convenience.

Although the major world markets may have experienced varying degrees of foreign investor activity during the break, the markets uniformly were besieged by enormous sell pressures. Thus, the staff examined how London, Tokyo and Hong Kong fared under this extraordinary pressure. London operates in a manner similar to the NASDAQ market and, although it continued to function throughout the break, experienced many of the same problems as the NASDAQ market. For example, instances of widened spreads and reduced quote sizes were reported. Market participants also indicated that some market makers were not answering their telephones and that locked and crossed markets were not uncommon.

Tokyo also suffered under the strain of huge sell-order imbalances. On Tuesday, October 20, the implementation of daily price limits and huge sell-order imbalances halted most trading in that market. Finally, in response to the unprecedented volatility around the world, the Hong Kong markets closed for four trading days in the hope that those markets would avoid the calamitous drops other markets experienced. Nevertheless, upon reopening, the Hang Seng index plunged 1,120 points, a 33 percent drop.

The growing internationalization of the markets presents many challenges to the world's securities regulators. The events of October 1987 brought to the forefront the degree to which events in one market can affect other markets and emphasized the need for greater international cooperation and initiatives. Regulators can respond positively to these developments by working together to develop trading, clearance and settlement linkages and other arrangements; international trade and quote reporting mechanisms; adequate financial oversight systems; and effective enforcement and surveillance arrangements.

CHAPTER TWELVE— INVESTOR COMPLAINTS

Chapter Twelve is devoted to the detailed analysis of investor complaints and inquires received by the Commission and the self-regulatory organizations in the aftermath of the October market break. The chapter describes the results of the intensive program undertaken to identify and categorize the types of problems experienced by individual investors, as well as to document the general perceptions of investors during this period. A brief summary of telephone complaints/inquiries is included with the primary focus on the analysis of the 1,283 letters received through December 15, 1987.

The findings of this study indicate that problems involving order execution accounted for the highest percentage (43.3 percent) of investor complaints by far. The next two most frequently cited categories, each representing approximately ten percent of the market break complaints, were confirmation problems (10.4 percent) and margin maintenance problems (10.1 percent). A public commentary category, that tracked letters containing general comments on the market break situation, accounted for an additional 10.7 percent of the complaints. A majority of these expressed concerns about program trading. Although emphasis was placed on identifying abusive sales practices, the market break complaint data revealed a slight decrease in this area when compared to the percentage of Fiscal Year 1987 sales practice complaints. It may be that these types of complaints were delayed while the investor attempted to resolve the problem with the broker-dealer. Consequently, this percentage may increase over time.

The staff concludes that it is important to move to address systemic problems that impacted order execution and confirmation of orders for small investors. The staff recommends review and modification where necessary of disclosure in account opening agreements concerning margin calls and options risk disclosures. Finally, the staff recommends review and modification where necessary of disclosure in account opening agreements concerning margin calls and options risk disclosures. Finally, the staff suggests that information contained in customer complaints be utilized in targeting broker-dealer examinations.

GAO

Financial Markets: Preliminary Observations on the October 1987 Crash

United States General Accounting Office

EXECUTIVE SUMMARY

Purpose. On October 19, 1987—a date now called "Black Monday"—the nation's financial markets experienced one of their most severe shocks in history. Amidst unprecedented volume and price volatility, the New York Stock Exchange's Dow Jones Industrial Average plunged 508 points, or 23 percent—comparable only to the percentage drop that occurred over two days in October 1929. Had the precipitous decline continued for even another day, massive disruptions to the United States financial system might have occurred. In all, during the first 19 days of October the Dow lost about 24 percent of its total value, almost $1 trillion.

Even though the Dow finished the year higher than it began, the specter of the Great Depression that followed the 1929 crash, and questions about how the decline occurred so quickly, have left the markets uncertain. Market participants are concerned about how such an event can be prevented from happening again.

In the wake of the decline, numerous studies, including that of a Presidential Task Force, were initiated to determine what happened, why, and what could be done, if anything, to prevent a recurrence. Several congressional committees asked GAO to address these issues and a number of related ones to help them consider legislative or regulatory actions that may be needed.

Background. The U.S. capital markets facilitate channeling funds from savers to users and thus provide for capital formation. An orderly and active securities market is essential for this process because it is an efficient mechanism for allocating resources, providing liquidity, and establishing prices. To assure the continued existence of these functions and to maintain the confidence of investors who supply capital funds, a system of self- and federal regulation was developed.

Options and futures markets function to transfer the risk of price fluctuations to persons willing to speculate on those movements for a potential profit. Futures markets operate differently than stock markets, and they developed their own system of self- and federal regulation.

In the 1970s and 1980s, options and futures markets began offering derivative products based on financial instruments that were intended to help their holders protect against price fluctuations (hedge). These products have been subject to continued study and controversy between those who sell and use them as hedging devices and those who fear that the products and trading strategies improperly influence the underlying capital markets. The October 1987 market decline renewed that controversy.

Results in Brief. Most market experts have agreed that the market decline of October 1987 was caused by a confluence of macroeconomic, political, psychological, and trading factors, and that isolating any one cause would be difficult. However, the events of October demonstrate that broad new trading interests and strategies have evolved in capital markets and that the previously segregated stock, options, and futures markets have become linked and international in scope.

Current market and regulatory systems were faced with unprecedented volumes and price changes for two days. In view of the circumstances, it is remarkable that the systems performed as well as they did. However, GAO found two areas needing immediate attention to help restore confidence in the markets and alleviate concerns that the markets could crash again soon.

Some automated systems had difficulty handling the extraordinary volume. Problems with the New York Stock Exchange's systems adversely affected trade executions and pricing information both in New York and in other markets. Several actions to try to correct problems have been taken; others need to be taken as quickly as possible. The Securities and Exchange Commission needs to reassess its oversight role and capabilities for evaluating automated systems.

Decisions of self- and federal regulators were made without benefit of any formal intermarket contingency planning. Such plans should be developed to deal with any future market emergencies that may occur.

No agency currently has responsibility for intermarket decisionmaking. Given the new intermarket linkages, the need to assure financial system liquidity, and the increased internationalization of markets, strong leadership is needed to develop and implement an appropriate intermarket regulatory structure. Moreover, if the current barriers between commercial and investment banking are relaxed, the need for such leadership becomes all the more important.

Over the longer run, a number of other issues, discussed below, will require careful consideration. GAO will continue to explore these issues.

GAO'S ANALYSIS

Markets are Linked

As GAO reported in 1986, the futures and securities markets, which evolved separately and have been regulated independently under different statutes, have become linked through the introduction of new futures and options products based on securities or broad groups of securities comprising major indexes. These new products create prices in two separate markets for securities. They are used in some cases as substitutes for ownership in the underlying stocks or for changing positions and exposures in those stocks. The users of these products trade in both markets, sometimes simultaneously.

During the October market decline, some traders tried to use both futures and securities markets to manage risk based on expectations of future market performance and thereby prevent portfolio losses. Market participants considered not only the actual activities of these traders, but also the anticipation of their activities, as important factors in the market break. Although there are disagreements about the exact extent and effect of this activity, it reinforces observations made earlier by GAO and others that the markets are closely interconnected. These links necessitate more coordinated intermarket regulation.

Foreign markets also experienced dramatic price declines and increased trading activity during this period. Unprecedented volumes and price changes could be tracked around the world.

Market Systems Stressed

The massive volume of trading activity strained some automated systems to meet the needs of traders. System backlogs caused intended trades to be delayed or unexecuted and contributed to an overall inability to conduct normal trading activities. This added to the confusion and panic in the markets. Investor complaints during this period most often related to poor or non-execution of orders or to problems with margin calls.

The unprecedented volumes, coupled with large order imbalances and rapid price movements, strained the marketmaking capacity, particularly at the New York Stock Exchange and in the primary over-the-counter market. Their inability to maintain orderly markets and, at times, to make any market at all in large numbers of stocks, was a major source of uncertainty for traders. Evidence about marketmaking in the securities and trading in the futures markets is still being evaluated.

Actions by Regulators

Self- and federal regulators implemented procedures to respond to high volatility in their markets during October 19 and 20. These involved primarily increased market surveillance, increased margins, rule changes, and more frequent communication with each other. Many decisions were made as events unfolded, and market participants generally praised the regulators' performance. For example, federal regulators clarified the rules affecting when corporations may buy back their own stock. This helped provide buying support in the falling market. In addition, the Federal Reserve System, which said it had developed contingency plans for a market disaster, provided needed liquidity to the markets on October 20, which probably prevented even more serious financial problems.

A critical communication problem that arose was confusion about whether the New York Stock Exchange would close on Tuesday, October 20. Trading in the Standard and Poors 500 stock index futures contract on the Chicago Mercantile Exchange closed for a short time because of the confusion, which disrupted trading activity for investors using both markets.

Regulators have recognized the linked nature of the securities and futures markets for some time and have begun to make changes to improve intermarket data sharing and communication. However, the regulatory structure has been established primarily for individual markets with no central intermarket leadership responsibility. The self- and federal regulators had no intermarket planning group nor any preexisting coordinated intermarket contingency plan. The events of October provide impetus for developing the leadership and intermarket planning necessary to restore confidence in the markets and protect consumer interests.

GAO Observations

Much of the information available to GAO at this time is incomplete and unverified, so observations about the events of October 1987 are preliminary. Nevertheless, steps should be taken immediately by the self- and federal regulators to reduce or eliminate problems, such as the following, that may create unnecessary market uncertainty.

Trading and information systems should be reevaluated and improved by the markets to ensure that they are capable of handling the new trading pressures placed on them. In addition, the limited federal oversight role in trading systems development and enhancement needs to be strengthened.

Self- and federal regulatory agencies should develop integrated intermarket contingency plans to deal with market breaks such as those demonstrated in October. These plans would contribute to confidence by assuring the market that a repetition of the October events has been considered by those responsible for regulating these markets, and an approach to dealing with the problems created by those events has been developed.

In addition, strong leadership must be exerted to develop an appropriate intermarket regulatory structure. Such a structure should be able to deal with issues such as:

- intermarket products and strategies,

- provision of adequate liquidity in normal times and in emergencies, and

- the growth in linkages across international financial markets.

Congress is considering the repeal of Glass-Steagall Act provisions which could allow the merging of the securities and banking industries. This would lend further emphasis to the need for an appropriate regulatory structure for linked markets and industries. GAO will continue to evaluate these issues.

Over the longer term, a number of other issues remain to be decided. In analyzing the events of October, the Presidential Task Force on Market Mechanisms and others have recommended certain changes to margins, regulatory structure, controls over market activity, and clearing systems. These recommendations help frame issues that should receive careful consideration, both individually and taken together, in terms of their potential effects on trading activity, market liquidity, international competitive positions of U.S. markets, and most important, the function of providing capital to the nation's businesses. In addition, other issues must be addressed including the adequacy of current market making systems, the long-term automation needs of market systems, the adequacy of current consumer protection requirements, and the need for regulation and coordination of increasingly linked international markets.

INDEX